Scholarly Reprint Series

The Scholarly Reprint Series has been established to bring back into print valuable titles from the University of Toronto Press backlist for which a small but continuing demand is known to exist. Special techniques (including some developed by the University of Toronto Press Printing Department) have made it possible to reissue these works in uniform case bindings in runs as short as 50 copies. The cost is not low, but prices are far below what would have to be charged for such short-run reprints by normal methods.

The Scholarly Reprint Series has proved a valuable help to scholars and librarians, particularly those building new collections. We invite nominations of titles for reissue in this form, and look forward to the day when, with this series and other technological developments, the label 'out of print' will virtually disappear from our backlist.

CANADIAN GOVERNMENT SERIES

R. MacG. Dawson, *Editor*

THE GOVERNMENT
OF NOVA SCOTIA

by

J. MURRAY BECK

Royal Military College
Kingston, Ontario

Toronto

UNIVERSITY OF TORONTO PRESS

1957

TO MY MOTHER

FOREWORD

IT IS PLEASANT to welcome to this series the second volume on the government of a Canadian province. This, like its predecessor on Prince Edward Island, deals with one of the oldest constitutions, one which was not created by statute but by the prerogative power of the Crown, and hence is less likely to fit into any standard mould. Nova Scotia has, of course, two major claims to priority in the history of Canadian politics: she was the first province to receive representative institutions and the first (by a few weeks) to win responsible government. Owing in large measure to Howe's inspired leadership, the latter was achieved through peaceful, constitutional means, though the rebellions in Upper and Lower Canada may well have proved the decisive factor.

It is obvious that a study of the government of Nova Scotia must dig deep into the past, and Dr. Beck has worked on this early history with great care and thoroughness. But he has not neglected the more recent period or the working of the government of our own time. The important changes, the interesting practices, and the colourful incidents have not all been in the distant past. There was, for example, the Legislative Council, that travesty on democratic institutions, which lasted until less than thirty years ago. It displayed an unexpected—and quite unfounded—belief in its own excellence; and it even managed to acquire some repute for the ingenuity, tenacity, and unscrupulousness with which it managed to postpone its inevitable extinction. There has been the odd phenomenon—unique in Canada—of the Liberal party having been in power for seventy out of the ninety years since Confederation, and the debilitating effect which Conservative success in the Dominion had on Conservative fortunes in the provincial field. There has been the long-standing resentment at the treatment of the province at Confederation and the effect of that event on the province's economic development, its standards of life, its revenues, and its attitude to the federal government. There has been, of course, the constant need to adapt the parliamentary practices and institutions, developed under quite different conditions, to the needs of a much smaller community, though one which was keenly aware of its heritage and was very jealous of any serious interference with it. Dickens' sensa-

vii

tion at the opening of the Nova Scotia Legislature (which Dr. Beck quotes so aptly) of "looking at Westminster through the wrong end of a telescope" could not have hit the mark more accurately.

In short, "the Nova Scotianess of Nova Scotia" (as the late Professor Archibald MacMechan used to describe it) finds an even greater expression in politics than in other directions. Or, to put the same thing a little differently, the government of Nova Scotia has within it unique material for an interesting study, and Dr. Beck has made excellent use of it.

R. MacGregor Dawson

PREFACE

THE GOVERNMENT of Nova Scotia has passed through three distinct phases since 1758: an initial period of more than seventy years during which an immature House of Assembly strove somewhat amateurishly and not always consistently to enhance its privileges, powers, and prestige; a middle period of about thirty years in which all the institutions of government underwent a thorough examination and were made over, so far as the colonial circumstances made it desirable, to the British exemplar; and a later period (since 1867) in which the political institutions have evolved in much the same manner as British institutions generally, but without the novel deviations which a previous volume in this series has shown to have occurred in Prince Edward Island. The story ends with a political revolution of sorts, since in November, 1956, for the first time in the history of the province, a Conservative government assumed office under non-crisis conditions.

With a few exceptions—Professor Brebner's two books on the period prior to 1783 and a very considerable body of literature on the movement towards responsible government—the secondary material on Nova Scotian government is slight. As a result, the principal sources of information for this study have had to be official documents and newspapers. In these circumstances a bibliography can have no practical use, and therefore none is included.

In limited aspects of the work the Public Archives of Canada and the Legislative Library of Nova Scotia have proved to be invaluable. But by far the greatest amount of material has been gathered at the Public Archives of Nova Scotia, where for many months the former Provincial Archivist, Dr. D. C. Harvey; the present Provincial Archivist, Dr. C. B. Fergusson; Miss Phyllis Blakeley; and Mr. George MacLaren have assisted me in a friendly and helpful manner. Any officials of the Nova Scotian government who were consulted were equally co-operative.

I must express my thanks as well to the Canadian Social Science Research Council for awarding me a pre-doctoral fellowship and a grant in aid of publication; to Colonel W. R. Sawyer, the Director of Studies at the Royal Military College, for providing the opportunity for research; and to Dr. David J. Dooley of the English Department at the Royal Military College for assisting with some of the writing. My principal acknowledgment must be to Professor R. MacGregor Dawson, who, over an extended period, has placed his wide knowledge and penetrating powers of criticism unstintingly at my disposal. The imperfections are, of course, entirely my responsibility.

The Royal Military College of Canada   J. MURRAY BECK
March, 1957

CONTENTS

I. COLONIAL GOVERNMENT TO 1830

CHAPTER I

THE BASIC DECISIONS
IN NOVA SCOTIAN GOVERNMENT

THE FIVE DECISIONS which determined the basic form and character of the government of Nova Scotia had all been made by 1867. Thereafter the development of the province's political institutions paralleled that of British institutions generally as they adapted themselves to the requirements of a new day. The first decision—effected by the Treaty of Utrecht (1713) after a century of sporadic conflict—decreed that Acadia was to be British. At first it was so in little more than name, since the only English inhabitants prior to 1749 were a few soldiers and merchants at Annapolis and Canso, augmented in the latter village by a transient fishing population. The governing of the province resolved itself, therefore, into supervising the Acadians who constituted almost its entire population. The striking fecundity of these people had resulted in the few hundred original immigrants, all of whom had arrived by 1671, multiplying to more than 1,700 by 1714 and to about 10,000 by 1749. Even before the final British conquest their settlement at Minas was larger than the original one at Port Royal, they had established themselves in considerable numbers at Cobequid and Chignecto, and had made their way as far west as Shepody Bay.[1]

By that time, too, they had been indelibly stamped with an attitude towards government which had irritated the French governors and was to become the bane of their English masters. Once they had moved far from the forts and the frontiers, they had declined to take an interest in high politics and had left the frontier fighting to others.[2] Under British rule they still continued to disregard the official regulations and to rule themselves. Successive English governors and administrators adverted to the "hard, and uneasy Task" it was to "manage a People, who will neither believe nor hearken to Reason (unless it comes out of the mouths of their Priests)."[3] But although they appealed time and time again for instructions on how to make English rule more secure, the authorities across the water provided little in the way of practical assistance. While the Board of Trade agreed to guarantee the consti-

[1]See J. B. Brebner, *New England's Outpost* (New York, 1927), 46.
[2]*Ibid.*, 45–6.
[3]Philipps to Board of Trade, May 26, 1720, P.A.C., N.S. A11, 93.

tutional rights of Englishmen as a means of attracting settlers and in 1719 provided Governor Philipps with a new Commission and set of Instructions which required the calling of an Assembly before laws could be enacted,[4] it treated all colonization schemes somewhat gingerly. The apparent explanation is that these proposals always involved New Englanders, and the Board's intention was to "purge Nova Scotia of the possible taint of New England republicanism and to make it conform to the character of the more admirable Virginia."[5] As a result, the province was left without the English elements which were required to work institutions similar to those of the ideal prototype.

The need for a law-enacting body was so compelling that Lieutenant-Governor Armstrong himself ventured on two occasions to suggest how a representative body might be convened. In 1725 his suggestion was to move the seat of government from Annapolis to Canso, and from its small and transient English population "Appoint a General Assembly Composed of twenty four of the principall Inhabitants to make Laws for the Good Gover[mt] of the Province . . .";[6] six years later it was to fashion a small Assembly which would include the Acadian deputies[7] in the hope of bringing them "through their own free and voluntary act to pay a greater obedience to the Government." In neither case, however, could he convince a dubious Board of Trade.

Even the two functioning institutions, the chief executive and the Council, passed through troubled waters during these years. The difficulties in the first instance stemmed from the almost continual absence of Richard Philipps who held the Commission as Governor between 1717 and 1749. If the Lieutenant-Governor of the province or the senior Councillor acted in his absence, the Lieutenant-Governor of the fort and town of Annapolis denied his assumption of the functions of Commander-in-Chief, "tho' it [was] the constant Rule and practice in all Civil Governments."[8] If there was no Lieutenant-Governor to act in his stead, the determination of who was senior Councillor sometimes proved a source of equal contention. The problem with the Council was likewise twofold in nature—how to recruit a quorum from the transient English population and maintain harmony among its members.

[4]But because Nova Scotia had not been "hitherto peopled or settled by His Majesty's Subjects," it was not considered necessary that either the Commission or Instructions should "be so extensive, as those for His Majesty's other Gov[rs] in America." See Board of Trade to Lords Justices, June 19, 1719, N.S. A10, 128–33.

[5]Brebner, New England's Outpost, 134.

[6]Armstrong to Mr. Popple, Sept. 5, 1725, N.S. A16, 162–3.

[7]Infra, 5. For the Lieutenant-Governor's plan see Armstrong to Council of Trade and Plantations, Oct. 5, 1731, N.S. A20, 106.

[8]See Mascarene to Newcastle, Oct. 14, 1742, N.S. A25, 223–9.

In the last analysis, however, the lack of legislative power proved the most serious impediment of all. Limited powers of action could be derived from the Governor's capacity as military commander and from the laws of Virginia;[9] an occasional order from England might fill a serious gap in the fabric of government; the Council might utilize the Virginian precedent and constitute itself a court for the trial of all causes.[10] Yet these devices were poor substitutes for the real thing. "Obviously . . . a province of complex problems like Nova Scotia could not depend for its entire administration on military authority, on the laws of another colony, and on the long-delayed and often ignorant orders of the Board on the other side of the Atlantic."[11]

To cope with emergencies and chronic problems the chief executive and his Council were forced, therefore, to resort to proclamations, and the home authorities co-operated to the extent that they rarely annulled what was, in effect, legislation. More interesting still were the "unique native instruments of government" which were evolved to provide a regular channel of communication between the governors and the governed. As early as 1710 the Acadians sent deputies to treat with their new masters who, appreciating the need for someone to receive and attend to the execution of their orders, proceeded to regularize their election and functions. Collectively the deputies became "the local government bodies of the Acadian population, and at the same time buffers between them and the English."[12]

All in all the scheme of government between 1710 and 1749 amounted to little more than a makeshift *modus vivendi*. It is doubtful, however, if a province with a public revenue of £30 a year[13] deserved anything better. Certainly its legal constitution had the best possible antecedents, and as Professor Brebner indicates, once local circumstances dictated something better it was a simple matter to graft new powers on the old.[14]

---

[9]Article 10 of the Instructions ordered the Governor, until such time as government by Council and Assembly was practicable, to conform to the Instructions originally given to the Governor of Virginia, insofar as they were applicable to Nova Scotia. See N.S. E1, no. 6.

[10]Eventually this function became a heavy burden; see Armstrong's reference to the Council being "daily Employ'd and harras'd with [Acadian] Affairs" because of the lack of any other court of judicature. Armstrong to Board of Trade, Oct. 5, 1731, N.S. A20, 104–5.

[11]Brebner, *New England's Outpost*, 137.

[12]*Ibid.*, 149–50.

[13]All derived from the quintal of codfish or equivalent value paid annually by every proprietor of a "fishing room" at Canso. Philipps to Board of Trade, Jan. 24, 1732, N.S. A20, 130–1.

[14]Brebner, *New England's Outpost*, 148.

II

The second decision—to make Nova Scotia British in form of government as well as in name—followed the realization by the authorities in England that something more than a feeble garrison at Annapolis was required to balance the French fortress at Louisbourg and to act as the custodian of the important eastern flank of North America. In record time they put in motion a scheme for the establishment of Halifax, and late in June, 1749, Edward Cornwallis, the newly appointed Governor, arrived at Chebucto with 2,546 settlers. He brought with him a Commission and set of Instructions far more comprehensive than those of Philipps, and in them is to be found the real origin of the provincial constitution.[15]

Meanwhile the Board of Trade was giving every encouragement to further immigration from Britain, New England, and some Protestant regions of the European continent. The result of this policy of settlement, when combined with the expulsion of the Acadians in 1755, was to give the province, in which Cornwallis had originally been unable to discover "the least glimpse of an English Government" or "one true subject without the Fort of Annapolis,"[16] a substantial, predominantly English population. Still more significant was the arrival of New Englanders to supplement the other settlers, for within a decade[17] they had become the core of the English-speaking population and stamped enduring marks on the governmental structure.

It was the first of the New Englanders who provoked a clash of opinion about what was legally necessary and what was practically possible in political institutions. The Governor's Commission still required the calling of an Assembly for the enactment of laws, but because the English population was largely restricted to the Halifax area, the Board of Trade permitted the Governor and Council to act temporarily in a legislative capacity, and the Instructions to the successors of Cornwallis appeared to provide this irregularity with some sort of legal basis.[18] Not until the New England element became restive under conciliar government and agitated for the rights of Englishmen did the Board decide to retrace its steps.

[15]See J. E. Read, "The Early Provincial Constitutions," *Canadian Bar Review*, XXVI (April, 1948), 626.

[16]*N.S. Archives Report*, I, 586.

[17]The New England influx was at its peak between 1760 and 1764, and it continued at a diminished rate until the seventies. By that time New Englanders accounted for about one-half of the population.

[18]Those of Lawrence read: "And in case you shall find it necessary for Our service to call an Assembly within Our said Province. . . ." N.S. E2, no.4, clause 11.

Although the right of the Crown to institute governments in British possessions had never been in question, the limitations to which it was subject in prescribing their character had not yet been precisely defined. The rule had long been established that in colonies settled by Englishmen the inhabitants enjoyed English law as of right and could be legislated for and taxed only by a legislature in which they were represented or by the King in Parliament. It had similarly been accepted, although not judicially determined, that in conquered colonies the original powers of the Crown were unlimited. It was not until 1774, however, that the courts made the pronouncement that once a conquered colony had been promised or granted an Assembly it could not be denied or deprived of its representative institutions merely by an act of the Crown.[19] Such a retraction could be made only by Parliament.

To fit Nova Scotia into this general scheme of things is difficult because of the lack of any authoritative statement upon whether the province was to be regarded as a settled or conquered colony. The historical evidence in favour of the latter view seems conclusive and it was upon this basis that its Chief Justice argued in 1755 that an Assembly was legally unnecessary.[20] Nevertheless, in 1753 the English commissaries for determining the limits of Acadia presented some dubious historical material to show that the province had always been British by prior discovery and settlement;[21] the First General Assembly attributed the grant of representative institutions and the establishment of English law to the fact that the province was a settled English colony;[22] and "the courts showed the same splendid disregard of the historical facts."[23] But the problem is of little more than academic interest since in responding to the pressures of the New Englanders the Board of Trade at no time attempted to apply the settled-conquered colony doctrine to Nova Scotia or considered whether the Crown still possessed an unlimited power to shape the political institutions of the colony by changing the Governor's Commission.

Its decision was dictated instead by general policy. A law-making authority of some kind was clearly required in Nova Scotia, and the law officers had ruled that the existing Commission and Instructions prohibited laws from being enacted unless an elected Assembly gave

[19]*Campbell* v. *Hall*, [1774] 1 Cowper 204.
[20]*Infra*, 8n.
[21]See *Memorials of the English and French Commissaries Concerning the Limits of Nova Scotia or Acadia* (London, 1755), 519.
[22]33 Geo. II, c. 3.
[23]R. MacGregor Dawson, *The Government of Canada* (Toronto, 1947), 6.

its approval.[24] There could be no question of issuing new instruments which would confer a temporary legislative authority upon the Governor and Council as no province with a substantial number of English inhabitants had been accorded that kind of treatment at any time during the century.[25] In fact, the Board unceremoniously rejected Governor Lawrence's argument that the Governor and Council had enacted laws in the early history of Virginia.

> . . . they derived the Power of doing it from their Commission, which was also the case of many other of the Colonies at their first Settlement, tho' it was a power of very short duration, and in later times, since the Constitution of this Country has been restored to its true Principles, has never been thought adviseable to be executed.[26]

The course which was pointed out by these considerations of policy had the additional merit of coinciding with the path of least resistance since the main opposition to representative institutions came from Lawrence whose opinions might be brushed aside at will. The natural outcome, therefore, was the convening of an elective Assembly at Halifax on October 2, 1758—the first in what is now Canada.

The decision of 1749 also broke new ground in that the British government, which had hitherto declined to participate in colonial projects that might involve outlays of money in time of peace, lavished £336,707 upon the Nova Scotian enterprise between 1748 and 1752 and thereafter defrayed a considerable portion of the cost of civil government by an annual parliamentary grant.[27] When a policy of providing additional support for the established church was later instituted, the annual grant rose from £5,845 in 1788 to £13,140 in 1823. After that time the insistence of a parliamentary opposition bent upon economy forced successive colonial secretaries into all sorts of financial hocus-pocus to conceal the grant until they could devise measures for its elimination.[28] The exact effect upon constitutional

---

[24]N.S. A57, 117–18. Their report was in conflict with that of C. J. Belcher who held that Nova Scotia as a conquered colony was not entitled to an Assembly as of right, and the Instructions (which were, in effect, an integral part of the Commission and therefore of equal weight) required by implication at least two settled townships each containing fifty families before an Assembly was to be called. See N.S. A57, 58–65.

[25]L. W. Labaree, *Royal Government in America* (New Haven, 1930), 176.

[26]Board of Trade to Lawrence, March 25, 1756, N.S. A59, 23.

[27]Between 1749 and 1764 the total expenditure was £613,969. Brebner, *New England's Outpost*, 187n.

[28]This was not accomplished until 1842. For the later story, see D. C. Harvey, "The Civil List and Responsible Government in Nova Scotia," *C.H.R.*, XXVIII (Dec., 1947), 365–82.

development of this continued support of the principal officers of the civil government is an imponderable, but it certainly meant that the power of the purse could not play the preponderant role in Nova Scotia that it did in other provinces.

III

The third decision—the determination of the provincial boundaries —was effected in stages over a period of seventy years. In the process considerations of extent of territory and population played a minor part; rather it was the fortunes of war, Imperial policy, legal niceties, and sometimes even the desires of the colonials themselves which were the real determinants.

A proclamation dated October 7, 1763, annexed St. John's and Cape Breton Islands to the peninsula of Nova Scotia. In the case of the former, henceforth to be known as Prince Edward Island, the action had little significance, for within six years the authorities in England had hearkened to the pleas of its proprietors and constituted it as a distinct province.[29] Cape Breton, however, was quite another matter and its final disposition awaited the passage of another sixty years. For the time being the government of Nova Scotia merely conferred upon it the status of a normal county.

The next two geographical and jurisdictional changes were effected during the 1780's by further acts of the Crown. One, in 1784, separated the new province of New Brunswick from Nova Scotia with its own Governor-in-Chief, reduced the status of the chief executive of Prince Edward Island to that of a Lieutenant-Governor subordinate (but, as it turned out, only in theory) to the Governor-in-Chief of Nova Scotia, and granted Cape Breton its own government under a Lieutenant-Governor subordinate to the same authority.[30] Another, in 1786, conferred upon Guy Carleton (Lord Dorchester) the governorship-in-chief of all the British North American provinces except Newfoundland, and placed Nova Scotia, New Brunswick, Prince Edward Island, and Cape Breton under lieutenant-governors, who, in the normal absence of the Governor-in-Chief from their environs, exercised the functions conferred by his various Commissions.

While it is possible to take the simple view and regard the creation of New Brunswick, for example, as merely "a natural development

[29]See Frank MacKinnon, *The Government of Prince Edward Island* (Toronto, 1951), chap. I.
[30]See Commission of John Parr dated Sept. 11, 1784, P.A.C., Nova Scotian Commissions to Governors 1778–1816, 240–69.

stimulated by the arrival of the Loyalists," it appears more realistic to consider all these changes as constituting a single scheme based primarily upon the broad principle of *divide et impera*.[31] But if one of its objectives was to promote efficiency in colonial administration by conferring the widest possible powers upon a Governor-in-Chief at Quebec, it proved to be a complete will-o'-the-wisp. Whether those responsible for the colonial policy decreed it or not, Nova Scotia was still far closer to London than to the backwoods of Canada and destined to remain so for many years to come. Hence the change, as Lieutenant-Governor Parr pointed out ruefully, answered "no one earthly purpose" in regard to Nova Scotia.[32]

The second objective—to govern "by means of division, to break [the North American colonies] down as much as possible into petty isolated communities, incapable of combination, and possessing no sufficient strength for individual resistance to the Empire"[33]—did not, as it might appear, mean a callous disregard of colonial interests by a distant tyrannical power.[34] Even if the policy-makers failed to appreciate it, the separations were practically desirable because the circumstances of the day made it impossible to bring the areas beyond the mainland of Nova Scotia within the influence of the centripetal forces of Halifax.[35]

The last territorial change—the re-annexation of Cape Breton—occurred in 1820 just as it had become apparent that the integration of the people of the peninsula into a compact and self-conscious whole was to be successful. Because of the troublous history of the island since 1763,[36] the Secretary of State welcomed a constitutional difficulty which afforded the opportunity to heal a long-running sore. This difficulty stemmed from the Instruction which permitted the Governor and Council to make rules and regulations for the peace, order, and good government of the Island until conditions were ripe for the calling of an Assembly, but forbade them to do or pass anything which affected the life and liberty of the subject, or imposed a duty or tax.[37]

---

[31]For discussion of this point, see Marion Gilroy, "The Partition of Nova Scotia, 1784," *C.H.R.*, XIV (Dec., 1933), 375–91, and XVI (March, 1935), 91–3; also J. B. Brebner, "The Partition of Nova Scotia," *C.H.R.*, XV (March, 1934), 57–9.

[32]Parr to Nepean, July 15, 1791, N.S. A116, 233–4.

[33]The opinion of Lord Durham, quoted by Gilroy, "Partition of Nova Scotia," 391.

[34]W. M. Whitelaw, *The Maritimes and Canada before Confederation* (Toronto, 1934), 49.

[35]*Ibid.*, 49–50.

[36]For the details see Richard Brown, *A History of the Island of Cape Breton* (London, 1869), 386–451.   [37]See N.S. E4, no. 11, clause 16.

In the face of this explicit prohibition, the courts had no alternative, when a duty on spirits imposed by the Governor and Council was challenged in 1816, but to invalidate it.[38]

Lord Bathurst, the Colonial Secretary, concluded that the representative body which was required to make taxation legal would be "destructive of the prosperity the island then enjoyed, limited as it was, and that there was not a sufficient number of persons in easy circumstances to attend an Assembly."[39] Hence the only practicable course was to reconstitute the island as part of the province of Nova Scotia. Naturally this step was thoroughly unpopular in Cape Breton, and for the next quarter of a century the House of Assembly at Halifax re-echoed with complaints of the neglect of its interests, and with descriptions of the island varying from "a kettle tied to a dog's tail" to "a jewel in a swine's snout."[40] Nevertheless, no Secretary of State could be induced to reverse the decision on grounds of public convenience or policy, and the Judicial Committee of the Privy Council eventually rejected the legal grounds upon which the Cape Bretoners objected to re-annexation.[41]

IV

The fourth decision—to make the Nova Scotian governmental system British in spirit as well as in form—was not fully effected until the mid-nineteenth century. Gradualism in constitutional matters was to be expected since the nature of the Commission and Instructions to the governors allowed the same type of development as had already occurred in Britain. Neither explicitly prevented the representative branch from using the legislative process as a means of modifying, restricting, or even overriding many of the powers which were originally considered to be vested in the Crown and had therefore been exercised by the Governor and Council. Nor did they expressly prohibit a Governor from permitting an Executive Council which enjoyed the confidence of a majority in the popular branch of the Legislature to wield the executive power legally vested in himself. The former of these developments went on for half a century prior to 1830; the second came to fruition in 1848 after little more than a decade of debate.

[38]For the implications of the decision of the Chief Justice of Cape Breton, see P.A.C., C.B. A37, 37–8.

[39]Brown, *History of Cape Breton*, 435.   [40]*Novascotian*, March 14, 1833.

[41]The question at issue was whether the Crown still possessed the right to alter the political institutions of Cape Breton in 1820. For the arguments, see *In re the Island of Cape Breton*, 5 Moo. P.C.259.

The earlier phase may be regarded primarily as a period of differentiation in which the simple original edifice of a Governor and Council controlling within themselves all the governmental powers became infinitely more complex. Partly by acts of the Crown performed by the King and his ministers in London or by the Governor and Council in Halifax, and partly by the action of the provincial Legislature, new institutions were created and the existing ones altered to make them suitable for a colony which had expanded well beyond its original confines at Halifax. Contemporaneously with these developments there went on unceasingly the working out of new relationships between the Governor, the Council, and the Assembly as the latter strove in a somewhat amateurish fashion to secure ends not dissimilar to those of the seventeenth-century British House of Commons.

V

Thus the source of authority for the first four decisions is to be found in acts of the Crown, exercised sometimes in the governors' Commissions and Instructions, and sometimes in proclamations and dispatches. The Sovereign put these decisions into effect on the advice of his ministers simply by resorting to the discretionary authority which, in these matters, still resided in the Crown because Parliament had not decided otherwise; in other words, he exercised his prerogative powers. The basic components of the Nova Scotian constitution were, in fact, two prerogative instruments, the Commission and the Instructions to the governors which, while purporting merely to invest the chief executives with their powers and to instruct them in their duties, went far beyond these limited objectives.[42] The Nova Scotian constitution was to rest solely on such a foundation until the fifth basic decision—Confederation—effected by an act of the British Parliament, placed it partially on a statutory basis.

[42]See Labaree, *Royal Government in America*, 6. The constitutions of Prince Edward Island and New Brunswick were likewise prerogative; those of Quebec and Ontario were statutory.

CHAPTER II

ACTORS ON THE GOVERNMENTAL STAGE

THE GOVERNOR

THE NOVA SCOTIAN GOVERNORS of the eighteenth century were no better and no worse than could be expected from the prevailing mode of appointment. "Governments have bin sometimes given," went a commentary of that day, "as a reward for Services done to the Crown, and with design that such persons should thereby make their fortunes. But they are generally obtained by the favour of great Men to some of their dependants or relations. . . . The Qualifications of such persons for Government being seldom considered."[1] Even those who aspired to the governorship of so poor a colony as Nova Scotia brought all the influences at their disposal to bear upon the appropriate authorities in England. Chief Justice Belcher, anxious to emulate his father's career as governor of a royal province, easily excelled the senior Councillor Benjamin Green at this kind of game, but he had to be satisfied, none the less, with a mere lieutenant-governorship when the antecedents and family influence of Henry Ellis apparently proved to be of a higher order. The most "typical example of eighteenth-century nepotism,"[2] however, was Francis Legge. Fortunate enough to be a kinsman of the Secretary of State for the Southern Department, Legge became Governor of Nova Scotia, not because he was personally suitable, but because it happened to be the best of three positions which opened up when he was prepared to accept and the Earl of Dartmouth able to offer a change of station.

Sometimes the appointee was one whose previous services to the Crown could not be ignored. The Nova Scotian instance, par excellence, was John Wentworth, ex-Governor of New Hampshire, who, for devotion to his Sovereign, found himself without gainful employment after the American Revolution.

My destination is quite uncertain [he wrote]; like an old flapped hat thrown off the top of a house, I am tumbling over and over in the air, and God only knows where I shall finally alight and settle to rest. . . . Benning

[1]*North Carolina Records*, II, 154 *seq.*, esp. 158, quoted in E. B. Greene, *The Provincial Governor* (New York, 1898), 46–7.
[2]J. B. Brebner, *The Neutral Yankees of Nova Scotia* (New York, 1937), 244.

[his brother-in-law] has been nearly four years a captain, and not being able to establish his rank as he expected, has sold out, and is now in the country; so that we are all seeking something to do.[3]

Wentworth was never one to hide his light under a bushel, and anyone in Britain who might have done anything about it, must soon have learned that his years of service and sacrifice merited something more than the mere office of surveyor-general of H.M. Woods in North America. Yet even then almost a decade elapsed before the governorship of Nova Scotia beckoned, and he finally alighted and settled to rest, determined to find in his new habitat the means of reviving the family fortunes.

The temperaments of the governors were even more diverse than the circumstances of their appointment and were an important factor in determining their attitude to the government of which they were the heads. To the worn-out soldier John Parr, who wanted a pleasant haven wherein to finish out his days, the Nova Scotia of 1782 was the very apotheosis of his highest hopes.

. . . the greatest civility and attention from all Ranks of People, a most excellent house and Garden, a small farm close to the Town, another of 70 or 80 Acres at the distance of two Miles . . . a snugg little farm house upon it, a beautifull prospect, with good fishing, plenty of Provisions of all sorts except Flower, with a very good French Cook to dress them, a Cellar well stock'd with Port, Claret, Madeira, Rum, Brandy, Bowood Strong Beer etc., a neat income . . . of £2200 Ster^g p Annum, an income far beyond my expectations, plenty of Coals & Wood against the severity of the Winter, a house well furnish'd, and warm Cloths . . . upon the whole my Dear Grey, your friend Parr is as happy and comfortably seated, as you could wish an old friend to be. . . .[4]

Naturally Parr was all for the maintenance of tranquillity no matter what it cloaked beneath its exterior. Alike in that respect was Wilmot, who was utterly complaisant about abuses in administration. Unlike Parr, he thoroughly detested the Nova Scotian environment. Sick with the gout when he arrived, he experienced three rigorous winters in Nova Scotia which added to the ravages of eight previous years spent in cold climates. It is little wonder, then, that his principal concern was to secure a successor with whom he might make a financial bargain which would facilitate his return to England.

As little enamoured of the Nova Scotian situation as Wilmot was his successor, Lord William Campbell. Long service in hot climates

[3]Wentworth to Captain Cochran, May 6, 1783, in *Acadian Recorder*, March 11, 1848.

[4]Parr to Grey, Oct. 23, 1782, Shelburne MSS, LXIX, 149–50, quoted in Brebner, *Neutral Yankees*, 352.

(he had served eight years in India) and "a wound formerly received in [his] left eye by an Iron Spike" had left him in an indifferent state of health and led to repeated requests for a posting to a part of the continent "as may be judged fittest to relieve me from the ill effects which the continuance so long in this cold climate has brought on me."[5] In these circumstances a Secretary of State, thoroughly confused by Nova Scotian politics anyway, decided that the transference of Campbell to South Carolina would be to the advantage of all concerned.

Both Wilmot and Parr carried out their functions apathetically, while Campbell, because of his frequent absence from the province, stirred himself only occasionally into bursts of real activity. Actually zeal in one's capacity as Governor brought with it, in two instances before 1792, the fate of supersession in office, although each time it was combined with defects in personality which made the incumbents obvious misfits. Jonathan Belcher should never have ventured from the judicial sphere where he possessed undoubted abilities into the political where he was completely outsmarted by the merchant oligarchy which dominated the province. Francis Legge's fanatical prosecution of the same interests, when combined with his alienation of that section of the Assembly which would have afforded him assistance, demonstrates all too well his almost incomprehensible obtuseness.

These are the individuals who administered the province between 1760 and 1808, no better, no worse than the prevailing mode of selection could have been expected to provide. Their predecessors and successors were military men who for the most part showed up to better advantage in colonial eyes. Prior to 1760, Governors Cornwallis, Hopson, and Lawrence were described as "Men of great Humanity and Disinterestedness. The trifling Revenue then raised, was applied to useful and humane Purposes, and tended to the public Good."[6] The resort to military men after 1808 coincided, but not accidentally, with a return to a period of relative quiet in the conduct of civil affairs. The first of these, Sir George Prevost, determined at all costs to keep up "that good understanding with [the Assembly] which so materially influences its proceedings when acting as one of the branches of the Legislature" and to leave "untouched the nice and difficult constructions on Colonial Legislation."[7] His successors followed the same policy

[5]Campbell to Hillsborough, April 13, 1771, P.A.C., N.S. A87, 53–4.
[6]*An Essay on the Present State of the Province of Nova Scotia* by A Member of Assembly (? Halifax, 1774), 7.
[7]Prevost to Castlereagh, May 4, 1809, P.A.N.S. 58, doc. 71.

with similar results. The price was a compromise which virtually surrendered part of the prerogative, but it at least brought tranquillity, and it was in accord with the general policy after 1783 to let colonial institutions develop as they would with a minimum of control.

Yet these outwardly conciliatory governors trusted the people and their representatives no more than their predecessors. Prevost's experience convinced him that as "Nova Scotia [became] sensible of her adolescence, her dislike to control [would] become more evident, and her attempts to shake off the restraints of the Mother Country more frequent.—In short her ties . . . [were] those of necessity and convenience, more than of gratitude and affection."[8] Even the amiable Sir James Kempt feared that, if the Assembly were made fully responsible for the civil list, it might regard "the Governors and all the Officers of the Colonial Government to be their servants rather than the King's."[9]

Divergent as governors, lieutenant-governors, and administrators may have been in other respects, all were fastidious about seeing that the dignity and prestige of the King's representative were not lowered. Several even used the threatened or actual impairment of their position in the eyes of the public to serve their personal ends. To regain the title of Governor-in-Chief,[10] Parr adopted the pretence that Nova Scotians desired to "have a Governor of their own, and not to be considered as a Dependance upon any other";[11] and to thwart the ambitions of persons whom he abhorred, Wentworth pictured Attorney-General Uniacke and William Cottnam Tonge as pursuing a course destructive of the Governor's position and, hence, of the very foundations of government.

Wentworth's successors had little need to scent out imaginary instances of subversive conduct because their leadership was often too slavishly followed. Dalhousie posed as the patron of agriculture, and his example

set all the Councillors, and officials, and fashionable mad about farming and political economy. They went to Ploughing Matches—got up Fairs—made composts and bought cattle and pigs. Every fellow who wanted an office or wished to get an invitation to Government House, read Sir John Sinclair, talked of Adam Smith, bought a South Down or hired an acre of land and planted mangel wurtzels.[12]

[8]Prevost to Liverpool, May 12, 1811, P.A.N.S. 59, doc. 4.
[9]See private and confidential observations of Kempt included with Kempt to Horton, Nov. 19, 1825, N.S. A166, 139.
[10]It had gone to Lord Dorchester as a result of the colonial arrangements consummated in 1786.
[11]Parr to Nepean, July 15, 1791, N.S. A116, 234.
[12]Joseph Howe, "Notes on Several Governors and Their Influence," *Collections of the N.S. Historical Society*, XVII, 197.

But this was a purely temporary state of affairs, for

no two Governors think alike or patronize the same things—when Sir James Kempt came he had a passion for road making and pretty women, and the agricultural mania died away. Agricola was voted a bore—a fat Scotchman—and his family decidedly vulgar, and the Heifers about Government House attracted more attention than the Durham cows.[13]

In addition to acting as the patron of all good works, the Governor had to keep up a style of entertaining befitting the King's representative. Wentworth performed this function so well that his salary as Lieutenant-Governor (£1,000 since the time of Cornwallis), even when augmented by his emoluments and fees as Surveyor-General of H.M. Woods, was insufficient.[14] Prevost, who had no outside source of income, found his salary still more "inadequate to the ceremonious and social duties of his high station."[15] The outcome was that it was raised to £2,000 to bring it into conformity with that of the Lieutenant-Governor of Lower Canada. Eventually the increase produced a problem of the opposite kind, for with a further provision of £1,000 in commutation of all his fees in 1824, the Governor's income reached a level which the Reformers of a later day considered grossly in excess of what colonial conditions warranted.

The administration of the government during the absences of the chief executive was an even more frequent source of trouble. Before 1786 these periods were frequent and prolonged. Henry Ellis failed to grace the province with his presence during his two-year tenure; Francis Legge left under a cloud never to return, but managed to retain the governorship and half its emoluments for another four years; Lord William Campbell spent at least one-fifth of his term in the more pleasant southern colonies. If anything, the lieutenant-governors and administrators who assumed their functions were more unsuitable than the normal run of governor.

While the absences of the lieutenant-governors were much less frequent after 1786,[16] the problem of succession became even more serious because fate decreed that the senior councillors who acted in place of the absentees should be men intensely disliked by the Assembly. The first of such was Judge of Vice-Admiralty Alexander Croke, whose exalted conception of the prerogative resulted in actual paralysis of the civil government, and who would undoubtedly have

[13]*Ibid.*, 197–8.

[14]Prevost to Cooke, April 27, 1808, P.A.N.S. 58, doc. 13.

[15]In addition to its being low in comparison with the incomes of some officers under his own government. Prevost to Liverpool, March 13, 1810, *ibid.*, doc. 102.

[16]Parr and Wentworth (1782–1808) were so enamoured of their position that they never left the province.

thrown a province less well ordered than Nova Scotia into complete turmoil. To prevent a recurrence, Prevost suggested that the Chief Justice[17] or the senior officer commanding the forces[18] should act for the Governor in his absence. Although the second alternative did not come into effect in time to prevent a second assumption of authority by Croke, it did effectually prevent a third.[19]

A reversion to the old practice occurred later with equally bad results. Five times Michael Wallace, the only member of an anything but liberal Council who could stomach all the proposals of the reactionary Croke, fell heir to the mantle, the last occasion being marked by the Council's rejection of the Appropriation Bill with Wallace's blessing.[20] After his death the senior councillorship passed to T. N. Jeffery, the Collector of Customs, who, by virtue of the office he held, if not by reason of his personal characteristics, was almost as unpopular. This time the protest against his assumption of the government became vocal. It was clearly preposterous, so the argument ran, that in case executive interference were necessary

as regards his Majesty's Council or the Customs Establishment,—a senior member *of the Council*, and the Collector of the *Customs*, will be the personage to whom the Country must appeal!! Evils may not result; but such regulations seem a trifling with the peace and prosperity of the most quiet and orderly colony under heaven. Surely, surely, it is time, full time, that *our* constitution should be altered. It was evidently intended, only for the miserable non-age of a poor and ignorant people, and is a disgrace to our present state and character.[21]

THE COUNCIL

The Council, which in one capacity advised the Governor and in another acted as the upper House of the Legislature, underwent the transformation experienced by similar bodies in the other royal colonies

[17]Prevost to Cooke (private), Aug. 19, 1809, P.A.N.S. 58, doc. 89. The prohibition against the Chief Justice acting as Administrator dated back to the time of C. J. Belcher whose incompetence in the office of Lieutenant-Governor led to its subsequent inclusion in the prerogative instruments.

[18]Prevost to Liverpool, July 30, 1811, P.A.N.S. 59, doc. 12.

[19]Duncan Darroch administered the government from Aug. 26 to Sept. 20, 1814; George Stracey Smyth from June 28, 1816, to Oct. 24, 1816.

[20]The description of Wallace quoted in George Patterson, *A History of the County of Pictou* (Montreal, 1877), 195, is not too inaccurate: "He is one of those who think the King can do no wrong, that the British constitution is the most perfect fabric the world ever saw. He hates a radical as he hates Satan himself. He would, if he had the power, shake all the liberals in the world over the crate of Vesuvius, but his heart would be too kind, to let them fa' in."

[21]*Acadian Recorder*, Sept. 15, 1832.

—it came to ally itself with the Governor in bolstering the prerogative. No other result was possible when, through a progressive change in the mode of appointing councillors—sometimes officially and sometimes conventionally recognized—the body came for all practical purposes to be appointed by the Governor.

This development was necessary to counteract the infirmities associated with the earlier method of appointment. Since the tenure at pleasure conferred by a Councillor's mandamus was, in practice, one during life, the result was to introduce all the usual evils of that tenure. While the quorum of five, which was the rule prior to 1784, appeared on paper to provide an adequate margin of safety, the toll exacted by illness, old age, and absence from the province, sometimes made it difficult to convene a legal meeting of the Council. The restrictions upon the Governor's right to make provisional appointments tended in the same direction. Until 1784 he could fill vacancies only when the number of councillors fell below nine, a contingency which rarely occurred, even though the Council might be barely capable of functioning because of the various types of casualties. Sometimes, in fact, the whole process of government hung by a slender thread.[22]

Although most of the early governors faithfully obeyed the Instruction to forward lists of persons suitable for councillorships, they might generally have spared themselves the trouble. Between 1760 and 1775, the nominees of the Board of Trade normally received preferment, and they were usually the candidates[23] of Joshua Mauger, the king-pin of the merchant-official oligarchy which dominated the province, and not those of the Governor. But with the decline of the merchant clique in the post-Revolutionary period, "interest in Council membership rapidly declined,"[24] and two innovations followed as a matter of course.

For one thing, almost all appointees were chosen from the Governor's

---

[22]For a time in June, 1772, Lieutenant-Governor Michael Francklin found himself with only six councillors in Halifax, and of these Benjamin Green, "it is apprehended will never be able to attend again," while "three of the other Five are upwards of Sixty years of Age, and rather infirm, either of which now falling sick would put an entire stop to all business in General Assembly." Francklin to Hillsborough, June 26, 1772, N.S. A88, 49–50.

[23]Sometimes the individuals suggested to the Board of Trade possessed merits as dubious as those of one Mr. Hutton: ". . . after having sold the greater part of his lands, he has gone to Boston; & . . . his return is very doubtfull. . . . His place of residence, whilst he was in this Province, was at Cumberland, a hundred miles distant from Halifax . . . [but he] is a man of honest Character." Legge to Pownall, Oct. 22, 1773, N.S. A89, 89.

[24]Brebner, *Neutral Yankees*, 218n.

nominees and generally in the order of priority which he suggested. For another, the making of provisional appointments, hitherto exceptional, was constantly used to ensure a quorum after an alteration in the Instructions permitted a Governor to fill vacancies up to the full membership of twelve. The combination of these two developments with Wentworth's long governorship meant a Council of Wentworth's friends. Any possibility that a body so constituted could act as a buffer between Crown and Assembly is ludicrous on its face. From the Wentworth period dates that entire identity of interest and feeling between the Governor and the Council which lasted as long as the Council of Twelve.

While Wentworth made provisional appointments only when the exigencies of the moment dictated, his successors dispensed with this formality after 1815 by filling all vacancies on their own initiative. Since the authorities in England always confirmed these provisional appointees and never objected to being continually presented with a *fait accompli*, the inference is that the innovation was not greeted with disfavour.

In their choice of councillors, the governors strictly observed the Instruction which required their nominees to be well disposed towards government. Legge, for example, recommended John Creighton as "a man of good character & understanding, in easy circumstances, well affected to His Majesty,"[25] while Wentworth described Delancey, Butler, and Barclay as "persons properly qualified by their distinguished loyalty and attachment to His Majesty's Person and Government."[26] The unquestioned support of government in this context meant, above all, the slavish acceptance of every executive and administrative act of the provincial bureaucracy from the Governor downwards.

Why no member of the Council ever chanced to be listed among the disaffected becomes even clearer upon an examination of the Council in 1760 and 1830, and at any intervening period:

1760

Jonathan Belcher	Chief Justice
Benjamin Green	Treasurer
Charles Morris I	Surveyor-General
Richard Bulkeley	Provincial Secretary
Thomas Saul	Merchant; commissary
Joseph Gerrish	Storekeeper of the Naval Yards

[25]Legge to Pownall, Oct. 23, 1773, N.S. A89, 98.
[26]Wentworth to Dundas, March 22, 1793, N.S. A118, 56.

1830

S. S. Blowers	Chief Justice
John Inglis	Lord Bishop
Michael Wallace	Treasurer
R. J. Uniacke Sr.	Attorney-General
Charles Morris III	Surveyor-General
T. N. Jeffery	Collector of Customs
Brenton Halliburton	Puisne judge
H. N. Binney	Collector of Impost and Excise
Enos Collins	Merchant
S. B. Robie	Master of the Rolls
C. R. Prescott	Sometime merchant; country gentleman
Samuel Cunard	Merchant

No surprise should be occasioned, therefore, by the contemporary pamphlet which pictured the Council as

chiefly composed of Persons who held Offices and received Salaries from Government, they considered themselves as envied by the Demagogues in the *Assembly*; and as every Regulation proposed by the *Assembly* affected one or other of them in their official Capacities, they were unanimous in Opposition, and brandished the shield of Prerogative to ward of [*sic*] the Attacks against their own Mal-Administrations. . .[27]

This description remained valid throughout the period, but the further point that each Councillor "violently resented the least Attempt in any of his Brethren in Office to controul him"[28] had little meaning after 1783 when the Council coalesced to defend both its general and particular interests from outside attack. More and more the councillors, and hence the principal office-holders, tended to be related by marriage, and more and more they became enamoured of their own happy situation.

The outstanding instance of family connection was the Gerrish-Brenton-Halliburton-Stewart-Cochran-Hill-George-Collins group which contributed eleven (or about one-fifth) of the councillors appointed prior to 1830 and was the closest Nova Scotia came to having a family compact. Its most distinguished member, Brenton Halliburton, belonged to a Council in which his father, two uncles, two brothers-in-law, his father-in-law, son-in-law, aunt's brother-in-law, brother-in-law's father-in-law, and the latter's brother-in-law all held seats at one time or another, and five of whom were members at the same time.[29]

[27]An *Essay on the Present State of the Province*, 1774, 8.
[28]*Ibid.*, 9.
[29]See Appendix C for the interrelationship of the Halliburton and associated families. A genealogist could, with two or three exceptions, link together all the councillors between 1760 and 1830. For example, the Uniackes with their Hill

Over a long period a substantial part of "government" was concentrated in this small group of associated families. Similarly the inter-related Green-Newton-Binney-Creighton group managed to secure five councillorships for themselves as well as a host of offices, major and minor. Even the two or three merchants who in later years held seats on the Council were closely tied in with the majority, sometimes by blood, always in general outlook, and they showed no more enthusiasm for altering the established order than their confrères.

Furthermore, in its practical operation the Council was a Halifax, not a Nova Scotian body. Of fifty-one councillors appointed between 1760 and 1830, only six can be said to have been resident outside the environs of the capital, and none of them gave anything like regular attendance. If attention to duty were the determinant, all deserved the fate of James Bruce and John Creighton who were superseded for non-attendance in 1788. Sebastian Zouberbuhler of Lunenburg made sporadic appearances in 1763 and 1764, but was hardly a nominal member in the eight years which followed; Col. James Delancey of Annapolis attended a total of four executive sessions out of 103 between 1795 and 1801; even Isaac Deschamps of Windsor, who held the reasonably remunerative post of assistant justice of the Supreme Court, was present only intermittently when the Legislature was not in session. Because of this dismal record, no Governor chanced his luck with an outsider for almost a quarter of a century, and when he did with Charles Ramage Prescott of Cornwallis, the results were only slightly better—attendance at twenty out of seventy-five executive sessions between 1825 and 1830. Despite its patent exaggeration, Thomas Chandler Haliburton's allegorical description of the Council was therefore pointing out a very real defect:

Two thirds of them have never been beyond Sackville Bridge, and think all the world is contained within the narrow precincts of Halifax. Two or three of the younger sisters indulge in a ride on the post road every summer, into the country, and have acquired the names of the villages and the inn-keepers, but that is the extent of their knowledge. They then return to town, talk sagely of roads and bridges, agriculture, rural affairs and common schools. They are looked upon as walking gazeteers, and living directories.[30]

Yet this unrepresentative character was not due to pure malice on the part of the governors. The proper conduct of provincial business clearly required a quorum on the spot, and a Council truly repre-

---

and Newton connection afford a means of connecting the Halliburton and Green families, as well as the Black, Jeffery, Morris, Francklin, Deschamps, and Wentworth families.

[30]See supplement to the *Novascotian*, March 29, 1827.

sentative of the province geographically therefore meant an unworkable Council. If the authorities in England could have foregone the notion that the councillors were on no account to receive remuneration, a workable and yet representative Council might have been constituted to perform legislative functions, but the difficulties of travel presented an altogether insuperable obstacle to genuine representation at the Council's two score or more executive sessions held intermittently throughout the year.

But the Council was not merely a Halifax body—it was also the nucleus of a loosely knit Church and State party which manifested "a tender regard for the British church and state policy," partly because it was congenial to the sympathies of its members, and partly because it would preserve and enhance a favourable opinion of them in English minds.[31] Early in the century Judge Croke, Attorney-General Uniacke, and Treasurer Michael Wallace, who represented the party's extreme wing at the Council Board, objected particularly to the public support of schools which did not have the established religion as a foundation. The latitudinarian principles of such institutions, they said, were "calculated to create a laxity in religion and morals, and a want of respect for the established forms of worship, and of the british Government & Constitution, which are closely connected with it."[32] Similarly, their counterparts of the twenties[33] declined to accept the counsel of the moderates[34] that "every attempt to give or retain exclusive privileges to the Church of England ha[d] invariably operated to its disadvantage."[35] As a result of their intransigence, criticism of religious favouritism, and of the composition and functioning of the Council itself, became important strands in the Reform movement.

But although the Council stood united in support of the status quo, its individual members were continually on the alert against efforts either by insiders or outsiders to reduce their status in the colonial

[31]See Norah Story, "The Church and State 'Party' in Nova Scotia," *Collections of the N.S. Historical Society*, XXVII, 33–57. Miss Story points out that the party, often "at war with itself," cut across denominational lines and included Anglicans, Congregationalists, Baptists, Methodists, and Roman Catholics.

[32]See P.A.N.S. 288, doc. 108, and *Journals of the Legislative Council* (*JLC*), March 31, 1815.

[33]The extremists were Bishop John Inglis, Michael Wallace, T. N. Jeffery, R. J. Uniacke, H. N. Binney, C. R. Prescott, and Enos Collins.

[34]Mr. Justice Halliburton, Mr. Justice Stewart, Master of the Rolls Robie, and Surveyor-General Morris. The extreme right and the moderate groups joined battle on the most hardy of perennials, the bill for the permanent support of Presbyterian Pictou Academy. Despite the pleas of the moderates, the extremists would do no more than vote a grant from year to year.

[35]*JLC*, March 22, 1826.

hierarchy. A Councillor's order of precedence normally depended upon seniority of appointment, but in time the Instructions conferred the first three seats upon the Chief Justice, the Lord Bishop, and the Judge of Vice-Admiralty. While special circumstances[36] allowed these exceptions to be established without incident, in two other instances the importance ascribed to precedence appears in its true light. In 1802 two councillors resigned simply because John Butler Butler was permitted to present a two-year-old mandamus enabling him to outrank five of the sitting councillors.[37]

Later the little colonial *élite* was shaken to its very foundations when Crofton Uniacke demanded admittance to the third seat at the Council Board by reason of his appointment as Judge of Vice-Admiralty.[38] This would have permitted a relatively young man, who had not yet indicated by long experience his entire affection to government, to rank ahead of the assistant justices of the Supreme Court and the oldest and most respectable members of the community, including his own father. The Lieutenant-Governor warned the Secretary of State that the matter was anything but trivial since it was "likely to affect that distinction in our Society which has hitherto attached to the Members of H.M. Council, & at [the] same time that unanimity which for years past has happily prevailed at our Council board."[39] This time his advice was heeded and the colonial *élite* breathed more easily. Thus the definitely charted course of preferment to the Council and establishment of precedence among its members and in society generally continued after 1830 with little alteration.

THE ASSEMBLY

The Assembly, which was the elected body, should be distinguished from the General Assembly, which included all three components of the legislative branch of government, Governor, Council, and

[36]The primacy of the Chief Justice had been recognized from the beginning in the case of the British jurists who held the office; the overwhelming Church of England majority on the Council naturally accepted the special recognition accorded to their Bishop without question; the third exception, "altho' very painful to several members," caused no flurry because in the case of the only individual who enjoyed the precedence, Alexander Croke, it was "associated with distinguished Talents—Family, and high official situation." Wentworth to Hobart, Oct. 10, 1803, P.A.N.S. 53, 454–6.

[37]For Governor Wentworth's final arguments against Butler's admission, see Wentworth to Hobart, May 26, 1804, *ibid.*, 505.

[38]Uniacke's demand raised the problem: Did the Instructions to the Governor to admit the Judge of Vice-Admiralty apply to the Judge of Vice-Admiralty *ex officio* or merely to the first holder of that office?

[39]Dalhousie to Bathurst, Nov. 11, 1817, P.A.N.S. 112, 40.

Assembly.[40] As was typical of British colonial governments, the elected Assembly grew steadily in power between 1758 and 1830. Two specific developments profoundly affected its nature and gave it the prestige to play a more substantial role in government.

The first was an improvement in its representative character. The legal system of representation had been "built up by fits and starts, in a higgledy-piggledy sort of fashion, without any regard to any of the principles by which a representative body is created except that fundamental one that it should represent something . . . it [was] neither according to population, intelligence, wealth, or class interests. It [was] according to no rule whatever."[41] Yet even if the system had been designed to provide genuine geographical representation, the Assembly could have been little other than a Halifax preserve in its early years. Professor Brebner has shown that its effective majority was normally made up of Halifax men, who, for the most part, were members or hangers-on of the office-holding clique.[42] The six members of the county and township of Halifax constituted a majority of its legal quorum, and the outlying counties and townships added to that total by always returning a generous representation of Haligonians. Although the celebrated Fifth Assembly (1770–85) initially contained only three residents of Halifax representing non-Halifax seats, the number had risen to six by 1775, and in that eventful year the Haligonians alone might have carried on a legal session of the Assembly.

The Halifax contingent, it is true, were not always a united phalanx, associated, in a minor role, with the dominant merchant-official oligarchy in the sharing of the loaves and fishes. Certainly John Day, who represented Halifax Township at one time, was "the leading, perhaps the only, independent, public-spirited statesman in [the] Nova Scotia"[43] of his day. But he was a *rara avis*. The evidence all goes to show that a display of real assertiveness only occurred in a well-attended House when the proportion of country members was high.

Yet even then there were ways of circumventing a lower House hostile to the Halifax interests. The Gerrish brothers organized a strike

---

[40]This use of "General Assembly," although still encountered, possesses no legal basis, and in 1777 it confused a Secretary of State who understood it to mean the lower branch of the Legislature. The Lieutenant-Governor enlightened him that "by long practice, the meeting of the Governor, Council, and Assembly for making laws, has been call'd the meeting of the General Assembly." Arbuthnot to Germain, Aug. 4, 1777, P.A.C., N.S. A97, 255.

[41]*Acadian Recorder*, Oct. 31, 1857.

[42]Brebner, *Neutral Yankees*, 210.

[43]*Ibid.*, 229n.

of assemblymen and thereby prevented the securing of a quorum and of legislation injurious to their own interests.[44] Usually a prolongation of the session or an adjournment achieved the same objective because it put the country members in a minority. Manœuvres of this kind prevented an address describing all too explicitly the Mauger domination of the province from being recorded on the Journals of the House in November, 1774. The later emasculated version reflects all too well the failure of the country members to return at an unpropitious season of the year.

While the governors cared little about the Halifax domination of the Assembly, they were most concerned about securing and maintaining a quorum. Legge stated the difficulty as he and other governors experienced it:

> . . . it often happens, that in the Beginning of the Assembly a Sufficient Quorum is not to be had, and which has obliged the Governors to prorogue oftentimes. . . . [later] the members absent themselves without leave of the Assembly or Speaker, before the Bussiness is half gone thro', whereby the Governors have been obliged to adjourn them to keep alive the Bills then under consideration, or otherwise reduced to the necessity of having no Quorum, & consequently a loss of the Whole Business of the Session. . . .[45]

A committee of the Council proposed a remedy which would have guaranteed legal sessions of the Assembly but at the same time rendered Halifax control even more complete. In essence, it reduced the quorum to nine[46] and increased the Halifax representation to ten, four for the town and six for the county. Naturally a well-attended Assembly bluntly rejected a plan "so subversive of our freedom. With a dependant Council & a Majority of such a Quorum of Assembly, what might not an ambitious Governor effect."[47]

Its counter-argument was that a quorum could always be secured in June, "the best time for travelling & the season most convenient for the interests of the generality of the Representatives."[48] But since the summoning of general assemblies was entrusted to the Governor and Council, who acted on grounds other than the convenience of the elected House, this suggestion never received a fair test. Accordingly the lower branch turned to remedies within its own power.

The Third Assembly resorted to punitive devices for non-attendance. To prevent the customary falling off in attendance as the session

[44]The helpless Lieutenant-Governor could only "prorogue and prorogue while ten faithful Assemblymen kicked their heels and swore at the others who were walking about the town." *Ibid.*, 79.
[45]Legge to Dartmouth, Nov.17, 1774, N.S. A91, 160–1.
[46]Including the Speaker. For report of the committee, see *ibid.*, 155–8.
[47]*Minutes of Council*, June 29, 1775.   [48]*Ibid.*

progressed, it ordered its members not to absent themselves without leave from the Speaker. At the same time it initiated a procedure which called for the summoning of delinquents by courier, and for their expulsion in the event of failure to appear by a fixed date.[49] Although these rules were generally not applied, the Assembly did not adopt mere half-way measures when it did choose to act. The Fifth Assembly, for example, declared no less than twenty-nine seats vacant, nine during a single week in December, 1774. Yet it was powerless to prevent the electors of Cornwallis from continuing to elect Dr. Samuel Willoughby, who had been expelled twice for constantly and wilfully neglecting to attend, and it was so soft-hearted that it could easily be persuaded to remit the fines of delinquent members.

Negative devices having accomplished little, the Assembly turned to positive measures for the alleviation of the evil. Like Governor Legge on a later occasion, it attributed the root cause of irregular attendance to the "Previledge granted to each Town of chosing among themselves, the Person to Represent . . . them, who perhaps is poor, & unable to support himself for any length of time, & is driven by necessity to return Home."[50] So when it had difficulty in assembling a quorum in 1770, it stopped recording its determination not to be remunerated for its services, and adopted an ancient English practice which required a county to pay any of its representatives who requested it at the rate of five shillings a day. None but the most naïve of optimists could have expected the grand juries of that day to assume this burden voluntarily, and the following year the magistrates in sessions were authorized to set up the machinery of assessment and collection if the grand juries failed to act.

When that resort also failed,[51] the Assembly turned to another mode of proceeding which had no English precedents to hallow it—payment by the Legislature itself. Although a small minority of the Assembly adhered to the English view that a legislative body which voted itself remuneration prostituted itself, the great majority thought otherwise. The two attitudes were brought out during an exchange in the Assembly in 1819:

[Dimock (Hants County)] could not afford to come there and devote so much of his time without remuneration—some of the members, he observed, had their friends houses to lodge at, and probably did not pay their eight dollars per week as others were obliged to do.

[49]*Journals of the House of Assembly (JHA)*, Nov. 5, 1763.
[50]Legge to Dartmouth, Nov. 17, 1774, N.S. A91, 161.
[51]The relevant statutes were: 10 Geo. III, c. 3 (1770); 11 Geo. III, c. 7 (1771); and 12 Geo. III, c. 4 (1772).

[Prescott (Cornwallis Township)] Candidates spent more money to get in, than they would receive for their pay in 7 years; was it not therefore plain, it was the honor of holding a seat in that House, which was the object in view, and not the pecuniary consideration which was now said to be necessary.

[Chipman (King's County)] . . . what is this mighty great word *honor?* The Hon. gentlemen should recollect, that the person who puts up at an Election expects his pay when he comes there—that was the object to which he looked; and not to that mighty big sounding word.[52]

Prescott was of the stuff councillors are made of, and he was soon elevated to the body where he could serve solely for the sake of honour. Yet his viewpoint had then been outdated by almost forty years. For after the Fifth Assembly had been blocked in one direction in 1772, it veered upon the other tack of making pay for members a charge upon provincial funds by statutory enactment.[53] Although the Council rejected the latter part of this proposal, it agreed in 1781 to a resolution for the payment of members who "reside[d] in the Counties and Towns distant from Halifax" at the rate of ten shillings a day out of the sum allowed for the contingencies of government.[54] Henceforth the Assembly saw to it that the contingency fund was sufficiently large to provide compensation at this rate, and once the practice of framing a general appropriation bill was adopted in 1786, it would admit of no tampering with that vote. When, in 1790, an irritated Council rejected the £650 item for defraying sessional indemnities because "a better time could not offer to Stop a growing Evil,"[55] the executive found itself without supply.

No other Council ventured thus far, but all looked with dubious eyes upon a practice which permitted it to approve the contingency fund only as a lump sum and left the money to be "divided among the Members of the House of Assembly ad libitum."[56] To reduce the evil, the Council tried, in 1811, to incorporate a fixed indemnity of ten shillings a day into the appropriation bill, and, in 1819, to restrict the indemnity to thirty-five days a session. While it succeeded on the second occasion, its victory was a Pyrrhic one, for the price of agree-

[52]*Acadian Recorder*, May 1, 1819.
[53]For the Assembly's later efforts in this direction, see bills initiated in 1777, 1780, and 1781, contained in folio "Unpassed Bills 1762–92" in P.A.N.S.
[54]*JHA*, June 21 and 22, 1781.
[55]Council to Grenville, May 4, 1790, N.S. A114, 113.
[56]Prevost to Liverpool, May 12, 1811, P.A.N.S. 59, doc. 4. It was on this occasion that Prevost asked the Secretary of State how to deal with "certain abuses grown familiar to the Legislation of this Province," and particularly the contingency fund vote of £800.

ment was an increase in the daily rate of remuneration from ten to twenty shillings.

The payment of assemblymen is by no means a matter of purely academic interest since, to all appearances, it was the major factor in enabling the outside counties to have their own members in regular attendance. After 1781, all the former indications of absenteeism on the part of country members—the wholesale vacating of seats, the difficulty of securing a quorum at the beginning and the end of sessions, the excessive number of Halifax residents representing country seats, the bewildering reversals of viewpoints in the closing days of the sessions—are missing. The lower House became, in fact, too assiduous in its duties for governors like Wentworth who terminated with pleasure sessions "protracted by those who found no disadvantage in receiving 10/ per diem."[57]

The Assembly was also transformed by the appearance of nascent party divisions. Beamish Murdoch attributed the province's first experience of party to the Loyalists,[58] and to support him, had the evidence of Governor John Parr, who, rudely disturbed as he slumbered away his last years, continually lamented the "cursed factious party spirit, which was never known here before the Emigration of the Loyalists," with their "levelling republican Principles."[59] Yet it is absurd to label the newcomers as "republican" merely because they agitated constitutional issues with some heat between 1789 and 1791. Their conduct may be explained partly by the refusal of even the Loyalists to accept all the procedures of an undoubtedly immature Assembly, and partly by the exclusion from government of persons who were accustomed more to governing than being governed. Once it became clear, as it did under their patron Wentworth (1792–1808),[60] that they were not to be denied a reasonable share of the patronage, constitutional agitation lost most of its old charm. The cleavage between Loyalists and pre-Loyalists in the Assembly melted away never to be revived; Loyalists once identified with the official group adopted the conservative and reactionary attitudes of that group,[61]

[57]Wentworth to Castlereagh, Feb. 3, 1806, P.A.N.S. 54, 82.

[58]A History of Nova Scotia or Acadie (Halifax 1865–7), III, 60–1.

[59]Parr to Nepean (private), March 18, 1790, N.S. A114, 18.

[60]See Margaret Ells, "Governor Wentworth's Patronage," Collections of the N.S. Historical Society, XXV, 55–6.

[61]Sampson Salter Blowers provided the first illustration of this phenomenon. Already Attorney-General and angling for the chief justiceship, he incurred the incriminations of his fellow Loyalists for his support of the judges whom they had impeached. That support to "government" in its hour of need brought the hoped-for reward in 1797.

while the descendants of others who failed to secure high office later became prominent in the Reform party.

The relative calm of the nineties did not carry over to the first decade of the nineteenth century. Outwardly responsible for the disturbance of the peace was a so-called "country" party which owed its appearance to an elemental characteristic of every Assembly—the conflict between the country members, who now comprised its majority in fact as well as in law, and the supporters of the merchant-official oligarchy, some within but most outside the Assembly. Their differences had many ramifications. They may be seen, for example, in the Assembly's opposition to the incorporation of a bank by legislative charter. Wentworth might ascribe the country assemblymen's behaviour to their unawareness of "the aid and support that such an Institution would afford to commerce and industry,"[62] but actually they were acquainted only too well with the persons listed in the proposed articles of incorporation and therefore highly suspicious of anything calculated to rivet more securely upon the totality of provincial life a group whose multifarious powers were already considered to be dangerous. According to the Assemblyman William Fraser of Windsor,

the interests of this town ha[ve] ever assumed a dangerous, an overwhelming preponderance. But sir give them this engine and it will become irresistable. Yes sir give them only a bank, allow them only to issue paper, permit them to deal in bonds and securities you confirm their power, you give them new influence, you enable them to lay their paw upon every freeholder in the country; and such will be the weight & extent of their influence that no man will be returned to this House unless they regard him as favourable to their interests—yes I pronounce it prophetically in all questions the voice of the country would be drowned.[63]

Immediately after 1800 another aspect of this deep-rooted conflict was dominant. Wentworth, to his credit, had got the Council and Assembly to agree, during the 1790's, to the increased impost and excise taxes needed to extinguish the public debt. That being accomplished, the Council took the position that the provincial trade required relief, while the assemblymen wanted the existing taxes retained to provide funds for the road and bridge service, which to some of them was fast becoming the principal end of their political existence. The same Wentworth who had once minimized the existing tax burden— "nobody feels them—they are scarcely known, being so highly dis-

[62]Wentworth to Hobart, Jan. 6, 1802, P.A.N.S. 53, 328.
[63]Novascotian, April 2, 1825.

perced, upon consumption only"[64]—now sided with the merchants and lamented their inability to secure relief from the country members who constantly outvoted the town members even though more than nine-tenths of the revenue was collected at the capital.[65] The subsequent intervention by the Governor and the Council in money bills forced a majority of the country members to act together, particularly since this intervention was aimed at reducing the sums voted for public works and limiting the members' control of their disposition.

Authoritarians who are obstructed in their designs try to paint the blackest picture possible of the opposing forces as a means of self-justification. Hence neither Administrator Croke's charge that the Assembly was actuated by the criminal purpose of making itself "absolutely necessary to the Government, for the payment of the interest, and other necessary supplies,"[66] nor Wentworth's warning that "views more republican than are congenial to the British Constitution, always attempt to obtain a guiding influence over the Treasury"[67] is surprising. Actually Croke's picture of the Assembly bore a close resemblance to fact; it was, he said,

as usual, composed principally of farmers, who have a little leaven of American democracy amongst them. They are consequently as a body, suspicious of Government, jealous of their rights, and strongly retentive of the public purse. Little or nothing whatever of party division prevails amongst them.[68]

But something akin to "party" could and did develop when a majority of the assemblymen had their normal "suspicions of Government" amply verified by its extravagant pretensions. Wentworth thought it was typical of political societies for a little acid leaven to ferment a large mass, and pictured that leaven as concentrated in the person of William Cottnam Tonge, an alleged sower of "discord and hatred both in and out of the House, more especially directed against those who are in the Kings service & longest established."[69] But while Tonge guided the constitutionalist forces in the Assembly, he by no means led a united following. More than once, the Assembly adopted a middle course in preference to the more extreme line which he had advocated. The "country" party of that day might, in fact, not have

[64]Wentworth to Scrope Bernard, Sept. 30, 1799, P.A.N.S. 52, 338.
[65]*Ibid.*, April 7, 1800, P.A.N.S. 53, 27–8.
[66]Croke to Castlereagh (private and confidential), Feb. 11, 1809, P.A.N.S. 58, doc. 66.
[67]Wentworth to Windham, Nov. 14, 1806, P.A.N.S. 54, 142–3.
[68]Croke to Castlereagh (private no. 1), Dec. 23, 1808, P.A.N.S. 58, doc. 60.
[69]Wentworth to Scrope Bernard, Feb. 24, 1800, P.A.N.S. 53, 20.

assumed even the nebulous shape that it did had not the whole system of road and bridge grants been challenged. Once a compromise had been reached which, in effect, entrusted the disposal of road funds to the assemblymen, all was peaceful for another two decades.

This period of relative calm was due, in part, to the tact displayed by Wentworth's successors, and, in part, to the strength of particularist forces in the Assembly.[70] Prevost, Dalhousie, and Kempt made certain that no arbitrary executive act could generate enough heat to provide the basis of united opposition; combined with particularism this meant the continuance of a partyless Assembly. Each representative joined in all sorts of complicated manœuvres with his fellow assemblymen to secure the maximum in road moneys for his own county or township,[71] and watched suspiciously to see that no other received more than its share. Similar conduct long prevented the Assembly from dividing two of the old counties and providing additional representation.[72] In this, as in other matters, the need to effect compromises on the actual floor of the Legislature always stood in the way of positive action.

Particularism also tended to conceal the irresponsible system which was the cause of all evil. To lay it bare, something more was needed than what the leadership of the twenties provided. It is true that country members like William Allen Chipman of Kings and Shubael Dimock of Hants were "conspicuous for good sense, firmness, and a readiness to defend the public interests," while lawyers like Ritchie, Robie, W. H. O. Haliburton, and Archibald "exhibited statesmanlike ideas, a power of subtle reasoning and much eloquence."[73] The last four guided the major deliberations of the Assembly, and when replacements were required in the late twenties, it was lawyers again in the persons of Charles Rufus Fairbanks, Alexander Stewart, Beamish Murdoch, and T. C. Haliburton who filled the gap. From the legal profession, too, the lower House invariably chose its Speaker. Between

---

[70]See Story, "Church and State 'Party' in Nova Scotia," 42.

[71]John A. Barry, annoyed by the Assembly's treatment of himself, described the process as "a most ingenious piece of manoeuvring and chicanery." "When I first took my seat in the Assembly," he said, "I did not expect to find gentlemen sauntering behind the cushions, and soliciting votes for particular measures." See Barry's letter in *Acadian Recorder*, May 2, 1829.

[72]The passage of any specific alteration, it was feared, would lessen the bargaining power of those who wanted alterations in other counties.

[73]Murdoch, *History of Nova Scotia*, III, 439. N. W. White, himself a lawyer, held that "if you deduct the Profession you leave a balance of ignorance, vulgarity & littleness personified." N. W. White to Cornelius, Dec. 23, 1830, White Collection in P.A.N.S., item no. 1248.

1806 and 1841 Lewis M. Wilkins, Simon Bradstreet Robie, and S. G. W. Archibald acted, in turn, as First Commoner and periodically descended from the rostrum to give the Assembly the benefit of their learning on the constitutional issues of the day. On occasions such as these, members of their profession alone possessed the education and the research facilities which were needed to present mature arguments.

Nevertheless, an acute sense of malaise slowly developed around the lawyers who constituted at least one-fourth of every Assembly after 1819.[74] Proof positive of the influence which they wielded was their ability to bestow "three easy chairs . . . upon the hungry profession"[75] in the 1820's despite the opposition of a highly vocal and not inconsiderable group of country members. Although the latter kept urging the electorate to "reduce the present number within narrower limits; and bring it into a more rational proportion with the other classes of which our representation is composed,"[76] they could hardly have realized that as long as this type of leadership continued, the Assembly could not hope to make headway against the prevailing irresponsible system. Not that any of the leading lawyers in the Assembly belonged to the extreme party in church and state,[77] for all of them felt perfectly free to make an occasional display of independence on specific constitutional issues.[78] Yet none carried it to the point where he could

[74]The following is an analysis of the membership of five Assemblies. See the *Novascotian*, July 13, 1826.

	Lawyers	Merchants	Farmers	Others
1809	7	16	13	3
1812	7	17	12	3
1819	10	17	10	2
1820	11	15	11	4
1826	10	16	13	2

[75]By the appointment of three lawyers to preside over the Inferior Court of Common Pleas and the Court of Sessions in three districts which included all counties but Halifax. *Infra*, 67. Three assemblymen, Chipman, Ritchie, and Haliburton, became the first holders of a not unattractive office. But they were not alone. Of approximately fifteen lawyers who served in the Tenth to the Thirteenth Assemblies, at least thirteen received appointments. See Gene Morison, "The Evolution of Political Parties in Nova Scotia, 1755–1848" (unpublished master's thesis in P.A.N.S.), 38. Four leading assemblymen of the 1820's, Robie, Fairbanks, Archibald, and Stewart, succeeded in turn to the Mastership of the Rolls.

[76]*Novascotian*, Jan. 28, 1830. For a more extreme view, see the letter of "Monitor" in the *Acadian Recorder*, March 20, 1824. "One or at most two lawyers in the House of Assembly might be tolerated; but under the fateful influence of TEN the weight is oppressive. The Lower House in New Brunswick contains but one; and this by some is supposed to account for her commercial prosperity."

[77]See Story, "Church and State 'Party' in Nova Scotia."

[78]While the lawyers were all in favour of removing the Catholic disabilities and restricting the Council's power to deal with money bills, lack of agreement was the usual order. On quit rents it was Stewart, Fairbanks, and Murdoch

conceivably be labelled as an unceasing critic of "government" and hence be deprived of the patronage lavished upon those of good report. It is quite significant that in the decade after 1830, when a definite stand had to be taken upon whether the governmental set-up was to be a transcript of the British model in fact as well as in form, not one of the leaders of the 1820's who was still politically active favoured a radical change in the status quo, and Stewart and Murdoch came to be labelled by their critics as congenital Tories.

S. G. W. Archibald illustrates best why the existing leadership could never have effected a real change. For sixteen years, as First Commoner of Nova Scotia, he walked a tight-rope without losing the confidence of an Assembly or a Colonial Secretary. This was possible only because he was "prone to be governed by expediency."[79] Behind the scenes he could afford to oppose giving the Assembly full control over the salaries of all colonial officials for fear that it would encourage Nova Scotians to imitate their republican neighbours in other respects,[80] but in the House itself he always espoused the moderate course. On the question of customs officers' salaries, he closed both eyes and regarded it as a difference on the construction of acts of Parliament rather than a constitutional issue which threatened the Assembly's control over revenue collected within the province. On quit rents, he favoured the policy of commutation on moderate terms rather than outright abolition. All of which adds up to the fact that the Assembly, before it could make further real advances, needed leadership of different stuff, which could forget that preservation of a reputation for respectability was a necessary requisite for preferment.

---

against Archibald and T. C. Haliburton; on customs house salaries it was Stewart and Fairbanks against Archibald, Haliburton, and Murdoch; while Stewart alone opposed a permanent grant to Pictou Academy.

[79]Murdoch, *History of Nova Scotia*, III, 534.

[80]See Archibald to Kempt (secret and confidential), Nov. 20, 1825, N.S. A166, 133–6.

CHAPTER III

THE EXECUTIVE FUNCTION

THE EXECUTIVE AUTHORITY of Nova Scotia, as in all royal colonies, was vested in the Governor. Yet because his Commission and Instructions were by no means explicit in distinguishing between legislative and executive functions,[1] constitutional development could take the form it had assumed earlier in England whereby executive power once stemming solely from the prerogative came more and more to be regulated by statute. For that reason problems like the following periodically presented themselves: What powers were distinctly prerogative, and hence to be exercised solely by the colonial executive? What powers, originally prerogative, might appropriately be transferred to the General Assembly? To what extent had usages of the Imperial Parliament which imposed checks upon the prerogative become part and parcel of the rights and privileges of the Nova Scotian House of Assembly? Did the colonial executive of a later day have to recognize inroads upon the prerogative which one of an earlier day had previously conceded?

In exercising the executive power, no Governor was a complete law unto himself since the Commission and the Instructions singled out specific matters in which he was to act by and with the advice and consent of the Council. As the Governor's advisers, the Council met under his presidency and their decisions were recorded in minutes of Council. Their power tended to be enhanced after 1783 when British statesmen "acted on the assumption that the still waters of colonial administration, no matter what pestilence they might be breeding for the future, were better left absolutely undisturbed."[2] The free hand which was given to the Governor in the naming of the councillors[3] produced a growing community of feeling between him and them, fostered by other factors tending in the same direction—the desire to present a united front against the challenge of a more mature and pretentious Assembly, and the need of most governors after Wentworth, because of their relatively short terms, to rely upon the Council

---

[1]These instruments continued in much the same form that they had assumed at the beginning of the eighteenth century and hence pre-dated Montesquieu and Blackstone. H. T. Manning, *British Colonial Government after the American Revolution 1782–1820* (New Haven, 1933), 100.

[2]*Ibid.*, 13.   [3]*Supra*, 19–20.

for knowledge of local affairs. Joseph Howe paints the classic picture of the new relationship:

It is mere mockery to tell us that the Governor himself is responsible. He must carry on the government by and with the few officials whom he finds in possession when he arrives. He may flutter and struggle in the net, as some well-meaning Governors have done, but he must at last resign himself to his fate; and like a snared bird be content with the narrow limits assigned him by his keepers. I have known a Governor bullied, sneered at, and almost shut out of society, while his obstinate resistance to the system created a suspicion that he might not become its victim; but I never knew one who, even with the best intentions and the full concurrence and support of the representative branch, backed by the confidence of his Sovereign, was able to contend, on anything like fair terms, with the small knot of functionaries who form the Councils, fill the offices, and wield the powers of the Government.[4]

But although these conclusions cannot be denied, like attitudes towards government and a natural identity of interest afford a better explanation of the complete accord between the governors and their councils than resort to bullying and cajolery.

The Governor's principal difficulty as chief executive was that he served two masters whose interests sometimes conflicted. Somehow he had to retain the good will of the people of his province and still satisfy his superiors in England that he was not sacrificing the interests of the Crown. The governors found the defence of the prerogative comparatively easy prior to 1784. The immaturity of the colony and its Assembly, the clear instructions that the royal province of Nova Scotia must on no account be permitted to move in the dangerous directions of the other American colonies, and the Assembly's inability to secure concessions by withholding the salaries of the principal officers of government[5] were largely responsible. The Nova Scotian Assembly was never able to subvert the principle that all governmental moneys were to be received and paid out by a Treasurer appointed by and responsible to the Crown; it was never permitted to place moneys granted for special purposes in the hands of commissioners named in the Appropriation Act; it was never successful in establishing the right to appoint financial officials. In these respects, at least, it did not follow the example of the admirable province of Virginia.

Undoubtedly the most extensive criticism of the executive during these years was levelled at its exercise of the power of appointment.

---

[4]J. A. Chisholm, *Speeches and Public Letters of Joseph Howe* (Halifax, 1909), I, 230.

[5]Since these were on the parliamentary grant and not subject to colonial control.

To even the ordinary onlooker, the provincial civil service must have appeared to be what, in fact, it actually was, "a crowd of rapacious . . . men, supposedly carrying on their work under the governor, but really dependent on their own efforts for the lining of their pocket-books."[6] All the evils of the prevailing British attitude towards patronage were incorporated into the system. Except for the major offices, the powers of appointment and dismissal were devolved upon the Governor, sometimes with the advice and consent of a majority of his Council. "From end to end of Nova Scotia, there is not one office in the gift of the people but that of Member of the Assembly. They cannot choose a Health Warden, or a Firewarden—or even a Scavenger," lamented the *Novascotian*.[7] The Governor could also recommend individuals for the more lucrative provincial offices to the appropriate appointing authority in Britain, and after 1783 his recommendations were normally, although not invariably, accepted.[8]

Wentworth used these powers to practise nepotism of the most brazen and far-reaching character. Brother-in-law Benning got the treasurership in 1793, a councillorship in 1795, and the offices of secretary, registrar, and clerk of council in 1796. Son Charles Mary received a councillorship in 1801, and his father's recommendation for his uncle's three offices upon the latter's death in 1808.[9] The behind-the-scenes manœuvring on this occasion demonstrates to advantage the manner in which forces operated in colonial government. One not without his own patrons in England, Attorney-General Uniacke, made similar overtures on behalf of his son Crofton, but although the new Governor, Sir George Prevost, considered Uniacke to be less objectionable than Wentworth,[10] he ranked him below the nineteen-year-old Samuel Hood George, whose membership in the colony's leading family group undoubtedly contributed to his eventual success.[11]

[6]Manning, *British Colonial Government*, 115.

[7]Oct. 27, 1836. The single exception was provided by the road commissioners over whose selection the assemblymen gained a preponderant share by extra-legal convention after 1800. *Infra*, 58–61.

[8]Wentworth failed to have his Loyalist friend Jonathan Sterns appointed Attorney-General over the head of R. J. Uniacke, but even then the home government by "devious means . . . at once carried out its own views and contrived that Wentworth should appear to 'be supported in the business of govt.'" Margaret Ells, "Governor Wentworth's Patronage," *Collections of the N.S. Historical Society*, XXV, 54.

[9]Wentworth to Castlereagh, Feb. 22, 1808, P.A.N.S. 58, doc. 3.

[10]Prevost to Cooke, April 27, 1808, P.A.N.S. 58, doc. 13.

[11]There is ample evidence of the same contention for minor offices. Lord Dalhousie, to whom an outsider was recommended for preferment, described "the press for any little office . . . such, that I am quite sure I shall never have the

Where consideration of family did not enter, the making of appointments followed the eighteenth-century principle that patronage was not only "a legitimate but an essential instrument of political manipulation."[12] Wentworth's long "experience in the technique of governance and familiarity in imperial government circles"[13] had equipped him to be one of its abler exponents, while his long residence in Nova Scotia left him in no doubt about who would be his friends and the friends of government.

Consequently no Secretary of State had to fear that any of his nominees would be found in opposition to authority. Those who seconded the Governor's views upon government were invariably singled out for advancement. Charles Morris III, for example, moved from the Assembly to the Council because he "uniformly maintained the Kings rights and interests in the House of Representatives . . . [at a time when] questions [had] been agitated with too much warmth, and needed the firmness and wisdom of considerate men, to prevent extending into unpleasant Dissention."[14] Hence Administrator Croke's assertion that the executive always possessed considerable control over the lower House because of its ability to bestow little favours upon the representatives and their friends[15] needs to be treated with caution. Certainly nothing which savoured of a Governor's party could be built up in the Assembly for the very reason that its prospective leaders were destined to have only a brief stay there.

Yet such intangibles as the desire not to ruin one's chances in the distribution of these favours served to prevent an extreme display of independence by the assemblymen. They understood how deep the roots of the prevailing system of favouritism were. They could see how the power to appoint justices of the peace and commissioners of schools[16] was used to build up little local cliques which bore the same relationship to the local communities as the Council did to the provincial sphere. They were aware, too, that the awarding of contracts for

---

opportunity of placing any stranger to his advantage." Dalhousie to Hyde, April 10, 1819, P.A.N.S. 112, 70. One of the Shelburne Whites who applied for a position was advised that "there are so many Candidates for every public appointment that it is impossible for a person to be too early in application." Jos. Prescott to Gideon White, April 24, 1811, White Collection (P.A.N.S.), item 947.

[12]Manning, *British Colonial Government*, 110.

[13]Ells, "Governor Wentworth's Patronage," 52.

[14]Wentworth to the Lords of the Treasury, July 23, 1803, P.A.N.S. 53, 438–9.

[15]Croke to Castlereagh, Dec. 23, 1808 (private no. 1), P.A.N.S. 58, doc. 60.

[16]See, for example, the complaint in the *Novascotian* (May 19, 1830) that the lists of commissioners of schools showed an unmistakable bias towards adherents of the Church of England.

supplying the military and naval establishment in Halifax, and the making of extensive grants of land contributed to the same end. In getting land the good favour of Michael Wallace, the Provincial Treasurer, was a sure road to preferment. Wallace never forgave the people of Pictou for their part in his defeat in the election of 1799. Years later his supporters and their relatives got every attention in their application for Crown lands, while "other parties . . . were told to 'go to Mortimer' [his Pictou opponent], and let him get them land."[17] All this, said the *Novascotian*, seriously weakened the position and influence of the Assembly.

We once inclined to the belief that the influence which His Majesty's Council enjoyed, from the possession of office—from the intercourse with . . . the Governor, in their executive capacity, was only a sufficient counterbalance for the controul which the Assembly held over the sympathies of the people. . . . But unfortunately the sympathies of the people cannot always be brought to bear upon matters of minor importance; and therefore, while the patronage, the power and the influence of the Council, are daily and hourly at work in support of their own measures and opinions, that which we considered a useful set off cannot always be relied upon as a sufficient counteraction.[18]

Above all, the Assembly discovered that once an office was created, its occupant could seldom be displaced and its abolition was well-nigh impossible. Actually the Nova Scotian office-holders appeared not to be accountable because the powers of suspension and removal were rarely invoked. When the Assembly finally tried to improve the administrative machinery, the vested rights which had grown up around the offices proved a major stumbling block. They had become, in effect, valuable pieces of property which need not be surrendered without compensation.

Since the fees of office were also inadequately regulated, there was little to prevent the office-holders from adopting the uniform colonial practice of conducting their business so as to maximize the receipts.[19] Neither the protests of the First Assembly against the fees of the Judge

[17]George Patterson, *History of the County of Pictou* (Montreal, 1877), 198. Favouritism, however, did not extend to Pictou alone. Elsewhere, too, those on the inside, like the Shelburne Whites, came in for special treatment. "If you find any good land let me know & I will humbug old Michael out of a few hundred or so for myself," wrote Nathaniel White to his brother Cornelius. "Perhaps Dean [another brother] would like some also—Now is the time for asking favors, for I am quite sure of getting anything I have impudence enough to ask for." White Collection, item 1175.

[18]May 19, 1830.

[19]Manning, *British Colonial Government*, 114.

of Vice-Admiralty[20] nor the efforts of later assemblies to reduce those of the Naval Officer[21] had any real success. In desperation, the lower House then attempted a complete statutory regulation of fees so as "to prevent any undue exactions or exorbitant demands, touching the same."[22] While the Council did not reject the bill, it upheld its contention that the right to regulate fees was part of the prerogative and therefore beyond the power of the Assembly by changing the title to "an act for the establishment of Fees, as Regulated by the Governor and Council, at the request of the House of Assembly." Thus its right to establish new scales of fees could still be invoked at its own discretion.[23]

The power of appointment was also the means by which the Governor and Council exerted a strong influence over local government. It was only natural, of course, that local administrative matters for the township of Halifax should at first be decided largely by the Council. In 1758, when the First General Assembly undertook to place these arrangements on a statutory basis, it had to decide between two alternatives. One was the New England practice, which vested local governmental functions in proprietors' or town meetings, and the officials whom they elected; the other was the Virginian system, which entrusted these functions jointly to the justices in sessions, who were selected by the Governor and Council, and the grand juries, which were composed of substantial proprietors chosen by lot. The decision being to introduce the Virginian mode of doing things, an "Act for Preventing Trespasses" authorized the grand jury to appoint the local officials who were deemed essential for the township of Halifax in the existing state of society.[24] The practice of the next few years was to widen this provision and to extend it to the newly established

[20]See *Journals of the House of Assembly* (*JHA*), Dec. 5, 1758. When the Assembly demanded an accounting of the fees taken in the Court, its judge, Councillor John Collier, replied that he held the office pursuant to an Imperial commission and subject to no obligations to the Assembly.

[21]Twice (see *JHA*, June 23, 1777, and *JHA*, July 2, 1782) the Council gave its stock answer that these fees were settled by Act of Parliament, but in the case of a third protest against the exaction of fees from small boats and coasting vessels, the Naval Officer considered his position so doubtful that he thought it imprudent to press his claim. See Tonge to Gideon White, April 8, 1796, White Collection, item 593.

[22]See preamble of 28 Geo. III, c. 15 (1787).

[23]See, for example, the regulation of the fees of the Attorney-General's office (*Minutes of Council*, July 13, 1799), and of those to be paid on grants of land (*Minutes of Council*, Jan. 12, 1811).

[24]32 Geo. II, c. 14. The first officers were: four overseers of the poor, two clerks of the market, two fence viewers, two hogreeves, and four surveyors of highways. A pound-keeper was added in 1759.

counties.[25] But after 1765 there was a growing tendency to change the grand juries' power of appointment to a purely nominative function, and to permit the justices in sessions to select the local officials from their nominees.[26] In other respects, too, the powers of the justices were steadily enhanced,[27] and as a result local government came less and less to mean government of property-holders chosen by lot, and more and more government of the sessions chosen by the Governor and Council.

As part of its programme to maintain the status quo, the oligarchical governing clique periodically requested the British government's support for its defence of the prerogative. Parr's usual practice was to picture a Council acting with moderation in support of the authority of the royal Instructions against the encroachments of the Assembly. Invariably he concluded with the warning that, if the Council were not given proper encouragement, its members would resign and suitable replacements would not be forthcoming.[28] Wentworth fully seconded his viewpoint:

Upon a steady support of [the Council], their selection and rank among themselves and in society, will greatly depend the peace, prosperity and proper attachments to Great Britain of this, and all the other Colonies on this Continent. The political influence which has for several years past excited an enthusiasm in the public mind in most countries, under the specious name of amendment of constitutions of Government require only a firm support of the measures and members of Government to prevent the nominal amendments from extending into actual prostration of legitimate authority.[29]

These views reflect the fear of the official faction that the working out of Council-Assembly relationships would necessarily favour the popular branch; colonial experience elsewhere had shown it and the operation of local pressures made it inevitable. So when Chief Justice Blowers offered his suggestions for adapting the royal Instructions to

[25]Perhaps the most important of the later statutes was 5 Geo. III, c. 6, which empowered the grand jury to appoint annually a County Treasurer, subject to the confirmation of the sessions, and upon the representations of three or more freeholders or of its own knowledge to make presentments for a wide variety of expenditures largely connected with the administration of justice. But, in keeping with the general tendency, the power of the grand jury to appoint a County Treasurer later became the power to nominate three suitable candidates from whom the sessions made the appointment.

[26]The preamble of 5 Geo. III, c. 1 declared the system of having the local officials appointed by the grand juries to be "inconvenient."

[27]For the details on local government prior to 1830 see chap. IX.

[28]Parr to Grenville, April 24, 1790, P.A.C., N.S. A114, 58–9; for similar views see Parr to Nepean (private), April 24, 1790, ibid., 60–1.

[29]Wentworth to Castlereagh, March 28, 1808, P.A.N.S. 58, doc. 7.

"the progressive alterations both in the law of the Empire at large, and in the condition of particular Colonies,"[30] he recommended "a code framed and established by Statute for the General Government of the Colonies published and made known [as] preferable to Instructions to the Governors which are to be communicated at discretion;—objections having often [been] made in the Assemblies to the Royal Instructions as not obligatory on them but on the Governors only."[31] Long experience had convinced him that the only way to avert more radical pretensions by the Assembly was to clip its wings by statute.

The official faction also considered it fraught with danger to have to rely upon the lower House for their emoluments of office. Parr was especially indignant because the assistant judges were "obliged to court the Favor of the leading members of the Assembly, or be made liable to complaint or Impeachment on every Occasion."[32] But the most extreme proposal for promoting official independence came from Alexander Croke. Why, he asked, could not all the members of the Council, "consisting principally of His Majesty's Officers, [and] always disposed to second the views of Government,"[33] be secured in the regular payment of their salaries, so as to avoid the need of applying to the Assembly? If the Secretary of State would impose additional taxes of £4,000 on the commerce of Nova Scotia and add that sum to the parliamentary grant, the King's business could be conducted in comfort.[34] While his associates were more moderate, they were opposed, none the less, to placing the emoluments of the officers supported by the parliamentary grant at the mercy of the Assembly. Lieutenant-Governor Kempt even prophesied that it would mean the disappearance of English habits and feelings from the colony.[35]

Attorney-General Uniacke had the insight to see that a Council

[30]The request for suggestions came in a despatch from Bathurst to the Officer Administering the Government of Nova Scotia, March 31, 1823, P.A.N.S. 64, doc. 70.

[31]But Lieutenant-Governor Kempt opposed any "very material alterations" on the ground that "the mischievous might represent the measure as a re-modelling of the Colonial Constitution." In his opinion Nova Scotians considered that a constitution derived from the Instructions rested upon a more secure foundation than one which had been created by Act of Parliament and hence could be repealed or amended at any time, especially as His Majesty could not "recall any rights which he ha[d] granted to his Subjects." See Kempt to Bathurst, April 3, 1824, P.A.N.S. 113½, 40.

[32]Parr to Grenville, April 24, 1790, N.S. A114, 56.

[33]Croke to Castlereagh (private no. 1), Dec. 23, 1808, P.A.N.S. 58, doc. 60.

[34]Croke to Castlereagh (private and confidential), Feb. 11, 1809, P.A.N.S. 58, doc. 66.

[35]See private and confidential observations which are included with Kempt to Horton (secret and confidential), Nov. 16, 1825, N.S. A166, 140.

containing the principal officers could not fail to be involved directly in controversy with the Assembly so long as it possessed legislative functions. On two occasions, therefore, he suggested the insertion of a buffer between it and the lower House. His plan was for the Crown to summon by writ, at the time each Assembly was elected, a specified number of persons of influence, ability, and fortune, from all sections of the province, to constitute a Legislative Council and to control any factious disposition on the part of the Assembly. The major officers of government would act only as an Executive Council and advise the Governor from their completely aloof position, independent of all authority except that of the King "at whose will they should hold their situations, and from whom they should all receive their salaries."[36]

At best, this proposal could have provided little more than temporary protection for the existing Council since the new Council would have meant a body chosen principally from the local compacts and in entire sympathy with the viewpoint of the master compact at Halifax. Any Assembly would quickly have realized that contending with it was really tilting at windmills.

[36]See Uniacke's Memorandum to Windham, Feb. 18, 1806, N.S. A138, 243–83. By 1819 the details of the plan had changed a little, but it remained the same in principle. Furthermore, Uniacke had new arguments to support his position: The officers of government had insufficient time to give legislative matters "that deliberate consideration which their importance require," and the province had developed to the point where it possessed an abundance of well-informed persons of property and influence to form a second legislative branch. *Minutes of Council*, April 22, 1819.

CHAPTER IV

THE LEGISLATIVE FUNCTION

THE LEGISLATIVE ARM of government instituted in Nova Scotia after 1758 was the empirical product of long colonial experience elsewhere. In its essence a General Assembly[1] was empowered to make laws for "the public peace, welfare and Good Government of the said province." The Governor's Commission restricted this delegation of power somewhat by stipulating that the "said Laws, Statutes and Ordinances [were] not to be repugnant but as near as local circumstances will admit agreeable to the Laws and Statutes of this Our Kingdom of Great Britain." The Instructions also had a limiting effect, particularly after 1767 when they prohibited any changes in the constitution of the Legislature which had not been approved in England or were not passed with a suspending clause.[2]

While the legal power for the enforcement of these restrictions was never in doubt, the human factor was always incalculable. One might have expected that the naval and military governors would not be unduly fastidious in their observance, and Hughes' assent to a bill limiting the duration of assemblies, even though it did not contain a suspending clause, is therefore not surprising. Nor is Kempt's acceptance of one which altered the basis of the franchise in Cape Breton and altogether outraged a Secretary of State.[3] It is somewhat astonishing, however, to find Wentworth encouraging the framing of a revenue bill at variance with the royal Instructions, and Belcher and Croke, the only two chief executives with legal training, straining their Instructions to suit themselves.

Generalizations about the policy pursued in England are simpler. At the outset, in keeping with the intent that Nova Scotia should not be a quasi-republic like Massachusetts, the Board of Trade expected Chief Justice Belcher to keep the laws free from republican taint. It was shocked, therefore, to discover that the acts of the First Assembly which differed from those of England had been taken from the statutes of Massachusetts Bay.[4] Its explanation that the latter had been accepted in the very infancy of that colony's charter, "when the

[1]*Supra*, 24–5.   [2]*Infra*, 55.
[3]See Bathurst to Kempt, April 15, 1826, P.A.N.S. 65, doc. 73.
[4]Board of Trade to Belcher, Dec. 12, 1760, N.S. A64, 288.

Administration of Government . . . at home was too well employed in Settling those principles upon which the present happy constitution of this Country rests, to attend to the lesser, tho' important, consideration of what might be the principles of Colony [*sic*] constitution and government,"[5] implied that a stronger hand was to be used in Nova Scotia, but this initial ardour for preventing the statute book from being contaminated soon dissipated and had little practical effect.

Much more significant was the stronger use of the prerogative during the late sixties and seventies, for not only was the Legislature's one attempt to regulate the system of representation denied in England, but the general restrictions upon changes in its constitution were rigorously enforced. After the Revolution, however, the policy again became one of a minimum of interference. Throughout the colonies disallowance was used principally to "protect the persons and property of individuals, . . . to render the colonial codes more workable and consistent," and not primarily to bolster the prerogative.[6] The dawning of the new day for Nova Scotia was indicated in 1782 when the Board of Trade, noting by pure accident that the County of Hants had been established the previous year by an order of the Governor and Council, advised that

Tho' the power of erecting Counties in all parts of His Majesty's Dominions is undoubtedly within His Royal Prerogative, nevertheless in Colonies like Nova Scotia where the Legislature is compleat, we are of opinion that this power ought not be exercised in any other Mode than by general Act of the whole Legislature, subject to the pleasure of the Crown.[7]

Although a sterner policy appears to have been pursued after 1815, it simply meant that the English officialdom was taking its duties more seriously. For while James Stephen, the legal adviser to the Colonial Office, "examined the laws carefully . . . he was loth to recommend disallowance even though the colonial laws might be carelessly drawn and not conform in every particular to the corresponding English law."[8] Yet it is a sign of the times that in 1809 a Lieutenant-Governor might assent without objection to an act barring justices of the Supreme Court from the Assembly, whereas in 1824 he was reprimanded for acquiescing in a similar prohibition upon the first justices of the Courts of Common Pleas.

In addition to their purely negative power of veto, the Governor and

[5]*Ibid.*, 288–9.
[6]H. T. Manning, *British Colonial Government after the American Revolution, 1782–1820* (New Haven, 1933), 81.
[7]Board of Trade to Hamond, Feb. 22, 1782, N.S. A102, 15 b–c.
[8]See *The Cambridge History of the British Empire*, II, 286n.

the appropriate authorities in England might recommend legislative proposals of their own. Since these suggestions normally required an additional financial outlay, their reception by the Assembly was invariably lukewarm. Lieutenant-Governor Hughes acquiesced in its failure to provide for provincial defence because he knew how far the Nova Scotian was prepared to go.[9] Lord Dalhousie, on the other hand, was so annoyed at the rejection of his plans for the survey of the province and the inspection of the militia that he declined the honours which the General Assembly had voted him.[10]

The Council's participation in the legislative process reflected its determination to uphold the interests of the class it represented. This is best illustrated by its continuing disagreement with the Assembly on the amount of revenue to be raised, the mode of raising it, and the manner of applying it to provincial needs. In pre-Revolutionary days the conflict sprang from the land-owning Council's objection to the taxation of unimproved lands; after 1784 it resulted from the desire of a Council keenly interested in mercantile and business pursuits to avoid heavy expenditures on roads, bridges, and bounties so as to keep down the impost and excise taxes which were anathema to it.

But the main cause of contention was the Assembly's attempt to whittle down the executive and legislative powers of the Council. To the councillors, the Governor's Commission and Instructions constituted the Alpha and Omega of the constitution. Their interpretation of these documents restricted the powers of the Assembly within the narrowest possible confines and extended their own to include anything which was not specifically prohibited. According to this view, the people's representatives could use the House of Commons as a model only so far as might be "necessary to preserve Order and Method in the arrangement of Public Business . . . but without assuming Rights, that can neither be inherent or implied in the Nature of our Provincial Settlement, and which, will never apply."[11] Since the Assembly rejected this interpretation in its entirety, the main thread in the evolution of government between 1758 and 1830 is the working out of its differences with the Council in the field of practical politics.

One result was that the lower House successfully asserted its right to a substantial share of the privileges enjoyed by the House of

[9]But the Secretary of State contended that since the province levied neither a land nor poll tax, a contribution towards defence in critical times would be "no more than a proper expression of Loyalty & Gratitude." Germain to Hughes, May 3, 1779, N.S. A99, 72.

[10]Beamish Murdoch, *History of Nova Scotia* (Halifax, 1865–7), III, 451.

[11]See letter of "Observer" in the *Royal Gazette*, June 22, 1790.

Commons.[12] The extent to which these privileges, many of them gained after prolonged struggles with the Crown, belonged inherently to a colonial Assembly, was not authoritatively decided until the 1860's. As early as 1759, however, the Assembly requested the customary privileges of British representative bodies, and Lawrence accorded it "all such privileges as His Majestys Instructions would permit."[13] While the House was demanding the privileges of the Commons, the Governor was granting those permitted by a document which intended no exalted position for the people's representatives. For the moment the latter avoided debate on the abstract question and applied the procedure of the Commons to each issue as it arose. So long as the process did not affect the interests of the merchant-official oligarchy, the "sparks of liberty" were few, but the situation altered when Wentworth attempted to turn the clock back in an Assembly which contained a strong "country party." From that period dates the practice of extensive research into British precedents.[14]

Generally speaking, the claims of privilege put forward by the Assembly fell into three categories, the foremost of which was freedom of speech and action for its members. At its first session in 1758 it arrested Archibald Hinshelwood, the Deputy Secretary of the province, for using "very threatening and scandalous words against . . . [the Assemblyman] William Pantree," a course of action it described as "Dangerous to the Lives of the Members, and distructive to the liberties of the people."[15] Twenty years later it required G. H. Monk to apologize for threatening the Assemblyman who had opposed the granting of his petition.[16] Sometimes the Assembly's action was to protect its members collectively rather than individually. That was true in 1829 when a group of assemblymen were "hooted and hissed along the streets [of Halifax], pelted with snow, mud, stones and other missiles, and assailed by every opprobious expression that could be vented by a heedless and unthinking rabble."[17] This time the lower House sought to vindicate its wounded dignity by voting £500 for

[12]This was typical of most colonial Assemblies. See Mary P. Clarke, *Parliamentary Privilege in the American Colonies* (New Haven and London, 1943), 269.

[13]*Journals of the House of Assembly (JHA)*, Dec. 4, 1759.

[14]In the most celebrated of these cases, John A. Barry contributed a year-long series of letters to the *Acadian Recorder*, attempting to prove that the precedents of the British Parliament had been ignored in the Assembly's handling of his alleged breaches of its privileges. See *Novascotian*, Feb. 4, 1830.

[15]*JHA*, Dec. 14, 1758.

[16]*Ibid.*, June 18, 1778.

[17]*Novascotian*, April 16, 1829. The crowd was protesting its having committed the Assemblyman John A. Barry to jail.

discovering, "prosecuting and bringing to condign punishment, the Authors, Parties, Aiders and Abettors, of and in the said Outrages."

A second objective of the Assembly was to remove those obstacles which barred a member from attending to his legislative duties. More than once it had to intervene on behalf of individuals who had been imprisoned for debt. At first it dealt with specific cases, as in 1783 when it censured an attorney for committing a member to jail, but when two incidents occurred in one year (1818),[18] it was fearful that the ill might attain epidemic proportions. Accordingly it resolved that, except for treason, felony, or breach of the peace, its members should be immune from arrest during a session and, in conformity with the usage of the Commons, for forty days before and after a session.[19] Even so, it occasionally had to provide relief for members who were not released from custody[20] or whose occupation constituted a deterrent to attendance.[21]

Finally, the Assembly took steps to protect its members from insult, libel, and slander. Prior to 1830 the violators of the Assembly's privileges in this respect made their humble submission without incident. That was certainly true of two members who cast insults upon the Speaker,[22] and of another who alleged that "the Majority of Members appeared to have come determined right or wrong to vacate the Election" of his friend.[23] It applies also to a constituent who charged his representative with improper motives,[24] and to a newspaper publisher who permitted a jocose criticism reflecting upon a member.[25] But it is decidedly inapplicable to the Assemblyman John A. Barry who, for continued contempt of the House, was committed to jail in 1829. In some of these incidents the Assembly may have exaggerated

[18]One of these incidents concerned Jacob van Buskirk, a member for the county of Shelburne, who was held in custody under a writ of attachment issued by the Court of Vice-Admiralty. To effect his release, the House had an English procedure adopted—the issuance by the Lieutenant-Governor, in his capacity as Chancellor, of a writ of discharge directed to the Deputy Marshal of the Court of Vice-Admiralty.

[19]JHA, 1818, 92.

[20]A Speaker's warrant directed to the Sheriff of Annapolis was needed to effect the release of John Robertson, a member for that county, in 1825.

[21]As in the case of a sub-collector employed in the Imperial customs establishment. See JHA, 1830, 613, 620–1, 714–15.

[22]Joseph Woodmass in 1762 and William Lawson in 1812.

[23]Major Thomas Barclay in the unseating of his fellow Loyalist David Seabury. See JHA, June 23, 1786.

[24]David Benjamin in 1817.

[25]Anthony Holland of the Acadian Recorder upon the Pictou member Edward Mortimer in 1818.

the seriousness of the breach of privileges because it was the easiest way to uphold its prestige at a time when its attempts at self-assertion were being circumscribed in other directions.

The Assembly attempted, in addition, to regulate any matter pertaining peculiarly to itself. This was the outcome of its realization that unless it could determine its own rules of procedure, the qualifications of the electors and elected, the duration of its own life, and the basis of representation, it would lack the authority which was needed to play a forceful role in the governmental process. Theoretically some restrictions in these matters remained up to 1867, but for all practical purposes it had established its pre-eminent position by 1830.

In regulating its procedures and in choosing its officers, the lower House at no time met any concerted attempt at interference by the Governor or Council. But in 1806 Governor Wentworth refused to accept his long-time abomination, William Cottnam Tonge, as its Speaker. Although the Assembly's rejoinder—a protest against the use of a power "long unused in Great Britain and without precedent in this province"—was woefully impotent, the authorities in England showed such a lack of enthusiasm for this exercise of the prerogative that no other Governor attempted it.[26]

The lower House was particularly anxious to secure some measure of control over the duration of the Assembly, especially after it became evident that the power of the Governor to adjourn, prorogue, and dissolve assemblies constituted a trump card in the executive's control over the legislative branch. More than once it was a means of reminding the lower House that its existence was dependent upon the caprice of a Governor. Lord William Campbell dismissed the Fourth Assembly (1765-70) after five years of failing to cope with the financial ills of the province. His successors let the Fifth Assembly drag on for fifteen because they realized that an election would not produce an Assembly more in consonance with their own wishes. Unwilling to remain a mere plaything in the hands of the Governor, the Assembly petitioned the King in 1775 for triennial parliaments to be elected on a day fixed by law, but its bill to that effect was rejected by the Council. It was no more successful in 1790 when Parr refused a septennial bill which did not contain a suspending clause. Two years later Wentworth managed to secure prior approval in England of a measure which was completely in harmony with the British practice, but its only result was to fix the outermost limits of an Assembly's life.

[26]Tonge, of course, had been elected in the first place by a majority of one and his "country" party by no means controlled the House.

Within the seven-year period the Governor still determined how long it was to exist.[27]

A second source of complaint, the use of an extended prorogation to render an offending Assembly impotent,[28] was remedied by a natural corrective without resort to legislation. Since the revenue solely at the disposal of the Governor became increasingly inadequate to carry on the government, annual sessions of the Legislature could hardly be avoided, and 1788 appears to have been the only year in which it was not convened.

The Assembly's efforts to exert some control over elections and the franchise were considerably more rewarding. Until 1789 the Council was the sole regulator of elections.[29] The Assembly's early attempts to gain a voice in these matters had only a modicum of success since the Council declared its first proposals to regulate elections (1759) to be "cont[r]ary to His Majestys Instructions and the Resolutions of the Governor and Council settled and confirmed by His Majesty,"[30] and rejected a bill even more extensive in its application in the mid-seventies. The one gain of the Fifth Assembly (1770–85) was a measure providing for the appointment of county sheriffs,[31] a result of its demand to be delivered from "a Provost Marshall presiding over this whole province, whose influence . . . must be excessive, and whose power in Elections is absolute."[32]

It was the Sixth Assembly (1785–92), operating as it did under a much less exalted view of the prerogative, which made the greatest headway. Acting on the premise that it possessed the "sole and exclusive power of examining and determining . . . all matters incidental to elections," it regulated both the franchise and election proceedings by statute.[33] This act broke entirely new ground in its attempts to reduce the disorders during elections by introducing some degree of certainty into the mode of conducting them and by providing penalties for fraudulent practices and other breaches of the election rules. As in other matters, once the Assembly had participated in the alteration of electoral procedures, the Governor and Council never again attempted to make alterations solely by themselves.

[27]Wentworth, for example, opposed a seventh session for any assembly to prevent the obstructives from devoting a large part of its proceedings "toward making popular interests, for the ensuing election." Wentworth to Castlereagh, Feb. 3, 1806, P.A.N.S. 54, 82.

[28]As Hughes did in 1779–80.

[29]For the first election regulations, see *Minutes of Council*, May 20, 1758.

[30]*JHA*, March 19, 1759.   [31]18 Geo. III, c. 2 (1778).

[32]This was contained in its celebrated address of 1775. See *C.H.R.*, XV, 174–81.

[33]29 Geo. III, c. 1 (1789).

For the first thirty years the Governor and Council also regulated the extent of the franchise. Originally, any freeholder, twenty-one years of age, and not a "Popish recusant," might vote and be elected for the district in which his freehold was situated.[34] In 1759 a provision requiring the freehold to have an annual value of forty shillings brought the qualification into conformity with English practice.[35] No further change occurred until 1789 when the General Assembly placed the qualifications of voters and candidates upon a statutory basis. Yet the temporary conferment of the right to vote upon the owner of a dwelling-house or one hundred acres of land constituted no real extension of the franchise.[36]

Once again the Assembly's entrance into a field meant that all subsequent changes would be initiated by itself. But the need to insert suspending clauses in all bills altering the constitution of the Legislature restricted its freedom of action before 1830, particularly in the enfranchisement of Catholics. For although the act of 1789 boldly proclaimed the principle of religious equality in voting, the land-holding regulations still constituted a very real disability.

The First Assembly had given Catholics the right to possess only those lands conveyed to them by the Crown,[37] and a later Assembly's attempt (1782) to give them the same rights as Protestants was denied in England because it was not in conformity with the corresponding English statute.[38] As a result, the Legislature could go no further than permit those Catholics to acquire and hold lands without restriction who took oaths which were highly obnoxious to them.[39] This state of affairs continued until the re-annexation of Cape Breton, with its considerable Catholic population, forced a reconsideration of the problem. Its initial phase developed when one of the island's first members, the Catholic Lawrence Kavanagh, declared his inability to subscribe to the declaration against transubstantiation which was required of all assemblymen. The solution was to admit Roman Catholics to membership upon their taking the state oaths and nothing more.[40] But since the Assembly of the day favoured the complete equality of all citizens before the law, it went further and repealed all the other

[34]*Minutes of Council*, May 20, 1758.
[35]*Ibid.*, Aug. 22, 1759.
[36]29 Geo. III, c. 1. The act also enabled Loyalists who were occupying land not yet escheated by the Crown to vote on licences of occupation.
[37]32 Geo. II, c. 2, s. 2 (1758).
[38]North to Governor of Nova Scotia, June 24, 1783, N.S. A103, 110–12.
[39]23 Geo. III, c. 9 (1783).
[40]See Bathurst to Kempt, May 8, 1822, P.A.N.S. 64, doc. 46.

restrictions upon Catholics, including those relating to land-holding, three years before similar relief had been provided in England.[41]

The re-annexation of Cape Breton was also responsible for the first real dent in the freehold basis of the franchise. Because of the general absence of grants in freehold on the Island, the Assembly considered it necessary, despite the misgivings of the Secretary of State,[42] to confer the right to vote upon the holders of Crown leases or licences of occupation in Cape Breton.[43]

In its efforts to regulate the qualifications of its members, the Assembly started out by opposing the inclusion of place-men, hoping thereby to prevent the Legislature from becoming a replica in minia-ture of the House of Commons. Thus, in December, 1758, it tried to debar any Councillor or Assemblyman from holding "any Place or Employment of Profitt under this Government."[44] If the bill had been accepted it would have meant the destruction at one fell swoop of the political power of an entrenched officialdom and might have rendered much of the subsequent constitutional agitation unnecessary. Yet even if it had not run counter to established colonial policy, the possibility that any Assembly could have functioned without the official element is highly problematical, while the construction of a Council without it was entirely out of the question.

After 1783 the Assembly was much more reluctant to restrict its membership. The Loyalist assemblymen got nowhere in 1789 when, during their campaign against an entrenched pre-Loyalist official element, they sought to exclude from the Assembly the judges of the Supreme Court and the customs officials in general,[45] and the three sitting members who held office in particular. Much later in the period the Legislature disqualified the puisne judges of the Supreme Court and the first justices of the Inferior Courts,[46] but beyond that it would not go.

In deciding upon the qualifications of the electors and elected, the Assembly secured an early concession without even requesting it when the Governor and Council made it the final determinant of contested elections in 1759.[47] At first the whole House heard the cases, but it soon transferred this power to select committees of from three to five

[41]7 Geo. IV, c. 18 (1826).
[42]Bathurst to Kempt, April 15, 1826, P.A.N.S. 65, doc. 73.
[43]4–5 Geo. IV, c. 22, s. 6.
[44]See *Journals of the Legislative Council* (*JLC*), Dec. 6, 1758.
[45]*JHA*, March 12, 23, and 31, 1789.
[46]*Infra*, 71.
[47]*Minutes of Council*, Aug. 22, 1759.

members. During the Revolutionary and post-Revolutionary periods, however, it reverted to its earlier practice, in the former case because it considered itself best qualified to adjudicate upon the loyalty of individual members, in the latter because it would have had to determine the contested elections involving pre-Loyalist and Loyalist candidates in any event. The election of 1793 introduced a new feature. Since a recent statute for the better regulation of elections required the ferreting out of fraudulent conveyances of land grants, a task for which the whole House, either in committee or otherwise, was unsuited, the House submitted a petition from Kings County to a committee selected according to the procedures laid down by the English Grenville Act of 1770.[48] At the same time, however, it rejected a bill which would have made this procedure generally applicable and it continued to decide the method to be employed in particular cases on a completely *ad hoc* basis.

Up to 1806 no one questioned the sole right of the Assembly to determine the validity of elections.[49] It was therefore unprecedented when Wentworth dared to review the propriety of the Assembly's action in vacating the seat of one Thomas Walker of the Township of Annapolis.[50] The ensuing difference of opinion between the Nova Scotian law officers and the Council raised for the first time the whole theoretical basis upon which privileges rested. Was it true that the *lex et consuetudo parliamenti* as "part of the Common Law of England . . . necessarily extend[ed] to this province and [afforded] the only safe rules to guide and direct its Legislature"? Or was "the Law of Parliament . . . peculiar to the High Court of Parliament in England and . . . not transferred to or vested in the General Assembly of Nova Scotia, which owes its creation to the Royal Instructions and is regulated by the Laws of the Province"? If the former viewpoint, that of Attorney-General Uniacke, was correct, the constitutionality of the Assembly's action was undoubted, for "one of the strongest Maxims of the Law of Parliament is that whatever matter arises concerning either House ought to be examined discussed and adjudged in that House to which it relates and not elsewhere." But if the latter, the opinion of the Council, was to prevail, the determining factor was the election act of

[48]This procedure called for fifteen members to be chosen by lot, of whom each party to the case was permitted to strike off five. The addition of a spokesman for each party brought the total membership to seven.

[49]By this time the Assembly had received at least 38 petitions alleging undue elections and had investigated six elections on its own initiative; of these, it had voided thirteen.

[50]See *Minutes of Council*, March 5, 1807.

1789, and, in its opinion, that act would not justify the removal of Walker until he had been convicted of bribery or corruption in due course of law.[51]

The Assembly fully realized the clear-cut threat to its independence. Before it loomed the unpleasant alternative either of "submitting to the mortification of seeing some of its Seats filled by persons whose practices had been illegal and corrupt . . . or of declaring such Seats vacant, and thereby leav[ing] the County or Town without representation."[52] Actually it had nothing to fear, for the English law officers unequivocally upheld its competency to "decide exclusively and without appeal on the validity of the Election of one of the members."[53] Although it never again had to meet a similar challenge, the unsuitability of its machinery for trying election petitions came increasingly to the fore. Eventually (1821) its inability to hear witnesses under oath[54] and the inordinate length of time which the first session of each Assembly was forced to devote to the hearing of election petitions led to a Nova Scotian version of the Grenville Act, and the delegation to committees, chosen in a special way, of the right to decide finally and absolutely all contested elections.[55]

Perhaps the Assembly's worst failure was in the regulation of the system of representation. Governor Lawrence and his Council instituted the only scheme of representation that was practicable in 1758 when they empowered the townships of Halifax and Lunenburg to elect four and two members respectively, and the entire province sixteen members at large.[56] They promised, in addition, two representatives to other townships upon their attaining a minimum of fifty qualified voters.[57] These townships, designed to "consist of 100,000 acres of lands, or about 12 miles square," and to "include the best and most profitable lands," were apparently expected to play a role somewhat analogous to the boroughs of the mother country, an anticipation which subsequent history was to prove a delusion.

Before the election of the Second Assembly (1759-61), the Council considered that the increase in population warranted the establishment of a county system. Accordingly it created the first five counties, Halifax, Lunenburg, Annapolis, Kings, and Cumberland, and granted

---

[51]For the opinions, see *Minutes of Council*, April 28, 1807.
[52]*JHA*, 1807-8, 58.
[53]See *Minutes of Council*, March 2, 1808.
[54]See *Acadian Recorder*, March 27, 1819.
[55]1-2 Geo. IV, c. 17 (1820-1).   [56]*Minutes of Council*, May 20, 1758.
[57]The promise was repeated in Lawrence's proclamation aimed to attract New England settlers. *Minutes of Council*, Jan. 11, 1759.

them representation along with three new townships.[58] During the next six years it established a sixth county, Queens, when the circumstances warranted it, and provided representation for five additional townships which qualified on the basis of population. Then, just before the election of the Fourth Assembly in 1765, it suddenly realized that the Halifax representation, normally identical in interest with itself, was in the process of being swamped. It concluded, therefore, that it would be wiser to try its luck with an Assembly of thirty in which Halifax elected six members than one of forty immediately and a much larger one later on in which the proportion of Halifax members was smaller.[59] So it increased the representation of Halifax County from two to four, while reducing that of Halifax Township to two, and of all other townships to one.[60]

Naturally the assemblymen regarded this action as an attack upon the foundation of their constitution and an obstacle to the speedy settlement of the province.[61] The only concession they could secure, however, was the Governor's promise to permit them to confirm by law the existing representation,[62] according to the cut-and-dried formula of the Council. Even this meaningless gesture ran foul of the growing tendency in England to regard tampering by colonial assemblies with representation and the franchise as evidence of democracy run rampant. Hence the first provincial statute regulating representation[63] was disallowed in England and shortly afterwards North American governors were enjoined in a General Instruction to reject similar bills as being inconsistent with their Instructions and prejudicial to the authority conferred by their Commissions.[64] Subsequently the Instructions were less restrictive, but they still required prior approval in England or a suspending class for this type of bill. As a result, the Governor and Council continued by themselves to alter the composition of the Legislature—the creation of Sunbury on the St. John and the granting of representation to five townships between 1765 and 1767, and then, after fourteen quiescent years during the Revolutionary period, the setting up of Hants County and provision of representation for Windsor Township in 1781.

Those were the last alterations made solely by the Governor and

[58]Ibid., Aug. 22, 1759.
[59]J. B. Brebner, Neutral Yankees of Nova Scotia (New York, 1937), 222.
[60]Minutes of Council, Jan. 30, 1765.
[61]JHA, May 30, 1765.
[62]Ibid., June 1, 1765.
[63]5 Geo. III, c. 10 (1765).
[64]Dated Sept. 11, 1767.

Council. The new mode of effecting them, as was indicated earlier, was necessitated by an unsolicited directive of the Board of Trade.[65] So when Parr wanted additional representation to "quiet the mind of the Loyalists,"[66] he had no alternative but to submit his proposals to the Legislature. Naturally the Assembly was delighted to have a part in separating the counties of Shelburne and Sydney from Queens and Halifax, and in providing representation for the townships of Digby and Shelburne,[67] because in so doing it was establishing an unquestionable right to place its *imprimatur* upon all future changes.

Over the next thirty years, however, this newly won power proved to be entirely negative in its effect. This was due to no lack of agitation, for petitions, particularly to divide the counties of Halifax and Annapolis, dot the *Journals* of the Assembly. Some governors, such as Parr, described the demands as "mere Pretences to gain an addition of two more Counties" and four more members;[68] others, like Wentworth, considered them "better accomplished now, than hereafter, when the Country is more populous, and a larger increase of Representatives would naturally be wished for."[69] Yet because the authorities in England exhibited a curious reticence to make any pronouncement at all on the subject until 1819, Nova Scotia carried on with its nine counties, eighteen represented townships, and Assembly of thirty-eight until the annexation of Cape Breton by a direct act of the British government resulted in the creation of a tenth county with two additional members.

Finally, the Assembly asserted its right to the powers of the House of Commons with respect to money bills. In its early years it sought to make the elementary point that no expenditure should be authorized by the executive which had not been previously voted by the General Assembly. The outcome was that by 1766 a half-conscious compromise had been reached whereby the Governor and Council had obliquely conceded its constitutional claims.[70] Thereafter the executive transmitted annual estimates to the Assembly which approved them singly and forwarded them to the Council for its concurrence.[71]

After 1783, a more mature Assembly became increasingly aware that

[65]*Supra*, 45.
[66]Parr to Sydney, Aug. 13, 1785, N.S. A105, 185.
[67]24 Geo. III, c. 5 (1784).   [68]Parr to Grenville, May 3, 1790, N.S. A114, 104.
[69]Wentworth to Hobart, Sept. 26, 1801, N.S. A133, 153.
[70]Brebner, *Neutral Yankees*, 348.
[71]Since the executive had not acknowledged the practice as a formal constitutional principle, it showed no compunction about circumventing it, particularly during times of emergency, and thereby provoked periodic wrangling with the Assembly.

it needed the privileges of the House of Commons in money bills to "preserve that just equilibrium between the three component Parts of the Constitution, upon which the Welfare of the whole depends."[72] It received considerable assistance from the Secretary of State who insisted that a regular Appropriation Act should be passed in place of the many resolutions for the expenditure of specific sums which had hitherto been approved singly by the Assembly and Council and assented to by the Governor without being collected into a single bill.[73] This meant that after 1786 the Assembly could refuse to vote any money at all if its wishes were not met on points of sufficient import to justify risking the total loss of supply.

As the contest developed between the Council and the Assembly, neither branch was content to accept the English analogy in its entirety. The Council was naturally anxious to have it established that resolutions for the expenditure of money should be recommended by the Crown before being submitted to the Legislature, a pretension which no Assembly could have accepted because of the peculiar position of the colonial executive of the day. In its legislative capacity, on the other hand, the Council rejected the English practice and claimed co-ordinate power with the Assembly on the ground that when the General Assembly was first convened, the Royal Instructions had authorized it both to frame and amend money bills.[74] Practically, however, it waived the right of initiation and contented itself with removing what it considered objectionable provisions from money bills. The lower House frequently rejected these amended bills,[75] but even so, after the stormy year 1790,[76] calm prevailed for a decade because of the generally conciliatory atmosphere.[77] The Council normally pre-

[72]Address of Assembly to the Governor, *JHA*, March 31, 1790.

[73]Somehow Sydney had got it into his head that a resolve of the House, concurred in by the Council, completed the grant, the result being to deprive the Crown of "a negative upon the Grant, however improperly made." Sydney to Parr, Oct. 6, 1784, N.S. A106, 28.

[74]*JLC*, March 27, 1790. See also Council to Grenville, May 4, 1790, N.S. A114, 107.

[75]See *JHA*, July 6, 1792; June 30, 1794; June 28, 1797; June 28, 1798.

[76]When the Assembly refused to accept Parr's compromise on the Revenue Bill, the Council yielded "without prejudice to their rights and privileges in future." *JLC*, April 3, 1790. It then secured a temporary, if illogical, success of its own by rejecting the resolution which provided funds for the payment of assemblymen, a part of each Appropriation Act since 1786. Naturally the Assembly refused to yield, and the entire supply for the year was lost.

[77]The Loyalist assemblymen had come to see that the existing system was by no means weighted against them, and the early Wentworth fairly exuded with the milk of human kindness.

sented its objections to money bills in conferences with the Assembly, and altered them only when the lower House declined to submit less objectionable measures; the Assembly, in its turn, often co-operated by initiating the same bill under a new title and in a form more palatable to the upper branch.[78]

After 1799, this mutual accommodation became increasingly difficult to maintain as a prerogative-conscious Wentworth and Council, which more and more regarded a popularly elected Assembly as suspect, came into conflict with a lower House which tended to consider non-concurrence in its acts as a violation of its inherent rights. In the new struggle the Assembly discovered that its earlier concessions had seriously attenuated its bargaining power, particularly its practice of allowing the Council the equivalent of an item veto in financial bills. This meant that one of the most useful devices of a representative body, that of passing financial bills containing some provisions by which it sets great store and which it knows are objectionable to the upper House, and placing upon the latter the onus of rejecting them in their entirety, was rendered ineffective. Even when the Assembly retained the revenue bills in its possession so as to secure favourable action on the supply bill, it invariably failed because of the Council's insistence upon an adequate revenue before it permitted any appropriations.[79]

Yet the Assembly, although rebuffed in one direction, succeeded in making inroads upon the control of the executive over finance, and Wentworth, who first permitted them, underwent the usual experience of one who attempts to turn the clock back. The differences centred around the expenditure upon roads and bridges for which the Assembly provided lavishly once the provincial debt had been extinguished. When it sought a voice in appointing the road commissioners, Wentworth denied its claim on the ground that as "Servants of the Crown [the commissioners] should be nominated and Commissioned by the Lieut. Governor,"[80] but practice was much more favourable than a Governor's dictum. Even under Wentworth, but more particu-

[78]The Assembly *Journals* keep up the fiction of non-acceptance of amendments to money bills throughout the period, but the Council *Journals*, which report the specific details of conferences much more adequately, indicate that the suggestions of the Council often became part of the enactments. Sometimes there appears to be absolute contradiction between the two sets of *Journals*.

[79]Wentworth's description of the practical operation of this device was not the usual outcome: "The Revenue Bills, often held back, as a coercion to obtain favorite concurrences—were then sent up and concurred in Council." Wentworth to Camden, July 31, 1804, P.A.N.S. 53, 528.

[80]*JLC*, 1801, 42.

larly under his successors, the nominees of the assemblymen were usually confirmed by the Governor and Council as road commissioners. In time, rejections became so rare that the Assembly regarded them as attacks upon its privileges. The lower House also took it upon itself to review the accounts of the road commissioners, to determine the adequacy of performance of their duties, to fix their rate of compensation within limits and, most remarkably of all, to initiate its own road estimates.[81]

Until 1804 Wentworth and his Council did not seem to care that "the mode of granting monies and the controul upon Expenditures had gradually deviated into a manner totally opposite to the practice of Parliament."[82] Then to re-institute propriety, they announced their intention to reserve to "the Executive Government the General Superintendance and direction of all appropriations of Money granted to the Crown for public Service."[83] But when they insisted upon the removal of the normal regulatory clauses[84] from the appropriation bill, the Assembly declined to give way and supply remained unvoted in the session of 1804.

While the Council gained a hollow victory in this instance,[85] its backtracking policy was by no means so successful in restoring the sole right of recommending votes of money to the Crown. Wentworth's method of re-instituting the British practice was to include his own road estimates in the normal estimates for the support of government.

[81]"Petitions for money," said Wentworth, "were presented to the Assembly, received and granted, and accounts settled previous to any communication with the King's Governor, or Council.—Hence solicitations for interest to carry votes, unavoidably excited little party pursuits—consumed time, obstructed the true business of the Province, and was but too fast diminishing the King's just and constitutional authority in the Legislature." Wentworth to Camden, July 31, 1804, P.A.N.S. 53, 527.

[82]*Ibid.*

[83]"These Powers being Prerogative Rights," Wentworth said, "although they may have been in some instances left to the Management of the Assembly, may be constitutionally resumed by His Majesty's Representative, whenever he thinks the general Interest requires it." Wentworth to Assembly, July 10, 1804, P.A.N.S. 303, doc. 55.

[84]The Assembly had adopted the practice of introducing clauses for regulating road expenditures into the annual appropriation bill, but even though they did little more than provide for the performance of these functions by the Governor and Council, their very admission implied the right of the General Assembly to have some voice in spending the money which it had voted.

[85]The following year the Assembly accepted an appropriation bill without regulatory clauses, and in a separate act regulating the expenditure of road moneys agreed to fix the compensation of road commissioners at 5 per cent instead of leaving the percentage variable within limits at the discretion of the determining authority. 46 Geo. III, c. 11.

Yet although he and the Council argued that only the executive had "the means of investigating the propriety, and of determining the utility"[86] of the allocation of road moneys, the Assembly clung tenaciously to the counter proposition that it was more competent to determine the distribution than the executive of that day could ever hope to be. While the memory of the lost appropriation bill made it adopt a more cautious role during the 1805–6 session, it was back to all its old tricks the following year. When it departed from the Governor's estimates more than it followed them, Wentworth finally acknowledged the futility of executive interference. Prevost was no more successful, and his successors completely abandoned the practice of submitting road estimates.

Thus the greater part of the provincial expenditures came to be initiated by the Assembly without prior recommendation of the executive. One reason for the Council's acquiescence in a departure from "a known and established principle of the british constitution"[87] can be traced to its being vested with both legislative and executive functions. Even it realized the absurdity of recommending votes to the General Assembly in its executive capacity which it would later have to consider in its legislative capacity. So, despite the lamentations of Attorney-General Uniacke, it followed the line of least resistance and in this instance gave its legislative arm precedence over its executive arm.

The outcome was a peculiarly Nova Scotian mode of procedure for the handling of road moneys which left a later Governor-General aghast. The Assembly ascertained from the Council (usually by test resolutions, often followed up by conferences through committees) what sum would be permitted for the road and bridge service. It then spent a day in deciding what amount should be allotted to the great roads, and in dividing the remainder among the counties for the maintenance of their cross roads. During this operation, normally performed behind closed doors, several scales of division were proposed "each varying from the others as the local interests of the mover's own County or Township, or his own feelings or prejudices, were concerned."[88] On these occasions logrolling was frequent, and the usual outcome was a victory for the western counties' interest since representation was heavily weighted in their favour. The final step was to subdivide each county's money among its cross roads. Here the

[86]Message from the Council to the Assembly, July 12, 1804, *JHA*, 1804, 36–7.
[87]See protest of Uniacke, P.A.N.S. 288, doc. 15.
[88]*Novascotian*, March 11, 1830.

decisions of a committee which included a member from each county and district were crucial, for although its subdivision was often challenged in day-long debates, the Assembly seldom made changes.

In its practical operation this system had highly objectionable features. Only by sheer accident would a county or a specific road receive an amount proportionate to its needs; the subdivision of the moneys into infinitesimally small amounts meant that no work of a really permanent character was performed; the commissioners who directed the work enjoyed only a transitory tenure and were wont to regard the assemblymen as their friends and guardians and not as their inspectors and critics.[89] But to these defects the rural Assemblyman was entirely oblivious. In his opinion, "nobody could be so competent to name commissioners as the Representatives from the several Counties, who knew the Country well. £10 laid out by a person who had an interest in the road would do more good than £25 expended by any one else."[90] He had come to feel that his participation in the distribution and expenditure of road moneys dwarfed all his other duties as an Assemblyman.

The more constitutionally acute member could, of course, see far-reaching implications in any proposal to alter the status quo in favour of the executive. "Can you turn out the Executive Council by a vote of this Assembly as the Commons of England can," asked Alexander Stewart, "and will you not, if you make this change, transfer the patronage from the hands of those who are directly responsible to the people, to a body who can defy you and them, and upon them no responsibility rests?"[91] To him and like-minded individuals the result would have been to destroy the existing power equilibrium, and to bring to an end a period of comparative peace, both of which might be traced to the comparatively free hand which the Assembly was permitted in the disposition of a substantial portion of the annual appropriations.

Fully conscious of its many gains, the Assembly began to give evidence of its own realization that it had actually "arrived." One indication was the appearance of Mr. Speaker Archibald and the Clerk, James Boutineau Francklin, in wigs and silk gowns for the first time on February 21, 1825.[92] A little earlier the House had tried to secure a

89Ibid., Feb. 25, 1836.   90Ibid., March 27, 1828.   91Ibid., March 3, 1836.
92The innovation prompted Nathaniel White to poke fun at Archibald: "His visit to our aristocratical parent has filled him with the flourish & humbug of pomp. . . . Those only who have had a peep under the wig have the courage to stand up & address such a majestic figure." Letter to brother Cornelius, March 7, 1825, White Collection (P.A.N.S.), item 1166.

mace only to discover that it was "a gift of the Crown to the Commons, and to procure one otherwise, would be like the Commons buying a Crown for themselves."[93]

Of deeper significance was the insistence by some assemblymen during the later twenties that no additional power should be granted to the executive, particularly in money matters, and that the utility of the existing structure needed to be questioned on specific points. Further strengthening of the Council, said Beamish Murdoch, might leave "the forms of a constitution; but the Assembly would be like the trunk of Hercules on the funeral pile, a body without a soul."[94] Simultaneously his colleagues were questioning the composition of the upper branch and the use of its power in its legislative capacity. Haliburton, for one, described its rejection of his common school bill, in effect a money bill, as unconstitutional.

It is a power which even the House of Lords, in modern times, has not exercised. . . . The House of Lords is hereditary, representative, and also elective. . . . But the Council! whom do they represent? of what body are they the hereditary representatives?—they are appointed at will; and may be suspended and removed at will; can it then be said, that a body thus constituted, however learned and respectable they might be, have a vote upon money bills; or that the Commons of Nova Scotia, who raise the revenue, have not a right to its appropriation, without their consent.[95]

Nevertheless the Council was foolhardy enough to raise a like issue in the Brandy Dispute of 1830. This time, in response to its contention that "the burthens imposed upon the Commerce of the Country were too great, and that many of the duties should be lessened," the House unequivocally declared itself "not only the most competent but the Sole Judges of the amount of the burthens to be borne by the people whom they represent."[96] The searchlight which the accompanying debates threw upon the Council and its committees augured badly for its future. "Who," asked S. G. W. Archibald, "were they that sat in judgment upon us 36? who formed the committee of Review, by whom our acts were scrutinized and our determination opposed? Two Officers of our own Revenue and a Gentleman deeply interested in Trade!"[97] And about the same time the youthful Joseph Howe was wondering if the remedy for these obvious defects must not be found "in a remodelling of the Council—in the exclusion of public officers from its Board, and the separation of its executive and legislative powers."[98]

[93]See the reference to the earlier event in the *Novascotian*, Jan. 30, 1840.
[94]*Novascotian*, Feb. 28, 1828.
[95]*Acadian Recorder*, Feb. 23, 1828.   [96]See *JHA*, 1830, 747.
[97]Supplement to the *Novascotian*, April 8, 1830.   [98]*Ibid.*, May 20, 1830.

CHAPTER V

THE JUDICIAL FUNCTION

THE PLENARY POWER in judicial matters which Cornwallis's Commission conferred upon the Governor and Council could not have been avoided under the circumstances which prevailed at the time the original government was set up. Neither could the bewildering interconnection between the judicial and other functions of government whereby judges participated actively in the executive and legislative processes and the highest executive and legislative officers performed judicial duties. The early period was marked, not by efforts to make the judiciary independent of the other branches of government, but by the expansion of judicial functions and procedures to meet the needs of a Nova Scotian society ever increasing in complexity. Since the English judicial structure was by no means a suitable plant for wholesale transfer, the natural result was the building up of a peculiarly Nova Scotian variant of the parental species. In the process of development the Governor and Council[1] and the Legislature both had a share.

Initially Cornwallis and his Council constituted themselves a General Court, established a County Court to deal with lesser offences, and adopted for their regulation the rules of similar courts in Virginia, the colony deemed to possess a form of government nearest to that of Nova Scotia.[2] Apparently the Court of Quarter Sessions for the trial of petty offences also began to function with no other authority than that it was part of the customary English procedure. The first change of substance occurred in 1752 when by minute of Council the County Court became the Inferior Court of Common Pleas and was thereby stamped as a court of civil jurisdiction. The practice of holding this court four times a year as regulated by the law of the colony, while the Courts of Sessions met at four different times "agreeable to the time and seasons of Holding Sessions in the Realm of Great Britain," led to complaints that four courts and four juries were being unnecessarily convened. The remedy was to make the times of meeting of these courts coincide, a provision which existed in most counties until the abolition of the Inferior Courts in 1841.

The efficacious working of the judicial system depended in the last

[1]The constituting of courts remained a prerogative power throughout the period.
[2]*Minutes of Council*, Dec. 13, 1749.

analysis upon the character of the judicial personnel designed to work it. Naturally the litigious spirit which prevailed in Nova Scotia, as in most infant colonies, seized upon the alleged incapacity and partiality of the judges as a real grievance, and a harassed Governor Hopson, anxious to promote the tranquillity of the settlement, pleaded in his dispatches for proper persons to manage and advise in law affairs.[3] For the moment there was no relief since no qualified Englishman could be found who was willing to undertake the duties of Chief Justice or Attorney-General upon "such an Establishment of Salary, as Government would be willing to grant,"[4] but eventually (October 21, 1754) Jonathan Belcher, pursuant to royal authority endowing him with "full Power . . . to hold the supreme Courts of Judicature at such Places and Times as the same may and ought to be held within our said Province,"[5] was sworn in as Chief Justice, and the Supreme Court superseded the General Court.

That completed the institution of the common law structure, but it was still left to the Governor individually, or to the Governor and Council collectively, to deal with a variety of causes outside the jurisdiction of the common law courts. Thus, when Cornwallis was confronted with a petition for divorce, he simply constituted himself and the Council as a Court of Marriage and Divorce in the absence of the ecclesiastical courts which tried similar causes in England.[6] In two other instances the setting up of courts depended upon the Governor's functioning in his capacity as Ordinary and Chancellor. As Ordinary, he granted letters of administration and the probate of wills, a power which in England belonged to the ecclesiastical courts. Even before the First Assembly, however, he had delegated part of his authority in this capacity to a Surrogate-General. As Chancellor, he possessed powers similar to those of the Lord Chancellor, and until 1825 he continued personally to preside in the Court of Chancery, assisted first by the councillors, later by trained lawyers acting as Masters of Chancery.

Two other types of causes, both involving the principle of extraterritoriality, necessarily required regulation in England. Although all the governors were commissioned as vice-admirals, they at no time presided over the Court of Vice-Admiralty, which enforced the laws of trade. Prior to 1801 that duty fell to a judge, sometimes commissioned in England, sometimes appointed by the Governor subject to confirma-

[3]Hopson to Board of Trade, March 28, 1753, P.A.C., N.S. A52, 109.
[4]Board of Trade to Hopson, July 9, 1753, N.S. A54, 12.
[5]P.A.N.S. 347, doc. 8.   [6]See *Minutes of Council*, May 15, 1750.

tion; after that date the whole establishment was altered, and the operation of Vice-Admiralty Courts in the western hemisphere was centred in Halifax and two of the West Indian Islands from which the three judges might issue their process to any of the other American colonies. In contrast, the Governor was provided with a Commission which empowered him, the Lieutenant-Governor, the Judge of Vice-Admiralty, the Secretary of the province, and all naval officers of the rank of commander and above[7] to try cases of piracy and other offences which had been committed on the high seas.[8]

The only court which owed its establishment to the legislative action of the General Assembly—and it did not possess an independent existence—was the Courts of Escheats and Forfeitures. This was set up in 1760 to enable the Crown to recover lands on the peninsula of Halifax upon which the conditions of the grant had not been fulfilled, and its jurisdiction was later extended to the rest of the province. The act provided that once a jury of twelve men acting under a Commissioner of Escheats and Forfeitures had made an inquest and submitted its return to the office of the Register of Chancery, the Governor-in-Council might escheat and re-grant lands on the basis of its determination.[9]

Thus a multiplicity of courts with divergent bases was thrust upon the infant colony of Nova Scotia. Prior to 1830 little progress was made to reduce them to a single hierarchical system. What did happen was that the existing structure was regulated and extended to bring it more into conformity with provincial needs.

EVOLUTION OF THE COURTS, 1758–1830

The credit of establishing the procedure of the Supreme Court and investing it with the dignity essential to its proper functioning belongs to Jonathan Belcher. Yet the Assembly of the early sixties which was critical of his activities as Lieutenant-Governor also found fault with the constitution of a court which was dependent upon "the Opinion and Judgment of any one Single Man, however capable and upright,"[10] and its request for a court "more conformable to the constitution of the courts at Westminster" culminated in the appointment of two assistant justices to conduct the sessions of the Supreme Court in conjunction

---

[7]Three of these persons, one to be of the first four named, constituted a quorum.
[8]See T. C. Haliburton, *An Historical and Statistical Account of Nova Scotia* (Halifax, 1829), II, 342, and *Minutes of Council*, March 28, 1814.
[9]34 Geo. II, c. 8.
[10]*Journals of the House of Assembly (JHA)*, Nov. 24, 1763.

with the Chief Justice. Ten years were to elapse, however, before the latter would permit the assistant justices to act in his absence.[11]

Because of the expanding population and the increased business of the court, its sessions at Halifax were increased from two to four a year in 1768 to avoid the ills arising from "a want of a more speedy administration of justice in capital offences" and "the great delay of the subject in recovering their civil rights and demands."[12] But it was in the other counties that the most serious difficulties were experienced. There the trial of felonies was by specially appointed commissioners of *oyer* and *terminer* and general gaol delivery, and where communication by land with Halifax was non-existent, the hiring of vessels to carry the judges and officers of the court not only proved expensive, but left the time of trial uncertain. A temporary remedy of transferring the alleged felons and witnesses to Halifax for a hearing in the Supreme Court[13] introduced as many evils as it sought to cure.

The eventual solution, a circuit system, was begun on a limited scale in Kings, Annapolis, and Cumberland counties in 1774.[14] Any two of the three judges were authorized to hold sittings in these counties, but instead of their courts being merely courts of *nisi prius* as in England, and hence limited to civil causes, they were invested with the powers of the courts of King's Bench, Common Pleas, and Exchequer in that country, that is, with the full powers and jurisdiction of the court at Halifax. In counties unconnected by road with Halifax the old procedures remained until 1794 when courts of *nisi prius* alone were established for the counties of Lunenburg, Queens, Shelburne, and Sydney, to be presided over by one or more judges of the Supreme Court acting in conjunction with one or more judges of the Inferior Court.[15] Not until 1816 had the means of communications sufficiently improved to permit the extension of the original system of circuit courts to all the counties.[16]

The augmented duties which these changes devolved upon the Supreme Court necessitated the appointment of a third assistant judge in 1809, and, for a time after 1816, an associate judge with the full powers of an assistant judge except at Halifax.[17] The real remedy was delayed, however, until 1834 when the inconvenient provision which

[11]*Minutes of Council*, Nov. 3, 1773. Belcher apparently heeded or ignored his two colleagues as he pleased.
[12]8-9 Geo. III, c. 5.
[13]8-9 Geo. III, c. 9.
[14]14-15 Geo. III, c. 6.
[15]34 Geo. III, c. 10.
[16]56 Geo. III, c. 2.
[17]*Ibid.*

required two or more of the assistant judges to try all causes was abolished, "any Law, usage or custom . . . notwithstanding."[18] Henceforth a single judge presided over all causes in the first instance.

First of the courts in their impact upon the populace were the Inferior Courts of Common Pleas and the Courts of Sessions. All the justices of the peace within a county were entitled to sit on the latter, but the records indicate a meagre attendance, sometimes less than the legal minimum of two. For the Inferior Courts the Governor and Council chose a varying number of the senior justices. Only in Halifax were the sessions held quarterly; elsewhere the normal practice was to have each court meet twice a year, the one immediately following the other.[19]

Both these courts suffered from the uncertainty of the law and the general unfitness of the justices. The course adopted when Cape Breton was reannexed—the appointment of a trained lawyer as Chief Justice of the Inferior Court of Common Pleas and President of the Court of Sessions—suggested one means of avoiding the second difficulty, but the proposal was strongly condemned by the "country" assemblymen who preferred procedures based on equity and common sense to strict legal forms, and regarded it as a lawyer's scheme to create offices of preferment for themselves. Nevertheless, in 1824 the mainland counties, Halifax excepted, were grouped in three divisions, in each of which the Governor was to appoint a lawyer to preside over the Inferior Courts and the Courts of Sessions.[20] While the change undoubtedly improved the quality of the justice meted out by these courts,[21] it also fostered the opinion that the judicial structure had become grossly overmanned.

By 1830 the Courts of the Justices of the Peace were also causing dissatisfaction. The commissions of the peace issued periodically by the Governor and Council contained the lists of persons who were to act as justices of the peace and possess "all the power of the ancient conservators at common law, in suppressing riots and affrays, taking securities for the peace, and apprehending and committing persons accused of crimes."[22] The unceasing effort to introduce speed and economy into the judicial process led, in 1807, to their being em-

18 4 Wm. IV, c. 4.
19 After 1785 the difficulties connected with the incarceration of prisoners over the long period between the sittings of the court led to a provision which enabled Special Sessions to hear cases by indictment or in a summary way. 25 Geo. III, c. 2.
20 4–5 Geo. IV, c. 38.
21 See Beamish Murdoch, *Epitome of the Laws of Nova Scotia* (Halifax, 1833), III, 60–1.
22 *Ibid.*, I, 132.

powered to deal with minor causes in a summary way.[23] Once this
development had begun the tendency was to increase the powers of
the justices despite a strong body of opinion which held that men
inexperienced in the law already had too much power. "The little
emoluments of the office, . . ." wrote Haliburton, "have occasioned the
commission to be eagerly seized after; and to use the words of Lord
Bacon—'There are many who account it an honor to be burdened with
the office of Justice of the Peace.' "[24]

The courts of a special nature experienced fewer changes than the
foregoing because provincial control over them was limited. This was
especially true of the Court of Errors and Appeals, for no less an
authority than the Governor's Commission authorized the Governor
and Council to act as such a court, while the Instructions specified
more precisely how they were to exercise this jurisdiction. But since
the amount at issue was required to be at least £300 sterling, the
Council seldom acted in this capacity.[25]

The First Assembly confirmed the Governor and Council as a Court
of Marriage and Divorce, and authorized them to void marriages on
the grounds of impotence or consanguinity within prohibited degrees,
and to grant divorces for adultery or wilful desertion.[26] While the
second of these grounds had to be repealed because it was "not agreeable to the Laws of England,"[27] in other respects the form and the
functioning of the court remained unchanged until 1841.

Similarly the First Assembly, while expressly declaring its intention
not to infringe upon the Governor's powers, regulated the activities of
the Surrogate Judge upon whom the governors had devolved part of
their authority, and provided for an appeal from his decisions to the
Governor and Council.[28] The later division of the province into
counties and districts necessitated the establishment of other registries
of probate and the appointment of Judges of Probate to act under the
supervision of the Surrogate-General at Halifax,[29] but since no unified
system of procedure was laid down, the judges were generally left to

[23]A summary jurisdiction was also conferred upon the other courts. See 48 Geo.
III, c. 12.

[24]Haliburton, *Historical Account of Nova Scotia*, II, 337.

[25]Appeals to the King in Council were permitted when the sum at issue
amounted to £500 sterling.

[26]32 Geo. II, c. 17.

[27]1 Geo. III, c. 7; see R. J. Uniacke, *Nova Scotia Laws, 1758–1804* (Halifax,
1805), 69n.

[28]32 Geo. II, c. 11.

[29]But Murdoch, *Epitome*, III, 39: "The judge of probates for Halifax proper,
claims a general jurisdiction over the province, but his authority in this respect is
by no means settled."

find their way by "the feeble light of analogy to the Ecclesiastical Courts of England."[30]

The Court of Chancery escaped regulation by the Legislature because of the assumption that the jurisdiction of the Chancellor was not subject to its control. Only when the governors[31] themselves recognized their incompetence to handle chancery matters was a part of their duties in this capacity delegated to individuals trained in the law. But even then the permission of the Secretary of State and the provision of a salary by the Legislature were necessary before Sir James Kempt could appoint the first Master of the Rolls in 1826.

By far the most unpopular of all the courts was the Court of Vice-Admiralty. Its judge established fees in accordance with Imperial statute or custom or, if necessary, at his own discretion; but no matter how they were determined, they were criticized as grievous, oppressive, and beyond the capacity of the subject to bear.[32] Thus in 1811 a Committee of the Assembly deprecated the court's exclusive power to try breaches of the Laws of Trade and Navigation, and alleged that the costs of its trials forced many persons to forfeit their property rather than "solicit [it], at a ruinous expence before a Tribunal, exercising a jurisdiction, unknown to the constitution of the Parent State."[33] Similarly in 1817 a group of Halifax merchants protested "a mode of trial that appears from history, to have originated in a state of society in the old colonies, very different from that which exists in this Province."[34] By this time, however, the Court of Vice-Admiralty had lost its most lucrative business, since the dawn of a long period of peace practically ended its function of disposing of prizes, while the steady attenuation of the Navigation Laws which began in the 1820's was eventually to render its other duties negligible.

In contrast, the Court of Piracies attracted little attention because it tried few causes. Nevertheless, its practice of not employing juries appeared questionable to legalists like Haliburton who suggested that while a commission might issue in the normal way,[35] the procedures of the court should be regulated by an earlier British statute which called for the use of a jury.[36] In 1827 that course was followed in the trial of

[30]Haliburton, *Historical Account of Nova Scotia*, II, 338.

[31]Dalhousie, for one, tried to have Chief Justice Blowers appointed Master of the Rolls, but the Secretary of State objected because of Blowers' connection with the common law courts.

[32]Even when the Council intervened in their regulation. See *Minutes of Council*, Jan. 9, 1801.

[33]*JHA*, 1811, 107.

[34]*Acadian Recorder*, April 12, 1817.   [35]*Supra*, 65.

[36]For details, see Haliburton, *Historical Account of Nova Scotia*, II, 342.

five seamen of the brig *Peggy* for mutiny,[37] but five years later there was a reversion to the older form.[38] Actually the functioning of this court seems to have been enveloped in the same cloudiness as the probate courts.

During this period it was at no time recognized as desirable that the judicial should be kept independent of the other functions of government. Similarly there was little concern about the Governor individually, or the Governor and Council collectively, performing judicial as well as legislative and executive duties. Yet this bewildering admixture of functions periodically raised knotty problems in various ways. Sometimes the difficulty arose as a result of the Governor exercising his functions as Ordinary and Chancellor. When Legge could not get his own delegate, Surrogate-General William Nesbitt, to comply with an order, the official to whom he had to turn for legal advice was Attorney-General William Nesbitt. When confronted with similar non-compliance of an order which he gave in his capacity as Chancellor, he found the Chief Justice unwilling to give a written opinion for fear the matter might come before him later in his judicial capacity.[39] Even when a full-time Master of the Rolls was appointed to assist the Governor as Chancellor, he was still left with the responsibility of hearing appeal cases, a duty he performed not without criticism:

The idea of taking some old, battered soldier who happens to be placed here as Lieut.-Governor, sticking him on a bench, and, day after day, keeping him away from his lunch and his *siesta*, upon the supposition that he is—trying a cause in Chancery! This is really carrying on practical joking on a very large, and a rather expensive, scale.[40]

Similar difficulties were experienced when the Governor and Council acted collectively. In the Court of Marriage and Divorce the problem was whether a majority of the Council could overrule a minority which included the Governor.[41] In the Court of Errors and Appeals it was to secure a quorum when the circumstances of the appeal disqualified

[37]The procedure followed was: the finding of a true bill by a grand jury, the setting up of a court as provided by the Commission to the Governor in his capacity of vice-admiral, the determination of guilt by a jury, and the passage of sentence by the court.

[38]In the case of Patrick Crane charged with murder on the high seas.

[39]Legge to Pownall (private), March 18, 1774, N.S. A90, 39–45.

[40]From the letter of "A Layman on the Court of Chancery," *Acadian Recorder*, Feb. 17, 1855.

[41]The law officers decided it could, since a judgment in this instance did not mean that the Governor could be "controuled in matters of Legislation or acts of executive Government which stand upon Grounds of a very different nature." Report of law officers of the Crown, Oct. 28, 1812, P.A.N.S. 62, doc. 63.

some members of the court. In 1826, six[42] of the twelve councillors had previous connections with a case, and the Governor was at his wit's end to convene the seven members who were needed for a quorum. When he did, it was a Council stripped of its judicial elements which passed judgment upon the Supreme Court.

Although few realized the unhealthy condition implicit in the far-reaching union of powers, the first tentative movements towards separation had begun before the period ended. Whereas the eighteenth-century Assembly had declined to debar the judges,[43] the nineteenth-century body had no such qualms. In 1809 it disqualified the assistant justices from holding any "Office, Post, Place, Appointment, or Situation," except those of Master in Chancery and Councillor;[44] and in 1824 it prohibited the first justices of the Inferior Courts from sitting in the Assembly and voting or interfering in elections.[45]

The rooting out of the judges from the Council proved to be a more formidable task. From the beginning the Chief Justice was the senior Councillor, while up to 1815 all but two of the assistant justices had been councillors, three prior to their accepting judgeships and four subsequently. The new order was instituted by a Secretary of State who, in order to give the Council a more independent character, forbade the admission of further puisne judges in 1830.[46] After that date the Chief Justice and the Master of the Rolls were the only senior judicial officials who still possessed executive and legislative functions.

The existence of a close correlation between the independence of the judiciary and its tenure and remuneration was recognized on several occasions prior to 1830. For years the Assembly strove to make the puisne judges removable by a joint address of the Council and the Assembly and, as a bargaining point, it declined to place their salaries on a permanent basis. Since the existing tenure at the pleasure of the Crown was actually one during good behaviour, the lower House appears to have been concerned more with making the judges dependent upon itself than with strengthening their independence. In the end, however, it had to confess failure, for although it added a face-saving provision when it made the salaries permanent,[47] the tenure of

---

[42]The three Supreme Court judges, the two prosecutors (the Attorney-General and his son-in-law, the Collector of Customs), and the defendant (Enos Collins). Kempt to Bathurst, Oct. 19, 1826, P.A.N.S. 113½, 85.

[43]*Supra*, 52.

[44]50 Geo. III, c. 15.   [45]4–5 Geo. IV, c. 38.

[46]Goderich to Maitland (confidential), Dec. 7, 1830, P.A.N.S. 67, doc. 88.

[47]The statute 29 Geo. III, c. 12, s. 2, provided for their removal at the pleasure of the Crown upon a joint address of the Council and the Assembly, but nothing in the act was to alter the tenure stated in the commissions.

the justices continued, in effect, to be at the pleasure of the Secretary of State.

The ensuring of independence through adequate salaries was the motif more of the interested parties themselves than of the Legislature. To make the office of Chief Justice attractive to suitably qualified Englishmen, a salary of £500 sterling was initially provided and placed upon the parliamentary grant. Soon after 1797, when individuals who called themselves Nova Scotians succeeded to the office,[48] it was increased to £850 sterling.[49] The puisne judges, who were dependent upon the Assembly for their remuneration, had their salaries raised from £400 to £500 in 1816 and £600 in 1822 because of the additional work resulting from the extension of the circuits, but by 1830 they were petitioning for a further increase, this time on the ground that they were finding it "impossible . . . to support the dignity, and independence which should attach to their situation."[50]

[48]Sampson Salter Blowers (1797–1833) and Brenton Halliburton (1833–60).

[49]Fees supplemented substantially the income of the Chief Justice, and those of the puisne judges to a lesser degree. See letter of Halliburton, *JHA*, 1836, Appendix 76, 150–1.

[50]*Acadian Recorder*, Feb. 20, 1830.

II. COLONIAL GOVERNMENT FROM 1830 TO 1867

CHAPTER VI

THE EXECUTIVE FUNCTION

"ONE HUNDRED YEARS AGO," wrote Dr. D. C. Harvey in 1933, "Nova Scotians had already prepared themselves by intense economic and intellectual activity for the greatest achievement of their history."[1] His examination of the forces and agencies which had been operating to produce an intellectual awakening led him to conclude that, without minimizing the achievements of Joseph Howe, the Reform leader must be regarded more as "the embodiment of the spirit of the age" than "as having sprung Minerva-like from the rocks of the North-West Arm." The general picture is that of Nova Scotians rubbing the sleep out of their eyes after 1812 until by 1835 they were thoroughly awake. In the process the descendants of the early settlers, their outlook determined in part by British and American experience, were producing in a new environment a distinctly Nova Scotian character which was reflected in their becoming "thoroughly aroused to the strength and weakness of [their] birthright, and eager to overhaul the entire ship of state, from the keel of commerce to the captain on the bridge."[2]

The result was that they subjected the existing institutions to a prolonged and intensive inquest, and within three decades they had attained self-government and remodelled the entire governmental machine. In the great debate which accompanied this searching inquiry the main divergence of opinion hinged upon the degree to which British institutions could serve as a pattern for Nova Scotia. Tories and Reformers were usually at variance upon whether the basic principles of the British constitution were suitable for colonial adoption, and, if they were, whether they could be instituted without involving the threat of independence. The Reformers wanted nothing less than the full application of the spirit of the British system which, to them, was

[1]D. C. Harvey, "The Intellectual Awakening of Nova Scotia," *Dalhousie Review,* XIII (April, 1933), 22.
[2]*Ibid.*, 2. In the past they had been a little too content to wring concessions piecemeal from the authorities across the water. The arrival of the packet from England had always caused a momentary flurry of excitement in the capital: ". . . speculations and rumours fly about in all directions; half a dozen members of the cabinet are in idea displaced, or reinstalled in office, with an ease and rapidity even outstripping that we have seen acted upon within the last hundred years." W. Moorson, *Letters from Nova Scotia* (London, 1830), 6.

a system of responsibility to the people extending through all the departments of the government.

The British laws [said Howe] are modified to suit the condition of the colonies and we see no reason why British institutions should not be, in like manner, adapted to our situation. . . . in England the people can breathe the breath of life into their government whenever they please; in this country, the government is like an ancient Egyptian mummy, wrapped up in narrow and antique prejudices—dead and inanimate, but yet likely to last for ever. We are desirous of a change, not such as shall divide us from our brethren across the water, but which will ensure to us what they enjoy.[3]

In contrast, the Tories argued that the wholesale introduction of the British model was impracticable and at the same time incompatible with colonial status. As for responsibility, they maintained either that it already existed or that it could be fully introduced by a few comparatively minor modifications.

The general positions of the two parties upon the adaptability of specific English institutions to the colonial sphere cannot be stated with the same degree of assurance, for, depending sometimes upon the recognition that the lesser of two evils must be accepted, they might advocate, deny, or advance beyond the British precedents. Here, too, Howe was the spokesman of the usual Reform viewpoint.

I do not think that the colonial legislatures should always shrink from the adoption of a sound principle till the Imperial Parliament sets them the example. . . . I will not advise pulling down and changing merely for amusement; but am anxious that this House should, without reference to what may be done in other countries, or said across the water, ascertain where the shoe pinches *us*, and having done so, with a firm hand remove the evil.[4]

Yet, after 1849, this position was equally true of the Conservatives since they were advocating a greater measure of democracy than existed in Britain, or than the Reformers admitted was desirable, in order to counteract the undesirable tendencies which they felt had been introduced as a concomitant of responsible government.

Towards a Responsible Executive

". . . I believe all monopolies are bad."[5] In those words Joseph Howe epitomized the basic view point of the Nova Scotian Reformers of the 1830's and 40's since fundamentally their efforts were directed against an oligarchy in which ecclesiastical, commercial, and political power

[3] J. A. Chisholm, *Speeches and Public Letters of Joseph Howe* (Halifax, 1909), I, 104. Hereinafter referred to as Chisholm.
[4] *Ibid.*, I, 111.   [5] *Ibid.*, II, 36.

was concentrated. By 1836 a majority of the Assembly favoured a programme of rational reform, but even then Howe was undecided about what changes were required to remedy "that gross and palpable defect in our local government . . . the absence of all responsibility to the Commons." He dismissed for the moment any idea of converting the Executive Council into an English ministry holding its position only as long as it retained the confidence of the elective branch. "I am afraid," he said, "that these Colonies, at all events this Province, is scarcely prepared for the erection of such machinery; I doubt whether it would work well here."[6]

In place of a responsible executive, he proposed an elective Legislative Council, in the hope that two elective Houses might impose an effective check upon an irresponsible executive.[7] But the address which was submitted to the Crown contained an alternative proposal—the separation of the Executive from the Legislative Council with just representation for the major provincial interests in each[8]—and although Howe described it as analogous to "cutting a rotten orange in two, in order to improve its flavour,"[9] it was this suggestion which a Colonial Secretary who was anxious to avoid too great a departure from the British model decided to accept. Howe's forebodings proved all too correct, for the usual influences were at work behind the scenes in determining the composition of the new Councils. The result was that neither was genuinely representative of broad provincial interests. Furthermore, the new executive councillors took special pains to deny that they held their positions in a collective capacity. Yet the change was significant in that it clarified the problem of the Reformers. Henceforth they concentrated their attention upon the Executive Council, knowing full well that, if they made it responsible, they could fashion the upper House as they pleased.

Howe revealed their new line of thought in his letters to Lord John Russell in September, 1839. "You ask me for the remedy. Lord Durham has stated it distinctly; the Colonial Governors must be commanded to govern by the aid of those who possess the confidence of the people and are supported by a majority of the representative branch."[10] But although he had veered round to the conclusion that the British machinery was not too cumbersome to be transferred to the colonial sphere, he failed to convince the Colonial Secretary of the day that a colonial Governor could act under instructions from the Crown and at

[6]Ibid., I, 125.
[7]Ibid., 230. See also Novascotian, March 9, 1837.
[8]Chisholm, I, 155.   [9]Ibid., 125-6.   [10]Ibid., 229.

the same time accept advice from ministers who commanded a majority in the colonial Assembly.

It required almost a decade to have that opinion reversed, and the delay has raised the question whether the rebellions in the Canadas acted as an accelerating or inhibiting force in the movement towards full colonial responsibility. Did the rebellions give a new lease of life to the various family compacts in the colonies and cause the Imperial government to "withhold the boon of self-government . . . [to Nova Scotia], because they had lost faith in the others despite the clear-cut recommendations of Lord Durham, their lord high commissioner"?[11] Or did the Papineau and Mackenzie uprisings compel the British government to face up to the problems of colonial government for the first time, and might Nova Scotians not have found "self-righteous moderation a harder virtue had it not been for the pioneering turbulence of the Canadian 'Ultras' "?[12]

Whichever was the case, the Nova Scotian Reformers continued to pursue their moderate course. Their strongest act—an address to the Crown requesting Governor Campbell's removal[13]—was sufficient to bring the Governor-General, Charles Poulett Thomson (soon to be Lord Sydenham), to Halifax, and his visit resulted in the institution of that type of ministry which was his peculiar contribution to colonial politics, a ministry in which "the governor was to govern, and the Executive Councillors were to be the governor's 'placemen' . . . diverting men's minds from awkward abstractions."[14] Governor Campbell, he decided, was an altogether unsuitable instrument for his purposes because he was "not only incompetent to Civil Government, but . . . too much mixed up with personal and party feelings."[15] The difficulty was to persuade the leaders of the contending factions to sit together in the Council and thereby submerge party feeling. With the moderate

[11]See D. C. Harvey, "Nova Scotia and the Durham Mission," *C.H.R.*, XX (June, 1939), 162. In contrast with the Canadians, "Howe, Young, Huntington, and the other Nova Scotian Reformers sought redress of grievances through the regular official channels, did not seek the assistance of [the Radicals] Hume and Roebuck, and consequently when they later had occasion to visit England officially or unofficially they were received with the utmost courtesy at the colonial office, while their loyalty to the empire as a whole and to British principles was accepted there at its face value." *Ibid.*, 163.

[12]Chester Martin, "Nova Scotian and Canadian Reformers of 1845," *Transactions of the Royal Society of Canada*, 1929, Section II, 12.

[13]Largely for his refusal (and properly) to interpret a circular of Oct. 16, 1839, as having conferred "a new and improved constitution" upon the colonies.

[14]Chester Martin, *Empire and Commonwealth* (Oxford, 1929), 196.

[15]Paul Knapland (ed.), *Letters from Lord Sydenham to Lord John Russell* (London, 1931), 83–4.

Tories there was no trouble; the problem was to convince Howe and the bulk of the Reformers.

By playing upon Howe's deep-rooted sense of loyalty—it was his duty to co-operate with the Governor-General in reducing discord and setting a good example for the rebellious Canadians—Sydenham achieved his end. Yet his boast that Howe had "made the amende honorable and eschewed his heresies on Responsible Government publicly in his newspaper"[16] was clearly wishful thinking. What the *Novascotian* had acknowledged was that the Governor-General's system, "though differing a little in theory, in practice . . . was essentially the same as, and in some respects better than, [its] own."[17] For although the Governor retained the responsibility for all the acts of government and the disposition of the patronage, he would be an idiot if he dispensed his favours contrary to his councillors' advice. Moreover, while the Reformers had contemplated an Executive Council, distinct from the heads of departments, but with sufficient control over them to see the business properly done, the Governor-General "tackles them into the team—he makes them conduct the Government, and he tells them distinctly, that if they cannot obtain sufficient Parliamentary talent to assist, they must move off, and hand over the offices to those who have the requisite weight and ability."[18]

This was the genesis of the coalition experiment which, under a new Governor, Lord Falkland, enjoyed a short troubled existence from September 30, 1840, to December 21, 1843. Inherently it possessed difficulties sufficient to debar it as a long-term solution of governmental problems. From the outset the extreme Tory element of the Council delighted in making definitions of its relations with the Governor which were wholly unacceptable to the Reform element. With the more moderate leader of the government, J. W. Johnston, the Reformers might have maintained a general agreement on broad principles, for he admitted a development towards direct ministerial responsibility which at the moment could not be defined precisely.[19] But since the two factions had to present an appearance of face-saving, one by contending that an important step had been taken towards their ultimate goal, the other by denying the reality of substantial change,[20]

---

[16]*Ibid.*, 81.   [17]*Novascotian*, Aug. 27, 1840.   [18]*Ibid.*, July 23, 1840.
[19]*Ibid.*, Feb. 25, 1841. In Britain, he said, "the principles were undefined, but adapted themselves to public exigencies. So should it be here."
[20]This was also the position of Herbert Huntington, who with a small following of Reformers remained outside the coalition on the ground that if "those who were previously at the board held the opinions that then distinguished them, those who went in from the liberal party had no influence,—if the latter had an ascendancy, then it would be fatal to the influence of the others." *Ibid.*, Feb. 18, 1841.

ministerial solidarity was an illusion. "There is something more required to make a Strong Administration," wrote Howe, "than nine men treating each other courteously at a round table. There is the assurance of good faith—towards each other—of common sentiments, and kindly feelings, propagated through the friends of each, in Society, in the Legislature and in the Press, until a great Party is formed . . . which secures a steady working majority to sustain their policy and carry their measures."[21]

The differences which developed upon non-constitutional issues further broadened the cleavage within the Council. Sydenham himself would have found it difficult to preserve the balance between the conflicting elements; Falkland did well to maintain it for almost three years. Of undoubtedly liberal sympathies at the outset, he found himself forced, as if by inexorable circumstances, to rely increasingly upon the Tory section of his Council and thereby doomed the administration.[22] Yet the coalition ministry was significant in more ways than one. It was the first to operate under some degree of collective responsibility; its existence depended upon its maintaining a majority in the Assembly; its members acknowledged the desirability of requiring the principal public officers to hold seats in both the Legislature and the Council;[23] its breakdown was proof positive that party could be no more submerged in a colony than in England.[24]

In its essence the great debate between December, 1843, and the election of August, 1847, hinged around the applicability of party government to the colonial sphere. The Tories—once again in office by themselves—would admit of no principles or issues in colonial politics which could in any way justify two clearly defined political parties such as existed in England. "Ask either [the Liberals or Conservatives] the same question with reference to their views of good government, or needful reform, and it is possible enough that a similar answer

[21]Howe to Falkland, April 3, 1843, Howe Papers, VI, 39, quoted in Martin, *Empire and Commonwealth*, 209.

[22]His conduct may have been determined in part, as the Reformers alleged, by his desire to "propitiate the favour of Sir Robert Peel's [Tory] Government, and ensure for himself some other employment when his term expires here." *Morning Chronicle*, March 13, 1844.

[23]When the offices of Secretary, Treasurer, and Surveyor-General became vacant, only those who acceded to these terms were to be eligible for appointment. See speeches of Dodd and Uniacke, *Novascotian*, March 6, 1843.

[24]Professor Chester Martin wonders how such masters of the traditions and functions of British political parties as Russell and Sydenham could have imagined that provincial assemblies could "function without political parties, or that disciplined political parties once they began to function should not prevail." See review in *C.H.R.*, XXVII (Dec., 1946), 434.

would be received from both."[25] A Liberal, they said, could be distinguished only by his desire to have the existing office-holders supplanted by his own friends;[26] a Conservative only by his opposition to the so-called Liberals. The animosities between the two, by being maintained at fever-pitch over a long period, were proving the bane of the country.[27] The Reformers, while admitting that the issues in Nova Scotian politics could never possess the same absolute significance as those in Britain, contended that they were just as important to colonials as those which agitated the larger sphere were to Britons. The principal colonial issue of the day, centring as it did around the utility of the existing oligarchical rule, was one illustration, even though the Tories did not recognize it because of a convenient myopic condition.

The two positions were just as far apart upon the implications of party government as upon its adaptability to colonial conditions. For one thing, the Tories contended, and the Reformers denied, that it would mean a government operating to favour a particular interest. The former wanted an administration in which the various provincial interests were represented in such proportions as expediency, the efficient conduct of public affairs, and the exigencies of the times dictated.[28] So constituted, it could devise measures for the public good independent of party considerations, and if it abetted corruption and waste, or was wanting in energy, it would be displaced by the Assembly.[29] The Reformers argued that this would make the Assembly either a nullity, or the instrument of a designing administration, since, if a cabinet were constituted of all the leading minds in the colony, any real opposition would disappear and with it the scrupulous sifting of government measures.[30] But practically the proposal could not work, for the binding together in this way of individuals with few private or public ties would never produce that "united personal influence upon society and public opinion, which the members of Council should steadily exert and without which they cannot expect support, either in Parliament or throughout the country."[31]

The two parties differed also upon the prospective status of the Governor under party government. The Tories prophesied that he would become a cipher,[32] the mere advocate of the Assembly, even if its actions were repugnant to his own sense of justice, prejudicial to

[25]Halifax *Times*, March 10, 1846. [26]*Ibid.* [27]*Ibid.*, Nov. 17, 1846.
[28]Falkland to Dodd, Feb. 24, 1844, P.A.N.S. 117, 162.
[29]Halifax *Times*, March 10, 1846.
[30]*Morning Chronicle*, April 1, 1844.
[31]Chisholm, I, 451.
[32]Falkland to Stanley, March 2, 1844, P.A.N.S. 117, 157.

the interests of the colony, and adverse to the rights of the Crown;[33] the Reformers that he would be raised sufficiently above the strife of party to seek only the common good regardless of personal enmities and predilections.[34]

The latter were especially fearful that if the Governor participated actively in the political process—a necessary concomitant of the Tory position in that he would personally determine his executive councillors —he would in time alienate one party and thereby be driven into the camp of the other. They were the first to admit that he could not stand in all respects in the same relation to the Assembly that the Sovereign did to the House of Commons.[35] Nevertheless, if the duties and responsibilities of colonial government were definitely delineated, he would no longer need to fear conflicting advice from his colonial ministers and the Colonial Secretary since he might always turn to the constitution of the colony, and show that he had neither trenched upon the rights of the colonials nor sacrificed the imperial interest.[36] Henceforth he would normally accept his ministers' advice on purely local matters; they, in turn, would defend his acts, and would be charged with whatever was wrong in the conduct of the administration.

The effect of another concomitant of party government—the introduction of the principal public officers into the Legislature—was likewise subject to various interpretations. The Reformers hailed it as a means of making these officers directly accountable to the representatives of the people; the Tories were certain that it would be fatal to the people's liberties.[37] The former described the opposition to it as just another attempt to maintain intact the existing system of vested rights; the latter declared it totally inapplicable to a colony in which public officers like the Treasurer were themselves engaged in receiving moneys at the public counter.[38] They feared that the influence of these

[33]*Ibid.*, May 29, 1845, P.A.N.S. 118, 109.
[34]Chisholm, I, 505.
[35]*Ibid.*, 528.
[36]*Ibid.*, 233.
[37]Falkland, who earlier favoured its introduction by degrees (Falkland to Stanley, Dec. 17, 1843, P.A.N.S. 117, 136) later described as salutary the opposition of the Tories to the "attempts which have been made here to render a system of Government by heads of departments accessory to party and personal aggrandizement." Falkland to Gladstone, March 2, 1846, P.A.N.S., 118, 175.
[38]See speech of Wilkins in the *Novascotian*, Feb. 9, 1846. But while the Tory member for Windsor, J. D. Fraser, concurred that the kind of talent which was required of these officers—an intimate knowledge of accounts, and regularity and system in their offices—was different from that to be looked for in an adviser of the Governor, he suggested the creation of new public offices to be filled by men who could "take at a grasp the whole machinery of Government and . . . bring to the Council and . . . Legislature information which we now in vain look for around

officers upon their colleagues at the Council Board and upon their party in the Legislature might diminish that vigilant supervision to which every public accountant should be subject.[39] Hence the exclusion of the Collector of Excise from the Legislature in 1846[40] was of sufficient import to them to be hailed as the final defeat of Reform principles:

Died at Halifax, aged five years and three months, Responsible, the youngest daughter of Corrupt Government, by POLITICAL QUACKERY. Her godfather, Lord Russell, at his political death willed a large fortune to the deceased on condition of her being brought up in Nova Scotia. . . . Johnston, Dodd, Stewart, Robie, George and Almon [the Tory leaders], proved so inexpert in the use of the spoon, that little Responsible Government never enjoyed a moment's health or exemption from suffering since she fell into their hands, and after languishing until the night of Friday last, she went off into a fit or spasm called *Excisomania.* Her death is supposed to have been accelerated by the injudicious treatment of the celebrated Dr. Marshal,[41] of Manchester, who . . . administered a strong dose of a purgative medicine. . . . This, however, by reducing the system, hastened the death of the child.[42]

Whatever the validity of these positions, Nova Scotia was driven relentlessly along the road to party and, as it proved, responsible government after December, 1843. Howe and his colleagues realized that victory was theirs if for the moment the Governor was compelled to carry on with a ministry composed entirely of Conservatives, and if at a succeeding election they secured a majority in the Assembly. The Tories realized it too, but, try as they might, they were unable to extricate themselves from their predicament. This time no Reformer could be induced to accept the seats in the Executive Council which had been left unfilled to seduce them.[43] Falkland's own despair is indicated by the nature of the remedy which he suggested to avert party and responsible government—"a Constitution defined by Act of Parliament" so as to vindicate "by high authority the free exercise of the prerogative by the Lieut.-Governor in official appointments especially in the nomination of his constitutional advisers."[44] But this suggestion fell on deaf ears, as did his appeal to "a third and moderate

these benches, and which can only be obtained and that imperfectly, through the medium of committees." *Novascotian,* Feb. 23, 1846.

[39]Falkland to Stanley, May 17, 1845, P.A.N.S. 118, 98.

[40]They had previously supported the Governor in having the Treasurer excluded from the Legislature. See Stanley to Falkland, Aug. 2, 1845, P.A.N.S. 84, 147.

[41]J. J. Marshall of Guysborough sponsored the bill.

[42]Quoted from the *Post* in the *Sun* of Feb. 27, 1846.

[43]Falkland made such overtures in February and July of 1844; his successor Harvey late in 1846.

[44]Falkland to Stanley, March 2, 1844, P.A.N.S. 117, 159–60.

party,"[45] distinct from both extremist groups, to rescue the country from the "exclusive domination which *Great* Liberalism would entail upon it."[46]

Meanwhile the Reformers pursued their stated task of generating a healthy tone of public feeling among the great body of the people, certain that in so doing they must win over a majority of the electorate.[47] They were successful too, for in the election of August 5, 1847, the differences between the parties were sharpened to an unprecedented degree. Hence, even though the Reformers' majority was only seven, their victory was certain, since they need not fear the loose fish who in the past had been accustomed to swim in any pool which chanced to be full.[48] Everything now depended upon the new Russell administration in England and the principles of colonial administration which it expounded.

Howe warned at the time of its inception in 1846 that, "if this Whig Government disappoints us, you will have the questions I have touched discussed in a different spirit, ten years hence, by the Enemies of England, not by her friends."[49] Actually he had nothing to fear, for in a minimum of time[50] the new Colonial Secretary, Lord Grey, had outlined a policy in his dispatches to the new Governor, Sir John Harvey, which was entirely satisfactory to the colonial Reformers. He rejected outright any idea that a coalition of political leaders could constitute a permanent foundation for a stable administration. The lesson of experience had been that "animosities exhibit themselves at least as keenly, in small, as in large societies; and . . . the public necessities are as little effectual there as elsewhere, in inducing those who are

[45]*Ibid.*, Jan. 1, 1844, 145.

[46]Halifax *Times*, Nov. 24, 1846.

[47]Chisholm, I, 646. In contrast, the extreme Tories argued that the issues in this election possessed not the slightest interest for the rank and file of Nova Scotians. The *Sun* (Nov. 30, 1846) quoted the *Post* as saying: "What the rural people want is fine weather, fat crops, lots of fish, and a clear conscience; and we much doubt the power of any of the Great Liberals to furnish them with either. Keep your money in your pockets then, good people, or spend it on a gown for your wives, and leave politics alone—They wont fatten you." The *Sun* replied with indignation: "How the Tories do pray the people to be quiet. . . . Pay your taxes regularly, and we'll dispose of them for you—but don't ask any questions. . . . This is Tory advice. Be thankful O ye people! that your Tory masters allow you the enjoyment of those favours which Heaven bestows."

[48]In Howe's opinion the Assembly which was elected in 1847 was the best in Nova Scotian history because it contained few members who were willing to sacrifice a North American measure for a road vote.

[49]"The Correspondence between Joseph Howe and Charles Buller, 1845–8," *C.H.R.*, VI (Dec., 1925), 319.

[50]Even before the Nova Scotian elections of Aug., 1847.

separated by personal and political repugnances to unite their counsels for the common good."[51]

His method of effecting the new principles was equally to the Reformers' liking. "You have no Act of Parliament to define the duty of the Sovereign when ministers are in a minority," wrote Howe; "we want none to enable us to suggest to a Governor when his advisers have lost the confidence of our colonial Assemblies. But what we do want . . . is a rigid enforcement of British practice,"[52] and in this view Grey concurred. The result was that a few dispatches from the Colonial Secretary were the means of transforming the existing Commission and Instructions into a new constitution without a single alteration in their text,[53] and on February 9, 1848, the first responsible ministry in the colonies was formed at Halifax by the Reformer J. B. Uniacke. But although it required a Colonial Secretary to concede it, the victory was, in the main, won by colonials. "We owe [the new constitution] to no Colonial Secretary," said Howe; "we wrested it, step by step, against the prejudices and apprehensions of various Secretaries from 1837 to 1847."[54] Yet if Nova Scotia became, as he boasted, a normal school for the other colonies to follow in the way of constitutional agitation, external circumstances, including the rebellions in the Canadas, played no mean part in enabling a radical change to take place without "a blow struck or a pane of glass broken."[55]

THE EXECUTIVE UNDER RESPONSIBLE GOVERNMENT

Theoretical speculation upon the form of the governmental institutions did not end in 1848. Until 1863 the Conservatives clung to their earlier opinion that the lack of those guards and balances which were furnished by English society and institutions militated against the successful working of responsible and party government. They had concluded that it required "the strictest maintenance of political integrity, of party obligations, and of law and constitutional usages,"[56] something which was unrealizable in a colony. The result was that government had been converted to the system "most debased and

[51]See Grey to Harvey, March 2, 1847, *Journals of the House of Assembly (JHA)*, 1848, Appendix 1, 7–8.
[52]Chisholm, I, 613–14.
[53]Particularly those of Grey to Harvey of Nov. 3, 1846, and March 31, 1847, which are contained in Appendixes 6 and 7 of W. R. Livingston, *Responsible Government in Nova Scotia* (Iowa City, 1930). Officially the Reformers were unaware of their contents until after the election of 1847.
[54]Chisholm, II, 53.
[55]*Ibid.*, I, 331.   [56]*Acadian Recorder*, April 26, 1862.

debasing in itself . . . that sustained by a clique and an oligarchy operated upon by the corrupting influences of bitter party feeling."[57]

This attitude was the natural reaction of a group to the collapse of the political world which they had hitherto directed to their own advantage. Yet they were pointing out some real weaknesses which were accentuated as the Reform party passed through the normal cycle in which the aim of realizing ideal purposes gives way to the mundane objectives of ensuring power for the party leaders and material benefits for their supporters. Certainly there was *prima facie* evidence that the government had come to be vested in a fourth estate, the Executive Council, which was independent of, and paramount to the Colonial Secretary, the Governor, and the Legislative Council;[58] that the dispatches of a Colonial Secretary who was subject to this executive despotism were an unsuitable mode of effecting constitutional alterations;[59] that a Lieutenant-Governor had to choose between sinking into insignificance and seriously challenging his ministers' decisions;[60] and that the Legislative Council had become either the subservient instrument of the provincial government or a source of obstruction to its legislative acts.[61]

Since it was impracticable to reverse a *fait accompli* and abandon the English idea of responsibility, the Conservatives undertook to correct the ills unavoidable in its application to a colony by casting the provincial institutions into such forms as would ameliorate the most patent evil, the overweening power of the executive.[62] "True Conservatism," they said, "must hereafter consist of a well adjusted, well regulated system of Democratic Institutions."[63] That is why during the fifties they were advocating an elective Legislative Council, elective municipal institutions, and even universal suffrage.

No part of the executive branch of government was left untouched by the establishment of the new order in 1848. One concomitant of responsible government was the recognition that the functions of the Lieutenant-Governor were analogous to those of the Sovereign. But while the Governor's general position was transformed, the change was one in practice and not in legal status. Both the Commission and the Instructions remained undisturbed and the new relations between the

[57]*British Colonist*, Feb. 9, 1854.
[58]*Ibid.*, April 19, 1852.
[59]*Ibid.*, March 8, 1852.
[60]*JHA*, 1850, 600.
[61]*Ibid.*, 600–1.
[62]*Ibid.*, 601.
[63]*British Colonist*, Feb. 9, 1854.

Governor and his advisers had no other authority to hallow them than Grey's dispatches of 1846 and 1847.[64]

The interpretation of these dispatches differed, however, with the colony and the Governor, and one Colonial Secretary frankly admitted that "the mode in which the powers conferred on the Council are worked affects so much the whole tone and details of Public business that neighbouring Colonies with the same scripta lex may nevertheless be at least practically living under different Constitutions."[65] In Nova Scotia the mode of interpretation varied from that of the aged Harvey, who practically abrogated any real powers appertaining to himself, to that of MacDonnell who, by introducing the procedures which he had employed in less constitutionally advanced colonies in Australia, clearly attempted to turn the clock back.

Harvey's experience made it clear that the English analogy was not fully applicable to a colony. To have made it so, his decision whether or not to use his reserve power[66] should have been accepted as final. Yet under the new order, protests continued to be taken to the Colonial Secretary against his official actions. He felt obliged, therefore, to defend himself whenever he forwarded any criticisms of his conduct, and his defence, when tabled in the House at a later date, was invariably interpreted as the work of a partisan. His policy of permitting his advisers to write his dispatches aggravated the difficulty.

Grey clarified this situation somewhat by subscribing to the proposition[67] that the dispatches of the Governor to the Colonial Secretary, when "signed by the Lt.-Governor [were], as they profess[ed] to be, those of the Lt.-Governor alone, and in his own custody." As a result, Harvey's successor, Sir Gaspard le Marchant, prepared his own dispatches.[68] Yet his success in preserving a reputation for impartiality was purely coincidental, for Mulgrave, who pursued a similar course during more trying circumstances, fared even worse than Harvey. The solution to this specific problem awaited the time when an easing in the bitterness of the political struggle would make the politicians less inclined to appeal over the head of a Lieutenant-Governor to a higher authority.

[64]*Supra*, 85n.

[65]Cardwell to MacDonnell (confidential), Oct. 15, 1864. See Report of the Public Archives of Nova Scotia, 1949, *JHA*, 1950, Appendix 29, 43.

[66]Broadly his right, if the occasion warranted it, to refuse the advice of his Executive Council.

[67]That of Sir Edmund Head, Lieutenant-Governor of New Brunswick, who had encountered the same difficulty. See Head to Grey (separate), Feb. 28, 1852, contained in P.A.N.S., Lieutenant-Governor's Correspondence, 1838–56.

[68]*Minutes of Council*, Aug. 18, 1852.

The point of contention during MacDonnell's governorship was the precise role to be played by the Governor in the Council's deliberations. The attendance of his three predecessors at its meetings had been little more than a formality. In contrast, MacDonnell thought of the Council chamber as a place where his ministers came with unformed opinions, where a free interchange of viewpoints occurred, and where the Governor had a perfect right to impress his views upon the councillors.[69] But although he placed his personal opinions upon the *Minutes of Council* with abandon, his greatest success on matters of import was to secure agreement in the abstract.[70] Actually he avoided an open break with his ministers only because he went no further than to make suggestions, and in the end his attempt to re-institute propriety was a complete failure, partly because his stay in the province was abbreviated, but more significantly because his successors realized its futility.

Grey's prophecy that the most difficult task of a Governor under responsible government would be to moderate the violence of party contests was well borne out in practice. He conceived the ideal mediator and moderator to be one who gave fair and public support to the Council of the day and who refused its measures only when they appeared to "involve an improper exercise of the authority of the Crown for party rather than for public objects." He warned, however, that even in this limited resort to the reserve power the Governor must act with discretion, for if his ministry resigned and public opinion disapproved his interference, he might find himself in the impossible position of attempting to govern in opposition to majority opinion within the colony.[71]

Although these rules appeared eminently reasonable in the abstract, it was clearly too much to expect that the Governor could be transformed overnight from an active participant in the political process to a detached all-wise arbiter. The very violence of the political process, which continued until the seventies, prevented it. The seeming paradox is that MacDonnell, the only active meddler in local affairs, escaped any serious criticism, while Harvey, who never questioned his ministers' advice, and more particularly Mulgrave, who aspired to be a truly constitutional Governor, were denounced as partisans. The

[69]For his views, see MacDonnell to Cardwell, Sept. 3, 1864, *JHA*, 1950, Appendix 29, 37–40. The Colonial Secretary's reply amounted to: "Enforce your ideas if you think they are politically feasible in Nova Scotia." See Cardwell to MacDonnell, Oct. 15, 1864, *ibid.*, 43–4.

[70]As upon the rules for regulating the tenure of subordinate officials. *Infra*, 98.

[71]Grey to Harvey, Nov. 3, 1846. See Livingston, *Responsible Government*, 254.

Governor's ability to remain a neutral in this transitional stage clearly depended more upon fortuitous circumstances than upon his natural prowess as a diplomat.

Usually it was the contention for public office which embroiled him in the political struggle. Harvey's cardinal sin was that he acquiesced in his Reform Council's destruction of the vested rights of a few high ranking office-holders, while it was Mulgrave's unfortunate lot to have to deal with a constitutional crisis in which the stakes were high and the possibilities of political knavery unlimited.[72] One side had to lose, and when it was the Conservatives who did, they pictured Mulgrave as "completely in the toils of Mr. Howe, Mr. Young, and their myrmidons."[73] His continued subjection to abuse[74] may have caused him to lose his objectivity and to be less than fair to his Conservative ministry in 1863.[75] Yet when his successor MacDonnell attempted to present their conduct in a fairer light, he too was chided for being "too anxious to enter the lists and do battle for his very dignified and very conservative Executive Council."[76]

In addition to his role as the constitutional head of the colony, the Lieutenant-Governor remained the defender of and spokesman for the Imperial interest. In only one instance did the performance of this function prove troublesome. But that was the Confederation issue which presented MacDonnell, Williams, and Doyle with their most trying problems.[77] MacDonnell, for all his determination to assert the power of the Crown, insisted that it be done openly and above board, and his reluctance, which sometimes amounted to recalcitrance, to press with vigour the British government's policy for the union of the colonies resulted in his removal to Hong Kong after a term of little more than a year. His successor, the native Nova Scotian, Sir Fenwick Williams, did not share the same misgivings and since his term was to end with Confederation, he had no need to fear the aftermath of the methods which he used to effect it. Indeed, in winning over wavering assemblymen, he so overstepped the bounds of strict constitutional propriety that he won the open hostility of the anti-Confederates. One

[72]*Infra*, 126–7.

[73]*Acadian Recorder*, Feb. 2, 1861.

[74]*Infra*, 98. Earlier he had discouraged his Liberal ministers from defending his conduct to avoid the possibility of his being identified with a particular party.

[75]They, in turn, suggested that it would be preferable to have an elective Governor or someone under the cognomen of plain Mister to "one who has descended through a long line until the blood of a Lord is only capable of stimulating the brain to the duties of a 'whip.'" *Acadian Recorder*, Feb. 13, 1864.

[76]*Morning Chronicle*, Sept. 5, 1865.

[77]See chap. x for a fuller discussion of these problems.

of them went so far as to prophesy that "as long as Nova Scotia is known [Williams's] name will stink in the nostrils of our people."[78]

Thus in 1867 the Governor appeared to be as deeply involved in politics as he had ever been. But that was only because the development in the conception of his functions since 1848 was being completely beclouded by an issue which for the moment overshadowed everything else. Once its repercussions were no longer felt the modern Governor would emerge.

The Executive Council experienced changes no less far-reaching than the governorship. Upon the Reform administration of 1848 fell the onus of establishing the machinery which would ensure "adequate control, by the majority of the Constituency over the Departments by which the whole Executive Machinery was moved."[79] Of particular concern was the precise number of public officers who were to sit in the Executive Council to effect the optimum degree of control. The Tories were still obsessed with the notion that departmental heads who are "converted into parliamentary officers . . . become possessors of an influence at the Council Board and in the Legislature, unfavourable to a faithful and vigilent [sic] scrutiny into their official conduct,"[80] while the Reformers ridiculed the idea that officers whose conduct was constantly under the scrutiny of their opponents in the Legislature and whose resignation followed automatically an unfavourable vote in the Assembly could evade accountability for their maladministration. The former naturally favoured a strict limitation of the number of ministers with office, on the ground that the displacement of a single minister would vindicate the principles of responsible government as efficaciously as the removal of a dozen;[81] the latter upheld their right to control seven offices, "the smallest number . . . by the aid of which, it could ever have been sup[p]osed, that Responsible Government could be carried on."[82]

The second position was the essentially practical one of men who realized that, if the Executive Council were to consist of one or two paid members with office and seven or eight unpaid members without office, it would be impossible to convene regularly a quorum of five to perform the routine business of the province between sessions, much

[78]Assembly Debates, 1868, 15.
[79]Minutes of Council, July 21, 1848.
[80]JHA, 1849, Appendix 6, 107. See also letter of Executive Council to Harvey, Jan. 30, 1847, Journals of the Legislative Council (JLC), 1848, Appendix 1.
[81]Speech of J. W. Johnston in Novascotian, Jan. 5, 1852.
[82]JHA, 1849, Appendix 6, 113. The seven offices were: the two Crown officers, the secretaryship, the Treasury, Land, and Revenue departments, and the office of Queen's Printer.

less carry out the task of policy-making in all branches of the public service. Yet at the outset they held only the attorney-generalship and the solicitor-generalship since the Provincial Secretary and the Treasurer would not resign their positions.

They experienced no difficulty in vacating the office of Provincial Secretary through a resolution of the Assembly,[83] but the real test of their success depended upon the Colonial Secretary's acceptance of the Departmental Bill which they regarded as the keystone of the new system. It replaced the Treasurer by a Receiver-General whose sole duty was to receive and pay out moneys at the direction of a Financial Secretary to whom the ministerial duties in connection with finance were entrusted. The point of contention was that the two new officers were to sit in the Legislature as members of the provincial administration. This provision was criticized as a deviation from the recognized practice and from good common sense, each of which dictated a single finance officer in the Executive Council. Nevertheless the Reform ministry stuck to its guns and after a year's delay a still dubious Colonial Secretary withdrew his objections to the bill.

While the Reformers requested no other changes, they fought every subsequent attempt to bar additional officers from the Council by statute. "I for one," said Joseph Howe, "would never give up the power which a Government ought to possess . . . of making the best arrangement of its officers for the transaction of public business."[84] Yet, whether he liked it or not, the resort to legislative action in 1848 to inaugurate the new order had established the precedent that all future changes in departmental organization and in the number and title of public officers in the Executive Council would be made, not by exercise of the prerogative, but by statutory action. It was therefore that method which Tupper used in 1867 to implement his belief that four ministers with portfolio—an Attorney-General, Provincial Secretary, Provincial Treasurer, and Commissioner of Public Works and Mines— would be sufficient to carry on the diminished duties of the local government under Confederation.[85]

The civil service, in its turn, was also adapted to the requirements of

[83]*JHA*, 1848, 42–3. The resolution simply asserted that according to a proper understanding of the new principles Sir Rupert George's resignation from the Executive Council vacated the provincial secretaryship as well.

[84]*Novascotian*, Jan. 5, 1852.

[85]30 Vic., c. 1. The act abolished the office of Solicitor-General, transferred the duties of the Financial Secretary to the Provincial Secretary, changed the designation of the Receiver-General to Provincial Treasurer, and provided that a new minister, the Commissioner of Public Works and Mines, should perform the functions of the Board of Works and the Chief Commissioner of Mines.

the new order. Once in office, the Reformers were anxious to introduce the further principle that the definition of the duties, salary, and tenure of every colonial officer should be subject to colonial regulation. Apart from any ideal considerations which would result from this control, they undoubtedly looked to patronage as a means of strengthening the government and of gratifying their supporters. Even before 1848 one Lieutenant-Governor had stated his opinion that although the province could not be ruled by means of patronage, yet "the necessity of some influence derived from this source in a country governed through the instrumentality of a parliamentary majority [was] as great here as . . . elsewhere."[86] But just as his attempts to break through "the hereditary transmission of offices"[87] provoked the hostility of the extreme Tories of his day, so the Reformers' efforts to regulate the civil service conflicted with the determination of the Conservatives to protect the vested rights of the local oligarchy. As Howe pointed out ruefully,

Not a drunken magistrate was dismissed, nor an officer of any kind removed; but home to the Colonial Office went remonstrance upon remonstrance, petitions and prayers without number, calling upon the Colonial Secretary for redress. Why, sir, the strongest man in this House would hardly be able to carry on his back the piles of these documents that one after the other, packet by packet, went across the water.[88]

In the end these representations did no more than delay the cleaning up of the top-heavy structure of the colonial bureaucracy. Even when the Reformers compromised, the solution tended to favour them, for they were in the driver's seat, and the contending parties were a Whig Colonial Secretary and a Reform Council. In order to get control of the casual and territorial revenues of the Crown, they were forced to make a somewhat costly permanent provision for the Lieutenant-Governor, the judges, the two law officers, and the Provincial Secretary,[89] but the settlement was a much closer approximation to their views than to those of their opponents.[90]

Everywhere the Reformers ran up against the same solicitude for

[86]Falkland to Gladstone, April 2, 1846, P.A.N.S. 113, 184.
[87]Falkland to Stanley, Sept. 13, 1842, P.A.N.S. 117, 40.
[88]Chisholm, II, 54.
[89]This interrelated problem of the civil list and the casual and territorial revenues of the Crown had been testing the ingenuity of British and colonial statesmen since 1833. To the Reformers these revenues were a "trust fund to be husbanded with economy and expended for the benefit of the whole people," not "personal property to be capriciously lavished . . . [upon] three or four public officers . . . whose only care appeared to be to see who should get the most of it." *Ibid.*, I, 342.   [90]12 Vic., c. 1 (1849).

protecting "the faintest shadow of claim which wealthy individuals . . . ha[d] upon the revenues. . . ."[91] Where an officer—like the Provincial Treasurer—had disregarded their warnings and accepted a position under a tenure during good behaviour, they would provide no compensation if the fulfilment of their plans required his removal, but where his appointment had preceded the discussion of the new principles, they were prepared to make him a reasonably generous offer. In contrast, the extreme Tories were satisfied with nothing less than full compensation,[92] which in the case of Sir Rupert George, the Provincial Secretary and Registrar, would have saddled the provincial revenues with an annual outlay of £2,000. Eventually George was wise enough to heed the Executive Council's warning that any concerted effort to amend its proposals might outrage public opinion and redound to his own disadvantage. As a result, a new group of officials, the country registrars of deeds, were brought under the direct supervision of the Executive Council, whereas in the past they had been accountable only to George and part of their revenues had been his perquisite.

A similar procedure was followed in dealing with J. W. Nutting, the prothonotary of the Supreme Court and clerk of the Crown for the province, who also acted through county deputies and "reaped where he sowed not, and [ate] the bread sowen by others."[93] By guaranteeing him one-third of the fees of the local offices,[94] the county prothonotaries and clerks of the Crown were also made directly accountable. As usual, the Conservatives opposed the continuing tendency to strengthen the executive. "The only reason given . . . for introducing the Bill," said Holmes, "was to transfer the Patronage to the Government . . . [whose] patronage was already sufficiently extensive."[95]

[91]Chisholm, I, 348.

[92]It was this position which had once drawn Huntington's contemptuous reply: "If the doctrine . . . were correct, the West India Slaves would be still held in bondage, because their masters once had an interest in their services. . . . let a man once get a situation, no matter through what corruption of the legislative bodies of the time, and no matter how ridiculously high the original emoluments, he should be continued the full amount during his existence." *Novascotian*, Feb. 6, 1840.

[93]*JHA*, 1856, 176.

[94]But his total emoluments, including those from the metropolitan prothonotaryship which he retained, were limited to £500. See 16 Vic., c. 13. Howe would have been prepared to give £600, "but he drew a wide distinction between the man who sat quietly in his office with no elections to run, incurring but little responsibility, and those office-holders which under the responsible system, were dependent upon the people's will." *Novascotian*, Feb. 9, 1853.

[95]*Ibid.*

In time, the fear of executive despotism aroused more concern than the destruction of vested rights. The Reform ministry effected a consolidation of the two offices[96] in the Land Department with a minimum of debate about vested rights, but the mere suggestion that the head of the department should be made a political officer with a seat in the Legislature evoked the usual gloomy forebodings that it would strengthen the executive arm unduly and destroy the independence of the Legislature.[97]

In two other instances, the altered policy of the British government permitted additional provincial control over the local bureaucracy to be established. A long-standing grievance had been the maintenance, side by side, of two cumbersome revenue departments to collect the Imperial customs duties and the provincial impost duties, and "the payment of exorbitant Salaries [to their officers], disproportioned to the duties to be performed, and to the station which the Public Officers, in a young and comparatively a poor Colony, should occupy."[98] By coincidence, the repeal of the laws relating to navigation and trade occurred almost simultaneously (1849) with the advent of the Reform administration. This proved to be the death-knell of the Imperial customs establishment, for the outcome was that the Executive Council replaced the Lords of the Treasury as controllers of the patronage of the customs.[99]

A similar development occurred in the regulation of the post office where colonial interference had always been denied "lest the uniformity and harmony of the system embracing the whole Empire

[96]One for the mainland and one for Cape Breton. "The Public Domain," said the *Sun* (Jan. 7, 1846), "has been quite long enough giving bread and butter to two families, and yielding nothing to the people but trouble and vexation."

[97]Johnston re-echoed the usual refrain: "In England it was different from this country—there it was not necessary for a Head of Department to be qualified to discharge the duties of any office—these being always discharged by a well paid Under Secretary. The Head took office because he was a Statesman, not from his business qualifications. Here the case was different. The Head of the office was the working man, and was expected to be an efficient officer." *Novascotian*, Jan. 5, 1852. The outcome was that the responsibility of managing the Crown estate remained largely with a non-political Commissioner of Crown Lands. A committee of the Executive Council was to decide difficult cases, but "their interference will only be occasional." See letter of Howe to John Spry Morris, Dec. 9, 1851, *JLC*, 1852, Appendix 6, 60–1.

[98]See *JHA*, 1839, 590–1.

[99]After 1849 the Imperial customs officers in Nova Scotia performed only two functions, the registration of vessels and the granting of certificates of origin (when required) for colonial produce. Since both were rendered for the benefit of the colony, their assumption by the local customs officers on Jan. 5, 1855, was not inappropriate. See Marion Gilroy, "The Imperial Customs Establishment in Nova Scotia, 1825–55," *C.H.R.*, XIX (Sept., 1938), 291.

should be disturbed."[100] The abandonment of this position enabled the Legislature to transfer the control of the provincial post office, including the appointment and removal of the Postmaster-General and his subordinates, to the Governor-in-Council in 1851,[101] but because of the usual objections, it could not make the Postmaster-General a responsible political officer.[102]

The only officers who were not brought directly under the control of the Executive Council were the sheriffs. Before 1849 the Lieutenant-Governor selected them from lists which the Chief Justice compiled annually for each county. Since the process had an uncanny faculty for singling out individuals of one political shade, the Reformers had endeavoured to endow the Executive Council with a greater measure of responsibility. Each time they were told the result would be to produce political sheriffs and to "place the liberties of the people altogether in the power of the Executive."[103] Even after 1848 the most they could accomplish was to transfer the nominating function from the Chief Justice to a group of four which consisted of the Chief Justice, an assistant justice, and two members of the Executive Council,[104] but since the Lieutenant-Governor-in-Council made the appointment from their three nominees, the responsible executive had been endowed with a substantial measure of control.

The effect of this general development was to place the authority for the appointment and the dismissal of all but a limited number of colonial officials in the colonial executive. "Our Deities of the olden time . . . were immovable on their pedestals," said Howe; "now we can bowl them out like ninepins."[105] The concomitant of self-govern-

[100]Novascotian, Oct. 17, 1839.

[101]The Russell administration which assumed office in July, 1846, decided that "it was no longer expedient for the general post office to continue responsibility for postal systems, which had to subserve interests understood only by those whom they concerned." See William Smith, The History of the Post Office in British North America, 1639–1870 (Cambridge, 1920), 263. Some years were required to perfect the arrangements for the transfer. The relevant Nova Scotian statute is R.S. 1851, c. 23.

[102]". . . the presence of the Postmaster General here [said William Annand] is part and parcel of the Responsible system. It prevails in England, in Canada and New Brunswick, and I do not wish the stain of his exclusion to remain on our Statute Book." Assembly Debates, 1856, 78–9.

[103]Huntington described this argument as "the old Tory doctrine. . . . They would give the people no power in the offices under consideration, but would place the patronage in the hands of a man that could not be made responsible in any way." Novascotian, Feb. 10, 1842.

[104]The immediate effect was to displace two sheriffs, one in Yarmouth where the Tories, it was alleged, had "from time immemorial . . . monopolized nearly every office of influence and emolument." Novascotian, Dec. 10, 1849.

[105]Novascotian, Jan. 5, 1852.

ment, the control of public offices, paid off in the introduction of a greater measure of economy and direct responsibility. Yet these gains were counterbalanced in part by a responsible executive's unfortunate, although natural, resort to patronage as a means of rewarding its political supporters.

Before 1848 the Halifax and local compacts had monopolized even the most paltry of the public offices; by 1867 the system of "to the victors belong the spoils" had been generally accepted as a proper mode for their disposition.[106] Thus the prophecies of the Conservatives that responsible government would enable an oligarchical clique to confer office upon the individuals who had made its existence possible were at least partially fulfilled. The adoption of this allegedly loath-some Americanism was an evolutionary process and any attempt to fix the blame upon one individual or party is therefore fruitless. Certainly the first Reform administration, except in its commissions of the peace,[107] was loath to use its power of dismissal even though most of the bureaucracy was ill-disposed to its principles.[108] Yet, when new offices were created, or vacancies occurred in existing offices, Reformers were chosen to fill them. It was not surprising, therefore, that the Conservatives were soon accusing Howe of practising nepotism and of creating a Joseph Howe compact in a vein which was strongly re-miniscent of his own earlier writings.[109] While the administration admitted that its appointments partook, by necessity, of a party character, it denied that any "prejudice to the interests or rights of the community [could] possibly result from this, if the vacant office [was] filled by an incumbent thoroughly qualified for the discharge of its duties."[110]

[106]This development occurred despite the initial warnings of a Colonial Secretary that "the small population and limited revenue of Nova Scotia as well as the general occupation and social state of the community, . . . [were] additional reasons for abstaining . . . from going further than can be avoided . . . in making the tenure of offices in the public service dependent upon the result of party contests." Grey to Harvey, March 31, 1847, see Livingston, *Responsible Government*, 258.

[107]*Infra*, 138.

[108]"After conducting the Administration for months, but four removals have been pressed, but two or three others are required. We have asked for no office that is not, or has not been made by the peculiar circumstances which have occurred here, political." *Minutes of Council*, July 21, 1848.

[109]Howe's opponents contended, for example, that his son was "neither of age or ability to fill the office which his father's influence has obtained for him. . . . it is a revival of an old-fashioned custom which Howe was the first to complain of and denounce. . . . Were there no other young aspirants . . . sons of staunch Liberals—who might fairly put in their claim for a share of the loaves and fishes?" *British Colonist*, Feb. 9, 1852.   [110]*Assembly Debates*, 1856, 117.

A more serious problem developed around the dismissal of subordinate officials. After 1848 the rank-and-file supporters of the Reform ministry simply could not understand why their political enemies were allowed to retain their offices: ". . . it would be doing the people of Cumberland a very great kindness," one wrote, "to make some of those vile and unworthy men, if men I may venture to call them, walk the plank."[111] An Annapolis Reformer put the issue in the bluntest of terms:

Why do you allow those opposed and bitterly opposed to you and the present Govt. who they are incessantly abusing to hold all the offices in your gift . . . look for yourself The Shff—Judge of Probate—Regr. Probate—Regr. deeds—Collector of Excise—Proy.—and numerous minor offices all in their hands,—I ask you my friend is it right? is it just? we have fought for our party and if we have not been successful it is not our fault, we have always got up an opposition that has annoyed Mr. Johnston much; it is no wonder we do not succeed for all the Officials are against us.[112]

Grey had made it clear that if the subordinate officials expected to retain their position they must not take an active part in political contests,[113] but in a day in which the open recording of votes registered an immutable testimony of a voter's political allegiance, the grounds for dismissal were rendered easy to conjure up. The striving for even the pettiest of offices and the growing venom of the politics of the late 1850's and 1860's provided additional stimuli for ferreting out instances of misconduct.

To the credit of the Reform ministers they withstood for a time the pressure of their supporters. Not until 1856 were they accused of introducing the American mode of dismissal in wholesale fashion, and even then the specific incidents which were used as an illustration were subject to such varying interpretations that any accurate assessment of the degree of guilt is out of the question.[114] It appears likely, however, that the Reformers' earlier inclination to observe the Colonial Secretary's rules to the letter had experienced the same fate as their early zeal for reform. Yet a short-lived Conservative administration could not avoid similar criticism for accepting "the most detestable of all principles . . . the principle of driving men from office in consequence of the political opinions which they entertain."[115]

[111]See letter to Howe from River Hebert, March 31, 1852, in P.A.N.S. (unfiled).
[112]See letter to Howe from Annapolis Royal, March 28, 1852, in P.A.N.S. (unfiled).   [113]Grey to Harvey, Nov. 15, 1848, P.A.N.S. 87, 289–92.
[114]While the leader of the government William Young would neither announce or denounce the principle that to the victor belongs the spoils, he denied that the government had "yet acted on that principle." *Assembly Debates*, 1856, 90.
[115]*Acadian Recorder*, June 20, 1857.

In these circumstances it was only to be expected that the three changes of government between 1857 and 1863 would produce a "prolific crop of personal and political rancour" and "a fresh debt of retribution to be in turn rigorously exacted."[116] Each was followed by an increase in the number of dismissals, 36 by the Conservatives from 1857 to 1860, 82 by the Liberals from 1860 to 1863, and 60 by the Conservatives in the six months after 1863.[117] Each time, too, new arguments, sometimes more ingenious than ingenuous, were used as a means of self-justification. The dismissals, it was sometimes alleged, were "mainly caused by the displacement of active political partizans from Offices from which the friends of the present Government were expelled to make places for them." On other occasions it was stated that "no party could maintain any influence with the Country who uniformly sustained in Office those opposed to them while a different policy was practiced by their Opponents."[118]

Since the Lieutenant-Governors were implicitly entrusted with seeing that the rules of the political game were observed, they were continually having to deal with alleged cases of wrongful dismissal. Mulgrave's stay in the province became a veritable nightmare on that account.[119] His successor MacDonnell realized that unless the electorate appreciated the danger of the existing practice, no ministry would exhibit sufficient firmness to resist its own office seekers,[120] and he therefore placed his own views before the public whenever possible[121] His aim was to get both the government and the opposition to accept the English system of tenure, and then hedge it round with constitutional safeguards,[122] but since no one considered the evil quite as serious as he did, his success was limited to his Council's ac-

[116]See MacDonnell to Cardwell, Sept. 3, 1864, no. 1, P.A.N.S. 127.

[117]*JHA*, 1864, Appendix 36.

[118]See reply of Executive Council dated Nov. 25, 1863, to Mulgrave's memorandum in *Minutes of Council*, 1860–7, 255, 257 (P.A.N.S.).

[119]After 1860, he was described as "bewildered and brainless" for permitting his Liberal ministry to go as far as they dared in the introduction of "the Yankee system of tenure of office." *Acadian Recorder*, Jan. 25, 1862.

[120]MacDonnell to Cardwell, Sept. 3, 1864, no. 1, P.A.N.S. 127.

[121]For his active participation in the Henry B. Lowden and Arod Grant cases, see Lieutenant-Governor's Correspondence, July–December, 1865.

[122]See *Minutes of Council*, Feb. 22, 1865. The agreement between the parties was to be confirmed by a statute which would devolve upon the Governor, acting under the advice of a commission which he himself appointed, the dismissal or suspension of any office-holders who were alleged to have participated in politics. To prevent the act from being subject to instant repeal, any change was to require a two-thirds vote of each branch of the Legislature. MacDonnell admitted that this guarantee would have been insufficient in the case of Parliament, but he felt that it could be effectually maintained in a colony where the Governor and the

quiescence in his general proposition.[123] Both parties had come to recognize that the disposal of patronage possessed undoubted virtues as a political device, and by Confederation they were tacitly accepting a close approximation to the American practice in the tenure of subordinate officials.

Legislature remained "as it were responsible . . . to the Crown." MacDonnell to Cardwell, Separate, Aug. 31, 1865, P.A.N.S. 127.

[123]See *Minutes of Council*, Aug. 19, 1864.

CHAPTER VII

THE LEGISLATIVE FUNCTION

It happened to be the opening of the Legislative Council and General Assembly, at which ceremonial the forms observed on the commencement of a new Session of Parliament in England were so closely copied, and so gravely presented on a small scale, that it was like looking at Westminster through the wrong end of a telescope. The Governor, as her Majesty's representative, delivered what may be called the Speech from the Throne. He said what he had to say manfully and well. The military band outside the building struck up "God Save the Queen" with great vigour before his Excellency had quite finished; the people shouted; the in's rubbed their hands; the out's shook their heads; the Government party said there never was such a good speech; the opposition declared there never was such a bad one, . . . and, in short, everything went on, and promised to go on, just as it does at home upon the like occasions.[1]

SUCH was Charles Dickens' description of the opening of the Nova Scotian Legislature in 1841. The discussion which follows indicates that between 1830 and 1867 the colonial statesmen were continually facing the problem of how far and by what means the practical operation of the Legislature might be brought into the same conformity with the British model as its outward forms.

THE LEGISLATIVE COUNCIL

Only the Council of Twelve had escaped the differentiation of functions which the other governmental institutions had experienced in some degree before 1830. In a new era its members continued to perform all their old multifarious duties.

Now they are legislators—to-morrow they are the arbiters of life and death— or the distributors of patronage. They form a Court of appeal in which the decisions of the gravest Judges of the land may be reviewed and reversed— and then they are suddenly changed to a Court of Marriage and Divorce, so that a man cannot get rid of a bad wife without their interference and consent. On all occasions they surround the Representative of Majesty, who in most cases does, and in many is bound to, act by their advice, and one of the Members succeeds him when he is absent.[2]

The initial proposals to reduce this concentration of authority came, surprisingly enough, from a Colonial Secretary who, in the early

[1]Charles Dickens, *American Notes* (London and Toronto, 1931 ed.), 21.
[2]See speech of Alexander Stewart in *Novascotian*, Feb. 27, 1834.

thirties, explored the possibility of creating two distinct and separate councils. He abandoned the idea, however, when a Governor, an Administrator, and the Council, individually and collectively,[3] threw cold water upon the project. As usual, the individuals who enjoyed preferment defended to the hilt a status quo which operated to their own advantage. Nevertheless the tendency grew to trace more evils than ever sprang from Pandora's box to the defects of the Council[4] and to the extension of its hundred arms over the whole administration.[5] The considered views of the people's representatives could be defeated, it was alleged, by a combination of two families whenever the Council was not quite full. The manipulations of the five bankers within its walls had left the country "without any standard of value . . . and with one currency for the rich and another for the poor."[6] The selection of its members almost exclusively from adherents of the Established Church who lived in Halifax and the close connection of its members by blood or in mercantile pursuits strengthened the impression that it was an instrument of favouritism and monopoly.[7]

The Reformers' conception of an ideal second chamber was one which would support the Assembly's efforts to impose proper checks upon an irresponsible bureaucracy. But instead of the elective Council which they advocated they received a miniature House of Lords for which they expressed no enthusiasm. The Colonial Secretary who conferred it likewise doubted its utility, while the Council of Twelve contended that a British-type second chamber could not be constructed in a colony.

The fluctuating state of the Colonial Society,—the universal division of the property of a deceased person among his children or relatives, and the general feelings and habits of the people, prevent the growth of Aristocracy among us. We cannot therefore found any branch of the Legislature here upon Aristocratic principles.[8]

Thus the Legislative Council started with no one prepared to own it, and after an initial flurry because its original members were no less unrepresentative than their predecessors, it passed into eclipse as the bulk of the political energy was diverted into more fruitful channels.

The Council's first problems were those associated with setting up

[3]See, for example, Goderich to Maitland (confidential), Dec. 7, 1830, P.A.N.S. 67, doc. 88; Jeffery to Goderich, March 20, 1833, P.A.N.S. 114, 101–2; and *Minutes of Council,* May 7, 1834.

[4]*Novascotian,* Jan. 21, 1830.

[5]See speech of Stewart in *Novascotian,* Feb. 27, 1834.

[6]J. A. Chisholm, *Speeches and Public Letters of Joseph Howe* (Halifax, 1909), I, 122.

[7]*Ibid.,* 113.   [8]*Novascotian,* May 11, 1837.

house. Should its members continue to sit around a table, or if the seats were to be rearranged, how could the councillors be drawn sufficiently near the fire to prevent them from being laid up by illness? How could the public be admitted to its sessions without harm to the valuable pictures on the walls? Should the rules of the House of Lords be adopted to regulate its proceedings?[9]

The councillors settled these matters with comparative ease, but in performing what was considered their main function—to "arbitrate between the opposite tendencies of the Monarchical and the Democratic Branches of the Constitution, and when necessary, to control and harmonize both,"[10]—they were frustrated through no fault of their own. Successive colonial secretaries adamantly rejected any suggestion of a monetary reward for the councillors, either from the Crown or from the people, as likely to militate against the uncompromising discharge of their trust. Accordingly every governor was strictly enjoined to preserve the analogy with the House of Lords by selecting "Gentlemen of sufficient means to keep up the independent character of the Body, and to render unnecessary the resort to paid Members."[11]

This injunction conflicted with a previous instruction to have regard for the representation of all interests, geographical or otherwise, in making appointments to the Council. The experience of time fully vindicated the prophecies of the Council of Twelve that the province was deficient in "sensible and well educated men, possessing large landed property, separated from office, and having influence in the different counties in which they reside"[12] who would serve without remuneration. The Council itself lamented the fact that many of its members accepted their appointments only under pressure, and that a speedy resignation or sporadic attendance usually followed.[13] Despite its peremptory summonses to the absentees it was often difficult to

[9]*Ibid.*, Feb. 15, 1838.
[10]Stanley to Falkland, Aug. 20, 1845, *Journals of the Legislative Council (JLC)*, 1846, Appendix 1.
[11]*Ibid.*, July 21, 1842, P.A.N.S. 81, 132.
[12]*Minutes of Council*, May 7, 1834.
[13]*JLC*, 1845, 60–1. Typical illustrations were: Peter Hall Clarke of Sydney, described at the time of his appointment as "an independent and opulent merchant," but who later resigned because of "a deficiency of pecuniary means to meet the expenses of a residence in Halifax during the session of parliament"; George Smith of Pictou, who resigned, a virtual bankrupt, to become a candidate for the Assembly; and Peter de Carteret of Arichat, who refused outright to accept his mandamus as Councillor. Falkland required more than a year to secure a successor for James Bond of Yarmouth. R. M. Cutler of Guysborough incurred the Governor's reprimand for his absence without reasonable excuse in 1842, yet, nothing daunted, retained his membership and later established an all-time record of absence for five consecutive sessions.

convene a quorum of eight, and only the faithful attendance of its Halifax members enabled it to function at all in its early years.

Five times[14] it demanded the remedies which would permit it to perform its functions properly. Rebuffed on each occasion by the Assembly and the Colonial Office, it finally took matters into its own hands in 1852, and rejected the usual remuneration to the members of the Assembly. The latter did not fail to appreciate a danger which imperilled their own interests, and two years later they abandoned a completely unrealistic conception of a second chamber by voting equal indemnities to the members of both Houses. As a result, the Council never again experienced any trouble because of absenteeism. The monetary reward also enabled the Council to secure its members from a wider geographical area. By Confederation the Halifax contingent had been reduced from ten to four, the number of unrepresented counties from eleven to five, and the movement to give all the counties some representation had begun.[15]

Actually responsible government brought in its wake a new upper branch even though not the slightest alteration occurred in the Council's formal constitution. Its new character was due instead to a purely incidental product of party government—the practice of conferring councillorships upon party stalwarts in sympathy with the ministry of the day.

The party character of the second branch was further reinforced by the skulduggery which accompanied the institution of the new system. Although Grey had feared intransigent opposition from the Council, he had warned that no appointments beyond the ordinary maximum of twenty-one would be approved except under circumstances of obvious necessity.[16] Fortuitous circumstances[17] enabled the Reformers to get their proposals through the Council in 1848, but to stave off defeat in 1849, the Liberal President of the Council had to adopt a practice of

[14]In 1840, 1842, 1845, 1848, and 1850. The majority of the Council requested, as a minimum, a suitable provision for travelling and living expenses for its country members, but a lone exception, Alexander Stewart, proposed instead a "defined constitution," preferably by act of Parliament, and particularly a life tenure, as a more suitable means of enhancing the prestige of the Council and guaranteeing an assured supply of suitable recruits to fill its ranks.

[15]*Infra*, 233.

[16]Grey to Harvey, Nov. 3, 1846, see W. R. Livingston, *Responsible Government in Nova Scotia* (Iowa City, 1930), 252.

[17]The absence of one Tory Councillor (R. M. Cutler), the general support of a moderate (William Rudolf), the resignation of President S. B. Robie because two bills violated the principles which he had cherished throughout his political career (*JLC*, 1848, 69), and the filling of that vacancy and two others with Reformers accounted for their success.

the Lord Chancellor which had never been used in Nova Scotia—he
voted as an ordinary Councillor and thereby prevented the Reformers
from being defeated on a vital measure.[18] This was one reason why
Johnston's crusade for a well-regulated system of democratic institutions included an elective Legislative Council among its objectives.
The Conservative leader contended that the existing second chamber
could not be expected to perform the functions of the House of Lords
since it was not composed of a class distinct from the Commons and
unmoved by popular clamour.

> Do [our legislative councillors] ward off the aggressions of the crown, or
> oppose any check to the popular branch? . . . Our Legislative Council at
> present is the tool and slave of the executive for the time being . . . sub-
> servient to the will of a few men who can manage, by any means, to
> clamber into the Executive Council. . . . Do they start at an act of gross and
> heinous injustice and violation of faith, and refuse to sanction it? they are
> instantly swamped by the introduction of creatures who have signed a
> confession of faith, and bound themselves hand and foot to work out the
> will of these Executive Councillors.[19]

His conclusion was that only popular election would render the two
branches "independent and entirely beyond the influence or controul
of the other."[20] The Liberals naturally dismissed this argument as the
offspring of an individual who, despairing of getting back to the old
order, desired to unsettle the entire framework of existing institutions.[21]
They were especially fearful that the election of the upper branch
under a restricted franchise would weaken the claim of the lower
House to speak as the sole representatives of the people.[22]

After the Conservatives assumed office in 1857, they quickly discovered the futility of trying to press radical changes upon the particularist Assembly of the day. So within a year they had given up their

---

[18]The Tory councillors were present in full force early in the session to press a
temporary numerical advantage. They hoped thereby to secure an address opposing
the Departmental Bill of 1848 which had been returned by the Colonial Secretary
for reconsideration. One of the two missing Reformers, William McKeen of Mabou,
as yet to be sworn in, had been prevented from crossing the Strait of Canso "in
consequence of a snow storm, unexampled in Nova Scotia for half a century."
Harvey to Grey, March 9, 1849, P.A.N.S. 120, 260. Because of the emergency, the
Lieutenant-Governor appointed Dr. William Grigor to the seat intended for
McKeen. Eventually, however, the Colonial Secretary agreed to McKeen's confirmation as a twenty-second member, the only instance of a membership in excess
of twenty-one prior to 1928. Grey to Harvey, June 26, 1849, P.A.N.S. 88, 149–50.
[19]British Colonist, Aug. 18, 1849.
[20]See speech of Johnston, ibid., March 8, 1852.
[21]Novascotian, March 18, 1850.
[22]See speech of Doyle, British Colonist, April 12, 1852.

proposals for the reform of the Council[23] and were seeking through the power of appointment[24] to make it serve their own ends. Thus an upper House which used to reflect the viewpoint of a particular class was superseded by one which reflected that of a particular party. While the earlier Council had contained individuals capable of speaking their own minds on specific issues, similar displays of independence henceforth involved a deviation from the party line and rarely occurred on matters of import. Yet nothing more should have been expected of a second chamber, originally constituted so as to win the approbation of none, and owing its fundamental character to an unplanned, accidental circumstance.

THE HOUSE OF ASSEMBLY

By 1830 the House of Assembly had vindicated its right to the privileges which it required to perform its functions with assurance and with dignity;[25] henceforth it could concentrate upon reforming the provincial institutions in general and its own constitution in particular. Yet its members persistently refused to deal with the notorious evils[26] in the disposition of road moneys for fear of losing the peculiar rights which were theirs by long usage. They rejected the warning of Lawrence O'Connor Doyle that "When we attempt to turn the money changers out of the upper end of the building, because they derange the currency and traffic in Bills of Exchange—may they not turn upon us and say, your Bank is the Treasury chest—you trade and deal in Road Warrants, which is equally dangerous and unconstitu-

[23]Johnston's abandonment of the elective principle occurred after the Committee of the Whole divided evenly on its merits in 1858. *Journals of the House of Assembly* (*JHA*), 1858, 476. Actually the closest the Conservatives came to success was in 1851 when a weakened Liberal government recognized the merits of the elective principle, but postponed any consideration of its practical implementation until after the general election. *JHA*, 1851, 708–9.

[24]Or through manœuvres of another kind, as in 1864 when Tupper took advantage of the unscheduled bout of rheumatism which had incapacitated the Liberal Samuel Chipman to rush his contentious Equity Court Bill through all its stages in the Council.

[25]The only instance in which it needed to assert its privileges during this period resulted from Johnston's criticism of the proposal that the government should itself embark upon the building of railways. For that he was confronted in the corridors of Province House itself by several hundred persons who "not only hooted and hissed him, but . . . attempted to kick him on the shins and . . . throw him down." *Novascotian*, Feb. 21, 1853. Subsequently the Assembly examined the Mayor of Halifax to discover whether the civil power of the city was adequate to protect assemblymen in the performance of their legislative duties. *JHA*, 1853, 269.

[26]*Supra*, 58–61.

tional,"[27] and accepted instead the counsel of Alexander Stewart that since the constitution was "a system of mutual checks and balances . . . the Commons must scrupulously guard their right to hold the purse strings, and deal with the monies of the people."[28]

It is true that after 1848 the Financial Secretary's resolution prescribing the lump sum to be expended upon the roads and bridges was normally accepted without alteration, although seldom without the type of proceeding which occurred in 1854:

Then Hon. gentlemen went at it. Then followed five hours of storming, home-thrusting, tongue-lashing, recriminating, crowing, threatening, coaxing, "soothering," whimpering, gammon, bunkum, balderdash, all round the House, about these road monies, and about everything else that could be thought of, and about everything that could be spoken upon without being thought of.[29]

It is also true that by the mid-fifties the percentage to be awarded each county had finally been determined after years of trial and error, and that with a slight modification these percentages were to remain unchanged for the next half century. But no administration had yet deemed itself strong enough to deprive the representatives of their right to divide the county allotments into smaller votes and to nominate commissioners to expend these sums.[30] Thus the worst evils continued to prevail simply because the assemblymen still regarded their personal participation in the process as the second most rewarding feature of their role as legislators.

The first was their monetary reward of £1 a day. Since the number of days with pay was normally limited to forty during any one

[27]*Novascotian*, March 3, 1836. The reference is, of course, to the Council of Twelve.

[28]*Ibid.*, Feb. 25, 1836.

[29]*Acadian Reporter*, March 4, 1854. These proceedings occurred on a motion to increase the amount proposed in the Financial Secretary's resolution from £40,000 to £50,000. The debate on his scale of division between counties was equally edifying: "Hon. members all went instantly into fits. Patriotic effusions came from every part of the House, everybody was wronged, everybody was indignant, everybody was determined never to give it up so; but the debate ended, as is also usual in such cases, by the scale being unanimously adopted." *Ibid.*, March 18, 1854.

[30]Complications arose when all or a majority of the members from a particular county were opposed to the government. In 1854, for example, the executive failed to honour nineteen of the recommendations of Johnston and his Conservative colleagues from Annapolis County. This action was condemned as an interference with a well-established prerogative for the exercise of which the assemblymen were constitutionally responsible to the people, and not someone "secret and unknown, and certainly unauthorized by, and irresponsible to, the people." See *JHA*, 1855, 630, and *Acadian Recorder*, Feb. 17, 1855.

session,[31] the Assemblyman's initial garrulity quite understandably gave way to more businesslike procedures as the fortieth day approached. At the beginning of the session he wandered at will from "the mysteries of pickled fish and winter wheat, from similes upon old women, and touches of metropolitan satire, to disquisitions on the lore of the ancients, and general views of the practice of the modern empires"; at the end he was "finishing in one day . . . as much business as took him three to talk about during the earlier part."[32] After 1855, however, he might talk to his heart's content, for the no longer gratuitous Council—its members had won the right to equal pay the previous year—henceforth neglected to limit the number of paid days in any one session as had been its custom for more than three decades.

In other respects the Assembly came to be markedly different between 1830 and 1867. The most significant change was the division of the assemblymen into two well-organized and highly disciplined political parties.[33] The Pictonian Jotham Blanchard first conceived of an *"organized party against misrule* in Nova Scotia"[34] at a time when Joseph Howe was still writing that "the party to which we belong *is the Province of Nova Scotia.*"[35] But it was Howe who, when confronted with the problems of practical politics, most clearly realized the necessity for party in the colonial sphere and most ably defended its practicability. It was he too who merged the politico-ecclesiastical radicalism of Pictou County represented by the *Colonial Patriot* and the friends of Pictou Academy, and the politico-social democracy of western Nova Scotia represented by the *Yarmouth Herald* and Herbert Huntington into the Reform party.[36] By that very act he forced the elements which were opposed to him to coalesce in similar fashion. To the contention that the colonies lacked the great questions or principles which might form the touchstones of party he replied:

. . . "little things are great to little men", and to little Provinces, and I could point to a dozen [past] questions of internal policy . . . and to a dozen [future] . . . that were or will be of just as much importance to the people of Nova Scotia, as were the questions upon which ministers have come in and gone out in almost every reign since 1688. It cannot be otherwise in the very nature of things.[37]

[31]The heavier duties of the Assembly during the thirties accounted for the increase from thirty-five to forty. *Supra*, 28.

[32]W. Moorsom, *Letters from Nova Scotia* (London, 1830), 81.

[33]*Supra*, 29ff.

[34]*Colonial Patriot*, Feb. 20, 1830.

[35]*Novascotian*, Oct. 28, 1830.

[36]D. C. Harvey, "Nova Scotia and the Durham Mission," *C.H.R.*, XX (June, 1939), 162.   [37]Chisholm, I, 361.

Howe was fully aware that the materials to build a Reform party were close at hand. When his opponents described mechanics and farmers as intellectually unfit to participate in politics, he offered to take a dozen young men from the forges in Halifax "who with a sledge-hammer in one hand and a hot horseshoe in the other, shall deliver a better speech on responsible government than [they] can make after a month's preparation."[38] It was the sturdy yeomanry, however, the men who had won their farms from the wilderness or had paid for them by the fruit of their industry, upon whom he placed his chief reliance.

Such men cannot be made to understand why a Government should be partial or extravagant, and therefore take their stand at once on the side of reform. . . . The village Lawyer may sneer at or oppose measures of retrenchment. . . . the Trader may take his cue from the Halifax merchant with whom he deals, but the sturdy agriculturist feels that he is the main support of them both, and therefore has a right to his opinions—and these are in favour of fair competition in public as in private life.[39]

While elements of the population such as these were persuaded to elect a majority of alleged Reformers in 1836, particularism could not be destroyed at one fell swoop, and stout Reformers constantly found themselves "at the mercy of that section of the members, which is made up of the men of no decided leaning—no fixed principles—the lovers of peace at all hazards—the timid or the indifferent."[40] Although some progress towards a sharper delineation of the assemblymen occurred after 1836,[41] it all went for naught when Howe led the bulk of the Reformers into a coalition with the moderate Tories in 1840.[42] Ostensibly he was still uncertain if either party could ever form a government which could sustain itself on party principles.[43] But after the breakdown of the coalition and the elimination of these doubts, he set out to complete the process which he had arrested for three years—to "rouse, to inform, to organize the two hundred thousand people who compose the Liberal party . . . to make their voices heard . . . with a weight and authority that cannot be misunderstood."[44] His

[38]Ibid., 548.   [39]Novascotian, June 25, 1840.
[40]Ibid., May 24, 1837. In 1838, for example, the Reformers could count upon the firm support of only twenty members, and success for their point of view depended upon the attitude of nine "loose fish." See M. Gene Morison, "The Evolution of Political Parties in Nova Scotia (1758–1848)," unpublished master's thesis in P.A.N.S., 151.
[41]The assemblymen who were elected in 1840 could be more easily labelled than on any previous occasion: 28 Reformers, 21 Tories, and 2 Independents.
[42]The extremist rumps of both parties declined to participate in the coalition.
[43]Novascotian, Feb. 24, 1842.   [44]Chisholm, I, 475.

success is written in the conduct of the twenty-nine Reform assembly-men of the Nineteenth Assembly (1848–51) who gave unflagging support to every measure designed to institute the new order.

By that time the Reformers had begun to call themselves Liberals just as the Tories were adopting the more palatable name of Conservatives. Johnston's task was infinitely more difficult than Howe's in that, although himself a moderate, he had the compromising support of all who desired to retain the status quo in its entirety. For that reason it was easy to identify moderate Conservatism with Toryism and "arrogance, domination, selfishness and rapacity."[45] Johnston also suffered under the disability of having to constitute a party to oppose the introduction of party government. The promulgation of the myth that his party possessed no organization deceived no one.

No Conservative Organization! What say the Charitable Societies to that? What the Engine Company? What say those who pull the wires in the Banks, and serve their friends and black bean their opponents? Who can enter our Courts, or any one of our public departments, without feeling that the atmosphere of all of those is breathed more freely by Conservatives than Liberals?[46]

Thus two well-disciplined parties were marshalled against each other immediately after 1848, and the time for testing the suitability of party government in the colonial sphere had arrived. Did principles and issues normally exist which would ensure the maintenance of stable alignments within a two-party system? During the fifties only two issues of substance appeared, whether or not to institute a well-regulated system of democratic institutions, and whether to construct railroads as public works or by private enterprise. But not even they were debated for long. The advocates of a greater measure of democracy were unable to implement it when they held the reins of office, while private companies could not be induced to venture upon railway construction in Nova Scotia.

The second issue was, in any case, a thoroughly disintegrating force. For the Liberals it meant the loss of the so-called Yarmouth school. Herbert Huntington broke with the Executive Council before his death in 1851; Thomas Killam with two assemblymen and a legislative councillor later seceded. In their opinion, the railway project proved that the aristocratic society of the capital was exercising an unwholesome influence upon the executive,[47] and since they professed

[45]*Acadian Recorder*, May 1, 1847.
[46]Quoted from the *Chronicle* in the *Sun*, May 29, 1846.
[47]Quoted from the *Yarmouth Herald* in the *British Colonist* of June 1, 1854.

to be guided by the principles of Huntington, they found it easy to ally themselves with a Conservative party which was both sceptical of constructing railways as public works and zealous in supporting a greater measure of democracy. But the programme of the Conservatives was almost as repellent as it was attractive. During the Twentieth Assembly (1851–5) five Conservative assemblymen deserted the party ranks, and one of them actually entered the Liberal ministry in 1854.

During this time, when defections were becoming the order of the day, the first doubts about the utility of the existing parties were expressed by onetime vigorous advocates of party government.

At the present juncture [said the Recorder] . . . it would nonplus the shrewdest politician to invent any cogent reason for the division of the Representatives of Nova Scotia into two parties, regularly organised for the annihilation of each other, in the halls of our Legislature. We are not aware of a single public question, of the least consequence to any class, being in suspense. . . .[48]

This was only the beginning. The Twenty-first Assembly (1856–9) brought with it a new Conservative member, Dr. Charles Tupper of Cumberland, who delighted in a rough-and-tumble type of leadership, which within a year resulted in the collapse of a ministry long riddled with dissension. The fact that one-fifth of the assemblymen[49] could change their political allegiance overnight and maintain another party in power without sacrificing their principles demonstrated the lack of meaning of Liberalism and Conservatism. The backlog of bitterness accruing from this incident was further intensified by the disputed election of 1859.[50] The result was three years of endless partisan manœuvrings in which the Lieutenant-Governor and the Colonial Secretary were themselves forced to become participants.[51]

[48]Acadian Recorder, Jan. 20, 1855.
[49]The estrangement of the Catholics and the Liberal government over a number of issues culminated in the withdrawal from the Liberal party of the eight Catholic assemblymen and two Protestants who represented Catholic counties.
[50]Infra, 126–7.
[51]The sheriffs' returns for the election of 1859 indicated the election of 29 Liberals and 26 Conservatives. Because the election committees confirmed the election of half a dozen Liberals who were alleged to be disqualified, the Conservatives proceeded to describe themselves as the Constitutionalists, and to label their opponents as the Corruptionists. The defection of two Conservatives (Colin Campbell of Digby and Isaac Hatfield of Argyle) left the party standing at 32 to 23, but the loss of by-elections in Cumberland and Victoria counties in December, 1860, reduced the Liberal majority to five, and resulted in a proposition of the Lieutenant-Governor that "any further diminution of their strength would necessitate either a reconstruction of the Government, or an appeal to the country."

Serious criticism of the wastage induced by the political process was to be expected, therefore, during the early sixties. "The game of politics," said the *Sun*, "is becoming a pretty expensive one, and so long as parties remain constituted as they now are, Bluenose must expect to pay for it."[52] The Lieutenant-Governor likewise questioned the utility of the existing parties:

There is now no great political question which divides them, and which should keep them in perpetual antagonism to one another. The matter in dispute is now simply one of men, not measures.

. . . [Hence] the business of the legislature would be far better cared for . . . if . . . the representatives of the people were left to exercise their free and independent judgment on all matters . . . without being trammelled by party ties, so strong, that the vote of every member of the party is reckoned on as a matter of course, and that any member venturing to exercise his judgment, is condemned as a traitor to the cause he has been elected to support. . . .[53]

Thus the Nova Scotia of the early sixties appears to have been moving towards the political impasse of the Canadas. Yet one caution is necessary. There are no differences at all analogous to those which resulted from race and religion in Canada. The Nova Scotian parties and groups all accepted the existing social order, and agreed both upon the role to be played by government and upon the specific means calculated to provide good government. The most suitable designations for the administration and its opposition had become the Ins and the Outs; the struggle between the two was one for place, power, and the spoils of office.

The conclusion is that a small provincial government could normally not provide issues which would permit a division of the electorate upon distinct principles. Yet it was of no practical consequence because the party leaders of the sixties showed no greater willingness to unite than those of the forties. Much more important was the discovery that the institution of responsible government had altered radically

---

Mulgrave to Newcastle, Jan. 8, 1861, *JHA*, 1861, Appendix 2—Constitutional Questions, 39. The varying interpretations which were placed upon this dispatch subsequently increased the violence of the debate and embroiled the Governor even more deeply in dispute.

[52]April 17, 1861.

[53]Mulgrave to Newcastle, April 3, 1862, *JHA*, 1863, Appendix 11—Civil List, 6. But although Mulgrave felt the time propitious for an amalgamation of the parties, Howe's overtures to Johnston and Tupper to that end went unrewarded. So did his offers to the Catholic members who since 1857 had been allied with the Conservatives. See *Acadian Recorder*, Feb. 21 and 28, 1863, and *JHA*, 1863, 30. In the end the Liberals had to rely upon the defection of the Annapolis member Moses Shaw to control the House during the session of 1863.

some of the institutions around which the game of politics was to be played. Until new rules could be prescribed to meet these new conditions, the political process would present anything but a dignified spectacle.

The representative character of the House, and particularly the organization of the constituencies, naturally came under close scrutiny after 1830. First to be considered were the existing units of representation, none of which had undergone any change during the preceding half century. Even when the Colonial Secretary made it clear that he would deny no justifiable alteration,[54] a particularist Assembly found it difficult to provide ameliorative action until the census of 1827 had laid bare the striking inconsistencies and anomalies of the existing system. Two alternatives were open to the Fifteenth Assembly (1831–6), either to enact a general law for the equalization of representation or to deal piecemeal with individual cases. The first method having failed to attract sufficient support,[55] it necessarily resorted to the second.

Properly enough the Assembly turned its attention to Cape Breton for the first legislative reform of representation in 47 years. One act (1832) provided the island with three additional seats; another (1835) divided it into three counties, Richmond, Cape Breton, and Juste-au-Corps, without increasing the representation.[56] Next the Assembly split the sprawling county of Halifax—long notorious for the administrative difficulties it created at election time—into the three counties of Halifax, Pictou, and Colchester.[57] Finally it cut expansive Sydney County in two, the Upper District becoming the county of Sydney (later Antigonish), and the Lower District the county of Guysborough.[58] Even this piecemeal reform of the most aggravated ills met an external snag. Some residents of Annapolis petitioned directly to England that the Halifax bill ought not to be approved until their own grievances had been remedied, and the Colonial Secretary demanded an explanation.[59] But an Assembly of the temper

[54]Bathurst to Dalhousie, July 10, 1819, P.A.N.S. 63, doc. 83.

[55]Solicitor-General Fairbanks tried this means in three successive years (1832–4), but although he relied upon the simple expedient of an increased membership to overcome the existing anomalies, he ended up in 1834 by admitting its impracticability. For one of his proposals, see the *Novascotian*, March 14, 1833. Between 1843 and 1845 Solicitor-General Dodd and J. B. Uniacke experienced the same lack of success with more revolutionary proposals.

[56]2 Wm. IV, c. 6, and 5 Wm. IV, c. 46. Juste-au-Corps later became Inverness County. 7 Wm. IV, c. 30.

[57]5 Wm. IV, c. 37.   [58]6 Wm. IV, c. 79.

[59]See Glenelg to Campbell, Aug. 12, 1835, P.A.N.S. 73, 220–6. For the petition from Annapolis, see *JHA*, 1836, Appendix 1, 4–6.

of that of 1836 would clearly not tolerate such interference. The presumption must be made, it said, that it had adjudicated fairly the rival claims of its constituents, and it bluntly declined to justify its conduct.[60] Its tactic was successful, for although a suspending clause continued to be inserted in this type of bill until Confederation, confirmation became automatic.

In dealing piecemeal with the other counties, the Legislature was mindful that the eastern section of the province, which had experienced the larger proportionate increase in population since 1785, was underrepresented. Hence when Yarmouth County was finally broken off from Shelburne in 1836 and Digby from Annapolis in 1837,[61] neither the old nor the new counties secured the extravagant increases in representation which were demanded. These new counties were the sixteenth and seventeenth, and when Victoria was separated from Cape Breton in 1851,[62] the counties were complete.

But the real reform awaited the removal of the evils in the township system. Although the townships which enjoyed representation had failed to play the part of the English boroughs, they were never without their supporters. Even moderate Reformers like Henry Goudge justified them on the ground that the "old and cultivated parts . . . paid for the improvements of the outer districts."[63] After 1848, however, a substantial body of opinion agreed with Lawrence O'Connor Doyle that the same arguments had been used to defend Grampound and Old Sarum,[64] and with the *Recorder* that

few of the townships in question could ever bear any resemblance to the Boroughs except in their possession of the privilege of sending members to Parliament. The town which was originally intended to spring up in the centre of these townships has, in many instances, not yet "begun to be"; in other cases, the only thing in the vicinity approaching to the nature of a town has persisted in growing up somewhere beyond the limits of the township. In no one instance, except perhaps that of the one containing the Provincial metropolis, do these townships embody any interests, not contained in as great a degree, by the surrounding portions of the country.[65]

Yet these artificial creations not only elected their own members, but also shared in choosing the county representatives. Of the twenty-

[60]See *JHA*, 1836, 906–7. The Annapolis petition reflected the general fear that, if the most far-reaching evils were removed, the members from a particular county would lose the bargaining power which they might use as a lever to effect their own ends.

[61]6 Wm. IV, c. 88, and 7 Wm. IV, c. 89.

[62]14 Vic., c. 4.

[63]*Novascotian*, March 25, 1841.

[64]*Ibid.*, March 13, 1834.

[65]*Acadian Recorder*, Sept. 16, 1854.

three, only the four in Shelburne and Yarmouth were unobjectionable since in those counties the townships together comprised the entire area and every voter balloted for one township and one county representative. Elsewhere there were wide discrepancies in voting power within the same county. Wilmot, by any criterion, was as entitled to representation as its sister townships of Annapolis and Granville in Annapolis County, while Douglas deserved the same treatment as Windsor, Falmouth, and Newport, the other three townships in Hants County. But it was the three pocket-boroughs in Colchester which incurred the most persistent criticism:

That County, which was one of the smallest as regarded wealth and inhabitants, had become the duchy of Cornwall of Nova Scotia. If a Speaker were to be chosen, where was he to be obtained, for the last twenty years,— but there? If a government leader were wanted, who but . . . the Attorney General [i.e. S. G. W. Archibald] was appointed? Why? Because he brought three township members to the House, and, by being backed by three or four votes, he could turn the scale on important occasions, and therefore government could not pass him by. That County received its full share, at least, of roads and bridges.[66]

The remedy ought to have come from the Reformers, especially since the townships were generally more favourable to the Tories than to them,[67] but they could never attack the ill as a united group. In voting upon the bills which were introduced between 1839 and 1843 to equalize the representation in particular counties, 75 per cent of the township members acted in concert to protect their vested rights.[68] While a few Tories always supported equalization, more Reformers voted to sustain the borough system. Since equalization could therefore not be made a party question, the only course was to probe for

[66]See address of Beamish Murdoch in *Novascotian*, Oct. 29, 1840.

[67]Between 1836 and 1847 the representation of the Tories and Reformers from the counties and townships was (R—Reformer; To—Tory):

	1836		1840		1844		1847	
	R	To	R	To	R	To	R	To
Townships	10	12	13	9	10	14	10	14
Counties	13	10	16	12	13	14	19	8

[68]The following are typical examples of divisions in the Assembly to equalize the representation of particular counties (T—Township, C—County, R—Reformer, To—Tory, I—Independent):

County	Year	Division on the basis of county and township		Division on the basis of party	
		For	Against	For	Against
Annapolis	1839	6T,16C	16T, 9C	1To,21R	19To, 4R,21
Annapolis	1840	4T,14C	15T, 6C	2To,14R,2I	13To, 8R
Colchester	1841	5T,13C	16T,10C	4To,12R,2I	11To,15R
Annapolis	1842	6T,13C	14T,12C	3To,14R,2I	17To, 9R

weak spots in the system. Eventually the townships of Colchester settled their own fate by being so imprudent as to elect three Conservatives in 1847. The Reformers then felt no compunction about forcing them to accept the kind of representation which prevailed in Yarmouth and Shelburne counties.[69]

Queens County experienced a similar adjustment in 1856, but Liberal administrations were unable to proceed further, and it was left to a Conservative government to enact the first general scheme for the equalization of representation in 1859. Johnston's tactic was to work out a compromise in caucus and then adhere to it rigidly despite its imperfections. By this means he contrived both to eliminate township representation altogether and to equalize the voting strength within seventeen of the eighteen counties.[70]

Logically the next step was to provide for a similar equalization between the voters of different counties, but Howe's proposal to permit every elector in sixteen counties to vote for two representatives was rejected by the Legislative Council in 1863.[71] Actually its defeat had no real significance because Tupper was shortly to implement the three rough-and-ready principles of representation which he considered would be adequate under Confederation: the lessened provincial responsibilities permitted a much smaller Assembly; no county could be adequately represented by fewer than two members; the two most populous counties merited special recognition. Accordingly the membership of the Assembly was reduced from 55 to 38, and Halifax and Pictou counties were to elect three members, all the others two.[72]

At the same time that the Legislature was seeking to equalize voting power it was also regulating the franchise. Two closely interwoven threads entered into the Assembly's consideration of the qualifications for voting. How could the existing ills, particularly the practice of temporarily transferring freeholds to create votes and the false swearing which necessarily accompanied an uncertain qualification, be surmounted? Ought the lower House to be representative of a broader cross-section of the population than the one constituted by the forty-shilling freeholders? During the thirties and forties the discussion centred around the practicability of a scheme for the registration of voters. After 1848, however, Lawrence O'Connor Doyle

[69] 12 Vic., c. 33.

[70] 22 Vic., c. 1. The exception was Halifax, the western district of which was to elect three members, the eastern two.

[71] Howe proposed to except Annapolis and Lunenburg counties, one of which was held by each party.

[72] 30 Vic., c. 2.

challenged the suitability of any system based on the tenure of land, and urged "labour and industry . . . the source of all wealth" as "the true foundation for the electors of Representatives."[73] He contended that the essence and spirit of British institutions, not the moth-eaten habits of the Saxon settlers, should prevail, and in this instance turned to the United States for a principle and precedent.[74] The counter argument was that

land was easy of acquirement in this country; so easy, indeed, [as to make it] the best foundation for a franchise. . . . a man . . . entered into a new state of social being on becoming a freeholder; [was] invested with a new dignity, and had new claims of attachment to his native land, and a new interest in framing its laws.[75]

Doyle's views won some recognition in 1851 when the franchise was widened to include those males who had been "assessed for, and paid, in the year next preceding [an] Election, Poor or County Rates,"[76] but this alteration ran directly counter to Johnston's main political tenet after 1848—opposition to anything which might conceivably enhance the power of the executive. In this case he and his followers painted the usual vivid pictures of the abuses which would follow the conferment of additional opportunities for evil upon the rabid partisans whom the Executive Council was admitting to the magistracy:

This is the body of men who are to select you assessors—they are to prepare the assessment rolls and every man whose name is on this roll to have the privilege of voting at elections. . . . How easy for them to assess those of their own political opinions alone. . . . in some places the amount is so small as to be no burthen at all, and could be paid by the veriest pauper in the Country.[77]

For once the voice of the prophet was all too correct. The election of 1851 indicated that a greater evil had been introduced than the one eradicated. Part of the melancholy story appears in the forged receipts of rates and manipulated lists of rate-payers; part in the conversion of the assessors to the business of political skulduggery.[78] Since the Assembly's investigating committee saw no possibility of devising a plan for "reducing the rate-paying franchise into a simple, uniform and practically working system," it recommended universal suffrage

[73]*Novascotian*, April 7, 1851.
[74]*Ibid.* (Extra), April 3, 1851.
[75]*Ibid.*, April 7, 1851.
[76]14 Vic., c. 2.
[77]See speech of J. J. Marshall, *Novascotian*, April 21, 1851.
[78]*JHA*, 1851-2, 15-28.

restrained by "a residence of considerable duration . . . to prevent the
mischief that might result from an influx of new electors, having no
fixed stake, local or provincial, and no interest in the county or township."[79]

This conclusion reflects once again the Conservative advocacy of a
well-adjusted system of democratic institutions. William Young railed
as usual against a hazardous experiment which, once taken, could
never be retraced, but by 1854 Johnston had convinced a majority to
support universal suffrage based on a residence of five years in the
province and one in the county or township.[80] No one cared for it
particularly, but since a return to the freehold basis was regarded
as a thoroughly retrograde step, it seemed a lesser evil than the ir-
remediable difficulties of the rate-paying system.[81]

For the moment the freehold qualification was also retained, but in
1858 the Johnston government rendered it practically meaningless by
attaching to it a three months' residence clause.[82] This restriction was
supposedly designed to permit residents to determine their representatives without interference from outsiders, to avoid the expense of
conveying non-residents to and fro, and to reduce the votes of doubtful
character.[83] None the less, the Liberals called it the most damaging
blow ever inflicted upon the Constitution[84] because it gave equal
voting rights to a resident with merely the rags on his back and a
freeholder with real estate in every county.[85]

As a result, they initiated proposals in 1863 to make voting conditional upon the possession of real property of an assessed value of $150,

---

[79]*Ibid.*, Appendix 87, 412.

[80]17 Vic., c. 6.

[81]During the final stages of the passage of universal suffrage the parties outdid
one another in a bid for popularity by advocating reductions in the restrictions
upon those in receipt of poor relief. As a result, only those who had received relief
a year prior to polling were disqualified. See *Acadian Recorder*, Feb. 25, 1854.
The absence of electoral lists, the incomplete nature of the returns, and the
inability to measure the normal incalculables at any election render it difficult to
determine what effect the changes of 1851 and 1854 had in enlarging the
electorate. The election of 1851 showed varying results ranging from no increase in
the Township of Pictou to increases of 52 per cent in the County of Lunenburg
and the Township of Shelburne. The change to universal suffrage in 1855 resulted
in an increase (over 1851) of at least 25 per cent in all the constituencies, and
increases of 81 and 64 per cent in the Counties of Halifax and Lunenburg.

[82]21 Vic., c. 37.

[83]See quotation from the *Express* in the *British Colonist*, May 20, 1858.

[84]See *Acadian Recorder*, April 24, 1858.

[85]Hitherto an individual might vote in any or all of the counties and towns in
which he possessed a freehold. Johnston's simple answer was that property ought
not to confer a double franchise.

or of personal, or real and personal combined, of $300, in order to "place the institutions of [the] country on a solid basis—to elevate the character and qualifications of the constituency who create [the] House, and thus elevate the character and qualifications of the House which that constituency creates."[86] Their intention was to implement the basic viewpoint of Howe prior to 1848, and one which continued to be held by him and his party:

The sterling men of the country [said Howe] will continue to exercise their franchise; but the refuse of society—the men who live by elections—who would be glad if a contest occurred every month provided they had the power of basely trading away their independence for lucre, will be as they should be, disfranchised.[87]

The government succeeded in forcing its bill through the Assembly only to have the Legislative Council postpone its operative date beyond the forthcoming general election. Hence it was an electorate voting upon the basis of universal suffrage which inflicted upon the Liberals their second most decisive defeat in provincial history in 1863. But if the electors anticipated the restoration of universal suffrage, it was their turn to be disappointed. For all the Conservatives' violent denunciation of the change they gladly capitalized upon the Council's opposition to further tinkering with the franchise to justify its retention.[88] Yet they could not avoid the responsibility for administering an act which, in effect, necessitated the annual preparation of voters' lists and the appointment of revisers to ensure their accuracy. As usual, they found strong opposition to the provisions which placed an additional burden upon the districts and counties, and as a result, the new machinery was barely ready for its first province-wide testing in the general election of 1867.[89]

One uncertainty in the qualifications of voters remained unsettled until 1851—the right of women to exercise the franchise. While the effect of the common law was undoubtedly to disfranchise them, the statutory law was silent and periodically one party or the other pondered the political advantage to be gained by marshalling lady

[86]See speech of Attorney-General Archibald in *Morning Chronicle*, March 21, 1863.

[87]Chisholm, II, 412.

[88]See comments of Tupper, *Morning Chronicle*, Feb. 9, 1864.

[89]The reluctance of the sessions and grand juries to implement the act necessitated its deferment beyond 1863 (27 Vic., c. 20), and eventually another enactment requiring the summoning of special sessions to set up the necessary machinery, and imposing severe penalties for any acts of omission (28 Vic., c. 17). See *Novascotian*, Jan. 9, 1865, for the specific circumstances in Guysborough County.

freeholders in force at the polling places.[90] An act of 1851, by confining voting to males, effectually ended such considerations.[91]

The Assembly's grand inquest into the governmental structure also left its mark upon the members of the Legislature. In 1843 the English practice was adopted whereby a person who possessed the basic property requirement might run for election in any of the townships or counties.[92] Most Reformers expected the change to enhance the privileges of both electors and elected. "To be free of Great Britain," said Howe, "a man need . . . hold only one property qualification,—to be free of Nova Scotia, with its 300 miles of length, and its 250,000 inhabitants, a man should hold three and twenty freeholds."[93] While a Briton could not be kept in obscurity because he had maintained his independence and asserted his principles, this might occur at any time in Nova Scotia. In Colchester County, for example, responsible government was not the burning political question of the day.

What then? The entire county is separated into two parts by a river, and the parties in opposition are those on each side of it, the question being on which side a proposed road shall run. . . . on such should a public man be judged, turned from the Assembly, and refused appeal to the whole people?[94]

The opponents of the measure pointed out that a provincial legislature, in contrast with Parliament, was called upon continually to legislate on particular or local matters.[95] That task could be done best by individuals who had a stake in the welfare of a township or county. If rich and influential outsiders were chosen in their stead, the Halifax

[90]A correspondent from Annapolis reported in the *Novascotian* of Dec. 3, 1840: "I rode down to Annapolis Town to see what was going forward in the enemy's camp, and lo and behold! what did I find the Tories there up to!! getting all the old women and old maids, and every thing in the shape of petticoats, to be carried up to the hustings the next and last day to vote for Whitman!! . . . no time was to be lost. I gave my horse an extra feed of oats. . . . I rode all Tuesday night, and roused up every farmer . . . they harnessed up their horses, went off, and each one by 10 of the clock, was back with a widow or a fair young fatherless maid, to vote against the Tory women from Annapolis Royal. . . . They found out we should outnumber them, and at last we had the satisfaction of seeing them return to Annapolis without voting. I believe they number 26, and our party nearly 40. This manœuvre on their side was kept very sly, but am happy to say we outgeneralled them."

[91]14 Vic., c. 2.

[92]6 Vic., c. 11.

[93]"Men in search of a horse, or a wife or a farm," he continued, "have the whole Province to choose from. You would not say to a man in search of a horse, you shall be confined to Lunenburg; where, perhaps, they set as much value on an ox as a horse" *Novascotian*, Feb. 13, 1843.

[94]*Ibid.*

[95]See speech of Smith, *Novascotian*, Feb. 20, 1843.

element might once more dominate with all the attendant evils.[96] In addition, the role of the House in educating the members and their constituents might be destroyed. Hitherto the assemblymen had returned home each session with a new stock of ideas; "once shut the doors of that school to them . . . and adieu to the advancement of the distant townships."[97]

As usual, the innovation realized neither the high hopes of its sponsors, nor the fears of its detractors. Most constituencies continued to return residents to the Assembly, although occasionally they exercised their right to elect non-residents to good end.

Ostensibly the Assembly sought also to secure its independence through the disqualification of further office-holders. Even before 1848, most of the full-time officers of government had been excluded from the Legislature.[98] The addition of the Judges of Probate and the prothonotaries to the list in 1858[99]—a measure deliberately aimed at a Liberal Judge of Probate—led the Liberals to press for and secure the adoption of the Canadian practice which excluded all persons holding offices of emolument.[100] Fate almost decreed that they be hoist by their own petard, for only the absence of machinery to enforce the act enabled half a dozen of their members who had at least technically violated its provisions to retain their seats in 1860, and thereby permitted a Liberal government to cling to office.

The repercussions of that election demonstrated the utter unsuitability of the act for the circumstances of the day. The Legislature could clearly not afford to deprive itself of the services of men of standing who had accepted the offices of coroner and way-office keeper more as a public service than for the trifling emolument. Hence the Legislature, by reverting in 1862 to the law as it stood before 1858,[101] removed a provision which had demoralized the community and contributed little to its own independence.[102]

The first change in the term of the assemblymen occurred in 1833 when the Legislature enacted that an automatic dissolution of the Assembly would not follow the death of the reigning Sovereign.[103] Later, however, a small group sought to repeal the act on the ground that it had been motivated solely by a new Assembly's fear of the

---

[96]See speech of Forrestall, *ibid.*, Feb. 11, 1841.

[97]See speech of Johnston, Halifax *Times*, Feb. 9, 1841.

[98]R.S. 1851, c. 2, s. 1. Executive councillors vacated their seats on the acceptance of office, but were permitted to re-offer for election in accordance with the British practice.

[99]21 Vic., c. 43.   [100]21 Vic., c. 36. This was the so-called Annand's Law.

[101]25 Vic., c. 31.   [102]*Acadian Recorder*, March 30, 1861.   [103]3 Wm. IV, c. 4.

imminent death of the sickly old William IV.[104] But to contend, as these members did, that the heir-apparent to Queen Victoria was actuated by political feelings entirely dissimilar to her own and that Nova Scotians would require a different class of assemblymen to defend their rights in the event of his succession, was more than a trifle preposterous. This time it was the Reformers who pointed out the inapplicability of the English analogy—in England the civil list had to be granted at the beginning of each reign to provide for the great officers of state whose authority was dependent upon their relation to the new Sovereign's household.

Does any of these changes take place in the Colony of Nova Scotia? Here we remain settled and stationary, notwithstanding the death of twenty Sovereigns, and . . . we are in much more need of a re-election when the Colonial Secretary departs from office, than on the demise of a Sovereign.[105]

In the end the act of 1833 remained as it stood even though Britain did not follow suit until 1867.

A second change in the duration of the Assembly was effected by the Quadrennial Act of 1840. While the Reformers saw in it a means of according the electorate more frequent opportunities to reward the faithfulness and punish the neglect of the assemblymen,[106] the Tories objected to its republican tendency. Where in Nova Scotia, asked Alexander Stewart, could one find means to control the democratic principle, like "the vast weight of the crown, of the church, and the patronage of the government, [or] the combined influence of a powerful and wealthy hereditary aristocracy?" In his opinion, the influence of the people upon the Assembly was already far too powerful for their own good[107] and the tendency of the bill would be to make changes in the House more and more frequent.

. . . their legislation would be unsteady and capricious, the first year of their Session would be occupied in settling controverted elections, the second in learning the rules, usages and forms of legislation . . . and the third they would prepare for the next election. . . . [The House] would embody and give form and substance to the wildest fantasies, the most levelling democratical projects.[108]

[104]See speech of the "unreformed" J. B. Uniacke in *Novascotian*, May 10, 1838.
[105]See speech of William Young, *ibid.*
[106]Chisholm, I, 110. Lawrence O'Connor Doyle and his fellow Reformers contended that they were introducing the practice of England where a Parliament seldom lasted longer than four years despite the Septennial Act. Halifax *Times*, Jan. 21, 1840.
[107]*Novascotian*, Feb. 9, 1837.
[108]*Ibid.*, May 17, 1838. For similar views see the speech of J. B. Uniacke, Halifax *Times*, Jan. 21, 1840.

It required the Reformers four years to make their views prevail; after that no change along these lines occurred for more than half a century.

For many years the Assembly refused to permit its members to resign even though the result was occasionally to deprive a county or township of representation for prolonged periods.[109] Whenever the advocates of change alluded to the English practice by which members of Parliament vacated their seats upon the acceptance of the Chiltern Hundreds or the agency of a regiment of militia, they were reminded that a statutory provision could be in no way analogous since the power of appointment to the Chiltern Hundreds belonged to the executive, while the agency of a regiment was difficult to obtain. The basic objection to legalizing resignation still remained the fear that some members would use it as a loophole to avoid a disagreeable duty, while those who faced up to their responsibilities might be sacrificed to a momentary unpopularity. In the extreme case all the members might resign and, in effect, remove the prerogative of dissolution from the executive where it rightfully belonged.[110]

In 1837 the Legislature finally admitted of a slight relaxation by permitting a member to resign whenever he was "so seriously sick and unwell as to be unable to attend his duty . . . or . . . about to remove from the Province without any intention of returning thereto,"[111] but it required the advent of much quieter days (1850) before it completely abandoned its old conception of an assemblyman's duty and allowed him to resign simply by giving written notice to the Speaker.[112]

In regulating the procedures of the Assembly, the Reformers themselves once departed from the British practice without justification—they permitted Howe to hold the speakership of the Assembly and an executive councillorship simultaneously from 1841 to 1843. Not even he escaped criticism, however, for failing to recognize that the Speaker's single duty was to protect the interests of the Assembly, if need be, against the government itself.[113] Hence when he resigned his councillorship in 1843, the House lost no time in declaring the two offices to be incompatible.[114]

109In its early years (1764) the Assembly vacated the seat of a member who desired to resign because of ill health, but it later denied this course, "in some degree at variance with the practice of the British House of Commons" (*JHA*, 1824, 368), in the case of a member who was about to depart for England, and who saw "no probability of his being able to resume his Duties." *JHA*, 1825, 519 and 526. But it always affirmed its own right to vacate a seat in the event of a member's continued absence, although never at his own request.

110*Novascotian*, March 2, 1837.   1117 Wm. IV, c. 64.   11213 Vic., c. 28.

113See speech of William Young, *Novascotian*, Feb. 11, 1841.

114*JHA*, 1843, 359.

In a much more important matter—the mode of handling money bills—Nova Scotia's distinct aberration from the British practice was carried over into the new era with good reason. The Assembly naturally declined to vest the sole initiation of money votes in a thoroughly irresponsible Council; the latter in turn continued to exact its own pound of flesh by demanding a separate negative on each item of a money bill. During the period of the coalition the Reformers were sharply divided on what changes were necessary. The extremists wanted the powers of the Assembly further increased by depriving the Council of its item veto, while Howe hoped to vest the sole right of initiating money votes in the executive on a trial basis with a view to "making the analogy with Great Britain as close as possible."[115] But the first suggestion received little support, and Huntington's refusal to give the bi-partisan executive "a certificate of character" because "he did not like them well enough"[116] resulted in the rejection of the second.

When the English practice was finally adopted in 1860,[117] a few Conservative members ran true to form by opposing an extension of the authority of four or five executive councillors who, in their opinion, already possessed too much power without being subject to the safeguards which existed in Britain. The counter argument was that although logrolling did not constitute the same evil as in neighbouring New Brunswick, yet a few instances had occurred in which the Financial Secretary had opposed in vain the lavish grants which were pressed upon the House by various combinations of members.[118]

The actual operation of the new practice also led to divided opinions. One was that it gave the executive the power which it ought to possess to prevent the expenditures from exceeding the revenues; another that it permitted the government to disregard the claims of those who were politically opposed to it.[119] A few assemblymen were so disturbed by their loss of power that they continued to present their

[115]*Novascotian*, March 4, 1841.

[116]*Ibid.* The Reformer Forrester made the second point that whereas in England sums were appropriated for the Army, the Navy, and the other great departments, of which the ministers in charge were the best judges, in Nova Scotia the main expenditures were upon the roads and bridges, of which the assemblymen alone possessed practical knowledge.

[117]The Conservative government of J. W. Johnston which proposed the change in the Speech from the Throne fell within a few days, but Young's Liberal ministry instituted it during the same session.

[118]*Novascotian*, April 9, 1860. Concurrently with this change, the Assembly no longer submitted each vote to the Council separately. The mildness of the Council's protest indicates the general weakness of its position under responsible government.

[119]*Ibid.*, Feb. 15, 1864.

petitions for the expenditure of money to the Assembly, and a Provincial Secretary finally acquiesced in a procedure which caused no inconvenience and at the same time demonstrated to the electors that their representatives were active on their behalf.[120]

The mode of conducting the elections themselves caused increasing concern after 1830. Prominent among the ills were the general turbulence of the electoral process, the unabashed resort to corrupt practices, and the difficulty of determining whether a voter possessed the proper legal qualifications. The establishment of a general scheme for the registration of electors would have alleviated some of these abuses, but, because of the elaborate machinery which it necessitated, legislation which provided for the preparation of electoral rolls was not adopted until 1863.[121] By that time other devices had remedied the worst ills.

These had stemmed particularly from the assemblage of huge throngs of freeholders at the two or three polling places in each county, where for periods of one to six days they would show a greater interest in partaking of the free hospitality of the public houses than in exercising the franchise. Occasional efforts to decide the outcome of the election by forceful means are therefore understandable. At Cheticamp in 1833

the house in which the Hustings were held, was surrounded by a large party of men, about One Hundred and Fifty in number, armed with Sticks, many of whom rushed into the House in a tumultuous and outrageous manner . . . and violently expelled from it . . . the Friends of Mr. Smith, some of whom suffered severe personal injury and the grossest insult and ill treatment.[122]

In this instance the intent was to prevent the polling of votes for one hour, and hence, as the election law provided, to have the poll declared closed in an area in which Smith was in the ascendant.[123]

It was in Pictou County, however, where the religious differences between Kirkmen and Secessionists spilled over into the political sphere, that the violence was most pronounced. There the dispute over Pictou Academy led the Kirkmen to support the pro-Council slate of candidates in 1830, and resulted in an "armed mob, a murder, and ministers of Religion . . . [becoming] political engines, endeavouring to move congregations at the Tavern."[124] In 1845 the sheriff built a barrier ten feet high across a main thoroughfare to keep the contending

120Acadian Recorder, March 20, 1874.   121Supra, 118.
122See JHA, 1833, 474.
123Of this deliberate and preconcerted plan the opposing candidate, subsequently a Premier and Chief Justice, was declared cognizant.
124Acadian Recorder, Oct. 9, 1830.

factions apart. He then proceeded to poll one voter from each side in turn, but even this well-intentioned plan failed when the Liberal electors refused to recognize the arbitrary rules of a Tory committee.[125]

While incidents of extreme violence were exceptional, the existing electoral system clearly failed to provide an atmosphere conducive to the free expression of the will of the electorate. The greatest single step to counteract the old evils was taken by Johnston and the Conservatives in 1847 when they divided each county into polling districts and limited polling to a single day. The Liberals doubted whether "excitement would be diminished and comparative harmony preserved"[126] by the Simultaneous Polling Bill; Howe, in fact, thought it might result in "a Grog Shop and a Fiddler for every place in which the Poll would be opened."[127] But the election of 1847 passed off with comparative calm,[128] and the succeeding elections were equally free of violence.

Not nearly the same success attended the efforts to remove "the compulsion, bribery, drunkenness . . . and mental chicanery" of the electoral process.[129] The Legislature made a start in 1835 by strengthening the law against bribery and the use of intoxicating liquors at elections;[130] four years later it prescribed more severe penalties for those who transferred their freeholds to multiply votes.[131] But statutes to the contrary, the use of every device that could be conjured up to manufacture votes went on unabated. In 1847 one party employed a schooner laden with liquor and other commodities to supply its local organizers along the eastern shore;[132] not one negro turned out for the Liberal meeting at Hammonds Plains because the Conservatives had arrived a little earlier and distributed "a glorious feed of sandwiches and a lot of Indian Meal besides";[133] some reputable citizens of Halifax threatened to dispense with the services of the milkmen and truckdrivers who did not vote as they were directed; and Howe, it was whispered, "actually drank a whole bucket of holy water . . . in his great zeal to shew the intensity of his [alleged] conversion."[134] The Legislature tried again in 1861 to define electoral malpractices more explicitly,[135] but it failed as in the past to provide any effective means of enforcing the election laws.

[125]Ibid., April 12, 1845.   [126]Novascotian, Feb. 8, 1847.   [127]Ibid.
[128]Except in the West Branch of River John where a group headed by the half-negro bully, Black Sam, chased their opponents into the woods. Quoted from the Eastern Chronicle in the Sun, Aug. 20, 1847.
[129]Acadian Recorder, Nov. 10, 1832.
[130]5 Wm. IV, c. 25.   [131]2 Vic., c. 35.   [132]Novascotian, July 19, 1847.
[133]Acadian Recorder, May 15, 1847.   [134]Ibid., July 31, 1847.
[135]24 Vic., c. 19.

Evils made their appearance too in the law pertaining to controverted elections. The Grenville Act procedures worked reasonably well prior to the appearance of disciplined political parties; thereafter they were subject to grave disabilities which seriously affected their utility. In 1848 the Conservatives petitioned against a few Liberals solely to abridge the chances of Liberal majorities on the committees[136] and their opponents responded with petitions of a similarly dubious character. Nevertheless the committees acted with reasonable propriety because the possibility of upsetting the government was slight.

This was not so in 1860, for although the sheriffs' returns gave the Liberals a majority of three, half a dozen of their members were allegedly disqualified for having held offices of emolument at the time of their election. Since Annand's Law provided no other means of having their eligibility determined the Conservatives were forced to resort to the normal controverted election procedures. This meant that the election committees were subjected to their sternest test, since they had, in effect, to decide which party was ultimately to constitute the government.

Both parties carried on the usual manœuvres to ensure an equal opportunity in the draw. The petitions against five Conservatives and one Liberal were, in fact, on such slight grounds that the committees adopted the unprecedented course of declaring them frivolous and vexatious. In the other committees the Conservatives naturally demanded a slavish adherence to the strict letter of the statute, while the Liberals adopted the broader view that the Legislature had never intended to disqualify those persons who held petty offices merely as a service to the community.[137] Hence they saw nothing eminently unreasonable in the committees' confirmation of the sitting members.[138]

Should [Johnston] not have said . . . These offices are within the Statute, if vigorously construed. Resign them. In that case, I shall be no party to any attempt to unseat any of you. . . . But what has he done? Why, kept this country in a state of agitation, at fever heat, for twelve months very nearly, to end in nothing.[139]

[136]This device took advantage of the provision that any member whose election was being contested was debarred from sitting on any other committee. It thus reduced the number of members of a party who were qualified to serve on the committees and thereby lessened that party's chances in the draw.

[137]Such as coroners, health officers, and way-office keepers.

[138]The luck of the draw favoured the Liberals, for in the most dubious cases involving their own supporters they were in the majority. But the Conservatives actually constituted a majority on two of the committees which upheld the election of Liberals.

[139]*Novascotian*, April 30, 1860.

Their opponents could hardly find language strong enough to describe "the shameless dishonesty of the men who, upon their oaths, came to and reported such decisions."[140] Their vehemence increased when the only member unseated was a Conservative who had the misfortune to have six Liberals on his committee,[141] and it reached almost violent proportions when the House declined to vacate the seat of Attorney-General Archibald after a committee containing six Conservatives had found him guilty of bribery.[142] Clearly the rules of the election game were unsuited to conditions such as these.

Earlier (1856) some assemblymen had contended that the secret ballot would lessen bribery and intimidation, and reduce the excitement and contention during the time of polling.[143] Their opponents preferred the example of "the noble state of Virginia," which "held [its] elections as we did, by open choice." They contended that a man who wanted to vote in secret was unworthy of the franchise "from the very fact that he want[ed] to practise deception."[144] This argument always roused the *Recorder's* ire:

A great deal of bunkum was uttered about the manly, old, British practice of coming up to the polls and voting openly and independently; but very little about the other unmanly, old, British practice of "putting the screws on" to a poor, or timid, elector to make him show his independence *in favour of the right candidate.*[145]

For the moment, however, the anti-American and anti-democratic forces proved too strong, and they were to continue so for more than a decade.

[140]*Acadian Recorder*, April 21, 1860.

[141]But not for a violation of Annand's Law.

[142]The law as it stood did not permit a committee to vacate a seat on the grounds of bribery. The opposition newspapers described this particular incident as "whitewashing the Briber General."

[143]*Morning Chronicle*, March 28, 1856.

[144]*Ibid.*

[145]March 1, 1856.

CHAPTER VIII

THE JUDICIAL FUNCTION

CHANGE CHARACTERIZED the judiciary between 1830 and 1867 as it did almost all the other branches of government. The same assemblymen who were bent upon remodelling the executive branch wanted also to establish a judicial structure more in keeping with Nova Scotian needs and resources. England, it was shown, had a population of 12,000,000 and twelve judges; Nova Scotia a population of 124,000 and nine judges. Even worse, the Chief Justice of Nova Scotia was receiving a larger salary than the Chief Justice of the United States and the judicial establishment of Nova Scotia was costing more than that of the state of New York.[1]

A reforming Legislature naturally turned first to the practically concurrent jurisdictions of the superior and inferior courts in both civil and criminal causes. While surprising unanimity existed upon the need for a reduction in overhead, the inability to determine whether to reduce the number of judges in each court or to transfer all their functions to the Supreme Court prevented any change between 1836 and 1841. As usual, the second alternative was denounced as a departure from the English analogy, although this time it was generally the Conservatives, rather than the Reformers, who advocated a close adherence to British institutions.[2]

But the most potent argument against a single court was the fear of lowering the dignity of the Supreme Court. Its judges admitted that they could try without difficulty the thirty-eight civil cases a year of the Inferior Courts and the forty-five criminal cases of the Courts of Sessions. They objected strenuously, however, to the idea of presiding over the county as distinguished from the judicial business of the sessions. The result would be, they felt, to make them county and local politicians, and to involve them in the divisions, heats, and animosities of the sessional districts. "Make it a part of the ordinary duty of the Supreme Court to decide whether a tavern licence ought or ought not to be given to A or B," said Mr. Justice Hill, "and to me, it would seem to follow, that you ought to alter the style of the Court."[3]

[1]See speech of John Young, *Acadian Recorder*, March 20, 1830.
[2]See speech of S. G. W. Archibald, *Novascotian*, Feb. 15, 1838.
[3]*Journals of the House of Assembly* (*JHA*), 1838, Appendix 39, 116.

Nevertheless, the second alternative was adopted in 1841, but with two supplementary provisions to make it more palatable. The more important was the retention of the Courts of Sessions to transact the county business. The other was the addition of a fourth assistant justice to the Supreme Court to help it perform its augmented duties. Thus the English analogy was destroyed, and until 1876 no body exercised judicial functions between the Supreme Court and two justices of the peace acting in concert.

For two decades these provisions operated without any serious failure in the administration of justice, because a more extensive jurisdiction was conferred upon the justices of the peace.[4] So when the Supreme Court found it impossible to clear its dockets in the sixties, the natural remedy was to give the minor courts still wider powers. This was opposed by those assemblymen who regarded the justices as "a most ignorant and narrow-minded set of men" who would "feel less inclined for litigation if they were obliged to pay all fees into the County Treasurer."[5] Their fears were well-founded, for whereas the small amounts at stake in the justices' courts had heretofore acted as a deterrent to appeals, the further extension of their jurisdiction[6] caused the Supreme Court to be overloaded with appeal cases. The difficulty was accentuated by the advanced age of all the judges of the Supreme Court—a natural consequence of the failure to provide retiring pensions. Occasionally sickness and infirmity reduced the number available for service below that required to travel the five circuits. The one attempt to ameliorate these difficulties, the appointment of a Judge in Equity to assume a part of the judicial burden,[7] afforded little relief and the position of the Supreme Court was anything but satisfactory in 1867.[8]

The movement to fit the other courts into a single vertically arranged

[4]For example, two justices of the peace were authorized to try cases of debt involving amounts up to £10 (5 Vic., c. 33, s. 1) and all common assaults and batteries (4 Vic., c. 3, s. 13).

[5]*Acadian Recorder*, March 8, 1862. The *Morning Chronicle* (April 10, 1862) concurred: "These jobbing justices have surely field enough under the present law, for the exercise of their peculiar talents."

[6]A single justice of the peace was empowered to hear actions for debt up to $20, two justices up to $80. R.S. 1864, c. 128, s. 1.

[7]*Infra*, 130–1.

[8]One improvement was effected in the minor common law courts immediately prior to 1867. That was the transference of the judicial functions of the mayor and aldermen of Halifax to a stipendiary magistrate (30 Vic., c. 82), a change which was generally hailed as the eradication of "the worst form of a democratic nuisance, a judicial ulcer, a disgrace to our Constitution." See *Acadian Recorder*, Jan. 29, 1866.

system was completed by 1867. One phase of this development was the absorption of the judicial functions of the Lieutenant-Governor into the common law courts. Although probate was actually granted by the Surrogate-General and the Judges of Probate, they were the delegates of the Governor, who, in his capacity of Ordinary, was theoretically responsible for their acts up to 1842. Then the Legislature rejected the old fiction by putting the organization and functioning of the Probate Courts on a statutory basis, and making them subject to whatever rules and orders the judges of the Supreme Court and the Master of the Rolls felt were necessary to establish a simple and uniform course of proceeding.[9]

The stripping of the Governor's remaining duties in his capacity as Chancellor—his right to hear appeals[10] from the decisions of the Master of the Rolls—was associated with the general collapse of the chancery jurisdiction. During the first real attacks on "the abominable, heartbreaking, pocket-picking system"[11] of the Chancery Court in the early 1830's, the Assembly accepted the argument that "it would be very easy to get rid of the nonsensical prolixity—the delay—and the enormous expenses . . . without . . . transfer[r]ing its jurisdiction to a Court of a totally different description,"[12] and it empowered the Master of the Rolls to make recommendations to that end. But when the complaints continued unabated after 1836, the Legislature began to restrict the powers of the Court. By 1850 the settlement of partnership dealings of limited amount, the partition of lands, and the custody and control of the estates of lunatics had been entrusted to the Supreme Court either exclusively or concurrently with the Chancery Court,[13] and in 1853 William Young, the most vocal opponent of the Court, demonstrated how the bulk of its remaining business—the foreclosure of mortgages—might easily be transferred to the Supreme Court and the entire jurisdiction eliminated.[14]

These proposals were anything but appealing to the Supreme Court. The mere transference of the functions of the Court of Chancery from one judge to five, it felt, could not effect a proper "combination of distinct principles of widely different powers,"[15] and would result in

9[5] Vic., c. 22, s. 64.
10Assisted by the judges of the Supreme Court.
11*Acadian Recorder*, Sept. 22, 1832.
12*Novascotian*, Feb. 28, 1833.
13See memorandum of William Young, *JHA*, 1853, Appendix 16, 265–7.
14Young later showed that, if the routine foreclosure orders were excluded, the Court had heard only twenty-four cases from 1851 to 1854. *JHA*, 1855, Appendix 19, 148–51.
15See opinion of Mr. Justice Bliss, *JHA*, 1853, Appendix 16, 270.

confusion and uncertainty. Hence the wisest course was to wait until the British Parliament had effected a fusion of the two courts in England. Nevertheless, the Liberals' dislike of Alexander Stewart, the Master of the Rolls, led them to adopt Young's proposals in 1855, and subsequent events indicated, as the critics had prophesied, that the Legislature "had not grasped the basis on which the fusion of law and equity could be brought about." The result, in the opinion of a later Chief Justice, was a serious muddle in the administration of justice.[16]

The restoration of a partial equity jurisdiction in the Supreme Court in 1864 was motivated by political reasons no less potent than those which determined the abolition of the Chancery Court in 1855. Since the whirligig of party fortunes had deprived the Conservative J. W. Johnston of the chief justiceship in 1860, his party proposed to make him Chief Justice in Equity with a status equivalent to that of his old rival Chief Justice William Young, ostensibly to relieve the congestion in the Supreme Court. But the idea of a court with two heads was unpalatable even to the Conservative legislative councillors, who reduced the title of the new office to Judge in Equity and its status to little more than that of an assistant justice.[17] The practical result of the additional judge was neither to alleviate the difficulties stemming from the impartial fusion of the two jurisdictions, nor to effect any appreciable reduction in the pressure upon the judiciary.[18]

The judicial functions of the Governor and Council experienced the same fate as those of the Governor. The complete exclusion of the judges from the Council in 1838 accelerated this development. Three years later the Legislature, while explicitly denying any intention of restricting the powers of the Governor and Council, authorized the appointment of any senior judge as vice-president of the Divorce Court. His function was to preside in the absence of the Governor and, with two or more members of the Executive Council, to try the

[16]C. J. Townshend, "History of the Court of Chancery in Nova Scotia," *Canadian Law Times*, XX, 115.

[17]"Create this double headed monster," said the Liberal Assemblyman Hiram Blanchard, "and you will excite perpetual jealousies and bickerings between the two Chief Justices, and endless differences of opinion as to the nature of the causes to be tried before them." See supplement to the *Morning Chronicle*, April 30, 1864.

[18]The new arrangement permitted the assistant justices to hear equity cases while on circuit, but not in Halifax. The Judge in Equity, on the other hand, was to travel the circuits of the Supreme Court when a sufficient number of other judges was not available. His own advanced age, however, sometimes acted as a deterrent.

causes.[19] This left the Governor and Council with purely nominal powers and vested the real authority in a vice-president with judicial experience.[20] Even these nominal powers disappeared in 1866 when the Legislature belatedly adopted the provisions of the English law of 1857.[21] Thereafter the legal power to try divorce actions was vested solely in the Judge in Equity under the title Judge Ordinary of the Court for Divorce and Matrimonial Causes.

Since the removal of the judges from the Council left the Court of Errors and Appeals also without judicial members, the functioning of the Council in this capacity passed practically into desuetude. The Governors' Commissions still permitted an appeal to England in the more important civil cases and the Judicial Committee Act of 1841 outlined the type of procedure to be used, but this right was seldom claimed.[22] Thus, for all practical purposes, the Supreme Court was a final court of appeal. It possessed the powers of the criminal, civil, and exchequer courts of England in the highest degree because its decisions were usually beyond the reach of revision.[23]

The problem of judicial independence appeared in several guises between 1830 and 1867. It has been shown above that the Governor, acting with or without the Council, had been stripped of all his judicial functions by Confederation. The reverse process of depriving the judges of the right to act as legislators was completed in the thirties when the Assembly excluded the Master of the Rolls from its precincts[24] and the Chief Justice was denied a seat in the Legislative Council.[25]

While this suited the Reformers, they were dissatisfied with the tenure which the judges enjoyed by statute.[26] The first Reform ministry

[19]4 Vic., c. 13.

[20]In 1865 it was further provided that the Judge in Equity *ex officio* would assume the vice-presidency. 28 Vic., c. 1.

[21]See Stanley to Lieutenant-Governor of Nova Scotia (circular), April 12, 1858, in *JHA*, 1859, Appendix 30, 437. The Nova Scotian act stated the intention of incorporating "as far as suitable and appropriate the principles and practice" that prevail in England. See 29 Vic., c. 13, s. 8.

[22]Especially since the procedure was not prescribed in detail. See *JHA*, 1863, Appendix 48. An Imperial order-in-council of March 20, 1863, remedied this deficiency.

[23]*JHA*, 1838, Appendix 39, 118.

[24]5 Wm. IV, c. 26.

[25]While the Colonial Secretary felt that a Chief Justice might offer invaluable advice upon the legal merits of bills, the Reformers insisted that "judges ought not to mingle in the heats and contentions of politics" (Chisholm, I, 114). Hence Governor Campbell had no choice but to exclude him, since he had been instructed to conform to colonial opinion.

[26]*Supra*, 71–2.

contended that, if British judges, who were subject to the checks of an old and well-established society,[27] could be removed by the Crown upon the joint address of both Houses of Parliament, the analogous provision was all the more necessary in Nova Scotia. The opposing view was that any attempt to make the judges more amenable to the influence of public opinion and the supervision of the Legislature would destroy their independence. Instead of being subject to dismissal by a Colonial Secretary whose influence they neither felt nor feared, they would be at the mercy of the colonial legislators with whom they were in frequent collision and who, to some extent, were under the influence of the local government.[28]

The Reformers had their way in the end, but only because they permitted a judge the right to appeal to the Privy Council within six months of his removal from office.[29] This provision won the Colonial Secretary over to their point of view, for although he expected the Legislature to be guided by the same considerations as Parliament, he felt it desirable to enable the Privy Council to apply a check if it acted otherwise.[30] Practically the issue was a case of much ado about nothing, for there is no instance of a resort to the device of a joint address.

[27]The Nova Scotian judge, it said, "administers the Law in distant Counties alone and uncontrolled. In the Capital there is neither so numerous and independant [sic] a Bar as in older communities, nor are the decisions of the Courts regularly reported." Harvey to Grey, April 19, 1848, JHA, 1849, Appendix 7, 119.

[28]See observations of C. J. Halliburton, JLC, 1848, Appendix 29, 102: ". . . whenever any Judge incurred the displeasure of any influential Member of the Government, a foe might be punished, and a friend provided for, under its provisions. . . . I am merely looking upon human nature as those who have had long experience in life know it to be."

[29]See 11 Vic., c. 21.

[30]Grey to Harvey, June 24, 1848, JHA, 1849, Appendix 7, 121.

CHAPTER IX

LOCAL GOVERNMENT

THE SYSTEM OF LOCAL GOVERNMENT remained practically unaltered in a period characterized by substantial change on the provincial level. This meant that the lack of general devolution of authority from the Governor and Council to local governing bodies, which was typical of early Nova Scotia, continued to apply after 1830, although not for the same reason. Originally those who desired local self-rule could not wrest it from the central government at Halifax; later their descendants would not accept the responsibilities which the central government and Legislature were anxious to confer upon them. In the intervening years some circumstance within Nova Scotia accounted for a radical change in outlook even in the areas settled by New Englanders who had a strong tradition of local self-government behind them.

There was, of course, a vital difference from the start. In New England the town organization came first, county and state organization afterwards, whereas in Nova Scotia the central government attempted from the beginning to make decisions even on details for the most remote settlements.[1] Naturally the adoption of this Virginian mode of doing things[2] proved highly distasteful to the New Englanders who poured into western Nova Scotia in a flood after 1760, the more so because they had been promised their customary privileges as an inducement to migrate. They desired, above all, recognition of the principle that the local functions of government should be administered by their own elected officials. But two attempts to have it introduced, one by the Assembly in 1758-9 and one by the Council in 1763,[3] failed of assent. In only one respect did the Nova Scotia system provide the palest imitation of a New England town meeting. An act of 1763 authorized the freeholders in any township or district containing more than fifty families to meet once a year to grant moneys

[1]For a complete discussion see D. C. Harvey, "The Struggle for the New England Form of Township Government in Nova Scotia," *Report of the Canadian Historical Association*, 1933, 15-22.

[2]*Supra*, 40.

[3]That the "monopolistic, semi-despotic Council" favoured, and the Assembly opposed, local elective institutions in the second instance is to be explained by the temporary winning over of the Council to support the New England form, while, as was not unusual, the Halifax clique was in a majority in the Assembly. See J. B. Brebner, *The Neutral Yankees of Nova Scotia* (New York, 1937), 215-6.

for poor relief and to appoint assessors and collectors to effect their decisions.[4]

In still another matter the New Englanders were disappointed. The one provincial statute[5] which permitted the proprietors to divide the lands which they held in common according to their usual custom was disallowed in England, and a subsequent proclamation of the Lieutenant-Governor indicated that the central government would "interfere actively in determining the personnel of the proprietary groups in the various townships."[6] So instead of the freeholders apportioning the lands in town meetings, the provost marshal or his deputy undertook it by inquisition of a jury in the presence of two justices of the peace.[7]

On several occasions the New Englanders forcefully denounced these violations of their customary privileges. The freeholders of Kings County were especially indignant at the admission of non-residents by the Lieutenant-Governor and his agent despite the promise that they would have "the Privilege of Naming and admitting Settlers of [their] own Country men in the several Townships in this Country,"[8] and the freeholders of Liverpool joined them in protesting the loss of their right to "nominate and appoint men amongst us to be our Committee & to do other offices that the Town may want."[9] Neither protest was effectual, and the informal arrangements for the management of local affairs which prevailed in the southwestern part of the province until closer contact with the capital had been established soon gave way to the undemocratic system provided by statute for the government of counties and townships.[10]

[4]The statute 51 Geo. III, c. 8 (1811) conferred an additional power upon the same meetings of freeholders. Henceforth, if the overseers of the poor in townships, districts, or settlements stated in their notices convening the poor meetings that the raising of money for establishing a school was to be voted on, a majority of freeholders at those meetings might authorize the levying of a tax for educational purposes and elect trustees to carry out their wishes in the matter of education. Needless to say, an optional act of this nature was in the main ineffective, but the Falmouth Town Records (in the Public Archives of Nova Scotia) afford one example where the same assemblage acted as both a poor and a school meeting.

[5]33 Geo. II, c. 5 (1759).

[6]Harvey, "Struggle for Township Government," 20.

[7]7–8 Geo. III, c. 2.

[8]See Harvey, "Struggle for Township Government," 20.

[9]*Minutes of Council*, July 24, 1762.

[10]The proprietors of the township of Liverpool met first in 1760 for such purposes as: "To Choose a moderator. To Choose a Proprietors' Clerk. To Choose a Comte. to manage the affairs of the Propriety. To Pitch upon some Convenient Spott for a Town, & also by what method Town Lotts shall be Laid out. . . . To

From this it was an easy step for the governors to consider town meetings purely as a vehicle of the disaffected to express their opposition to established authority. Perhaps, in view of conditions in the southern colonies, Governor Legge may have been justified in banning all assemblies of the people as tending to "Disturb the Peace, & to promote Illegal confederacies, combinations, public disorders and the highest contempt of Government."[11] In much less dangerous times, however, the authoritarian Wentworth went so far as to take steps to remove several justices of the peace in Hants and Annapolis counties for daring to participate in the calling of meetings of freeholders to protest his dismissal of William Cottnam Tonge as Naval Officer.[12]

The upshot of it all was that "Nova Scotia, like Tudor England, made the Justice of the Peace its man-of-all-work."[13] Year by year the tendency continued to subtract from the authority of the grand jury, itself no democratic institution,[14] and to add to that of the even more undemocratic sessions. The former lost not only the direct power to make appointments, but also the absolute control over the presentment of moneys required for county purposes to the Supreme Court or the justices in sessions, who might amerce the county if they felt the grand juries had made inadequate provision for any service.[15] In the sessions, too, was vested an ever increasing power to hear appeals from the decisions of the county officials on such matters as poor rates, county rates, and the laying out of roads. Still more important was the growing tendency of the Legislature to confer upon them the right to make regulations on a wide variety of subjects.

Yet even after 1830 there was little agitation to change this thoroughly irresponsible system. Part of the reason for the acceptance of the status quo resided in the contradiction between appearance and reality.[16] Neither the grand juries nor the sessions were as unrepresentative as they seemed, since the former constituted a cross-section

---

agree upon some method of calling meetings for the future." But although, as indicated above, much of the power originally assumed by the town meeting was transferred to the sessions and grand jury, the meetings of the proprietors of Liverpool did continue to be held, if always more infrequently, until Sept. 20, 1866, in the latter years largely to deal with lands and rights they still possessed in common. See volume entitled "Liverpool Records" in the Public Archives of Nova Scotia.

[11]*Minutes of Council*, Sept.. 19, 1774.   [12]*Ibid.*, June 10, 1807.
[13]Harvey, "Struggle for Township Government," 22.
[14]While the qualifications for a petit juror in 1796 were a freehold of 20s. or personality of £10, those for a grand juror were £10 and £100 respectively (36 Geo. III, c. 2), and by 1833 the latter had been increased to £15 and £300 respectively (3 Wm. I, c. 51).
[15]8-9 Geo. III, c. 6 (1768).   [16]Brebner, *Neutral Yankees*, 217.

of the substantial citizenry, while the latter were the leaders of their communities.[17] Under the existing provincial franchise the freeholders' choice of local officials would have been little different. An even more compelling reason was the cheapness of the existing institutions. In the early 1820's the township and county of Halifax were spending less than £1,000 annually for local purposes, while as late as the 1850's the yearly amounts levied in the county of Queens and the township of Yarmouth were a mere £200.

In 1851 the Legislature finally recognized the obvious fact that any restrictions upon the objects for which the grand juries might make presentments were unnecessary[18] by empowering them to present any sums of money for any public purpose within the county.[19] Yet this change did nothing to counteract a tendency which had become deeply rooted in the political consciousness of the country. So the same individuals who kept unceasing pressure upon their local assemblymen for larger sums for the road and bridge service continued to provide mediocre and even wretched local services. The road funds came, of course, from customs duties and were therefore extracted painlessly, while the administration of justice and poor relief were supported by a tax on property, the most obnoxious form of obnoxious direct taxation.

How well the sessions and the grand juries performed this minimum of business is difficult to assess, but certainly the attendance of the justices was decidedly irregular despite the provision[20] which enjoined a faithful performance of their duties upon pain of removal. In Halifax County the records from 1829 to 1834 usually show no more than three justices and sometimes only a single justice attending the regular sessions,[21] and there, where the combined business of the county and town was more substantial than elsewhere, the weakness of the system gave rise to an agitation which laid bare all its shortcomings.[22]

---

[17]At least up to the time when the introduction of clear-cut party divisions provided a new criterion for selection.

[18]". . . the Grand Jury [said one Assemblyman] were the substantial labouring classes of the Province. They were generally hard working men—careful of lavish expenditure, and in his opinion rather stingy than otherwise. At any rate they were not inclined to expend public money without reason." *Novascotian*, Feb. 4, 1850.

[19]R.S. 1851, c. 46, s. 2.   [20]See 39 Geo. III, c. 10.

[21]See *Minutes of Council*, Jan. 26, 1835.

[22]The complaints of the grand jury had led a committee of the Council of Twelve to recommend a number of reforms which were carried out anything but effectually. That prompted Joseph Howe to make his celebrated denunciation of "the hardship, inequality, and oppression of the assessments, the disposition of the fire taxes, the miserable but costly corruptions of the Bridewell and Poorhouse, the

Although a movement to bestow local self-government upon the metropolitan area failed in 1838 because of a divergence of opinion upon the property qualifications to be required of the electorate, the opposing factions reached a compromise in 1841 which limited the franchise to the £20 householder, and upon that basis the first elected local government was instituted.[23] It was to enjoy that distinction for more than thirty years before a second permanent corporation was established. In the interval, however, one township had experienced a brief period of local self-government.

Its genesis goes back to 1848 when the incoming Reform administration discovered that its predecessors had been over-generous to the local compacts in selecting the justices of the peace. To redress the balance in the five counties where the disproportion was most serious,[24] it issued a new commission of the peace which displaced forty of its opponents. This action drew a severe rebuke from Lord Grey who feared that the tenure of judicial officers might become dependent upon the results of political struggles.[25] Although he relented somewhat when he discovered that the justices transacted considerable business of an administrative character, he recommended the setting up of machinery like the district councils of Upper Canada to perform the non-judicial functions.[26]

Two gestures in that direction during the 1850's got nowhere. The first was Howe's plan to divide Halifax County into townships, in each of which five elected officials, a warden and four councillors, would assume both the administrative and judicial functions of the justices of the peace. Grey was told that, if the measure were approved, it would "probably be extended to the other Counties, and confer upon the people of this Province the enlarged privileges" which he intended

inefficiency of the police, the malpractices of the brick building, the delay of justice in the commissioners' court, and the confusion of the accounts." J. A. Chisholm, Speeches and Public Letters of Joseph Howe (Halifax, 1909), I, 59.

[23]The most striking feature of the original Halifax charter was the conferment of judicial functions upon elected officials. The mayor, and in his absence the aldermen in rotation, assumed the functions of the police magistrates and presided at the daily sessions of the police court. In addition, the mayor and one alderman in rotation met twice a month for the hearing of civil cases. See 4 Vic., c. 55, ss. 53 and 54. In view of subsequent events, it is difficult to see how these provisions escaped the attention of the supervisory authority in England. Infra, 139n.

[24]The figures were as follows: Hants, 14 Reformers to 33 Tories; Kings, 13 to 32; Annapolis, 7 to 35; Cumberland, 16 to 32; Lunenburg, 5 to 20.

[25]See Grey to Harvey, Feb. 23, 1849, Journals of the House of Assembly (JHA), 1858, Appendix 51, 377–8.

[26]Grey to Harvey, May 21, 1850, ibid., 387–8.

them to enjoy.[27] This time the Colonial Secretary objected to the election on a short-term basis of judicial officials who would be "subject to influence from the popular feeling . . . on the questions which [might] be brought under their magisterial cognizance,"[28] while to Nova Scotians on the spot a system with a dual set of magistrates seemed so cumbersome that they declined to adopt it.

The second scheme was the offspring of J. W. Johnston's persistent attempts to reduce the power of the executive under responsible government. Now that a Liberal Executive Council was redressing the balance by appointing its supporters to the magistracy, he found the indirect control of the justices in sessions over the making of electoral lists quite intolerable.[29] Municipal corporations were to be the remedy. With difficulty he persuaded the particularist Assembly of the day to allow four counties to incorporate themselves at their own discretion in 1855,[30] and to extend the same privilege to the other fourteen in 1856.[31] As a result, the counties and districts might elect councils to assume the administrative functions of the sessions and grand juries and to appoint commissioners to perform the judicial functions.

Even then a substantial body of opinion advocated a more extensive devolution of authority. Under their urging the Legislature required any municipal councils which were instituted under the foregoing legislation to divide the counties or districts into townships, each of which was to elect five councillors.[32] These councillors were to perform twelve of the sixteen functions formerly entrusted to the municipal councils and were, in addition, to elect a reeve who, with the other reeves, would henceforth constitute the municipal councils and perform the remaining functions. "The local self-government is [now] complete," said Adams G. Archibald, "and the feelings of a Township in its own affairs are not over-ruled by the feelings of the whole country."[33]

Although this machinery remained on the statute book until 1879, it was unused and, in fact, unnoticed after the first three years. Its

[27]Harvey to Grey, June 4, 1850, *ibid.*, 1851, Appendix 6, 10.

[28]Grey to Harvey, July 15, 1850, *ibid.*, 11. This objection contrasts sharply with the acceptance of similar provisions in the act for the incorporation of Halifax.

[29]The type of franchise in effect from 1851 to 1854 (*supra*, 116–17) meant that the assessors and collectors of poor and county rates, who were appointed by the sessions, determined what persons were qualified to vote.

[30]18 Vic., c. 49. The provisions were based upon a New Brunswick act of 1851.

[31]19 Vic., c. 12. Four counties, Guysborough, Shelburne, Yarmouth, and Digby, were each to have two divisions for the purposes of the act.

[32]19 Vic., c. 11.   [33]*Novascotian*, April 7, 1856.

adoption was limited to Yarmouth Township which incorporated itself in October, 1855, and reverted to its old status in November, 1858.[34] In the interval the freeholders of Queens, Annapolis, Hants, Colchester, Pictou, Antigonish, and Guysborough counties and Argyle Township had all rejected the principle of incorporation. In each case the settled communities cast an affirmative vote, but they were baulked by intense opposition in the backwoods.[35] Thus the deeply rooted fear of heavier county rates continued to provide the real deterrent to change.[36] The prevailing attitude was that of the newspaper correspondent who urged that "the clarions of war should be sounded, and Taxation, Taxation, Taxation proclaimed throughout the county."[37]

The provincial press was almost unanimous in recognizing the need to educate the public to the desirability of the new institutions, but it received little assistance from the assemblymen, who were extremely reluctant to abandon their right to nominate road commissioners.[38] In the local communities the same influences were at work. Those who boasted of a "J.P." appended to their names, or hoped to some day, or were on the right side of the sheriff and therefore figured on the grand jury list; in other words, those "who love[d] to dictate local laws to their neighbours and who glor[ied] in the prospect of cutting what is popularly called a 'swell', . . . at the Court of Sessions"[39] threw their influence against local elective institutions. This combination of circumstances permitted the old system to perpetuate itself into the post-Confederation period.

[34]The affirmative vote in 1855 was 300 to 90; the negative vote in 1858 was 619 to 520.

[35]Acadian Recorder, Jan. 17, 1857.

[36]The adoption of the new system in Yarmouth Township had resulted in increasing the cost of local government from £190 to £250. See Novascotian, April 13, 1857.

[37]Ibid., Oct. 6, 1856.

[38]Acadian Recorder, March 11, 1854.

[39]Ibid., Oct. 4, 1856.

III. PROVINCIAL GOVERNMENT

CHAPTER X

CONFEDERATION

FROM THE LEGAL POINT OF VIEW, Confederation was the most revolutionary of the five basic decisions in Nova Scotian government, since for the first time the political institutions and the status of the province were altered, not by exercise of the prerogative, but by an act of Parliament. This did not mean, however, that the British North America Act conferred a written constitution upon the province, for the constitution of the executive, legislative, and judicial branches of government—much of which rested on the prerogative—was continued except as the Act otherwise provided.[1] Nevertheless, a considerable portion of the former authority of the provincial government was vested in new federal institutions created immediately or subsequently by virtue of the provisions of the Act.

The institution of these far-reaching changes by tortuous means in a province which for 109 years had been developing its own constitution, and which for twenty years had enjoyed responsible government, could not fail to provoke bitter controversy. The outstanding feature of their consummation was the failure to consult the people either directly or indirectly at any juncture of the proceedings. Colonial union of any kind was not an issue in 1863, yet four years later the electorate could do no more than express its approbation or displeasure of a *fait accompli*.

The story of why Nova Scotians were not permitted to place their *imprimatur* upon union began in 1864 when the Legislature accepted Dr. Tupper's proposal that delegates should be appointed to confer with the representatives of New Brunswick and Prince Edward Island on the subject of maritime union. Through it the leaders of both parties hoped to soften the asperities of political life by substituting the advocacy of broad public questions for petty personal bickering.[2] The five Nova Scotian delegates to Charlottetown, three Conservatives and two Liberals,[3] acquiesced wholeheartedly in the decision to go to

[1]See ss. 64, 88, and 129.
[2]See speeches of Tupper, *Assembly Debates*, 1864, 183; A. G. Archibald, *ibid.*, 184; and Johnston, *ibid.*, 184–5.
[3]The three Conservatives were Charles Tupper, Premier and Provincial Secretary; W. A. Henry, Attorney-General; and R. B. Dickey, M.L.C.; the Liberals were A. G. Archibald and Jonathan McCully, who led their party in the Assembly and Council respectively.

Quebec to discuss a wider union, and although they disagreed upon details during the conference, they were unanimous in accepting its conclusions.

That was indeed remarkable, for prior to his becoming a delegate Jonathan McCully, editor of the *Chronicle*, had thrown cold water upon the idea of federal union as designed to *"utilize the Maritime Provinces as make-weights for balancing the machinery of a new, untried, and more than doubtful expediency adapted to the exigencies of Canadian necessities."*[4] While all five may have been carried away by grandiose conceptions of nation-building at Quebec, their opponents alleged that their primary motivation was the prospect of personal preferment, and the high position which each of them attained under the new order added a degree of plausibility to the argument.

The next step was to have some stamp of approval placed upon the conclusions of the conference in the province itself. It could not be through the medium of a direct appeal to the people because the unleashing of vigorous opposition to the Quebec scheme after December, 1864, made that course impracticable. The problem therefore resolved itself into getting a majority in both branches of the Legislature to accept the proposal. For the moment, however, Tupper had to mark time because of the temporary defeat of the Confederation cause in New Brunswick. Not even his temporary return to maritime union could prevent three of his supporters from opposing the Quebec scheme in the Legislature, and the Assembly would certainly have rejected the project in 1865.

Yet by this time the forces had been set in motion which were destined to overcome the initial set-backs. The key to the subsequent course of events lay in the attitude of the British government. By December, 1864, it had approved the conclusions of the Quebec Conference[5] and had instructed Lieutenant-Governor MacDonnell to "render the Governor-General [full] support in those further measures which he [was] about to take in the furtherance of the scheme";[6] in June, 1865, it peremptorily rejected a reversion to maritime union unless as an ancillary to the larger union,[7] and to further its objective

[4]*Morning Chronicle*, Aug. 4, 1864.

[5]Cardwell to Monck, Dec. 3, 1864, *Journals of the House of Assembly* (*JHA*), 1865, Appendix 3—Union of the Colonies, 26.

[6]Cardwell to MacDonnell, Dec. 8, 1864, *ibid.*, 25.

[7]At the same time it insisted that "the Colonies must recognize a right and even acknowledge an obligation incumbent on the Home Government to urge with earnestness and just authority the measures which they consider[ed] most expedient on the part of the Colonies with a view to their own defence." Cardwell to MacDonnell, June 24, 1865. See *JHA*, 1866, Appendix 10—Union of the Colonies, 4.

it eventually resorted to the displacement of the Lieutenant-Governor.

Despite MacDonnell's extravagant conception of a Governor's role, he refused to become a tool either of the Colonial Secretary or the Governor-General in forcing the constitutional change which they were bent upon concluding. In no uncertain terms he told Cardwell that "the carrying so extensive a plan without an appeal to the country would savour somewhat of a 'Coup de Main,'" and that no representative of the Queen would therefore be likely to permit it "unless English interests were greatly concerned in the immediate establishment of such a Confederation."[8] Even after being warned not to oppose his judgment to that of his ministry for fear he should be unable to obtain another,[9] he continued to reflect the popular Nova Scotian viewpoint in his communications.[10] To him, the wisest statesmanship was to "lay the foundations of the new Edifice at its proposed base and not on its roof—and to begin by a legislative Union of New Brunswick and Nova Scotia . . . and . . . put the roof on by & by."[11] It is understandable, therefore, why a pretext was conjured up for sending him to Hong Kong after little more than a year in Nova Scotia.[12]

His successor, the native Nova Scotian Sir Fenwick Williams, shared none of MacDonnell's misgivings, and since his term was to end with union, he had no need to fear the aftermath of the methods he used to effect it. According to the *Chronicle*, wining and dining at Government House were part of his over-all strategy:

[8]MacDonnell to Cardwell, Nov. 22, 1864 (separate), P.A.N.S. 127.

[9]Cardwell to MacDonnell, Dec. 8, 1864, P.A.N.S., Lieutenant-Governor's Correspondence, July–Dec., 1864.

[10]Nova Scotia, he told Cardwell, could hardly be expected to "see any overwhelming immediate necessity for acceding to the exclusive requirements of a portion of Her Majesty's Canadian subjects" or to "barter the future interests of the Province at large" merely to provide inducements to her public men. MacDonnell to Cardwell, Dec. 8, 1864 (separate), P.A.N.S. 127. His dispatches to Monck questioned the Canadian ministers' "politic[al] manipulation of the subject with so keen a Spectator as Bluenose watching the game." MacDonnell to Monck, March 20, 1865 (private), Lieutenant-Governor's Correspondence, Jan.–June, 1865.

[11]*Ibid*. MacDonnell's total effort in the furtherance of Confederation went little beyond placing in the *Gazette* two of Cardwell's dispatches making the Quebec scheme the keystone of British policy in North America, and "squeezing as much as possible of civility" out of an unsatisfactory dispatch from Monck. Sir Joseph Pope, *Correspondence of Sir John Macdonald* (Toronto, 1921), 28.

[12]"If I had remained here another year or 15 months—unless by the *express desire* of Mr. Cardwell—there would have been a great risk of my throwing away all my previous long services—a sacrifice too great to be expected—or at least a risk of my not obtaining in a reasonable period a gov^t that would qualify me for a first class pension. Those things are very few—and difficult to get." See MacDonnell to Tupper, July 20, 1865, Tupper Papers (P.A.C.), item 32.

Dazzled with the sight of the fringe and fittings supplied by the tax payers, their constituents, astonished at the brilliant small talk of Dundreary aid-de-camps, bewildered with a hero's condescension, plied with wine and false promises, drugged with dead men's tales preserved in the gubernatorial repertoire, who can wonder that men, fashioned as are Caleb Bill, Robichau and others, forgot their honor and their country, and consented to commit the treason which has rendered them infamous.[13]

These talents of the Governor were incapable of full exercise until the Legislature met on February 22, 1866. While the Speech from the Throne made no mention of federation, the omission deceived no one. "My total abandonment of Confederation is too much like Punch even for [my opponents'] sincere belief," Williams himself acknowledged. "They know what I was sent here for."[14] Already a three-way correspondence had begun between MacDonnell, the Governor-General, and Lieutenant-Governor Gordon of New Brunswick in which, through the medium of coded telegrams, each of the provincial governors kept urging some concrete action by the other, while Monck applied the pressure to both.

Fate conspired in every way to assist Williams. He began the session with two trump cards—the determined attitude of the British government combined with the growing hostility of the United States and its determination not to renew reciprocity. In the month of March a third appeared when the possibility of Fenian attacks enabled the Confederates to exploit the necessity of a strong union for the purposes of defence. Even before the Governor called out the militia on March 17, he had already reported a "great change" in opinion to Monck.[15] That change, however, was not in public opinion, but in the attitude of the assemblymen.

The argument that federation was inevitable and that they who opposed it would not share in the allocation of the loaves and fishes to follow in its wake placed the Conservative members in a quandary. But before they had to make up their minds, Williams—likely not unaided—had conceived a plan which, if it had succeeded, would have rendered his opponents completely impotent. On March 13 he suggested to William Annand, the anti-Confederation leader in the Assembly, that he should propose the appointment of delegates to London where the British government would act as a final arbiter upon a scheme of union which would be of mutual advantage to all

[13]*Morning Chronicle*, Oct. 24, 1867.
[14]See Williams to Gordon, March 7, 1866, Lieutenant-Governor's Telegram Book (P.A.N.S.), no. 13.
[15]Williams to Monck, March 12, 1866, *ibid.*, no. 18.

the contracting parties.[16] Annand, like the Conservatives, knew full well that, if the resolution carried without his support, he would neither share in the appointment of delegates who would press his viewpoint with vigour nor participate in the bestowal of patronage. Nevertheless, relying on information from Smith, the anti-Confederation leader in New Brunswick, that the latter's lines would hold, and aware that federation required the inclusion of the sister province, he turned down the Governor's proposal.

It was in these circumstances that on April 3 William Miller, an independent member for Richmond who had previously opposed the Quebec scheme but not federation in the abstract, advanced the suggestion which Annand had rejected. Despite Miller's protestations that he had acted upon his own initiative, the Governor appears to have had advance knowledge of his action and considered it as the initial step in the Assembly's acceptance of some scheme of federation.[17] What followed has all the appearance of a cut-and-dried affair. Tupper followed Miller with a resolution for the appointment of delegates to "arrange with the Imperial Government a scheme of union which [would] effectually ensure just provision for the rights and interests" of Nova Scotia,[18] and the Assembly accepted it on April 17 by a vote of 31 to 19.

In this division twenty-six Conservatives, four Liberals, and one Independent were aligned against thirteen Liberals and six Conservatives. The significant factor was that only six Conservatives bolted the party ranks, while six Conservatives and one Independent who had previously opposed union in general or the Quebec scheme in particular provided the support which carried the resolution.[19] Without exception the viewpoint of these seven members was that of the Victoria member C. J. Campbell:

Whatever objections the people entertained to the Quebec scheme twelve months ago matters have entirely changed. There is not a man in my County who is not loyal to the heart and who would not consent to any scheme that would save us from annexation or from invasion. . . . All the trifling disputes which have engaged our attention should be at once buried before the great object of maintaining British connection. . . . I had objections to the Quebec scheme but when the great necessities to which I have referred arose these objections vanished like smoke.[20]

[16]See *Morning Chronicle*, March 23, 1869.
[17]See Williams to Monck, April 3, 1866, Lieutenant-Governor's Telegram Book, no. 51. [18]*JHA*, 1866, 60.
[19]See speeches of Longley, *Assembly Debates*, 1864, 191; Bourinot, *ibid.*, 1865, 265–8; Miller, *ibid.*, 238–9; McFarlane, *ibid.*, 1866, 283–4; McKay, *ibid.*, 294–5; C. J. Campbell, *ibid.*, 240–1; McDonnell, *ibid.*, 191–2. [20]*Ibid.*, 1866, 240–1.

With much less ado the Legislative Council confirmed Tupper's resolution, thereby deciding once and for all Nova Scotia's future status.

The opponents of federation contended that a resolution of a three-year-old Assembly which had been passed against "the well-understood wishes of the people" was an insufficient basis upon which to incorporate Nova Scotia into the new federal union. As a result, the debate which followed hinged around the extent to which a representative of the people is to be regarded as a "delegate." With great glee the Conservatives turned the arguments of the Liberals during the constitutional agitation of 1860–1 to their own advantage.[21] Tupper, in fact, became positively Burkian in his opposition to securing the approval of the people. "No man . . . in the history of constitutional legislation," he said, "ever heard of so unstatesmanlike a course as a government dissolving the parliament in which they have a clear, undoubted majority to carry a measure which they believed would promote the general prosperity of the country."[22] No anti-Confederate espoused an extravagant conception of the "delegate" theory, but all were in agreement that "colonial legislators . . . entrusted for a definite time with limited powers and sacred trusts, could not strip the people of their rights without their own consent," or transfer their legislative power to others.[23] Those in the driver's seat, however, were men who accepted the opposing view.

Yet their tactics left a feeling of resentment which time has not

[21]In particular, they could point to a dispatch of Lord Mulgrave in 1861 which stated that an assemblyman is "elected a representative and not a delegate, and the constituency have given up to him for the limited period fixed by law for the duration of the Parliament the power which they possessed. They have a right to represent to him their views, and to refuse to re-elect him . . . but they have no right during the duration of the Parliament, to coerce his actions." Mulgrave to Johnston, March 30, 1861, *JHA*, 1861, Appendix 2—Constitutional Questions, 51.

[22]*British Colonist*, March 21, 1867. For the general argument, see also Tupper's, *A Letter to the Earl of Carnarvon*, Oct. 19, 1866. Tupper held that an election would not reveal with certainty the people's wishes respecting federation while his measure for the support of schools by compulsory assessment was still agitating the country. Actually, when an election came in 1867, union of the colonies altogether dwarfed all the other issues.

[23]Chisholm, II, 483–4. See also Joseph Howe's *Confederation considered in Relation to the Interests of the Empire* (London, 1866), 28, in which reference is made to the Assembly's act as striking at "the Constitution of the country which the representatives were chosen to guard and not to violate." Tupper made the telling reply that if this position were accepted, "Nova Scotia is yet unfit to enjoy the free institutions which were conceded to her a quarter of a century ago, and that it is necessary that the Imperial Government should interpose and override the constitutional action" of her General Assembly. *A Letter*, 61.

entirely obliterated. While Tupper's arguments against the resort to direct democracy may have been valid, the behaviour of the Assembly which made the decision left much to be desired. Even if the less worthy motives were not dominant,[24] its members accepted too readily the argument that external pressures necessitated union and concerned themselves too little with the effect of that union upon Nova Scotia. The real debate occurred only after the die had been cast once and for all. But a final judgment of the Assembly's conduct is contingent upon first deciding to what lengths the leaders of a representative democracy are permitted to go in overriding an electorate which refuses to be convinced of the wisdom of their high policy.

To all indications the federation idea received little in the way of genuine popular support even though at the outset the Confederates had "the writing and printing and speaking power—and an immense deal of executive energy on their side . . . in putting the matter before the country."[25] By November, 1864, the Governor had found so many leaders of the community opposed to federation that he doubted the possibility of its being carried;[26] in February, 1865, he described its opponents as "gentlemen of the highest social standing here and in fact . . . most of the leading bankers and merchants, the wealthiest farmers, and the most independent Gentlemen in the Province."[27] Yet although the Halifax mercantile interests formed the advance guard of the anti-Confederation forces and contributed heavily to the funds of the Anti-Confederation League,[28] their views prevailed only because they coincided with those of the ordinary Nova Scotian. Until Joseph Howe made a belated appearance on the public platform, the opponents of federation lacked an orator to espouse their cause, but in this instance the function of the great tribune was not to mould public opinion, but to make it fully vocal.

The fundamental point upon which the majority of Nova Scotians were in agreement was that the province should not be forced pre-

[24]Samuel McDonnell of Inverness admitted that Miller won him over with the argument that "Confederation was bound to come; and we . . . had better get into line or we should be left out in the cold and lose all chance of obtaining any of the good positions." See "An Unexplained Incident of Confederation in Nova Scotia" in George Patterson, Studies in Nova Scotian History (Halifax, 1940), 110–11.

[25]MacDonnell to Monck, March 20, 1865 (private), Lieutenant-Governor's Correspondence, Jan.–June, 1865.

[26]MacDonnell to Cardwell, Nov. 22, 1864 (separate), P.A.N.S. 127.

[27]Ibid., Feb. 16, 1865.

[28]See "Howe and the Anti-Confederation League" in Patterson, Studies in Nova Scotian History, 116.

cipitately to accept revolutionary changes of more than doubtful utility. "We have fifty seaports carrying on foreign trade," said Howe. "Our shipyards are full of life and our flag floats on every sea."[29] Neither he nor his supporters should be criticized unduly, therefore, for not possessing the hindsight of the students of a later day that this high level of economic activity was directly connected with the American Civil War, or for not realizing the extent to which technological changes in the construction of ships would destroy the basis of the province's mercantile industry.

The anti-Confederates pointed particularly to the lack of genuine arguments by their opponents. Tupper's revelation of a crisis in which the province had to choose between annexation to the United States and a firm connection with the Mother Country,[30] and the *British Colonist*'s assertion that Her Majesty had placed herself at the head of the Union party[31] were typical, they felt, of the "Lickspittlerism" which the federationists were employing in the place of logic.[32] In their opinion Tupper had forsaken the public interest and was simply arguing: "The Queen wants this Confederation. The Ministry wants it. The General and Hero of Kars want it. The Archbishop is willing."[33] Instead of preventing annexation, the proposed federation would abet it by fostering discontent, and yet do little to put the North American colonies in a position to defend themselves more effectively.

More positively, the anti-Confederates considered the Quebec scheme as a sacrifice of Nova Scotian interests to suit the convenience of Canada. From its establishment the colony had always looked seawards. What it had seen in its few glances westward was not reassuring. Nova Scotians had regarded the rebellions in the Canadas with distaste and had attributed the fact that they were not consulted in the discussions on reciprocity in 1854 to the deliberate mismanagement of Canadian politicians. When, at a later date, Hincks had showed little sympathy for the attempts of Nova Scotians to gain control of their coal mines, Howe unleashed his long-smouldering sense of indignation. What would Canadians do in similar circumstances? "They would resort to their modern and more effective expedients—a successful or an unsuccessful rebellion. They would burn a Parliament House and pelt a Governor-General."[34]

Now they were attempting to draw Nova Scotia into the political

[29]Chisholm, II, 511.
[30]*Assembly Debates*, 1866, 222.
[31]May 2, 1867.
[32]*Acadian Recorder*, March 7, 1866.
[33]*Ibid.*, March 20, 1867.   [34]Chisholm, II, 319.

turmoil of the Canadas with their racial antagonism, sectional rivalries, dual leadership and double majorities, ever recurring crises and deadlocks. Even worse, all the gains of responsible government were to be surrendered at one fell swoop.

> . . . self-government, in all that gives dignity and security to a free state, is to be swept away. The Canadians are to appoint our governors, judges and senators. They are to "tax us by any and every mode" and spend the money. They are to regulate our trade, control our Post Offices, command the militia, fix the salaries, do what they like with our shipping and navigation, with our sea-coast and river fisheries, regulate the currency and the rate of interest, and seize upon our savings banks.[35]

To accord that treatment to a province with a long history of representative institutions was "an atrocious proceeding, out of which would grow undying hatreds and ultimate annexation."[36] "The wisdom of Solomon and the energy and strategy of Frederick the Great", said Howe, "would . . . be required to preserve and strengthen such a people . . . into 'a new nationality.' "[37]

Subsequent events appeared to confirm the fact that it would have been preferable if the natural forces which were operative after 1867 had pulled Nova Scotians of their own accord into some type of union with Canada. But for better or worse, the misgivings of the smaller entity had to give way to the compelling reasons for the immediate establishment of a united British country on the northern half of the continent.

The anti-Confederates experienced only one minor success in their opposition to federation. In the elections of September, 1867, they returned eighteen of nineteen members to the Commons, thirty-six of thirty-eight to the Assembly. Yet the only concession which their delegation to England could secure was a promise that the Dominion government would be requested to review its trade, fisheries, and taxation policies, and to "relax or modify any arrangements on those subjects which [might] prejudice the peculiar interests of Nova Scotia, and of the Maritime portion of the Dominion."[38] Much more effective tactics were open to the anti-Confederates than the innocuous ones of resolutions, addresses, and delegations. However, not only did the decision of their eighteen members of Parliament to go to Ottawa tacitly recognize the new régime, but it permitted the governing

[35]Ibid., 513.
[36]Ibid., 464.
[37]Ibid., 473.
[38]Buckingham and Chandos to Monck, June 4, 1868, JHA, 1868, Appendix 9—Confederation, 3.

powers to exercise their talents to the full upon those most susceptible to persuasion. To have refused to set foot within the Parliament Buildings of Canada would have proved a much more convincing gesture.

The anti-Confederates discarded an even more promising opportunity. Their convention during the summer of 1868 had to face the fact that the British government had left it the single possibility of securing better terms. Howe suggested that the Executive Council should resign and thereby make it impossible for the Lieutenant-Governor to secure a ministry. In the elections which followed the anti-Confederates would make certain of a majority which would convince the British government of the actual state of affairs in Nova Scotia. While his critics later questioned the seriousness of his proposal,[39] the evidence is clear that none of the executive councillors showed any inclination to divest himself of office.

No less a personage than the Attorney-General[40] put forward a naïve proposition which had the merit of disturbing no one. It was his contention that the effect of the Treaty of Utrecht had been to make Nova Scotia the absolute property of the Sovereign, who therefore possessed the sole power to legislate for it. When the English law officers could discover "no limit to the authority of the Imperial legislature over a colony in the situation of Nova Scotia,"[41] he argued further that the Imperial Parliament, which itself had no power to tax a colony, could not create another legislature with that power.[42] Yet not even the anti-Confederation Assembly would carry his argument to the highest court of appeal.

By mid-1868 the repeal movement was doomed. The Macdonald-Tupper policy of "striking off the tallest heads" was proving successful. With Howe's acceptance of better terms late in 1868 it won its greatest victory. After that date the anti-Confederation members struggled ineffectually to preserve cohesion among their members. While Purdy of Cumberland was demanding that Confederation should be accepted as an irrevocable fact, seven members led by Dr. Murray of Pictou and

[39]See the correspondence in the *Morning Chronicle* starting on Nov. 7, 1868.

[40]Martin I. Wilkins, whose critics described the argument as a "mass of Buncombe prepared especially for the eye of the clique of annexationists in the neighbourhood of New Glasgow." *British Colonist*, June 10, 1869.

[41]See *JHA*, 1868, Appendix 10—Repeal Delegation, 29–30.

[42]*Assembly Debates*, 1869, 158. Wilkins' rather fantastic proposal for invalidating the British North America Act was to force an action on an unstamped promissory note with the expectation that the Judicial Committee would declare the note valid despite its non-compliance with legislation of the Dominion Parliament. *Ibid.*, 1868, 161.

Kidston of Victoria were highly critical of the government for its tacit acceptance of the new order. Between the extremists of its own party the executive councillors clung determinedly to the sweets of office, acquiesced in meaningless resolutions passed by the Assembly, and contented themselves with maintaining and worsening their bad relations with Ottawa. Thus they were no more mindful of their responsibilities to the public than the Conservatives had been before 1867.

CHAPTER XI

POLITICAL PARTIES

ALTHOUGH the long-run effect of federation upon the established parties was slight, its immediate results were catastrophic. For the moment even the old shibboleths of Conservative and Liberal were discarded in favour of Confederate and anti-Confederate, and while the nucleus of the Confederates was Conservative just as that of the anti-Confederates was Liberal, the break in party ties was on such a scale as to create new parties in fact as in name. In the grand shuffle of supporters the Confederates had much the better of it at the leadership level, but the arguments of the anti-Confederates were far more appealing to the rank and file of Nova Scotians.

These phenomena quickly made themselves felt in practical politics and were instrumental in determining the course of the relations between the provincial parties and their new federal counterparts. From the beginning the Confederates constituted one section of the Dominion Conservative party, and their leaders, unable to win elective office by their own resources, took advantage of the beneficence of John A. Macdonald to ensconce themselves in judgeships, senatorships, and the like. The anti-Confederates, on the other hand, although overwhelmingly triumphant at the polls, could not long forestall the difficulties which inevitably follow the failure of a party to realize the high hopes it has held out to an electorate. By 1869 their solid bloc in the Legislature was beginning to crumble. Their inability to adopt any strong policy for the liberation of Nova Scotia was alienating their extremist followers at the same time as their opponents were using every possible device to wean away the lukewarm supporters of repeal. The only tie which could have kept the Liberal Annand and the ultra-Tory Martin Wilkins in the same cabinet was their opposition to union with Canada, and after that proved ineffectual, neither could provide the leadership which was essential to keep the discordant elements of their party in line.

The single desire of the anti-Confederation ministers, once the impracticability of their principal objective had become apparent, was to retain office. So although they adopted the wrongdoing of the Dominion government as their leading argument in the provincial election of 1871 and professed to believe in the eventual release of Nova

Scotia from Canada, this was merely one more effort to capitalize upon the bitter resentment which could still be aroused by recalling the cardinal sins of the Confederates. Moreover, even though they lost a dozen seats, they undoubtedly breathed a sigh of relief that five of the seven anti-Confederate extremists were missing from the new Assembly.

The relations of the anti-Confederates with the federal political parties presented further difficulties. Their early experiences with their representatives in the House of Commons demonstrated the futility of expecting those members to remain in splendid isolation. "Going up to Ottawa as red-hot Antis," complained the *Chronicle*, "they have been successively wheedled, with four or five sturdy and honorable exceptions, into giving an almost unbroken support to a Government which includes Howe and Tupper."[1] Hence, in the months which preceded the federal election of August, 1872, the anti-Confederation newspapers were carefully exploring the line of conduct which should be pursued in the next Parliament. They concluded that, if an alliance was sought, it would have to be with the Blake and Mackenzie party in preference to "the designing faction . . . now . . . denying us an honest, vigorous and economical government."[2] The other possibility was to maintain their independence, get all the federal grants they could put their hands on for the local services, and make an alliance only after questions of principle had superseded the existing struggle for power in the Dominion.[3]

Apparently the second alternative was decided upon—Nova Scotians were to create a moderate Reform party which would eventually join similar organizations in the other provinces.[4] The Confederates' victory in the federal election of 1872 could be dismissed, therefore, as of purely temporary significance. It was different, however, in 1874 when the Pacific Scandal and a return to honest government constituted the single issue on which the province elected a majority of anti-Confederates or Reformers, all of whom became faithful adherents of the Mackenzie government and two of whom entered the cabinet. "Now we have a government at Ottawa prepared to act fairly and justly towards our Government and people," exulted the *Recorder*.[5] The stage had thus been set for the anti-Confederates to become, like their opponents, the provincial wing of a national party. The events

[1]*Morning Chronicle*, July 8, 1872.
[2]*Ibid.*, Jan. 8, 1872.
[3]*Ibid.*, July 8, 1872.
[4]*Ibid.*, July 15, 1872.
[5]*Acadian Recorder*, Nov. 26, 1874.

of 1867–74 had also provided the first indication of the difficulty, if not the impracticability, of sustaining a party which favours withdrawal from the Canadian federation or opposes any of the basic national policies.

The integration of both the Confederates and the anti-Confederates into the national parties meant the submergence of the one issue which had permitted a meaningful cleavage of the electorate along party lines. Thereafter the limited nature of the provincial legislative field and the restriction of governmental activity by reason of the financial weakness of the province made it even more difficult than before for either party to base its attitude towards provincial problems upon a genuine philosophy. The *Acadian Recorder* had concluded as early as 1876:

> There is not, nor can there ever be, any policy dividing the people as far as local matters are concerned. The policy of the opposition will be to struggle by every means . . . to reach the treasury benches, and the policy of the Government will be to checkmate them, and retain the place and power they hold. A change of government in Nova Scotia now-a-days, would only mean changing the officials in some four or five heads of departments. . . . Hereafter the local elections will turn on purely local matters. . . .[6]

While the politicians are sometimes loath to agree with this diagnosis, it still constitutes a reasonably accurate appraisal of the political struggle. Not a Conservative leader since Confederation has, in fact, pretended to be the exponent of a conservative creed or sought inspiration from English or American conservatives, and those Liberal leaders who have attributed their own success and the province's well-being to their acting in consonance with liberal tenets were treating the intelligence of the electorate with scant respect.

Indeed, in their attitudes towards the liberalization of provincial institutions, the two parties have on more than one occasion reversed the roles which are expected of parties bearing their names. The explanation is that their stand upon specific issues is determined more by the exigencies of practical politics than by principle. Thus the Liberals refused for more than four decades to introduce universal suffrage because it could not assist them politically, while the Conservatives favoured it because the complexities of a property franchise facilitated malpractices on the part of the dominant Liberal party.[7] Again, the Liberals more or less acquiesced in the continuance of a second chamber of dubious merit when they discovered that it could be

[6]*Ibid.*, May 9, 1876.
[7]*Infra*, 257–8.

employed to strengthen their party organization, while the Conservatives, for the same reason, sought for more than half a century to have it abolished. In like manner the Liberals resisted the creation of new departments with responsible ministers long after a clear need for them had arisen.[8]

Similarly no generalization can be made about the attitude of the parties towards social legislation. While the Liberals, as the perennial custodians of power, have enacted the bulk of the existing legislation, the Conservatives have periodically pressed for additional measures as a means of securing public favour, so much so in 1937 that Premier Macdonald felt compelled to take up their challenge: "If social security, if social legislation is to be the issue on which the merits of the two parties . . . are to be decided there is not a man . . . behind me . . . who will not welcome the opportunity to put that issue to the proof."[9] Both the Liberals and Conservatives emphasize, however, that too much can be expected of governments and that paternal legislation is not the remedy for economic and political ills.[10] Both hold that the duty of a government is simply to "create conditions under which its citizens [can] work out their own destiny."[11] This, in fact, is the closest that either comes to having a philosophy. But although the statement appears vague and platitudinous, it is at least flexible enough to permit a government to meet the needs and desires of a small community which is not characterized by a sharp conflict of interests.

Undoubtedly the most striking feature of the operation of the Nova Scotian party system has been that the voters elect Conservative governments merely by spasms and those spasms are of short duration —a phenomenon which has left its mark on all the other political institutions.[12] Up to 1956 the Conservatives had administered the provincial affairs for only nineteen years since 1848 and for only twelve since 1867; the electorate had normally shown its satisfaction with Liberal governments and had not tried an alternative except in times of crisis. The first of the four Conservative periods of office—the Johnston administration from 1857 to 1860—was the result not of a victory at the polls but of the defection from the Liberal party of the Catholic assemblymen during a bitter religious controversy; the second—the Tupper government from 1863 to 1867—followed the general collapse

[8]*Infra*, 188–90.
[9]*Halifax Chronicle*, March 5, 1937.
[10]*Halifax Herald*, Feb. 9, 1923.
[11]*Halifax Chronicle*, March 19, 1946.
[12]See Appendixes F and G.

of a Liberal administration from old age and economic depression; the third—the Holmes-Thompson administrations from 1878 to 1882—was the outcome of depression and the impoverishment of the provincial finances; the fourth—the Rhodes-Harrington administrations from 1925 to 1933—may be explained in considerable measure by the failure of the province to recover from the economic ills which beset it at the close of the First World War.

Yet despite their lack of electoral success the Conservatives have polled at least 38 per cent of the popular vote in all but two general elections and always one-third except in the *débâcle* which followed the entrance of the Farmer-Labour group into practical politics in 1920. In every part of the province the Conservatives still constitute the substantial solid core to which Attorney-General Longley adverted in 1894:

Under the party system whole families maintain with a sort of proud tradition an unbroken history as partizans for generations. . . . a party convention will muster the same men and especially the same families it did twenty years before. Political issues may have changed, leaders may have changed and the party may have gone utterly wrong in the interval, it matters not. The old party traditions have gone on and its adherents have remained serenely blind. . . .[13]

The solid core of Liberal voters, however, is substantially larger than that of the Conservatives and in most provincial elections the Liberals have also attracted a higher percentage of the floating vote. This continuing phenomenon is due not so much to the mass shift of the electorate under the emotional stimulus of the Confederation issue— the Confederates made a rapid recovery from near extinction in 1867 to take over the control of the government in little more than a decade —as to a combination of factors, cumulative in their effects, which became operative in the period after 1878. The circumstances of history, good fortune, good organization, and good leadership have all played a part in the continued Liberal successes, and, as is to be expected, the absence of any clear-cut party philosophies has tended to accentuate the value of leadership and organization.

Paradoxically it was the continued success of the federal Conservatives which helped initially to establish the dominant position of the Liberal party. On the same day—September 17, 1878—the Nova Scotian electorate showed its preference for Conservative governments at Halifax and Ottawa; on the same day—June 20, 1882—it rejected the

[13]*The Week*, Jan. 5, 1894, XI, 126-7.

provincial Conservatives, but gave their federal counterparts a renewed vote of confidence. Nor was this second circumstance unique, for it was to last another decade.[14] The unbroken series of victories of the federal Conservatives affected the provincial party in two ways. For one thing, the Conservatives were called upon to fill not only the bulk of the seats in the Commons but all the other attractive positions which the federal government had in its power to bestow. Thus the local party was constantly being deprived of leadership material. The outcome was that the men whom the party recruited for the provincial field were unable to match those of a party whose leaders were obliged by the force of circumstances to be contented with the three poorly paid ministries at Halifax.

In addition, the provincial Conservatives found it disheartening to be held responsible for the unpopular fiscal and tariff policies of the federal government and yet receive little sympathy from the Nova Scotian members of the Dominion cabinet for the unfortunate plight in which the federal government's action, or lack of it, often placed them. John A. Macdonald's failure to give assistance to a Conservative premier of Nova Scotia who was in distress belies the reputation for which he became notorious in his dealings with the Conservative premiers of other provinces, while his government's cavalier treatment of Fielding's administration after 1884 was responsible for the provincial Conservatives' having to fight an election in 1886 on what for them was a hopeless issue—the repeal of Confederation. These were not isolated cases; in 1890 the local Conservative organizer was again bewailing the federal government's failure to show any consideration for the provincials:

. . . if Mr. [Charles Hibbert] Tupper had set himself to work to destroy the liberal-conservative party in local politics he could not have adopted methods more likely to effect his purpose than those he has pursued in his treatment of the saw-dust and lobster questions. The very pettiness of his recent restrictions upon the lobster fishery only serve to increase the annoyance. Then too the twenty-five cents extra-duty on flour will play a more important part in the next local contest than the scandalous record of the local government in regard to repeal. Such is undoubtedly the unpleasant fact. . . .

[14]Comparative figures are as follows:

Federal elections			Provincial elections			
1878	7 Lib.	14 Con.	1878	8 Lib.	30 Con.	
1882	7 Lib.	14 Con.	1882	24 Lib.	14 Con.	
1887	7 Lib.	14 Con.	1886	29 Lib.	8 Con.	1 Ind.
1891	5 Lib.	16 Con.	1890	28 Lib.	10 Con.	

We are really fighting a federal contest without the aid of federal leaders, federal patronage, and federal rallying cries. We have in every county the odium which the Dominion government may perchance have incurred. . . .[15]

Thus to all appearances the federal cabinet was distinctly apathetic about the health of the local Conservative party, and it complacently relied upon the return of Sir Charles Tupper from London to set the province right in the House of Commons and ignored the party's position in the provincial Assembly.

Local circumstances also played their part in establishing the primacy of the Liberal party. The financial plight of the province forced the Holmes Conservative administration to adopt a negative role calculated neither to catch the public eye nor to arouse enthusiasm even among its supporters. Its economy on the road and bridge service during a period of financial stringency antagonized the rural inhabitants who felt they had been robbed of part of their birthright, while its institution of elected local governments which would assume part of the provincial services became a source of acute political embarrassment because it increased the burden of the property-holder.

In contrast, the Liberals who assumed office in 1882 acted as "a progressive government having faith in the future of the province" instead of "a stick-in-the-mud combination preaching the doctrine of despair."[16] The somewhat improved economic and financial conditions permitted Premier Fielding to undertake an extensive programme of building roads and bridges as capital projects and to induce outside interests to develop the provincial coal resources. While he was extolling this "waking-up . . . from a Rip-van-Winkle sleep,"[17] the opposition was condemning the capital expenditures as a gigantic slush-fund specially timed to buy elections, and the concessions to outside capital as the beginning of a gigantic monopoly which would control every manufacturing industry in the Maritime Provinces for a century to come. But to the electorate these appeared to be the purely negative criticisms of a party which had shown little initiative when it held the reins of office. During this period the Conservatives at Halifax were, in fact, playing the same negative role as the Liberals at Ottawa. Hence their opponents could put to good use the comparisons between the accomplishments of Liberal and Conservative governments which have proved to be the perpetual bane of the provincial Conservatives.

[15]C. H. Cahan to Thompson, March 28, 1890, Thompson Papers (P.A.C.), item 12017. Charles Hibbert Tupper was the federal Minister of Marine and Fisheries in 1890.
[16]*Morning Chronicle*, May 1, 1890.
[17]*Acadian Recorder*, March 9, 1894.

Their position once established, the Liberals have had no difficulty in maintaining their primacy. The party workers attribute this continued success to superior organization on both the provincial and county levels. The Liberal constituency executives meet periodically and their supporters in the various polling districts are ready to spring into action at a moment's notice. If nothing else, the sharing of the lower levels in the allocation of the local patronage requires the Liberal poll organizations to maintain a coherent existence. Normally the Conservatives have possessed nothing like the same organization. In the intervals between elections their only activity has been the annual meetings of the provincial and constituency associations and their organization at the polling division level has been non-existent or at least quiescent in most counties. Yet, when an election is called, they have usually been able to enlist a sufficient number of the old faithful to provide at least the semblance of a contest in every constituency. Generally their only solace after the counting of the ballots on election night has been to register surprise at the size of their popular vote despite the strength of the contending forces.

Often, of course, the disposal of patronage, if handled maladroitly by the local organization, may be a source of dissension and redound to the Liberals' disadvantage. Any leakages from this source, however, have been more than counterbalanced by the complete assurance with which the Liberal workers have made the rationalization that their participation in the electoral process is designed, not to provide personal gratification, but to ensure a great public good—the retention in office of a Liberal government. Yet their ability to reason in this manner has stemmed beyond doubt from the good, if not always spectacular, leadership which they have steadily enjoyed. Thus the strength of their organization, like their electoral success, has, in reality, been more effect than cause.

Good political leadership consists, above all, in making the most of every opportunity. Unfortunately for the Conservatives the ablest of their leaders have had to contend with difficulties completely beyond their effective control. In contrast, fate seems to have conspired to lavish realizable opportunities upon their Liberal counterparts, and they have capitalized upon their good fortune to the full. This explains, in large measure, why three men, Fielding, Murray, and Macdonald, have led the party for 58 of the last 73 years, held the premiership for 55 years, and never suffered an electoral defeat.

By his own admission, Murray refused to place himself in the vanguard of public opinion and to persuade it to accept policies which he conceived to be conducive to the provincial interest. "New ideas cropped up from time to time," he said, "and it was the duty of the government to discern the wishes of the public and to meet those wishes as occasion demanded."[18] His opponents were wont to attribute his political success to his "systematic use of legislative and executive power for personal, party and corrupt purposes,"[19] and it is true that under his direction the executive machinery was adapted to a form which enabled the government to rid itself of some of its responsibilities, the Legislative Council was closely geared to Liberal party strategy, and the Legislature was unostentatiously called upon to rearrange municipal districts and to alter the tenure of election revisers whenever the Liberals appeared to be placed at a disadvantage in provincial elections. But nothing more was required at the time, since Murray's chief opponent, Charles Tanner, seldom offered constructive proposals for the conduct of the provincial business and usually contented himself with criticism purely for the sake of criticism.

Nevertheless the Murray administration was continually on the down grade after 1901. By 1916 the Conservatives had increased their percentage of the popular vote to 48.8 and a shift of 300 votes in key constituencies would have upset the government. Four years later the Liberals polled less than 45 per cent of the popular vote, and managed to cling to office only because of the division of the opposition votes between the Farmer-Labourites and the Conservatives. Fortunately for them, however, the downfall of their worn-out and discredited administration in 1925 coincided with a combination of economic ills which would have upset any government. Hence they were able to undertake the work of rebuilding while their opponents were obliged to cope with problems which were insoluble through their own resources.

Under Angus L. Macdonald the Liberals secured once more the Fielding type of leadership. On his assumption of office in 1933 he proclaimed the Old Age Pensions Act, which his predecessors had enacted but left dormant on the statute book, and embarked upon an ambitious programme of hard-surfacing the trunk roads. At the outset he had no guarantee that the provincial revenues could sustain the new services, but eventually the upturn of the business cycle permitted a type of governmental services which the province had hitherto not enjoyed. To the electorate he consistently expressed the view that no government ought to be content with the mere routine of ad-

[18]*Assembly Debates*, 1906, 114.
[19]Excerpt from the Conservative manifesto of 1906 quoted in the *Halifax Herald*, May 25, 1906.

ministration and that all its departments should give real leadership in their respective spheres.[20] But while Angus L. Macdonald and George Murray differed markedly in their conceptions of leadership, each possessed in abundance the personal attributes which appeal to an electorate. As a result, the apt analysis of the *Chronicle* in 1916 has been more than once applicable to the political situation: "King Charles once said to his brother James Duke of York:—'James, the people of England will never behead me to make room for you.' Similarly, it may be said that the people of Nova Scotia will never turn down the Honourable George H. Murray . . . to make room for Mr. Charles Tanner and his incurable 'quibblership.' "[21] These factors have combined to make the problem of leadership a difficult and, in fact, an insoluble one for the Conservatives. It is rendered all the more trying because not a single riding can be counted upon to provide a safe haven for any Conservative candidate. While the Liberal leadership is automatically equivalent to the premiership and therefore attracts men of the highest capabilities, the rival party can offer no such alluring prospects. An individual of moderate means may be persuaded to neglect his own affairs for a time in the slim hope of capitalizing upon a change in public opinion, but eventually he has no choice but to lay down the burden. The valedictory of L. W. Fraser in 1946 might well have been pronounced by several of his predecessors:

A Leader, if he is properly to lead, must lead both usefully and hopefully. You are the judges as to whether I have or can lead usefully but I alone must be the judge as to whether I can lead hopefully. In view of the results in the [last] two elections . . . I am forced to the conclusion that I can no longer lead this party hopefully and that leaves me only one course to follow.[22]

Others before him had likewise given up in despair. Thompson had accepted a judgeship; Cahan had gone to the Commons; John F. Stairs had failed even to reach the floor of the Assembly although he tried twice;[23] and Tanner had been elevated to the Senate after undergoing more than fifteen years of changing vicissitudes of fortune which had culminated in a near victory for his party at a time when he was experiencing personal defeat. The single consolation to a prospective leader is that the party is not a hard taskmaster, for despite its dismal

[20]See excerpts from the Liberal manifesto of 1937 quoted in the *Halifax Chronicle*, June 15, 1937.
[21]*Acadian Recorder*, June 15, 1916.   [22]*Halifax Chronicle*, Feb. 22, 1946.
[23]See *Acadian Recorder*, March 5, 1897.

record it has deposed only one leader against his own wish and consent.

The only two Conservative leaders who acted as premier between 1882 and 1956—Rhodes and Harrington from 1925 to 1933—were not satisfied with the negative roles of their Conservative predecessors, Holmes and Thompson. They cleaned up the laxity in administration inherited from their predecessors, dispensed with the services of an outmoded second chamber, reorganized the executive branch in accordance with modern concepts by creating three new departments, and introduced pensions for teachers and allowances for widowed mothers. But none of their innovations was of a character to capture the public imagination and during their last three years of office the unrelieved blackness of the province's financial prospects precluded their entrance into new fields which might have gained the indelible stamp of public approval.

The result is that the political history of the province since 1925 has repeated much of the cycle of events after 1878. The Conservative victories in 1925 and 1928 actually redounded to their own disadvantage. For more than two decades they had the unenviable task of defending their record in office as compared with that of their successors under completely altered circumstances. While the logic of comparing the financial records of governments whose revenues were so grossly disparate was dubious, the psychological basis was sound and it was pressed to the point of monotony. The electorate was persuaded by sheer repetition that Conservative leadership was inherently deficient and that Conservative governments could do little but harm, Liberal governments nothing but good. The Conservatives, said Premier Macdonald, were "condemned to an eternity of hopeless effort for misdeeds and errors of judgment in the past."[24]

Until recently the method of choosing the party leaders was itself related directly to electoral success since a leadership convention was convened only as a means of rescuing a party from the political doldrums. It was not until 1930, as the sequel to two electoral defeats, that the Liberals held their first convention. Under dramatic circumstances it hearkened to "the clarion call of the young Liberals" and chose Angus L. Macdonald. The *Chronicle*'s prophecy that "an historic episode . . . was being enacted"[25] proved correct, for the new leader was soon to achieve the same personal ascendancy over his party, the government, and the province as his predecessors. After a wartime tour of duty in the federal cabinet a second convention re-elected him

[24]*Halifax Chronicle-Herald*, March 25, 1950.
[25]*Halifax Chronicle*, Oct. 2, 1930.

as leader and the Liberals continued to win elections on such slogans as "all's well with Angus L." On his death Harold Connolly assumed the premiership in a caretaker capacity until another convention chose Henry Hicks as leader on September 10, 1954. Since 1945, therefore, the Liberals have used the convention as a regular, rather than as an exigent device.

For the Conservatives, leadership conventions have long been an accepted practice, but an unsuccessful one until recently. In 1948 their sixth convention chose Robert L. Stanfield, who was in a position to devote to his new duties the time which they required. Under his direction the party improved its standing in the elections of 1949 and 1953, and on October 30, 1956, it staged a mild political revolution when, for the first time in its history, it won an election under non-crisis conditions. Its previous experience had been that electoral successes which resulted from economic recession were likely to be Pyrrhic victories. In such cases the ills responsible for an overthrow of the Liberals could hardly be remedied within five years and might even be accentuated, and thus another link would be forged in the chain of evidence that Conservative governments are wanting in capacity. But since the two old parties agree broadly upon what governments ought to do and since Liberal governments generally perform these functions at least reasonably well, the Conservatives normally find themselves reduced to the ferreting out of minor misdeeds and until 1956 this role had proved to be more a public service than a key to electoral success.

Except for one-party dominance, the Nova Scotian party system exhibits little that is unusual. Normally the Liberals constitute the government, and the Conservatives serve to prevent an abuse of power on their part by questioning their acts and by standing prepared to form an alternative government. The critic's role is often inadequately performed, however, because the members to the left of Mr. Speaker constitute little more than a corporal's guard. Nevertheless, the spirit of competition which infuses life into the party struggle continues with little diminution, and a relatively small shift in the popular vote can tip the balance at any time and bring in the opposing party.

A second function of parties—that of adjusting the conflicting claims of religious, racial, occupational, and sectional interests in the society so as to secure sufficient support to constitute an effective government —is much less significant in the provincial than in the national sphere. The one racial minority—the French Acadian—normally has no special viewpoint upon the major public issues, and in any case its interests were adequately protected by the Acadian minister without portfolio who was included in all ministries between 1896 and 1948. The principal religious issue has long been rendered politically innocuous by permitting the local school boards to decide what privileges a specific religious faith is to possess within the public school system.[26] Much more difficult to adjust—and a crucial problem of practical politics since 1800—has been the allocation of the public expenditures among the various sections and counties.[27] The parties also cater to interests other than geographical. While the temperance organizations which once constituted the most watchful interest[28] now operate with diminished influence, the Union of Nova Scotia Municipalities has retained all its old prestige. Certainly it acts as a powerful influence in maintaining the status quo in municipal organizations, and no party would advocate substantial changes in local government if it offered vigorous opposition.[29] The other organizations which present briefs to the cabinet are far less influential and often defeat their own ends by the extravagance of their claims. All in all the parties seldom operate in the *milieu* of a vigorous expression of public opinion or attempt to mould public opinion to novel undertakings or points of view.

Since 1900, however, the advent of a limited industrialism has required them to play some part in moderating class interests. Each has, in fact, been zealous in posing as the party of the little man while labelling its opponent as the friend of the big interests and ascribing to it the support of sinister forces which are always at work behind the scenes.[30] Since the Liberals have enjoyed the public confidence almost uninterruptedly, they have had to bear the brunt of the charge of catering to the invisible party. This was particularly true of the Murray régime (1896–1923) which spanned the period in which the province was having its first experience of serious clashes between the interests of capital and labour. Murray candidly admitted that his policy was to secure the greatest possible development of the province by making the burden of capital as light as possible, and though on the platform he espoused the interests of labour and the masses in the abstract, in practice he pursued a middle-of-the-road course which was more acceptable in the final analysis to capital than to labour, although not so much so as to alienate the support of the latter until

26*Infra*, 205–7.
27*Infra*, 205.
28*Infra*, 279.
29*Infra*, 309.
30See, for example, *Halifax Herald*, May 21, 1937.

1920. Indeed, by venturing no further into the field of social and labour legislation than was unavoidable and by tacitly accepting the principle of protective tariffs he convinced the leaders of the corporate and business world that nothing was to be gained by upsetting his government.[31]

The Conservatives naturally gibed at the Premier's change in attitude towards the National Policy, particularly as they had been crucified so often at its altar after 1878. "The fact is, Mr. Murray," they said, "that before 1896 you were anything and everything politically to suit the exigencies of party, and chiefly a seeming enemy—uncompromising enemy—of the policy of protection. You are now by reason of political exigency—an out and out protectionist."[32] Towards capital their own attitude was somewhat less reassuring than that of Murray. Their longtime leader Charles E. Tanner was outspoken in condemning corporate actions that he considered pernicious to the provincial interest, while his supporters were highly critical of the Liberals for having "given away to their political pets, or bartered for a mess of pottage, nearly all the great Public Utility Franchises of the People, such as coal, minerals, light, power, transportation, and telephone privileges."[33] But after the election of a Conservative government in 1925 the shoe was on the other foot. Its critics expressed amazement at the precipitate cutting off of the flood of crocodile tears against corporate tyranny. More explicitly they accused the new administration of restricting the export of pulpwood in the interests of its friends in the Mersey Paper Company, and of conferring special privileges upon a second group of its friends by permitting them to merge their associated companies with the parent Nova Scotia Light and Power Company "so that they [would] no longer stand separately on their own bottom."[34] Why, the critics asked, were " 'the lynx-eyed guardians of the people's rights' in former days . . . now so strangely silent?"[35]

Since 1933 the attempt to identify a particular party with the big interests has become much less pronounced. Possibly both parties realize the futility of reviving a threadbare and meaningless argument now that it has become all too obvious that each of them counts considerable elements of Nova Scotian big business among its adherents. Certainly business itself is well aware that it has little to fear from the results of provincial elections. So it makes contributions to the

[31]See "Secret History of the Week," *ibid.,* Oct. 30, 1937.
[32]See the open letter of Tanner to Premier Murray, *ibid.,* Jan. 13, 1910.
[33]See manifesto of Tanner in *Morning Chronicle,* June 12, 1916.
[34]*Morning Chronicle,* March 20, 1933.
[35]*Ibid.,* March 17, 1933.

campaign funds of both the old parties, knowing full well that it will be permitted to conduct its activities in much the same way no matter which is successful.

Tactics such as the foregoing have played a considerable part in enabling the old-line parties to accommodate all the major provincial interests within their ranks. The only exceptions have been provided by the groups which were attracted to the Farmer-Labour movement after the First World War and to the C.C.F. movement of more recent date. The labour delegates who met in 1919 to establish a Provincial Federation of Labour were certain that the old-line parties had gone the limit in labour legislation since neither could proceed further without altogether alienating "the enormous interests of capital."[36] Hence within a year they proceeded to set up a Nova Scotian branch of the Independent Labour Party. Almost simultaneously the annual convention of the Nova Scotia Agricultural Association decided to establish a new party along the lines of the United Farmers of Ontario and New Brunswick, and the Farmers' Associations of the West. In April, 1920, it adopted the platform of the Canadian Congress of Agriculture as its policy and the constitution of the United Farmers of New Brunswick as its form of organization. The local farmers' groups cooperated with the Independent Labour Party during the provincial election of 1920 in presenting a single slate of Farmer-Labour candidates in the four industrial counties of Cape Breton, Pictou, Cumberland, and Halifax; and except in Hants County its candidates were not in conflict with those of the I.L.P.

Together the two groups polled 30.9 per cent of the popular vote and elected eleven members to the Assembly, but subsequently their fortunes declined as rapidly as they had mushroomed. By 1922 the membership of the United Farmers of Nova Scotia had fallen from 2,500 to 254, and the Labour party was undergoing a similar species of disintegration. The Conservatives, who invariably display striking powers of rejuvenation whenever their position as a second party is threatened, had reorganized by that time and afforded the best opportunity of displacing a government which was steadily alienating the labour vote. Hence in 1925 only ten third-party candidates ventured to contest seats and they polled only 2.8 per cent of the popular vote.

In its bid to become a provincial party, the C.C.F. has experienced a more moderate rise and decline. The decision of District 26 of the United Mine Workers of America to affiliate with it in 1938 provided it a solid basis upon which to build, but undoubtedly diminished its

[36]*Halifax Herald*, March 1, 1919.

chance of attracting support elsewhere. The party increased its popular vote from 7 per cent in 1941 to 13.6 per cent in 1945, but to date that has been its high-water mark. Even at its peak the C.C.F. failed to make a broad appeal to the electorate. In 1945, 90 per cent of its support came from the four counties which contain a substantial trade union vote and almost 50 per cent from Cape Breton County alone. In other counties the electorate still continues to be suspicious of a party with much philosophy and to support their fathers' and grandfathers' parties through thick and through thin. C.C.F. organizers may conduct an educational campaign by means of study clubs over long periods and then poll only a few hundred votes, while the old parties will rouse their quiescent organizations into activity a few weeks before polling day and without difficulty poll at least 40 per cent of the electorate. The present prospects are, therefore, that the successes of democratic socialism will continue to be confined to heavily unionized Cape Breton County, and even there the C.C.F. party ran a poor third in 1956.

Yet the limited success of a third party in one of eighteen counties ought not to be surprising. In Cape Breton the C.C.F. reaps the fruits of the seeds sown earlier by English trade unionists among the province's only large concentration of industrial workers, and finds less resistance than is normal from a considerable foreign-born element which is not traditionally attached to Nova Scotian Liberalism or Conservatism. But where such industrial concentrations do not exist, and where the population has long been established and few outsiders have been introduced over the course of generations, the hold of the old parties remains as secure as ever.

This state of affairs is further reinforced by the nature of the economy and the social structure. The economic development of the province up to now has not been such as to evoke any pronounced feelings of class-consciousness, and divisions based upon class have therefore no real political significance. Furthermore, there is no substantial economic group which, in the manner of the grain growers of Western Canada, is able to maintain a cohesive political existence by attributing the insecurity of its material position to dependence upon outside financial interests. For while the Nova Scotian primary producers may subsist in what Professor Macpherson describes as a state of "quasi-colonialism,"[37] their problems are so diffuse that combined action to improve their lot is rendered extraordinarily difficult.

The existence of a party which could appeal to the latent resentment

[37]C. B. Macpherson, *Democracy in Alberta* (Toronto, 1953), 245–7.

against the operation of federal policies has also proved to be impracticable even though some Nova Scotians have always questioned the value of federation. Whenever an opportunity presents itself, neither party hesitates to exploit this resentment to embarrass a government of the opposing party at Ottawa, but they have never carried their opposition to the point of jeopardizing the patronage, public works, and other hand-outs which the great milch cow at Ottawa can supply in bountiful measure. Certainly the Nova Scotian members of Parliament have followed a thoroughly conservative course, never resorting to the radical procedure of threatening to break up a government or even deviating from the party line to strengthen their bargaining position.

All in all, the old-line parties, to appropriate Lord Bryce's description of their American counterparts, "now continue to exist, because they have existed. The mill has been constructed and its machinery goes on turning, even when there is no grist to grind."[38] Furthermore, one of these parties, by the circumstances of history and its own unerring faculty for choosing leaders with popular appeal (and often with statesmanlike qualities), has in the past attracted such a large solid core of voters to its ranks and built up such a formidable organization that its electoral success is assured under any but the most unusual conditions. Yet, since the death of Angus L. Macdonald in 1954, the difference in relative strengths has not been so pronounced that some political event of significance, such as the provision of able and energetic leadership by a Conservative administration, might not alter the old balance and usher in a new era in provincial politics. This new era would be marked, however, not by any substantial change in the nature of the parties, but merely by their sharing more equally in the responsibility of governing.

[38] James Bryce, *The American Commonwealth* (New York, 1907), II, 24.

CHAPTER XII

THE LIEUTENANT-GOVERNOR

THE FULL EMERGENCE of a Governor entirely aloof from the party struggle dates back not to 1848 or 1867, but to 1871 when the Nova Scotian politicians had at last begun to accept the province's status as a part of the Dominion. For a very good reason the trying task of making the new federal system work smoothly in an anti-Confederation province was left to the Imperial soldier Hastings Doyle—no Nova Scotian Governor favourable to Confederation could have maintained harmonious relations with his ministry and no anti-Confederation one would have suited Ottawa.[1] Doyle's secretary, Harry Moody, paints a picture of a Governor, inept in the science of politics, confining his activities to the military and social duties which he could perform admirably with the help of a French cook and his Irish humour, and permitting Moody himself to chart the political course.[2] But whoever was the architect, the policy was that described by Doyle—"to steer my course by the pole-star of impartiality" and to permit the representatives of the people full latitude in "making such laws, expressing such opinions . . . as a regard for their own interests might counsel, and [the] constitution and the allegiance which we all owe to the Crown, might countenance."[3] By this means he prevented an admittedly dangerous situation from ever getting out of hand.

The outcome was that by 1871 the violence of the political struggle had begun to diminish, never to be raised to quite the same pitch it had reached during the terms of Harvey, Williams, and Doyle (1867–70), when the Governor's intervention or lack of intervention served equally well to identify him as a partisan and in the first two instances actually destroyed his neutral position. Like Harvey and Mulgrave, Doyle wanted no share in the normal business of government, and the Nova Scotian-born, Conservative-appointed, and hence pro-Confederation governors (1873–1900) who succeeded him fully understood that playing the part of the truly constitutional Governor

[1]Tupper had been instrumental in securing Doyle's appointment. See Doyle to Tupper, Dec. 28, 1872, Tupper Papers (P.A.C.), item 131, in which Doyle states: "I know *you* had more to do with my appointment of Lt. Governor than *any one else.*"
[2]H. Moody, "Political Experiences in Nova Scotia, 1867–9," *Dalhousie Review,* XIV (April, 1934), 67.   [3]*Acadian Recorder,* April 29, 1873.

afforded the best chance of their maintaining friendly relations with the Liberal, but no longer anti-Confederation ministries which held office almost continually until 1925. These circumstances helped to establish the new position of the Lieutenant-Governor as part of the unwritten constitution of the province.

The new attitude of the governors, combined with the infrequent adoption by their ministers of any course of action which could justify their interference, has served to prevent any constitutional issue of note involving the Lieutenant-Governor in the modern history of the province. Almost simultaneously with the falling into disuse of the Governor's exercise of intervention there passed his direct participation in the transactions of his Executive Council. Although Doyle appears to have attended the meetings of the Council as a matter of routine until January 17, 1873, the groundwork for the subsequent change had already been laid as the rough jottings which had hitherto provided the agenda for Council meetings gave way to a more elaborate "memorandum for Council" containing the fully drafted minutes and appointments to be approved by the Governor at the formal meeting of the Council. From that point it was but a step to the course adopted on January 20, 1873—the submission to Doyle of the proposed minutes signed by a quorum of the Council which, when initialed by him, were entered by the Clerk or his deputy in the Council Book.[4] After that date no Governor appears to have attended Council meetings in person and the communications between him and his Council took place through the leader of the government.

It had not been decided by 1871, however, to what extent the Lieutenant-Governor continued to be a true representative of monarchy and to what extent he had been relegated to the role of agent of the Dominion government. The circumstances surrounding Confederation in Nova Scotia raised this question earlier and more acutely than elsewhere. Even before the departure of Doyle,[5] the last Governor of the old school, the anti-Confederates delighted in singling out incidents which seemed to indicate the Governor's loss of status. Thus the withdrawal of the salutes to which he had previously been entitled and the removal of sentries from Government House were regarded as evidence that the British government did not recognize governors of

[4]At a later date strict formality was sometimes lacking. To a transmission of Aug. 17, 1893, which was signed by only four members of the Council, one short of a quorum, a pencil note is appended: "Another signature will be added before entering in Council Book"; while on Feb. 3, 1899, Lieutenant-Governor Daly himself was forced to make the notation: "Please have other signatures added."

[5]The *Recorder* (May 7, 1873) mournfully described the event as "the severing of the last link which connected Nova Scotia with England."

Canadian appointment.[6] Their worst fears (or hopes) were confirmed by Sir John Macdonald's contention—a natural one for a person who hoped to relegate the provincial governments to municipal status—that, since the powers of the lieutenant-governors were simply those conferred by the British North America Act, they possessed "no right to deal with matters of prerogative as representatives of the sovereign."[7]

Some anti-Confederates like Attorney-General Martin Wilkins naturally proceeded to espouse the opposite and even more extravagant view that all the prerogative powers which had not been specifically conferred upon the Governor-General by the written constitution were still vested in the lieutenant-governors.[8] But the Nova Scotian exponents of the enhancement of the Governor's status and of the executive authority of the provincial governments were of comparatively minor calibre compared with Premier Mowat of Ontario. For two decades he contended that many prerogative duties devolved upon the Lieutenant-Governor by the very nature of his office and that the executive government which the B.N.A. Act vested in the Queen included that of both the Dominion and the provinces.[9] By 1892 the courts had accepted unequivocally this view of things;[10] in effect, they recognized the appointment of a Lieutenant-Governor by the Governor-General-in-Council as an act of the Crown, and he was accordingly "as much the representative of [the Sovereign] for all purposes of provincial government as the Governor-General himself [was] for all purposes of Dominion Government."

Nevertheless the course of constitutional development has been to destroy some of the analogy between the Governor-General and the Lieutenant-Governor, since the former has been denuded of his capacity as an Imperial officer, while the latter remains in a very real sense a Dominion officer whose conduct is continually subject to review by the Governor-General-in-Council. On two occasions this dual capacity threatened to cause trouble in Nova Scotia. The central character in the first episode was Sir John A. Macdonald, who was somewhat inclined to regard his appointees to the governorship as his special instruments and who was by no means averse to using them to pull his own political chestnuts out of the fire. Hence his gratuitous

6*Ibid.*, Jan. 27, 1869.
7W. E. Hodgins, comp., *Dominion and Provincial Legislation, 1867–1895* (Ottawa, 1896), 656.
8See Wilkins to Moody, May 23, 1868, Lieutenant-Governor's Correspondence, 1868.
9*Dominion and Provincial Legislation, 1867–1895*, 117.
10*Maritime Bank* v. *Receiver General* [1892], A.C. 437.

(but unheeded) advice to Lieutenant-Governor Richey not to be derelict in his duty as a Dominion officer by permitting his Liberal administration a snap election upon the repeal of Confederation was
not surprising. Nor was his offer to support this allegedly improper
ground for a dissolution by the whole weight of the Dominion government.[11]

On the second occasion the initiative came from a Lieutenant-
Governor who took advantage of his role of Dominion officer to avoid
personal responsibility. His Conservative ministry had communicated
its intention of submitting for his approval the appointment of a
number of legislative councillors in excess of the normal maximum of
twenty-one, its object being to vote the upper House out of existence.[12]
This raised serious considerations, for although the cabinet was supported by an opinion of the Deputy Attorney-General that appointments above the number of twenty-one were valid, its constitutional
position was by no means on sure ground. The consequences might,
in fact, have been disastrous if a legislature, shorn of its upper chamber
by an illegal act, had attempted to perform the normal legislative
functions.

This circumstance appears to have been one in which a Lieutenant-
Governor might legitimately have counselled his ministers to withhold
their proposals until the questions at issue had been judicially determined, but instead he informed the Secretary of State at Ottawa that
he intended to approve them on a specific date unless he were given
instructions to the contrary by the Governor-General-in-Council.[13] By
that time a Dominion order-in-council had been passed directing him
to refuse his ministers' advice to appoint the additional councillors.[14]
Thus the cabinet at Ottawa undertook, in effect, to inject itself into a
purely provincial matter to prevent possible confusion in the governmental process. While the normal Liberal doctrine is that a province
should be permitted to suffer for the sins of its government within its
own sphere of action, undoubtedly Mr. King and his colleagues felt
impelled to adopt a supervisory role in this instance because it com-

[11]Sir Joseph Pope, *Correspondence of Sir John A. Macdonald* (Toronto, 1921),
379.

[12]For the constitutional background of this question see chap. xv. The *Chronicle*
(March 11, 1926) felt that the government's policy afforded "a great opportunity
to hold a grand re-union of all the defeated Tory candidates who are alive, who
have contested elections during the last forty years."

[13]The full correspondence between the Governor and Ottawa was published
in the *Halifax Herald*, March 17, 1926.

[14]The federal cabinet based its action upon a report of its law officers at
variance with that of the Deputy Attorney-General of Nova Scotia.

bined the merits of finding favour with the provincial wing of their own party without endangering themselves politically.

The Rhodes administration at Halifax found no fault with Lieutenant-Governor Tory's reference of its advice to Ottawa nor with the federal cabinet's subsequent instruction to the Governor, but it objected with some justification to Prime Minister King's premature disclosure to the Liberal leader in the Assembly of the Governor's dealings with the federal authorities. Premier Rhodes was appalled that a prime minister of Canada should be "so lacking in appreciation of constitutional procedure,"[15] while the *Herald* accused him of treating "the confidential communication of the Governor as an irresponsible politician might be expected to treat a piece of Sparks Street gossip."[16]

Although the possibility always exists that the Dominion cabinet may use the Lieutenant-Governor to subvert the normal constitutional relations between the Governor and his provincial executive, the political implications of this line of conduct, if not its general impropriety, are usually sufficient to prevent any blatantly indefensible cases of interference. Normally, therefore, the functions of the Lieutenant-Governor within his lesser orbit correspond closely to those of the Governor-General. Like him, he opens and prorogues each session of the Legislature with speeches which, since the time of Confederation at least, he has had no share in preparing; like him, he transmits annually to the Legislature estimates of expenditures which he has had no share in compiling; like him, in his capacity as an integral part of the Legislature, he gives an automatic assent to legislation which he has had no share in framing.

The old forms which were connected with these events have died hard in Nova Scotia. That was particularly true of the custom which called upon the members of the Assembly collectively to present the address in reply to the Speech from the Throne to the Governor. In 1893 the Conservative leader C. H. Cahan suggested the abandonment of a "formality done away with in England . . . and not observed anywhere else," but Premier Fielding, "a staunch conservative," deprecated any interference with the old customs and prerogatives.[17] Sometimes the practice became the object of newspaper witticisms.

After the opening, Mr. Speaker walked forth in all his glory,—including his magnificent wig,—and, followed by his faithful commoners, proceeded, some on foot, some in carriages, to storm Government house. . . . his honor

15*Halifax Herald*, March 11, 1926.
16*Ibid.*, March 12, 1926.   17*Acadian Recorder*, Jan. 21, 1893.

was not taken at any disadvantage. He had the gates open, and was armed with the answer, carefully indited on parchment or paper, which the constitution requires him to hand to Mr. Speaker after the speaker has delivered the commoners' address. One has to get up very early to catch the governor unprepared.

So, the ceremony concluded—and the constitution being saved from further breakage—Mr. Speaker led his faithful commoners back to the legislative halls, doffed the historic, though not the elegant looking wig— and after producing the little paper which the governor had given him assured the house that the constitution was without a crack.[18]

The practice survived the 43-year period of Liberal administrations, but the Conservative government which assumed office in 1925 swept it into the discard. Since then the task has been entrusted to "such members as are of the Executive Council."

In addition to his purely formal duties, the Lieutenant-Governor possesses those other powers of British chief executives, which, although they normally involve little or no discretion on his part, make his existence imperative even if he has only to deal with the emergencies which may arise from time to time in constitutional procedures. Above all, he must see that he has a responsible ministry. Prior to 1900 by virtue of the pre-Confederation Commissions, and since then by statute, the Executive Council has been "composed of such persons as the Lieutenant Governor from time to time thinks fit."[19] In practice the performance of this duty is confined to the selection of a first minister, but since the confusion which sometimes arises from a multiplicity of parties has been unknown in Nova Scotia, this has generally involved no personal discretion on the part of the Governor— his choice is restricted to the recognized leader of the successful party in an election, or the nominee of a retiring premier or a party convention in the period between elections.

The only difficulties have occurred when a party has been without a recognized leader or when the leadership has been in dispute. The last instance followed the election of 1925 in which the victor was E. N. Rhodes, who had been chosen by a joint assemblage of the provincial executive and the Conservative candidates to succeed W. L. Hall, who had been elected at a full-dress convention. The *Chronicle*, which was keenly aware that the publisher of the *Herald* had been active in securing Mr. Hall's removal, delighted in suggesting that the

18*Halifax Herald*, Feb. 20, 1908.

19See R.S. 1954, c. 89. The change occurred simply because the commissioners responsible for the Revised Statutes of 1900 undertook on their own initiative to put on a statutory basis a variety of matters which had hitherto rested on the prerogative or upon convention. See *Assembly Debates*, 1900, 20–8.

retiring Premier might not advise the Lieutenant-Governor to ask Mr. Rhodes to head an administration. Mr. Hall, it declared, was "deposed . . . by a mere group of Conservatives who had no authority from the Provincial Convention. . . . He is still the elected Leader of the Conservative party, and there is no constitutional obstacle or reason why he should not be called upon to accept the responsibility of forming the new Government."[20] But despite its apparent serious-ness, it clearly did not expect any recognition to be given to the vagaries which are associated with the transactions of the extra-legal political party and it therefore offered no criticism when the Lieutenant-Governor selected Mr. Rhodes as his first minister.

On two other occasions, both of which occurred during the days when the party leadership fell to one whose personal attributes won him recognition rather than to the formal choice of a party gathering, a victorious Liberal party found itself without an accepted leader. In each case the Governor turned to a former Executive Councillor of the majority party to constitute an administration, but neither choice —R. A. McHeffey in 1867 and Albert Gayton in 1882—won the ap-proval of the party caucus which was summoned to determine the composition of the ministry. While the details of these proceedings are somewhat obscure, the Governor had no alternative but to accept the leader[21] chosen by the caucus even though it meant the relegation of his own nominee to a subordinate position.

Whether the Governor would play the same role in appointing and dismissing his ministers individually and collectively as the usual practice had come to demand was not determined with certainty until 1884. The difficulty was that the legal guides in these matters— the pre-Confederation Commissions and Instructions—dated back to the time when a Councillor was the personal choice of the Governor and his removal required the approval of a majority of the Council; they had not contemplated an Executive Council which had its com-position determined by a first minister and which operated under a system of collective responsibility. So when Attorney-General Weeks was dismissed by the Governor in 1876, it was upon the advice, not of the Prime Minister, but of the whole Council.[22]

It required the unravelling of a constitutional "snarl"[23] in 1884 to decide once and for all that the normal constitutional practice was to

[20]July 2, 1925.
[21]Annand in 1867; Pipes in 1882.
[22]*Morning Chronicle*, Nov. 13, 1876.
[23]So described by Sir John A. Macdonald. See Pope, *Correspondence of Macdonald*, 316.

prevail in Nova Scotia. The issue on that occasion was the right of Premier Pipes to present his resignation and on the Governor's request[24] to nominate William Stevens Fielding as his successor,[25] apparently without the knowledge and certainly against the wishes of some members of the cabinet. Again, as in 1876, the viewpoint was expressed that the usual practice was not applicable to Nova Scotia because the Lieutenant-Governor was bound in such matters to follow the advice, not of a so-called "premier,"[26] but of a majority of his Executive Council. This time, however, Governor Richey, while admitting a degree of informality in his mode of proceeding, acknowledged that the resignation of the first minister automatically meant the dissolution of the ministry; that the retiring premier had the right, not to appoint, but to recommend his successor if the Governor requested his advice; and that the premier-designate was in no wise restricted in naming the members of the new ministry.[27] He was able, moreover, to give this unequivocal recognition to the English constitutional procedure without introducing any conflict with the pre-Confederation prerogative instruments, which once again permitted new arrangements to be effected within the executive branch of government by means of purely conventional understandings.

No Governor has had to deal with a ministry guilty of corruption or gross dereliction of duty, nor has he had to take action on his own initiative against individual ministers. One Governor was advised unofficially, however, as a result of the long delay in getting rid of an Attorney-General who had been barred from cabinet meetings because of the idiosyncrasies of his personal conduct, to call to his Council men whose presence would not be an insult.[28] On two other occasions a Governor would have been led to depart from strict

[24]Macdonald feared that Governor Richey, in requesting Pipes' advice, might have "given away . . . the only *personal* prerogative remaining to the Sovereign," i.e., "the absolute, uncontrolled right to choose a Premier." *Ibid.*

[25]Pipes is reputed to have indicated his intention to resign to Fielding, and on the latter's query as to his successor, to have referred him to II Samuel 12:7—"And Nathan said to David, Thou are the man. . . ."

[26]An office declared to be non-existent in Nova Scotia. For this position in full, see the letters signed "Nova Scotia" in the *Morning Herald*, July 19, 21, 23, 1884.

[27]Because the ministry had not lost the confidence of the Legislature, Richey merely requested the name of a suitable person to "further such arrangements as may be necessary in the reorganization of the Ministry." Richey to Pipes, July 15, 1884, in Lieutenant-Governor's Correspondence, 1884–5. But since Fielding was permitted a free hand in the selection of ministers and the allocation of portfolios, the Governor's course of action by no means constituted a substantial deviation from the accepted practice.

[28]*Morning Herald*, Nov. 10, 1876.

constitutional usage if he had followed the gratuitous advice of critics with their own axes to grind. Richey was correct in spurning the suggestions that he should warn Attorney-General J. W. Longley not to "grind out annexationist rubbish . . . in the columns of the two subsidized organs of the local government, [or] the province [would] be under the necessity of obtaining another attorney-general."[29] Equally judicious was J. D. McGregor's refusal to dismiss Attorney-General Daniels for allegedly using his official position to promote his private interests, because a royal commission subsequently cleared him of malfeasance and thereby indicated that the Governor's intervention could not have been justified during any stage of the proceedings.[30]

To what extent the Lieutenant-Governor's undoubted right to encourage and to warn his ministry has been and is exercised cannot be gauged with any assurance of certainty.[31] But the probability is that in a province which for three-quarters of a century has generally retained its premiers for lengthy periods and its lieutenant-governors for a single term the right has been seldom exercised. While there is evidence that it was still the custom in 1895 for the governor to be kept informed of governmental policy in other than routine matters,[32] it is doubtful if he now has more than a superficial acquaintance with the acts of his ministry.

None of the governors since Doyle has found it necessary on his own responsibility to refuse the advice of his ministers. Nor could they properly have intervened in those cases where their refusal to do so invited criticism. A. G. Archibald was clearly justified in accepting his ministers' advice not to publish the correspondence relating to the abolition of the Legislative Council until it had been brought to a

[29]*Ibid.*, Feb. 3, 1888.

[30]In this case the Murray administration was censured by its Conservative critics for improperly releasing 150,000 acres of Central Railway Company lands which it held under mortgage from the Halifax and Southwestern Railway Company, thereby permitting its friends to "deal with such lands with the object of personal gain." *Assembly Debates*, 1914, 737. Although the commission acquitted Daniels of wrong-doing, it considered him to be highly imprudent in placing himself in a position which might have "involved at some later day a possible conflict between his private interest and public duty."

[31]Its last disclosed use, which dates back to 1884, was undoubtedly sound—it was Governor Richey's suggestion that the procedure which had been adopted in one case under the Canada Temperance Act of having the same individual act both as the informer and convicting justice should not be allowed to become a precedent. Memorandum for the Executive Council, April 22, 1884, in Lieutenant-Governor's Correspondence, 1884–5.

[32]Fielding to Daly, June 20, 1895, in Lieutenant-Governor's Correspondence, 1895.

conclusion, despite the fulminations of the opposition that the delay was an act "worthy of the Star Chamber" and utterly "disastrous to the principles of Responsible Government."[33] He was equally correct in permitting a Conservative government to fill a few offices following its defeat in 1882 since he had accorded a Liberal government the same right in 1878 in the case of appointments which were, if anything, less pressing. In both instances, however, he was careful to decline others which could in no sense be considered urgent.[34]

The most recent criticisms of a Lieutenant-Governor stemmed from a somewhat similar incident—the approval by J. Robson Douglas of four pre-dated appointments to the Legislative Council which were not gazetted until the day of the provincial election of 1925. Fearful that the popular will might be defeated through the medium of the non-elective chamber, the Conservatives blamed the Governor for permitting "the balance to be weighted down in favour of a Government that was absolutely out of touch with public opinion."[35] Yet their attempt to invoke as a precedent the Governor-General's refusal to confirm a number of non-emergency post-election appointments in 1896 clearly failed, for no constitutional student would agree that a government which has still to be judged by the electorate and which is under no cloud of grave irregularities ought to be deprived of its power of appointment.[36]

The intervention of the Lieutenant-Governor in legislative matters has experienced similar disuse, but legally at least his legislative powers remain unimpaired, and without an amendment of the British North America Act his status as a integral part of the Legislature cannot be altered even with his own consent.[37] Section 90 permits him to adopt one of three courses towards the bills which are presented for his approval: he may give or withhold his assent in the name of the Governor-General,[38] or he may reserve a bill for the signification of the pleasure of the Governor-General. Since 1867, however, only nine bills have been denied assent or reserved, and none since 1883 when

---

[33]*Acadian Recorder*, April 7, 1880.

[34]*Morning Herald*, July 22, 1882. Archibald stated his position thus to Premier Thompson on July 4, 1882: "I think the Country can get on for a while with the Justices already created, and with other officers of a similar kind, and I must do with your friends as I did with their opponents four years ago when under similar circumstances I refused to appoint Justices." See Thompson Papers (P.A.C.), item 2884.

[35]*Halifax Herald*, June 27, 1925.

[36]See *Morning Chronicle*, July 3, 1925.

[37]*In re Initiative and Referendum Act*, [1919] A.C. 935.

[38]S. 90 when read in conjunction with s. 55.

the courts were still in the initial stages of defining the legislative fields of the Dominion and the province.

The first case of reservation had to do with a private member's bill which was designed to prevent the militia from leaving the province without the assent of the Lieutenant-Governor-in-Council. In this instance it was neither the authorities at Ottawa nor Governor Doyle who assumed the initiative. Rather it was the Governor's private secretary Harry Moody who, because of the magnified importance which he attached to the bill, induced the federal authorities to advise that the Governor's assent should be made contingent upon the approval of his Council and the opinion of Attorney-General Martin Wilkins that it fell within the provincial legislative powers. It was he, too, who was so insistent upon receiving a categorical affirmative or negative opinion upon its validity that Wilkins finally admitted the bill was of "so little consequence that the Attorney General would recommend the Lieut. Governor to be guided entirely by his own inclinations and assent or not as he pleases."[39]

One of the two other reserved bills received the Governor-General's assent after the courts had ruled that a similar act of another provincial legislature was within the provincial competence,[40] while the federal Minister of Justice concurred in the propriety of reserving the third; otherwise, he said, there could have been no course but disallowance.[41]

These last two cases of reservation and all the six cases of refusal of assent[42] occurred during the governorship of A. G. Archibald (1873–83), himself a former Attorney-General, and for that reason more qualified than any of his predecessors and most of his successors to play an active role in the legislative process. Although Archibald considered the bills from which he withheld his assent either as unworkable or as *ultra vires* in part of the Legislature, he was careful not to use his powers until he had made certain that no legitimate objection would be taken by either the Dominion or provincial governments. His personal assumption of the initiative enabled him to avoid the objection of Sir John A. Macdonald to the procedure which had been adopted in Ontario on the Orange Incorporation Bills—the ministerial use of the Lieutenant-Governor's legislative power to defeat the will

[39]Wilkins to Moody, Sept. 19, 1868, in Lieutenant-Governor's Correspondence, 1868.

[40]The bill was entitled "an Act to facilitate arrangements between Railway Companies and their creditors." The courts decided that a similar measure of the Quebec Legislature did not, in its essence, relate to bankruptcy and insolvency. See *Dominion-Provincial Legislation, 1867–95*, 484–8.

[41]*Ibid.*, 504.　[42]Two in 1875, one in 1879, one in 1880, and two in 1883.

of the Legislature and to pass a legitimate provincial responsibility to the Governor-General-in-Council.[43]

The other and more serious objection might have been that his failure to approve part of the cabinet's legislative programme appeared to be a vitiation of responsible government and, in the event of his ministers' disapproval, would have placed him under the necessity of being "prepared . . . to form a new ministry, by whom the act proposed could be constitutionally advised and justified to both houses."[44] He countered this difficulty, however, by making his refusal of assent dependent upon the advice of his Executive Council. For example, in dealing with the bill entitled "an act to amend the Law relating to Witnesses and Evidence," he addressed a memorandum to the Executive Council suggesting that he should be advised not to sign it, and "if time permit, in this session, if not in a subsequent session a Bill be introduced free from the defects of this one."[45] While this course of action involved the logical absurdity of a cabinet securing the passage of legislation and then advising a Governor to withhold his signature, it was perhaps the best way out of a difficulty caused by the Governor's ability to detect flaws which escaped the Attorney-General and his law officers. Certainly it obviated any possibility of the Governor losing the support of his ministers, for once they acquiesced in his refusal of assent they were compelled to accept the responsibility for the act and, if necessary, to defend it at the succeeding session of the Legislature.[46]

The failure of Archibald's successors to make a similar use of their powers has been the result of no strange freak of circumstances. Few have possessed the legal training needed to detect the imperfections which evade the scrutiny of the Legislature, while a general improvement in the drafting of legislation and the more precise definition of provincial legislative powers by a long series of judicial decisions have diminished the possibility of technical or constitutional defects. In fact, unless somethng occurs which causes the Legislature to depart from its traditional avoidance of radicalism in its enactments, it may

[43]*Dominion and Provincial Legislation, 1867–95*, 104–5.

[44]Alpheus Todd, *Parliamentary Government in the British Colonies* (London, 1894), 587.

[45]Folio in P.A.N.S. marked "Unpassed Bills, 1880–5."

[46]Archibald was also not averse to giving uninvited opinions upon the advisability of particular bills and the need for amending existing statutes. See *Thompson Papers*, items 2508 and 697. In addition, he advised Thompson to make a strong protest against Sir John Macdonald's conception of the prerogative after the Dominion government threatened to disallow the provincial legislation on escheats. *Ibid.*, item 2454.

safely be concluded that the Governor's assent to all bills will continue to be given with the same automatic regularity as in all cases since 1883.

The almost complete abandonment by the Governor of any active participation in the executive and legislative fields by no means applies to the social sphere, for Government House still continues to be the centre of high society. The prestige which is attached to invitations from that quarter is illustrated by the indignation of one city resident at being excluded from a garden party to which Lieutenant-Governor Daly had invited eleven hundred guests. "Merchants and citizens," he reminded the Governor, "naturally look toward Govt. House as the door of entrance into social life."[47] There is a suspicion that this individual is to be included in that large group which measures the success of a Lieutenant-Governor by the extent and the character of his entertaining. Both Doyle and Archibald won praise for dispensing the duties of hospitality with liberality, while J. D. McGregor's exclusion of wines from his table in conformity with the principles of his private life was anything but popular and failed to establish a precedent.

Invitations to dinner at Government House, which in the early days had been confined to the military and naval commanders, the Council of Twelve, the judges, and the Bishop, had been widened by Confederation to include the city aldermen, but not until the term of A. G. Jones (1900–6) did the old exclusiveness give way to a democratic simplicity, the constant aim of which was to "gather around the Governor for social intercourse the representatives of all that was best in the business, professional, industrial and official life of the Province."[48] The process was carried further, too far in the opinion of some, by his successor D. C. Fraser. At the New Year's levee in 1907 the callers at Government House were not divided, as from the early history of the province, by "the invidious distinctions of the much discussed 'private entree' into the elect few 'and many others.' "[49] This alteration stood the test of time, but a second—the substitution of the frock coat and silk hat for the Windsor uniform and cocked hat at the opening ceremonies of the Legislature in 1907—was not continued beyond Fraser's term of office even though the ultra democrats did not conceal their criticism of his two successors for returning to a custom "foreign to this democratic land and contrary to the spirit of our

[47]See letter to Daly, Aug. 21, 1894, in Lieutenant-Governor's Correspondence, 1894.
[48]*Morning Chronicle*, March 16, 1906.
[49]*Halifax Herald*, Jan. 2, 1907.

people."[50] More recent proposals to reduce the last bits of colour at the opening ceremonies were equally unsuccessful. This time Premier Macdonald, after noting that a part of the provincial press favoured the adoption of Premier Hepburn's innovations in Ontario—the absence of a guard of honour and an almost complete lack of ceremony— deprecated the levelling of shots at the office of Lieutenant-Governor. "Where is there," he asked, "a greater example of democracy than in the Mother Country which adheres jealously to traditions and yet is alive to the needs of the present? . . . I don't think we can go far wrong in following the example of the Mother Country."[51]

Although the Lieutenant-Governor is the representative of the Sovereign for all purposes of provincial government, no particle of patriotic sentiment attaches to the holder of the office; the best he may hope for is that by upholding the dignity of his position he may command general respect. The office should go, Premier Macdonald once stated, to men who have a record of "long and distinguished public service or have given of their talents to some form of general endeavor,"[52] and that course has invariably been followed. Until 1916 all the appointees were active political partisans. Of the first eight beginning with Howe in 1873, seven had been members of the House of Commons, and the eighth, J. D. McGregor (1910–15), a defeated candidate for the Commons and a senator when he assumed the governorship. It was therefore an innovation when Prime Minister Borden appointed a personal friend, MacCallum Grant, who had on no occasion been an active participant in the political arena. Grant and his lady contributed so much to making Government House the centre of every good work and the governorship a popular institution that the King government adopted the unprecedented course of appointing him—a supporter of another political party—to a second term of office.[53] Possibly it was his complete success which explains why six of his nine successors have likewise not played an active part in politics.

Active claimants for the office of Governor are normally not numerous and on a few occasions the term of the incumbent has had to be extended until a successor could be secured. The reasons for this lack of enthusiasm are obvious. Few can afford the office and those who possess the financial resources to perform its functions adequately

[50]*Morning Chronicle*, Feb. 24, 1911.
[51]*Halifax Herald*, March 3, 1938.
[52]*Halifax Chronicle*, March 7, 1940.
[53]*Halifax Chronicle*, March 22, 1922.

are not always anxious to assume a position in which one of the more successful holders is reputed to have spent $30,000 in excess of his remuneration. The acceptance of the governorship necessitates, in addition, the abandonment of any previous occupation and to this fact may undoubtedly be attributed the advanced age of most of the governors. The inclinations of most men do not move them to exchange with alacrity the role of an active participant in business life or the carefree devotee of unfettered retirement for that of chief patron of the learned and charitable societies and chief layer of cornerstones.

Even those who accept the office are not always satisfied with their lot. One who found the financial burden beyond his means sought refuge in resignation, while the family of another discovered that the office did not bring the prestige which had been anticipated. Until recently the condition of Government House itself was no inducement to prospective tenants, for the intermittent criticism of the economically minded Nova Scotian assemblyman against the cost of its upkeep had meant that the driblets of public funds provided for its maintenance were totally inadequate.[54] The buoyant revenues of the post-World War II period placed the government in a position to remedy the ill, and dismissing the suggestions of the C.C.F. assemblymen that the building should be converted into a museum or art gallery for the public and that a more modest residence should be provided for the chief executive, the Macdonald administration proceeded to rehabilitate Government House.[55] Hence it is now a fitting edifice from which to carry out the legislative and executive functions which by constitutional development have become largely routine and the social duties which have, in the eyes of many, become the sole reason for the continuance of the office of Governor.

[54]In 1942 the Minister of Public Works described its bathrooms as inferior to "what you would have in your own house." *Halifax Herald*, March 17, 1942.
[55]See *Halifax Herald*, April 22, 1948.

CHAPTER XIII

THE EXECUTIVE COUNCIL

ALTHOUGH in theory the executive power of Nova Scotia is still vested in the Lieutenant-Governor, in practice it passed to other hands in 1848. The individuals who actually wield it receive varying appellations in their collective capacity—most frequently the cabinet, but sometimes the government or the administration. Like its counterpart at Ottawa, the Nova Scotian cabinet (or government or administration) has no legal existence as such. To exercise its authority in a form recognizable in law, it must assume its official title, the Executive Council, which is the Nova Scotian counterpart of the Canadian Privy Council.

There are distinct differences, however, between the Canadian and Nova Scotian practices. Although Canadian privy councillors, like the British, retain their title during life, they by no means continue to share in the wielding of the executive power; that is left to the active part of the Privy Council which the Governor-General on the advice of his Prime Minister summons to advise him for the time being and which is identical in membership with the cabinet. In contrast, the Executive Council of Nova Scotia follows colonial usage; its members do not retain the title of executive councillor for life, and as occasion demands, present their resignations as executive councillors to the Lieutenant-Governor. Thus at any one time the Executive Council and the cabinet consist of the same individuals.

Moreover, while the Privy Council was instituted by the British North America Act, the Executive Council of Nova Scotia pre-dates the Canadian federation by twenty-nine years. Hence section 64 of the Act simply provided for the continuance of the provincial executive authority as it existed prior to Confederation subject to any modifications which were introduced by the Act itself. Since these changes, apart from restricting the executive authority, did no more than vest the appointment of the Lieutenant-Governor in the Governor-General-in-Council rather than in the Sovereign directly, the real effect of the section was to leave intact not only the clauses of the Commissions, the Instructions, and the provincial statutes which related to the executive function, but also the more subtle workings which were introduced as the concomitant of responsible government.

That clause of the Commission which set at nine the number of councillors who might be provisionally appointed by the Lieutenant-Governor proved to be the most controversial of all the provisions relating to the executive. Prior to 1900, a government's failure to maintain a full complement of members was invariably interpreted as a confession of weakness. This phenomenon may be traced directly to J. W. Johnston's inability or refusal to reconstruct his ministry after the withdrawal of the Reformers from the coalition government in 1843. "Our constitution required the Government to consist of nine members," said a leader of the opposition in 1884. "For a year it had consisted of only eight members; there was no reason on the same principle why it should not as well consist of six members or even one."[1] A little earlier Premier Pipes had considered this criticism sufficiently serious to refer it to his legal advisers,[2] but despite their opinion that the Executive Council need not be kept at its maximum, intermittent objections continued to be raised on this score until the Revised Statutes of 1900 finally set the matter at rest.[3]

Today few of the original provisions of the Commission which created the Executive Council[4] remain unaltered, but the fundamental one that there shall be an Executive Council still rests on the prerogative. The most far-reaching changes were introduced by the three devices which were used to adapt the Council to responsible government: dispatches from the Colonial Secretary explaining the new relationship between the Governor and his Council; convention requiring that all its members should secure a seat in one branch of the Legislature; and a statutory enactment prescribing which of the public officers should sit in the Executive Council to ensure adequate control over the entire governmental machinery. The resort to legislation in the last instance having established a precedent, that means was employed to make the Commissioner of Crown Lands a responsible minister in 1871,[5] and to reduce the ministers with office to three during the financial difficulties of the late seventies.[6] Thereafter

[1] *Assembly Debates*, 1884, 221.
[2] *Ibid*, 35.
[3] *Infra*, 188.
[4] That of Lord Durham dated Feb. 6, 1838.
[5] 34 Vic., c. 7. The intent was to create a responsible spokesman for a department which had long been subjected to criticism because of its failure to reduce the large number of unsettled land claims.
[6] In 1877 the Commissionership of Crown Lands was conferred upon the Attorney-General *ex-officio*. See 40 Vic., c. 3. The sharp diminution in the business of the department provided an additional argument for the change. The Attorney-General was selected to assume the new duties partly because much of the department's remaining business consisted of highly controversial

the number and title of ministers remained unaltered for forty years.

Two significant features stand out in the constitution of the Council during this extended period. The first was its complete inflexibility. Even before 1867 all premiers were severely restricted in determining the composition of their cabinets. Two new acts which appeared in the Revised Statutes of 1900 added the finishing touches. The Public Service Act[7] defined the functions of each department and designated the public officer, Provincial Secretary, Attorney-General, or Commissioner of Public Works and Mines, who was to preside over each. The Executive Council Act[8] put in statutory form a stipulation hitherto conventional—the Lieutenant-Governor was to choose the three ministers with office from his Executive Council—and rendered more explicit another which had been implied in the pre-Confederation Commissions—the Council was to have a maximum of nine members.

Although the strait-jacket with which these statutes circumscribed the provincial cabinet was little different from that which now confines its counterpart at Ottawa, it was none the less a limiting factor of no mean proportions. Implicitly, if not expressly, it prevented the Executive Council from establishing new departments or adding further departmental heads to its membership on its own initiative. It likewise precluded any variation in the combination of departments which were entrusted to the three ministers with office. The Attorney-General could not, for example, give up the commissionership of Crown Lands, which he held *ex officio*, to the Commissioner of Public Works in exchange for the Commissionership of Mines. Thus the rigid bar of statutory enactment prevented the Premier from effecting those transfers which the experience and the capabilities of individual ministers sometimes rendered expedient. There could be no more than three men, each of whom must fit into the unalterable grooves which had been defined in a day long past under circumstances which were no longer applicable.

More significant than the rigidity of the Council was the departure from the normal practice of increasing the number of ministers with

claims, and partly because the incumbent Attorney-General was highly conversant with the problems of the Land Department. *Assembly Debates*, 1877, 17. In 1878 the Provincial Secretary assumed the functions of the Provincial Treasurer whose duties had been light. See 41 Vic., c. 20. One Assemblyman had, in fact, once suggested that he "did not spend an hour a day in his office, taking the whole year, Sundays excepted." *Assembly Debates*, 1871, 192.

[7]R.S. 1900, c. 10.

[8]*Ibid.*, c. 9. This was the first statute which designated the Executive Council by name; previously reference had been made to "the members of the Provincial Administration for the time being." See, e.g., R.S. 1873, c. 14.

portfolio to cope with the expanding functions of government. Of all the provinces, Nova Scotia was the only one to reduce the number with which it entered Confederation. By the time it decided that three were insufficient Prince Edward Island alone retained a like number; in New Brunswick there were six and in all the other provinces seven or eight.[9] Yet the reason for this static condition was by no means financial. Rather it is to be found in the political philosophy of Premier George Murray who was the architect of government when the other provinces were pursuing a different course. It was he who extolled the Nova Scotia practice of setting up minor departments headed by experts subject only to the most general control by the three ministers with portfolio.

> . . . we took these men, enacted statutes and clothed them with jurisdiction and authority and that was why with these men we had been able to carry on Government with three departmental heads. Was it not better in the interest of the people, and wiser in respect to good government that the Ministers of the Crown should collect around them, not mere officials, but experts in the various departments, and let the people instead of having the judgment of a partisan . . . have men clothed with a fair measure of responsibility who, whatever the faults of the Government, could not be accused of being in political sympathy with this administration.[10]

This policy fitted in well with Murray's contention that no broad questions of policy existed in the limited provincial field that could provide a basis of division for parties. For that reason he saw little ground for a display of partisanship in the management of local affairs,[11] and to prove that his adherence to this point of view was more than academic, he delighted in singling out Conservatives who were administering important branches of the public service.[12] His critics refused to admit, however, that the Premier was not primarily a policy-making officer or that local administration was only a matter of personality. To them the argument was a subterfuge under the cover of which an astute politician was divesting himself of the responsibilities of his office. Murray, they alleged, had "put a 'buffer' between himself and every department of the public service. Let a member of the opposition, in his place in parliament, point to anything wrong in any of the departments, and the premier is on his feet ready to place the blame on some departmental head—or tail—

[9]See Appendix I.
[10]*Assembly Debates*, 1913, 291.
[11]*Ibid.*, 1909, 16.
[12]Two of his examples were Dr. MacKay, the Superintendent of Education, and Dr. Sinclair, the Inspector of Humane Institutions. See *Morning Chronicle*, Feb. 14, 1914.

who, he points out, is 'of tory antecedents,' and therefore can do no wrong, or if he has happened to do something wrong, the premier and his government are absolved from all blame"[13]

The result of this attitude—one not dissimilar to the Tory position before 1848—can best be illustrated by the nature of Murray's own duties in 1918. As first minister, he presided over the Council of Public Instruction which performed the ministerial duties of the Department of Education; as Provincial Secretary, he supervised a wide range of functions ranging from the incorporation of companies to the collection of municipal statistics, and was, in addition, *ex officio* Provincial Treasurer and King's Printer; finally, because of the practice of requiring the Provincial Secretary to oversee all the functions which had not been expressly assigned to other departments,[14] he exercised a general surveillance over three minor departments headed by the Secretary of Agriculture, the Secretary of Industries and Immigration, and the Provincial Health Officer, and in varying degrees over a large number of other officials and boards.[15] This state of affairs could exist only so long as Nova Scotians continued to expect the government to play a purely negative role in the working out of their destiny. By 1917 Murray himself acknowledged that three men were insufficient to attend to the expanding functions of governmental operations.[16] Since then the system has run the gamut from utter rigidity to almost complete flexibility. Four devices have played a part in the process.

The first was the amendment of the Public Service Act to permit the Governor-in-Council to create one or two new departments and to appoint a member of the Executive Council to preside over each.[17] It was this provision that was used to set up a Department of Natural Resources in 1925, a Department of Health in 1930, and a Department of Industry in 1939, each with a separate minister.

Another was the amendment of the Executive Council Act to remove the statutory limitation on its size.[18] Thus the Executive Council consisted of eleven members in 1953, eight in 1956, and might continue to vary in number at the Premier's discretion.

A third device was the creation of new departments and the separa-

---

[13]*Halifax Herald*, Feb. 17, 1914.

[14]See A. S. Barnstead, "Development of the Office of Provincial Secretary," *Collections of the N.S. Historical Society*, XXIV, 6.

[15]Such as the Inspector of Rural Telephones, the Game Commissioners, the Public Utilities Commission, and the Workmen's Compensation Board.

[16]See *Halifax Herald*, May 5, 1917. "He had not been able to leave the province but three times in ten years," said Murray, "and he thought the burden was too great to impose upon one man."

[17]7-8 Geo. V, c. 19.   [18]11-12 Geo V, c. 22.

tion of combined departments by specific statute. The first break with the past came with the establishment of a Department of Highways in 1917.[19] It was followed by a Department of Labour in 1932,[20] a Department of Municipal Affairs in 1935,[21] and a Department of Public Welfare in 1944,[22] the first to be administered by a cabinet minister whom the Governor-in-Council designated, the others by the Attorney-General and the Minister of Health respectively. Public Works, hitherto associated with Highways, became a separate department in 1955.

Finally, the statutory provisions which required some executive councillors with office to assume the administration of other departments were removed. Until 1946 the Minister of Public Health and the Provincial Secretary were each required by statute to administer a second department and the Attorney-General two additional departments;[23] then the Macdonald administration abolished the *ex officio* holding of portfolios in its entirety.[24] The new provision was put to immediate use, and in 1947 for the first time in almost seventy years the same individual was not acting in the dual role of Provincial Secretary and Treasurer, while the Attorney-General had relinquished an even longer tenure as administrator of the Crown lands. The process was carried further within the next three years by the appointment of individual ministers to head the Departments of Education and Municipal Affairs.

The cumulative result of the four devices has been the creation of fourteen separate departments which might be headed, if the Premier considered it desirable, by fourteen members of the Executive Council.[25] While this theoretical right is not likely to be used because some departments like Labour or Lands and Forests clearly do not warrant separate ministers at the moment, it does permit a first

[19]7-8 Geo V, c. 3. Premier Murray appointed the first Minister of Highways in 1918 but made him little more than a link between the cabinet and a bipartisan Provincial Highways Board which was entrusted with the full responsibility for maintaining and constructing highways. The Conservative government abolished the Board after its assumption of office in 1925. In 1939 Public Works was transferred from the Mines Department to become an integral part of the Highways Department. 3 Geo. VI, c. 56.

[20]22 Geo. V, c. 3.

[21]25-6 Geo. V, c. 5.

[22]8 Geo. VI, c. 2.

[23]In addition, the first minister, who was normally the Provincial Secretary, presided over the Council of Public Instruction.

[24]10 Geo. VI, c. 2. The change was effected during the consolidation of the Public Service Act.

[25]1 Eliz. II, c. 63, and 4 Eliz. II, c. 41.

minister to make any allocation of portfolios to whatever number of ministers he deems requisite. He may lighten the load for an inexperienced minister until he has become acclimatized to his new surroundings; make a reallocation of portfolios whenever a vacancy occurs to suit the training, the experience, and the capabilities of both the old and the new ministers; and establish one or two new departments on his own initiative at any time that he feels the public service requires it.

The considerations of race, religion, and geography which can never be neglected in the selection of a Dominion cabinet play only a minor role in the composition of the Nova Scotian Executive Council. Hence no premier needs to balance the intricate claims of varied groupings and to allot them representatives regardless of the qualifications of their candidates for high office. Nevertheless all the premiers keep the representative character of the cabinet broadly in view, and the modern tendency has been that, whenever feasible, at least one Executive Councillor shall be chosen from each of the six regions into which the province divides more or less naturally.[26] Normally the decisive nature of the general elections has ensured that the victorious party will elect one member of cabinet timbre in each of these regions, but occasionally the electorate has deprived itself of representation by its own action. Cumberland, Colchester, and Pictou counties, because of a more pronounced tendency to elect Conservatives than the province generally, have suffered most,[27] and in the reorganized Hicks administration of June, 1955, they were not represented.

But while each premier recognizes to a limited degree that he cannot "long neglect to give Cabinet representation to any considerable section without jeopardizing his Government,"[28] this normally constitutes no real limitation upon his freedom of choice, for he is unfettered by geographical considerations in his selection of the remaining four or five ministers. Four members of the MacMillan administration (1940–5) came from the Annapolis Valley, while a similar number represented Halifax in the Macdonald ministry from 1950 to 1953. This evident flexibility makes it certain that no person of ability

[26]See Appendix H. The reduction of the total representation of Antigonish and Guysborough counties to two (since 1933) constitutes a serious impediment to their retaining permanent cabinet representation.

[27]Up to 1956 no assemblyman from Colchester had presided over a department since 1867.

[28]Eugene Forsey, "Sectional Representation in Maritime Provincial Cabinets since 1867," *Public Affairs*, VI (Autumn, 1942), 30.

will be denied a place in the cabinet merely because his own or an adjoining county already enjoys such representation.

Religion and race play a similarly limited role in cabinet-making. From 1867 to 1933, two Roman Catholics generally held positions in the Council, but more recently there have normally been three, a number more in keeping with the proportion of that religious faith to the total population. It also accords best with the percentage of seats in the Assembly which are usually held by Catholics.[29] The allotment of the Catholic seats to Irish, Scottish, and Acadian representatives seems to have depended more upon the circumstances of the moment than upon deliberate planning. The Scotch have maintained their representation fairly consistently since 1867, the Acadians since 1896,[30] and the Irish since 1918. It is theoretically possible under the existing circumstances to afford each of them representation at the same time, but it is to be hoped that no hard and fast rule will be established to that effect, for while a general Catholic representation of three usually constitutes no impediment to the creation of a strong cabinet, limiting the Premier's choice by forcing him to recognize racial claims within a religious group might well necessitate the inclusion of mediocrity to the exclusion of superior ability.

Until recently the specialized knowledge or training of the individuals who fill specific portfolios has been a subject of recurring interest. In 1923, the leader of the opposition adverted critically to the fact that for twenty-one years the head of every department in the government had been a lawyer by profession.[31] The legal profession "number less than one-half of 1 per cent of the population," ran another complaint, "and from that one-half per cent practically all the government is drawn!"[32] The spectacle of a lawyer administering the Mines portfolio invoked special criticism:

The solution of the difficult problems arising constantly in relation to our mines call for a lawyer as much as they do for a plumber. They require a professional expert of capacity and experience, and to put a lawyer in it, is to repeat the old blunder of trying to make a square man fit a round hole.[33]

[29]Between 1933 and 1948 there were normally eight or nine Catholic assemblymen in a House of 30 members and the number remained unchanged after the increase to 37 members in 1949.

[30]Premier Murray inaugurated Acadian representation and between 1896 and 1948 it was only rarely that a Comeau or a Leblanc was not included in the cabinet. Between 1949 and 1953 no Acadian sat on the government side of the House.

[31]See speech of W. L. Hall as reported in the *Halifax Herald*, Feb. 13, 1923.

[32]*Ibid.*, March 26, 1907.　　　　[33]*Ibid.*

But although the Conservatives advocated the appointment of ministers who had a practical knowledge of departmental problems,[34] their programme was that of a party which had long been denied of the practical responsibilities of administration, and in the ministry which they themselves formed in 1925 four of the five salaried portfolios were, as usual, held by lawyers.

Actually no premier can afford to choose otherwise. Through the operation of natural forces the legal profession generally comprises about a third of every Assembly and a large proportion of the members who by training and ability merit inclusion in the administration. Fortunately much of the deeply rooted bias against lawyers—as evidenced by one minister's opinion that they had held the attorney-generalship long enough—has been submerged in recent years. Less progress has been made, however, in convincing the public that the specialized knowledge of the expert must give way to the fresh approach and balanced judgment of the amateur cabinet minister.

Yet one development of the past thirty years has made it all the more necessary to recruit individuals of the highest attainments as members of the Executive Council. Whereas six of its nine members held no office prior to 1918, the present practice is to have no more than one without portfolio. This development was, of course, inevitable as the functions of government steadily widened, but it has made cabinet-making infinitely more difficult, since, instead of needing only two members of real cabinet calibre, a premier must somehow acquire at least seven or eight. Thus the days in which individuals with little merit other than long and devoted service to their party could expect a seat in the Executive Council without office are clearly over. But if the members who are debarred for obvious reasons are excluded, the Premier's choice is confined within narrow limits and he must of necessity resort to the inclusion of mediocrity.

The salaries of the departmental heads who were to sit in the Executive Council were established by statute in 1848 and have since continued to rest on that basis. When Tupper reorganized the departments in 1867, he continued the established practice of providing different rates of remuneration for their heads—$2,400 for the Provincial Secretary, $2,000 for both the Treasurer and the Commissioner of Public Works and Mines, and $1,600 for the Attorney-General[35]—

---

[34]*Ibid.*, Feb. 13, 1923.

[35]30 Vic., c. 1. Later, when the Legislature conferred ministerial status upon the Commissioner of Crown Lands, it placed a value of $2,000 upon his services as well.

the implication being that the value of a minister's services was determined, not by his contribution to the council's deliberations, but by the nature of his departmental duties. Although this attempt to maintain a meaningful relation between a minister's duties and his remuneration was, in effect, abandoned when the financial difficulties of the late seventies required the Provincial Secretary and the Attorney-General to assume additional portfolios without an increase in salary, it was not until 1887 that the modern practice of according equal treatment to all the ministers with office except the premier was definitely established. Since then, their remuneration (apart from their indemnities as assemblymen) has been increased from $2,500 to $3,200 in 1891, $5,000 in 1907, $6,000 in 1921, and $8,000 in 1945,[36] while the additional amount received by the first minister, originally set at $800 in 1887, has been $1,000 since 1907. Supplementary allowances of $3,000 for the premier and $2,000 for the other ministers with office have also been provided since 1954.[37]

Although the Legislature has been moved to make these increases only when some inducement appeared necessary to retain the services of the existing ministers and to attract men of ability into public life, on no occasion have they escaped criticism.[38] A favourite method of defending them has been to compare the Nova Scotian emoluments with those prevailing in the other provinces, but perhaps the most eloquent testimony in their favour was that of W. T. Pipes, who resigned the premiership in 1884 because he could not afford it and only returned to public life after he had made himself financially independent.

He was here twenty-five or twenty-six years ago and he thought that bankruptcy would stare him in the face if he stayed any longer. He went home and attended to his business, and he thought financially he was all right, and he was about the only man in this government who could stay in it at the salary now being paid. He looked around him and found that the men were suddenly wanting to get away from this government. They had a far distant look in their eyes and were looking forward to something else. They wanted to be judges or senators, or something like that. . . . We had two judges and a senator, and they had got out from the house. . . . If he had not been able to work in his profession to put something by, he would not be here.[39]

[36]See 50 Vic., c. 31; 54 Vic., c. 7; 7 Edw. VII, c. 8; 11–12 Geo. V, c. 23; and 9 Geo. VI, c. 3.

[37]3 Eliz. II, c. 42.

[38]For examples, see *Assembly Debates*, 1891, 137, and 1907, 460–3; *Halifax Herald*, April 20, 1922, and March 30, 1945.

[39]*Assembly Debates*, 1907, 463.

In somewhat similar fashion Premier Macdonald defended the supplementary allowances of 1954 by comparing to advantage the contemporary cost of living with that in 1907 when the salaries were $5,000.[40]

Even the picayune amounts which the ministers without office received by way of allowances and travelling expenses were sometimes drawn into the realm of political disputation. On one occasion the *Recorder* maintained that "three men [we]re sufficient for an Executive Council, without paying out hundreds of dollars every year for travelling expenses for men to drop down here to Halifax to solemnly deliberate and vote upon the appointment of some paltry officer."[41] Perhaps it knew whereof it spoke, for a minister without portfolio in the very government which it was subjecting to criticism actually penned the following note to the Attorney-General: "I would like to run down [to Halifax] about the last of next week. Don't you want to appoint a magistrate or any thing."[42]

Recently (1950) Nova Scotia became the first of the Canadian provinces to tackle the problem of making provision for its ministers with office through the modern device of a contributory pension scheme.[43] Hereafter ministers who have reached the age of sixty may draw pensions after ten years of service; to draw the maximum benefits, however, fourteen years of service are required.[44] Naturally an opposition party which had held office for only nineteen years in widely scattered intervals since 1848 could not be expected to look favourably upon a measure which, if history continues to repeat itself, promises to be inapplicable to its own members. One of their criticisms was that the scheme, instead of being genuinely contributory, involved an outright gift of $50,000 to each pensioner,[45] but they also condemned it for introducing undesirable features into government. By providing the ministers with pecuniary reasons for becoming "yes-men," it would enhance unduly the power of a premier, and by appearing to endorse the idea of long periods of service by ministers and hence one-party

---

[40]*Halifax Chronicle-Herald*, April 10, 1954.

[41]July 28, 1880. For additional instances, see *Morning Herald*, March 4, 1876, and *Acadian Recorder*, March 12, 1881.

[42]James S. McDonald to Thompson, Dec. 29, 1881. Thompson Papers (P.A.C.), item 2344.

[43]14 Geo. VI., c. 17.

[44]Seventy per cent of the minister's salary which, in the Premier's case, would be $6,300; for the others $5,600.

[45]The minister's contribution is a deduction of 8 per cent from his salary or $640 annually. If he serves fewer than ten but more than three years, he is entitled to have his payments refunded.

rule, it would strengthen a tendency which already operated to the province's disadvantage. "If a man is interested in security," concluded R. L. Stanfield, "he shouldn't be in politics."[46]

Premier Macdonald denied that the scheme would be costly since the average term of a cabinet minister in the preceding half-century had been only 6.7 years. But in any case the measure provided no more than simple justice to individuals who had to put their political life in balance every four or five years.[47]

If any man thinks that a Cabinet Minister receiving the pay he does receive in Nova Scotia, devoting as he does his full time to that work, abandoning his profession or business, endeavoring in most cases to bring up a family, subject to all the demands that are made upon public men . . . if anybody thinks that a Cabinet Minister's salary of $8000 can provide for his retiring years . . . then he had discovered a method of finance totally unknown to me or to anybody else in the Cabinet.[48]

The long-term effectiveness of the pensions act in making available an improved brand of material for cabinet-making is apparently not to be tested, since the Conservative election manifesto of 1956 promised its repeal.

The formal procedures which the Executive Council employs to conduct its business exhibit little of the unusual, although in many respects they date back to the distant past. The Council meets regularly on the second Tuesday of every month, and is convened on other occasions as the circumstances require it, on the average of once a month. While the Premier has not always formally assumed the title of President of the Executive Council,[49] he invariably presides over its sessions. These are governed by the customary rules of cabinet secrecy, but some relaxation may occur in the event of special circumstances.

Until January of 1893 the Provincial Secretary was the Clerk of the Executive Council, but subsequently the Deputy Provincial Secretary has acted in that capacity. Matters are brought formally before the Council on the report of a minister, which is lodged with the Clerk in advance of a meeting. Collectively these reports constitute the agenda for the Council. It expresses its approbation (or disapproval) of their contents; the Premier initials any changes which the Council

[46]*Halifax Chronicle-Herald*, April 14, 1950.
[47]*Ibid.*
[48]*Ibid.*, Feb. 20, 1951.
[49]The origin of the title dates back to 1860 when William Young declined an office of emolument and created the unpaid office of President for himself to avoid the need of standing for re-election in politically doubtful Cumberland County.

decides are necessary; and the Clerk, whose contact with the Council is through the Premier, prepares them for submission to the Lieutenant-Governor, who, in accordance with long-established practice, gives his approval to the entire record of the meeting. Thus in Nova Scotia, as in Prince Edward Island, executive orders are, in effect, extracts from the minutes of Council.[50] Although no formal distinction exists between the cabinet—the deliberating body—and the Council, which registers the decisions, minutes of Council have been kept from the earliest days of English rule at Annapolis, while minutes of cabinet meetings are non-existent.

The principle of cabinet solidarity finds full expression in Nova Scotia without the astonishing aberrations which are constantly recurring in Prince Edward Island. This phenomenon stems from the practice of the first ministry after Confederation, for Annand, a rather severe disciplinarian, insisted that his ministers should adhere strictly to the settled programme of the administration.[51] In modern history, the most pronounced instance of disagreement among the members of the cabinet to become common knowledge occurred in 1923 on a somewhat inconsequential bill to amend the Costs and Fees Act.[52] "A battle royal between members of the government in open Legislature in regard to a government measure," commented the *Herald*, "creates a new and startling epoch in constitutional government, as we understand it from British tradition and practice."[53] In this instance, the cabinet proceeded to settle its differences within the secret confines of the council chamber, but when, during the next session, the opposition sought evidence of further rifts to build up its case that the administration was disintegrating and gratuitously offered the advice that it was the duty of some member of the government to resign, its suggestions were treated with levity. "Which one?" asked a cabinet minister. "Let them draw lots," was the facetious reply from the government benches.[54]

These incidents occurred during the administration of Premier

[50]See MacKinnon, *Government of Prince Edward Island*, 183.

[51]Once, when the Hon. John Fergusson failed to support the cabinet's determination, the Premier warned him that, in the event of a similar incident, one of the two would have to resign. " 'Well,' said Mr. Fergusson in a very kindly and conciliatory tone, 'We shall all be very sorry to lose you, Mr. Annand.' " Benjamin Russell, "Reminiscences of a Legislature," *Dalhousie Review*, III (Spring, 1923), 7.

[52]The differences centred around the amount of authority which prosecuting officers should possess in determining the witness fees of medical men.

[53]*Halifax Herald*, March 30, 1923.

[54]*Morning Chronicle*, April 11, 1924.

Armstrong, whose prestige with his colleagues was probably the least of all the Liberal premiers. The disintegration of the Conservative administration of Simon Holmes between 1880 and 1882 must likewise be attributed to a lack of confidence in the Premier. Holmes's preoccupation with dubious railway projects of which his colleagues had an imperfect knowledge, his failure to have the government's legislative programme discussed by the full cabinet before the Legislature convened, and his complete lack of concern for the state of his party's organization were primarily responsible.[55] "We are to meet the 22d inst.," wrote one of his ministers. "Will our labour consist simply of disposing of such routine work as Mr. Holmes may think proper to bring before us and then run away home again or will we take the necessary time to try and master the details of the public business, as men having the responsibility of governing the Country? Shall we create Mr. Holmes an autocrat and dictator of the party, or shall we insist that we will be consulted in every thing relating to the conduct of public affairs?"[56] Even though the magnitude of the differences was concealed from the public eye and a reorganization was effected under new leadership, the ministry never overcame the fatal decay from within.[57]

With these exceptions the various cabinets have managed without difficulty to present a united front. Since 1893 no minister has found it necessary to withdraw because of a difference with his colleagues on a matter of public policy.[58] The cynic might attribute this phenomenon to the unvarying willingness of the executive councillors to swallow their principles, or in the alternative, to the absence of any issues upon which adherence to principle would justify the sacrifice. Actually it should be accounted for in other terms. While the ministry's jurisdiction is sufficiently extensive to avoid the parochial politics of more limited spheres, the prestige which most premiers have enjoyed has induced their ministers to defer to them on what is best both for the province and the party.

All premiers have appreciated the need for their ministers to be

[55]See Thompson Papers, items 1548, 1566, 1608, 1621, 1653, 1661, 1723, 1751, 1769, 2344, 2586, 2628, and 2647.

[56]Hon. James S. McDonald to Thompson, Sept. 10, 1880, *ibid.*, item 1545.

[57]Before Holmes resigned he was barely on speaking terms with Attorney-General Thompson, and at least three of his ministers without office were thoroughly disgusted with the conduct of the administration. In the end, Thompson went to the electorate with three vacancies in his Executive Council.

[58]The last instance was the resignation of Hon. Daniel McNeil, who differed with his colleagues upon the granting of railway subsidies to Inverness County. See *Morning Chronicle*, Sept. 5, 1893.

entirely above suspicion in the public eye. Although no minister has found it necessary to resign because of his delinquency in administering a department, two whose activities threatened to embarrass the government found it wise to withdraw. One was president of a company which had been fined for trespassing on Crown lands and violating the Lands and Forests Act;[59] the other admitted to shortages in the joint expenditure funds of Cape Breton County which he was administering at the same time that he held the office of Provincial Secretary.[60] These and more recent incidents clearly demonstrate that anything which savours in the slightest of improper conduct on the part of a minister is certain to be aired in public.[61]

Today the cabinet at Halifax is no less the mainspring of Nova Scotian government than that at Ottawa is of Canadian government. Even though every administration since the 1850's has possessed almost complete control over the provincial bureaucracy,[62] a minister without portfolio might still refer in 1865 to his "honourable tho empty position."[63] Actually the collective deliberations of the cabinet played second fiddle to the ministers' departmental duties until 1884 when Fielding's government began to take "the initiative in all the most important measures of the session."[64] Subsequently this development assumed a thoroughly typical form. In 1908 the Assembly heard the first reference to the despotism of the cabinet and the subserviency of the Legislature;[65] today few public bills are introduced other than those sponsored by the ministry. Between 1943 and 1954 private members introduced only 4 per cent of the total and they were for the most part of a semi-public nature and involved no important considerations of public policy.

While the cabinet must not be regarded as a one-man show, never-

[59]The minister concerned, C. W. Anderson, disputed the evidence and requested that the case should be submitted to arbitration; in the meantime he considered it his duty to place himself in a position where he could not be accused of influencing the arbitrators. See *Halifax Chronicle*, April 10, 1937.

[60]This incident, which centred around D. A. Cameron, stemmed from the loose practices which prevailed under a forty-year-old administration. There was no question of Cameron's personal honesty. No Premier would now permit his Provincial Secretary to hold the additional positions of Municipal Treasurer and Solicitor of Cape Breton County, and Secretary-Treasurer of its Joint Expenditure Board.

[61]During the election campaign of 1953, the leader of the opposition adverted to the undesirability of a minister holding shares in a wine company which sold its wares to the N.S. Liquor Commission.

[62]In 1883 they were finally accorded the right of appointing sheriffs instead of having to share it with the judiciary. 46 Vic., c. 9.

[63]See John McKinnon to Tupper, Feb. 3, 1865, Tupper Papers (P.A.C.), item 27.

[64]*Acadian Recorder*, April 27, 1885.   [65]*Assembly Debates*, 1908, 97.

theless the Premier is to be regarded much more as *inter stellas luna minores* than as *primus inter pares*.[66] Over a long period of years, the personal characteristics of the premiers—particularly Fielding, Murray, and Macdonald—have had much to do with determining the basic outlook of the administration. George Murray, it has been noted earlier,[67] pursued a course of infinite caution. To bills of a radical character, he invariably put his unfailing test. Has it been tried elsewhere and with what success? Under him the Ontario statute book became the utmost limit to which Nova Scotia might hope to aspire in many matters.[68] Angus L. Macdonald, on the other hand, seemed to possess an unerring ability to divide public attitudes without resort to an omnipresent caution to maintain himself in office. Not only did his administration introduce social and developmental legislation during a time of financial uncertainty, but it departed from the beaten track in its measures relating to gasoline licensing, collective bargaining, and pensions for cabinet ministers.

Where the possibility of political repercussion is slight an administration may introduce far-reaching legislation with complete assurance of the support of its backbenchers. This is illustrated by one measure in 1950 which changed the provincial fiscal year. Even before it had made its way through the legislative mill, the Premier had introduced his estimates to conform with its provisions. Naturally the opposition seized upon a golden opportunity to reiterate its charge that the House had abrogated its authority to the executive. "The whole thing was cut and dried for weeks. How can any private member of the Government side examine the bill on its merits now?"[69] asked the Conservative leader.

If the contemplated legislation is likely to have political implications, however, a full preview of its provisions is exhibited to the government caucus. This not only affords a means of presenting a united front on the floors of the Legislature, but it also enables the Premier to supplement his own opinion of what the public reaction

[66]See Ogg and Zink, *Modern Foreign Governments* (New York, 1949), 90.
[67]*Supra*, 189.
[68]The following exchange occurred in the Assembly in 1911 (see *Assembly Debates*, 1911, 145–6):
Murray: "Is there similar legislation to this in any other province of Canada or in England?"
Hall: "I am unable to say . . . [but it] will not hurt Nova Scotia to be a pioneer. . . ."
Murray: "While . . . I have some sympathy with it . . . I feel that if it were justifiable it would be found on some of the statute books of other provinces, or countries where they have had progressive ideas. . . ."
[69]See *Halifax Chronicle-Herald*, April 19, 1950.

will be by the opinions of the caucus generally and more particularly by those of its members whose judgment he has learned to respect. The bill which provided pensions for cabinet ministers was especially unique in that the decision to introduce it was left to the back-benchers because of the personal considerations which it involved and the certainty that it would be used as a public canvass against the government. "The Ministers of the Crown had absolutely nothing to do with forcing this legislation," said one of them. "We, the members insisted that this legislation be brought in."[70]

The circumstances under which a government will withdraw a bill which its caucus has approved but which is subjected to heavy criticism outside the Legislature admits of no easy generalization. The Petty Trespasses Act of 1906 passed through all its stages in both Houses before it produced an "unreasonable panic,"[71] and the Murray government hastily introduced a second bill to repeal one which had not yet become law.[72] A Conservative government withdrew its bill to create a Department of Municipal Affairs in 1932, but two years earlier it had insisted on the passage of a measure which was designed to conserve the forest resources (Bill 151) despite the out-spoken criticism of a not inconsiderable group of its own supporters. Possibly the proximity of election day constitutes the main determining factor.[73]

The cabinet is, of course, not confronted by any highly organized pressure interests with a coterie of paid agents whose function it is to twist the legislative process in their favour. During the past two decades, however, an increasing number of organizations have made representations to the cabinet shortly before the opening of each session.[74] Their normal procedure is to request far more in the way of legislation than they expect, but the very extravagance of their claims often militates against a successful outcome. "I wonder if they ever sit down with a pencil and piece of paper and figure out the costs of some of the things they ask for," said Premier Macdonald in 1950. "It wouldn't be very difficult and only requires a little addition, multiplication and subtraction."[75]

[70]*Ibid.*, May 6, 1950.

[71]*Assembly Debates*, 1906, 340.

[72]Hence the public statutes of 1906 contain the following: Cap. 57 An Act respecting Petty Trespasses; Cap. 58 An Act to repeal an Act respecting Petty Trespasses.

[73]Both 1906 and 1933 were election years.

[74]Such as the N.S. Federation of Labour, the N.S. Teachers' Union, the N.S. Temperance Federation, and the Union of N.S. Municipalities.

[75]*Halifax Chronicle-Herald*, March 25, 1950.

Often the collection and interpretation of data are required before the cabinet can determine what course of action it is to pursue, and when departmental officials cannot perform these functions to advantage resort is had to a royal commission. "This is the day of Royal Commissions," the *Chronicle* once complained. "The Government of Nova Scotia seems to find it impossible to turn round without a Commission for one thing or another . . . the mental strain being apparently too great for [it] to look after the business for which it was elected."[76] Yet the device serves a useful purpose when it is properly used. The modern Workmen's Compensation Act, for example, is the product of a commission which made a painstaking examination of similar legislation in the other provinces and carefully considered the additional burden which might safely be placed upon industry before it presented its recommendations.

But the royal commission may serve also as an instrument of delay, a means of placing the onus for an unpleasant decision upon a non-political body, or a last forlorn gesture for coping with a problem which the government itself knows is insoluble. Premier Murray set the vogue for this type of commission in response to the first vocal demands for social legislation. The findings were as he expected—one commission (1908) reported that the limited financial resources of the province prevented the enactment of a general scheme of old age pensions for all workmen;[77] another (1910) that a compulsory eight-hour day would be fatal to the industrial prospects of the province.[78] Thus the government had provided itself with ample grounds for its refusal to enter the new fields.

Succeeding governments have used the device with equal alacrity. Premier Rhodes might have made a plausible case for the appointment of a royal commissioner in 1928 to estimate the cost of participating in the federal government's old age pension scheme, but certainly not to investigate how the revenue was to be raised.

> The chief thing Mr. Mahon . . . will have to do, is to find out where the money is to come from. That . . . he is by no means particularly qualified to determine. That is peculiarly a function of government itself. . . .
> The government is shifting responsibility, and in so doing is spending time and money, and accomplishing nothing, for in the end the Government itself must inevitably decide where it shall get its money.[79]

It was similarly argued in 1953 that the appointment of a royal com-

---

[76]*Halifax Chronicle*, April 22, 1930.
[77]*Journals of the House of Assembly* (*JHA*), 1908, Appendix 15.
[78]*JHA*, 1910, Appendix 26.   [79]*Halifax Chronicle*, Aug. 16, 1928.

missioner to delve into the financial aspects of the educational system was a device for forestalling discussion upon the vexed questions of teachers' salaries in the elections to follow. Yet in 1955 the government implemented the basic recommendations of the commissioner's report even though they meant a substantial increase in property taxation for many municipalities.[80]   The last administration which adopted a measure with similar effect—that of Holmes and Thompson (1878–82)—failed to survive the next election.

Since all governments realize the exaggerated concern of the Nova Scotian voter with financial matters, they make a special effort to present surpluses in the public accounts. But as the two Conservative administrations since 1867 discovered to their cost, the attempt to keep revenues and expenditures in balance is politically dangerous if it is accompanied by an increase in direct taxation or by a reduction in the moneys spent on public works. Even today, in many of the rural sections, "road work" provides a substantial and expected supplement to ordinary income. The longevity of Liberal governments is due, in part, to the circumstances, often not of their own making, which have enabled them both to keep the revenues buoyant and to finance additional public works without resort to new taxation.

It may also be attributed to their skill in dealing with a not inconsiderable number of competing interests all of which insist upon the recognition of their particular claims as an integral part of public policy. Sometimes this means a facility for conjuring up expedients to avoid the responsibility of decision-making; sometimes adeptness in fashioning acceptable compromises. The regulation of the liquor traffic affords one particularly convincing demonstration. On three occasions the electorate itself was required to determine the basic policy in this matter even though the plebiscite has normally been frowned upon in Nova Scotia as un-British,[18] while over a long period of time the private member has been permitted a far freer hand in deciding upon minor changes in liquor regulations than in any other item of public policy.[82] Premier Murray once rationalized his

[80]*Infra*, 323–5.
[81]In 1894, 1920, and 1929.
[82]In 1950, for example, the Legislature turned down a measure of the minister in charge of liquor administration which would have permitted the voters of rural polling districts to determine by plebiscites whether they favoured the sale of liquor with meals in hotels. One Liberal member changed his opinion after he had received 173 telegrams and numerous telephone calls over the week-end registering opposition to the proposal. *Halifax Chronicle-Herald*, May 2, 1950.

ministry's excessive caution with the pious hope that a great moral question would not be made a political issue.

Similarly each cabinet exercises the utmost precaution in distributing the public largesse among the various sections and counties. Sometimes, as in the division of the provincial road moneys prior to 1917, the price of agreement meant the sacrificing of the public interest. Even after the ministry assumed the initiation of money votes in 1860 it declined to reopen old sores and maintained intact the scale of division which the assemblymen had arrived at in 1852 after years of controversy. Indeed, with one slight alteration, that scale lasted until 1917 although it was "neither based on the area of the counties, nor their assessment, nor on the basis of population, nor on the mileage of highways in the several counties,"[83] and in the end it was discarded, not by a responsible executive which was willing to endanger its political existence to effect a necessary reform, but by a non-partisan and independent Provincial Highways Board.

Although the purposes to which provincial moneys are now applied have altered markedly over the years, the considerations which guide any cabinet in their distribution remain basically the same. Hence in allocating funds for the construction of rural high schools and the hard surfacing of highways, a major consideration is still to ensure that no section or county will be in a position to allege inequitable treatment. While the cabinet has likewise learned to exercise the utmost caution in placing burdens upon the municipalities,[84] in one instance where no objection was likely to be raised—the recognition to be accorded the claims of religious minorities in education—it has been more than content to cast the responsibility upon the local authorities. After the issue of separate schools had played a minor, if somewhat obscure role in the disintegration of the Liberal cabinet and party in 1857,[85] all ministries treated it gingerly. Tupper declined either to consider the introduction of denominational schools or to accord lesser

[83]*JHA*, 1917, Appendix 7A. While it was customary to describe it as the Road Scale of 1882, the relative proportions of funds to be allocated had actually been fixed for all counties except Guysborough by 1852. The final scale of division by percentages was as follows: Annapolis, 5.14; Antigonish, 4.82; Cape Breton, 5.62; Colchester, 5.77; Cumberland, 5.77; Digby, 4.82; Guysborough, 5.99; Halifax, 7.27; Hants, 5.92; Inverness, 6.52; Kings, 5.34; Lunenburg, 5.93; Pictou, 7.12; Queens, 4.67; Richmond, 4.82; Shelburne, 4.82; Victoria, 4.82; Yarmouth, 4.82. See *JHA*, 1882, Appendix 2.

[84]For a full discussion see chap. xix.

[85]See, for example, *Novascotian*, Oct. 5, 1857; *British Colonist*, Oct. 26, 1858; and *Acadian Recorder*, Nov. 1, 1858.

privileges to religious minorities in education when he introduced a system of free schools supported by compulsory assessment in 1865;[86] he likewise refused the requests of the Catholic bishops prior to Confederation either to add "a general clause . . . to the Quebec scheme guaranteeing freedom of Education to Turk Jew & Heathen"[87] or to confer upon the religious minorities who required it the rights which they possessed in Upper and Lower Canada.[88]

Although no government of that day would have dared to provide legal guarantees of this nature, the process had already begun by which the second of the bishops' requests came, in effect, to be unofficially conceded. It originated in Halifax where the school trustees rented the former Catholic schools as part of the public school system and continued to appoint Catholic teachers to staff them. These schools were obliged, however, to follow the course of study and observe the regulations of the ordinary public schools, and no religious instruction was permitted during the regular school hours. Later the Cape Breton towns with large Catholic populations adopted a similar practice. Today in these communities the local school authorities not only rent church property, but actually construct buildings which are designated as Catholic or Protestant schools.[89]

One Superintendent of Education once extolled in glowing terms arrangements which conflicted neither with the Education Act nor the regulations of the Council and which, although unwritten, were distinctly understood and loyally observed by all classes of citizens. "While, therefore, we have none of the disadvantages of a system of Separate schools," he said, "we have the advantage of a single Public school system, with the local elasticity allowing Catholics the essential advantages of a separate system for Catholics."[90] The one

[86]See *Assembly Debates*, 161–5 and 192–5.

[87]Archbishop Connolly to Tupper, Oct. 25, 1866, Tupper Papers, item 52.

[88]*Ibid.*, (about) April 8, 1867, item 55. Connolly told Tupper that if he secured this concession, it would "blend the whole Catholic body from Cape North to Yarmouth into one solid and serried phalanx . . . and earn for you their eternal gratitude." Furthermore, the bishops and clergy would "solemnly pledge themselves to take up your cause as their own and to promise for you and Confederation nearly every Catholic vote in this Province."

[89]An investigator for the Orange Lodge once commented upon the practice: "And the strange thing about the whole situation is that it has been brought about so gradually and so quietly that its very presence has become familiar, and . . . it is difficult to say who is responsible or whether anyone is responsible." See pamphlet published by the Grand Orange Lodge of Nova Scotia entitled *Educational Conditions in Nova Scotia Showing how the Excellent Non-Sectarian Public School Law is violated in the interest of the Roman Catholic Church*, 22.

[90]*Ibid.*, 25–6.

concerted attempt of the Orange Lodge to effect his removal for permitting the spirit of the Education Act to be violated under the principle of "local elasticity" was unceremoniously rejected by Premier Murray and his colleagues in 1922,[91] and the local arrangements have since been maintained and extended. The result has been to remove as a source of provincial conflict an issue which every administration shuns like the plague. The cabinet will be more than content if it can continue to devolve this responsibility elsewhere.

[91]*Morning Chronicle*, March 29, 1922.

CHAPTER XIV

THE ADMINISTRATION

BIG GOVERNMENT has come to Nova Scotia during the past quarter of a century. The annual revenues of the province, which had not reached $1,000,000 in 1900 and amounted to less than $5,000,000 in 1925, were about $60,000,000 in 1956; the fewer than 300 government employees in 1900 have grown to approximately 4,000; executive orders, which in 1900 could be contained in 83 written pages, required 206 typewritten pages in 1918 and 516 in 1949;[1] the number of departments is now fourteen instead of the three which existed before 1918.[2]

No one would suggest, however, that the existing departmental system is exactly what a student of public administration would design if he were permitted an entirely free hand, with only the principles of pure administration as the determinant. Rather it has been the product of a haphazard type of development in which the considerations of cost and the political implications which no premier dare ignore have played a not inconsiderable part. The problem is further complicated because many of the governmental services have appeared almost overnight and still remain in such a state of flux that no one can appreciate their final form. Yet such weaknesses have a way of righting themselves in time. Services which have grown up elsewhere are eventually transferred to the department to which they appropriately belong and are in time fully integrated with its other services to form a coherent whole.

Although none of the fourteen departments can be considered large, they vary widely in their number of employees, ranging at the extremes from a dozen to several hundreds. In one respect their comparatively small size complicates the business of administration since to all appearances some ministers have been far too prone to exercise supervision over the most minute details thereby usurping the functions of their deputies. This is all the more likely to happen when a minister lacks confidence in his own ability to act as a policy-maker.

The existing departments of government and their primary functions are as follows:

[1]See article by A. S. Barnstead, *Halifax Chronicle-Herald,* April 10, 1951.
[2]*Supra,* 191.

The Department of the Provincial Secretary, which boasts the deepest roots, traces its beginnings to the early days of English rule at Annapolis. The normal duties of the Provincial Secretary are to keep the Great Seal of the Province, to issue patents and commissions by virtue of its authority, and to conduct the correspondence of the province. This Department is also required by long-established practice to administer all matters which do not fall naturally within the purview of the other departments, and while these extraordinary functions have diminished substantially in recent years with the establishment of new departments, it still administers the legislation which regulates the incorporation and registration of companies, associations, and partnerships; one of its officials, the Queen's Printer, is responsible for publishing and printing the Royal Gazette, the statutes, the Journals of the Assembly, and the departmental reports; the inspectors of credit unions and rural telephones are under its supervision; and the Nova Scotia Housing Commission is attached to it for administrative purposes and makes its annual report to the Provincial Secretary. In some instances, as in the Board of Censors established under the Theatres and Amusements Act, the connection with the Department exists without a statutory requirement of any kind.

The Department of the Provincial Treasurer—also of early origin—achieved full autonomy under a separate minister in 1947 after being presided over by the Provincial Secretary for almost seventy years. It exercises a general control and direction over all matters relating to provincial finance. To that end the Provincial Treasurer supervises the payment of the revenues from all sources into the Consolidated Revenue Fund and directs their appropriation to the ordinary and usual services of the province. At the request of another department he takes steps to secure the Governor-in-Council's approval of any expenditure in excess of a legislative vote. Within ten days of the opening of each session he submits the provincial accounts to the House of Assembly for examination by its Public Accounts Committee; within the next two weeks he presents a budget in which he outlines the general financial condition and prospects of the province. The Provincial Auditor and his staff are included among his Department's personnel.

The Department of the Attorney-General goes back to 1750 when Otis Little was acting in the capacity of King's Attorney in Halifax. By statute it possesses, to the extent that they are applicable to Nova Scotia, those functions and powers which by law or usage belong to the office of the Attorney-General of England, and any others which it exercised prior to Confederation and which still remain under the jurisdiction of the provincial government.[3] The Attorney-General is the law officer of the Crown, the official legal adviser of the Lieutenant-Governor, and the legal member of the Executive Council. As such, he sees that the administration of public affairs is in accordance with the law, advises the other departments upon questions of law, conducts and regulates all litigation for or against the Crown in the right of the province, settles and approves the instruments which are issued under the Great Seal, and exercises a general supervision over the administration of justice.[4] On the advice of the Attorney-General the Governor-in-Council may exercise the power of clemency or pardon in respect to penalties inflicted under provincial statutes, but the right is seldom invoked.[5] Within recent years the government has initiated steps to remove the magistrates, the registrars of probate and deeds, and the prothonotaries from the old fee system and place them on salaries within the Attorney-General's Department. In this instance, one of its own supporters criticized it for introducing a principle which would

[3]R.S. 1954, c. 240, s. 4.

[4]Even by 1867 the Attorney-General personally prosecuted only a small fraction of the criminal cases and in his absence from a court room the presiding judge appointed the senior Queen's Counsel as Crown prosecutor. But when Attorney-General Wilkins attempted to have his responsibilities defined more explicitly in his celebrated "illness or preoccupation" bill, the Legislative Council baulked. "The country paid a large salary for [Wilkins'] services," said one legislator, "and should not have to pay a lawyer to do his work in consequence of his being pre-occupied." *Assembly Debates*, 1869, 123-4. It was not until 1887 that the Legislature authorized the appointment of paid prosecutors by the Governor-in-Council. In 1923 Attorney-General W. J. O'Hearn announced his intention of conducting in person "all criminal cases of an important character" throughout the province and other litigation of consequence in which the Crown was concerned when the Supreme Court was sitting *in banco. Halifax Herald*, Jan. 4, 1923. None of his successors has thought fit to follow his example.

[5]Possibly because of its political implications. Strong criticism developed because of the release from jail of one Michael McLean of Baddeck in 1900: "Now the jail at Baddeck is a beautiful new building, clean and healthy. . . . There was in the jail also a widow of three score for selling liquor. . . . His [McLean's] confinement was not rigorous. He was put to no hard labor. He was given a large upstairs front room as a parlor where, without a key turned against him, he might receive his friends. His food was from the jailer's table, good and wholesome. The sound of his merry violin as he whiled away the weary hours, filled the air with music. . . . [But] as he got fatter, dyspepsia lent teeth to grief. He then petitioned the lieutenant governor for release. Nobody knows how he backed up his petition or who helped him.

"But he was a good grit, also a good Roman Catholic, albeit he sold rum. . . . A few days after his release he was seen on the roof of one of his buildings

result in "an undesirable mingling of the judicial and executive functions of the law." He felt that a magistrate or registrar of probate might be placed in an embarrassing position if, as an employee of the Department, he was called upon to make decisions and exercise judgment.[6]

The Department of Education which Tupper set up in 1864 retained most of its original structure until 1950 even though it had been subjected to criticism over an extended period. In 1903 the body responsible for policy-making in education, the Council of Public Instruction (that is, the Executive Council with the Superintendent of Education as its Secretary), was labelled as "unique among organizations of its kind in the English-speaking world."[7]

In matters in which his advice might . . . be of great value, the Superintendent can get no more than an impatient hearing—because of "politics." In matters in which any single man is peculiarly liable to fall into errors of various sorts, he has the sole and ready ear of the Council [of Public Instruction]. In consequence, successive tenants of the Education Office have been at full liberty to impose their various personal fads and fancies, for the time being, upon all the schoolrooms of the Province.[8]

In more recent times a royal commission suggested that a responsible minister who offered advice upon the basis of informed opinion would be preferable to the whole body of ministers exercising a purely general supervision over education. This course was adopted in 1950 when the duties of the Council of Public Instruction and the Superintendent were reallocated among the Executive Council and a Minister of Education.[9] The abolition of the eighty-six-year-old Council, however, was not the significant feature since the same group of ministers remains the final determinant of educational policy; the real innovation is that it makes its decisions upon the advice of a minister whose special concern is educational matters.

The Department of Highways was the first of the modern departments (1918) to be created, but not until the Provincial Highways Board was abolished in 1926 was its minister endowed with the same responsibilities as his colleagues. Broadly the Department exercises

---

where they were shingling. The stipendiary magistrate did not recommend the release, in fact he was totally unaware of any proceedings. It would seem strange. Why was not the feeble old woman also released? Why was this rum seller released?" Quoted from the *Montreal Daily Witness* in *Assembly Debates*, 1900, 39. Attorney-General Longley's explanation was by no means convincing. *Ibid.*, 40.

[6]*Halifax Chronicle*, March 13, 1941.
[7]*Morning Chronicle*, April 14, 1903.   [8]*Ibid.*   [9]14 Geo. VI, c. 22.

supervision and control over the highways and roads in accordance with the provisions of the Public Highways Act. Since its size permits a degree of specialization not possible in most of the other departments, its purposes are achieved through four main branches—accounting, mechanical, roads, and motor vehicle.[10] The Motor Vehicle Branch not only registers motor vehicles, but also administers the Motor Carrier Act, the Gasoline Tax Act, and the highways safety programme. The Purchasing Bureau, which until recently was a branch of this Department, is now attached to the Department of the Provincial Treasurer,[11] while Public Works, once associated with Mines, but a branch of the Highways Department after 1939, was constituted a separate department in 1955.[12]

The functions of three other new Departments—Agriculture and Marketing, Public Health, and Public Welfare—were included in a restricted form in the manifold activities once supervised by the Provincial Secretary, and were later performed by the Department of Natural Resources which the Rhodes government set up by order-in-council in 1925. Today the Department of Agriculture and Marketing exercises the powers relating to agriculture which are conferred by the Agriculture and Marketing Act. To that end its work is divided into a number of services—agricultural engineering; animal and poultry; chemistry, soil, and fertilizer; dairy; extension; field crops; horticulture and biology; immigration and land settlement; and marketing—each of which is headed by a director responsible to the Deputy Minister. The Nova Scotia Agricultural College is also regarded as a separate service. Co-operation for the purpose of integrating the provincial agricultural policies with those of the Dominion is promoted through the Nova Scotia Advisory Committee on Agricultural Services which consists of officials of the two levels of government.

Since 1947 the Minister of Agriculture and Marketing has also been Minister of Lands and Forests in place of the Attorney-General who had acted in that capacity since 1877. The Department of Lands and Forests is the instrument for performing the three functions which are implicit in the Lands and Forests Act—the management, lease, and sale of Crown lands; the conservation of forest and timber lands; and the protection and propagation of game and game fish.

[10]For the organizational chart of the Department, see *Journals of the House of Assembly* (*JHA*), 1952, Appendix 10.
[11]*Infra*, 225.
[12]4 Eliz. II, c. 41.

The Department of Public Health was created in 1930 by the transfer of functions from the Department of Natural Resources (later Agriculture). Through a somewhat haphazard type of development the jurisdiction of the Department was gradually widened to include a loose aggregation of services, some of which had grown up in other departments.[13] By 1944 these functions had become sufficiently extensive to justify the creation of a separate Department of Public Welfare.[14] By statute the Department of Public Health is administered in accordance with the Public Health Act which empowers the Minister to supervise and regulate all matters relating to public health, vital statistics, hospitals, and sanatoria;[15] the Department of Public Welfare exercises similar functions with respect to social welfare, public charities, old age assistance, pensions for the blind, child and family welfare, juvenile delinquency, probation and parole, and reformatory institutions.[16] In some instances the Departments provide these services at the provincial level, in others they supervise the services which are provided by the local authorities. More than any other departments these two remain in a state of flux and for that reason their final organizational pattern is still far from certain.

The Department of Labour, which was created in 1932, takes cognizance of a variety of matters related to labour. Practically all its functions are co-ordinated by a Chief Administrative Officer (since 1955 a Deputy Minister) who is directly responsible to the Minister. These include a Fire Marshal Branch, a Boiler Inspection Branch, a Factory Inspection Branch, an Engine Operators Board, an Industrial Training Division with Apprenticeship and Trades School Branches, and a Minimum Wage Board. The one exception is provided by the Labour Relations Board which reports directly to the Minister of Labour.[17]

The smallest Department, Municipal Affairs, was established by legislation enacted in 1935 and is administered in accordance with the

[13]See Dr. George F. Davidson, *Report on Public Welfare Services*, no. IV of the *Report of the Royal Commission on Provincial Development and Rehabilitation*, 1944, 27.

[14]Sometimes it is difficult to separate the health and welfare functions. Dr. Davidson therefore suggested a single department with two deputies to facilitate the transfer of borderline services. He admitted, however, that by placing a single minister in charge of the two departments these difficulties could be minimized. *Ibid.*, 28n. But in the reorganized Hicks administration of June, 1955, they were headed by different ministers.

[15]10 Geo. VI, c. 2, s. 33.

[16]*Ibid.*, s. 42.

[17]For the organization chart of the Department see *JHA*, 1954, Appendix 28.

Municipal Act, the Towns' Incorporation Act, the Assessment Act, and the Municipal Affairs Act. Broadly, its objective is to effect an improvement in the administration of municipal affairs, and to that end it supervises the borrowings of the local governments, regulates their sinking fund payments, prescribes a system of estimates, book-keeping, and accounts for their use, and studies and advises upon the existing system of municipal administration.

The Mines Department, which had enjoyed a joint existence with Public Works since Confederation, secured recognition as a separate department in 1939. Its specific functions are prescribed by the Mines Act, the Coal Mines Regulation Act, and the Metalliferous Mines Regulation Act. In addition, it maintains a mobile mining plant and other technical equipment to assist in opening up new mining industries.

The Department of Trade and Industry, which was instituted under another name in 1939, is the major governmental instrument for promoting industrial development. At one time it was organized in five divisions—Commercial, Engineering (with an associated Handcrafts Section), Fisheries, Economic Research, and Administrative (which also supervised loans)—but the loss of senior staff and other difficulties necessitated their consolidation.[18]

II

The fourteen departments by no means carry on all the work of Nova Scotian government, for in conformity with modern practice a substantial part is transacted by boards and commissions some of which possess complete independence from, and others of which are closely connected with, the existing departments. Although it was urged before the Jones Commission that their haphazard emergence indicated a lack of planning and organization in the governmental administration as a whole,[19] this judgment may be somewhat harsh since the Nova Scotian development followed the only pattern possible in a rapid transition from the negative to the positive state. Public administration is nowhere more empirical than in determining the appropriate form of an organization, and when Nova Scotian governments were confronted with the task of deciding how the new advisory, regulatory, or operating functions were to be performed, they often deemed it best to create a board and to endow it with the powers

[18]JHA, 1954, Appendix, 32, 3.
[19]See memorandum of R. MacGregor Dawson on the civil service, Royal Commission, Provincial Economic Inquiry, 1934, Appendices, 53.

and the degree of independence requisite to the purpose which they had in mind. Experience alone afforded a means of determining what transformation or modifications were required to provide a more efficient instrument.

Two of the boards, the Nova Scotia Power Commission and the Nova Scotia Liquor Commission, are primarily operating bodies which conduct a governmental activity possessing much the same character as a private business. The Power Commission, which dates back to 1919, is mainly concerned with the operation of the larger hydro stations and with high tension transmission. Through nine separate systems it supplies power at cost to local distributing agents. In limited areas it also acts as a distributing agency and this function has been substantially widened since the Rural Electrification Act of 1937 facilitated the extension of electric power to the rural areas through government subsidization.

The Royal Commission on Provincial Development and Rehabilitation expressed its satisfaction with a power system which contained substantial elements of public and private ownership, but it felt that the Power Commission, since it had no interest beyond that of generating and selling electricity at cost, was the logical instrument for drawing together and integrating the small and isolated generating systems.[20] Earlier (1941) the government had taken steps to give the Commission complete control of the power situation after a private company "threw a monkey wrench into our works."[21] As a result, it is now empowered, with the approval of the Governor-in-Council, to regulate the generation, transformation, transmission, and distribution of electric power; and to restrict, prohibit, divert, or apportion its supply so as to effect the most economical, efficient, and equitable distribution.[22]

The Nova Scotia Liquor Commission administers the Liquor Control Act and as such operates the government liquor stores which have become the third largest source of provincial revenue.

A second group of boards have primarily advisory functions. Of particular significance since 1935 have been the authorities established to further industrial progress. From 1935 to 1941 the Nova Scotia

[20]See Alexander Brady, *Report on Electric Power*, no. XIII of the *Report of the Royal Commission on Provincial Development and Rehabilitation*, ss. 65–79.

[21]By starting to erect a plant in Trenton whereas the Commission intended to build one of the most modern coal-burning plants in Stellarton, *Halifax Chronicle*, March 13, 1941.

[22]5 Geo. VI, c. 39.

Economic Council had as its primary duty the task of advising the Governor-in-Council upon the industrial and economic development of the province.[23] Since 1946 the Nova Scotia Research Foundation has been studying the problems of the provincial industries and assisting them in utilizing the results of modern scientific research. It also has the responsibility of making long-term studies of natural resources with a view to exploiting them to better advantage.[24] Today there is also an Industrial Loan Board which examines and recommends applications for industrial loans and guarantees,[25] while an Industrial Development Board has been projected by legislation, although not yet appointed, to advise the Minister of Trade and Industry on the establishment of new industries.[26]

By far the largest number of boards, however, are those which perform regulatory, supervisory, or administrative functions, or any combination of these. Although boards in this group differ widely in character and status, first in prestige is undoubtedly the Board of Commissioners of Public Utilities which makes "such orders as it deems just in respect to tolls, rates and charges to be paid to any public utility." From the very nature of things the Board's regulation of utilities must be somewhat negative, for although it has the power to prevent "private companies from sacrificing the interests of consumers in the effort to accumulate profits, . . . it is less effective in the positive task of spurring the private companies to create carefully planned systems of electric [or other] supply."[27]

Yet it has acquired such expert knowledge during its more than forty years of experience that the Legislature continues to impose additional duties upon it of a quasi-judicial character. Since 1923 it has been supervising and regulating motor carriers, and issuing the certificates of convenience and necessity which are required for their operation;[28] since 1934 it has been administering a Gasoline Licensing Act which requires it to regulate the distribution and sale of gasoline, including the granting of licences to wholesalers and retailers;[29] since 1944 it has been acting as a commission under Part XVII of the Agriculture and Marketing Act and as such has been regulating the price

[23]25–26 Geo. V, c. 10.
[24]JHA, 1954, Appendix 35.
[25]15 Geo. VI, c. 6.
[26]15 Geo. VI, c. 7. Earlier (1948) it had been intended that an Industrial Assistance Advisory Board should combine the last two functions. 12 Geo. VI, c. 3.
[27]Brady, Report on Electric Power, s. 91.
[28]13 Geo. V., c. 1.
[29]24 Geo. V, c. 2.

of fluid milk in the controlled areas;[30] and since 1945 it has been determining the actual value or the approximate cost of improvements under the Bonus Act which regulates the granting of fixed assessments to industries by municipalities.[31] It appears likely, however, that the Board's span of control has been extended over too broad a range of activities, and that a contraction rather than a further expansion of its duties would be to its advantage.[32]

A second quasi-judicial body, the Nova Scotia Labour Relations Board, is constituted by the Trade Union Act to determine whether specific groups of employees are appropriate units for collective bargaining and to certify them for that purpose if they have conformed with the provisions of the Act.[33] While the Board has wide discretion in deciding who is an employer and who an employee, the courts once brought it sharply to a halt when it attempted to deny certification for a reason nowhere stated in the Act.[34]

The function of the Workmen's Compensation Board since its establishment in 1915 has been to administer the Workmen's Compensation Act which, like similar acts elsewhere, established the collective responsibility of employers for accidents and specific industrial diseases. The Board possesses extensive powers in the settlement of cases, but a guarded right of appeal on points of jurisdiction and law lies to the Supreme Court. On occasion its prestige with the employees who fall within its purview has been low because of its failure to maintain adequate public relations and to furnish them with a clear conception of its functions.[35]

A number of other boards wield somewhat less substantial, but no less necessary functions than the foregoing. Two of the more recent are the Old Age Assistance Board which determines the eligibility of applicants between sixty-five and sixty-nine years of age for financial assistance,[36] and the Public Accountants Board which prescribes the standards of education and the other qualifications required of a licensed public accountant.[37]

This conglomeration of boards and commissions with their varying

[30] Geo. VI, c. 39, and 9 Geo. VI, c. 61.
[31] 9 Geo. VI, c. 16.
[32] See Brady, *Report on Electric Power,* s. 95.
[33] 11 Geo. VI, c. 3.
[34] Upon the ground of mere apprehension that one Communist in a parent organization might succeed in perverting the applicant-union's purpose in labour relations. See *In re Labour Relations Board (Nova Scotia),* 29 M.P.R. 399.
[35] *JHA,* 1937, Appendix 33.
[36] 1 Eliz. II, c. 11.
[37] 1 Eliz. II, c. 14.

compositions and tenures constitutes an attempt to provide authorities with the powers and the independence needed to perform a substantial part of the functions demanded of modern government. While the Lieutenant-Governor, the Chief Justice, the Premier, the leader of the opposition, the President of Dalhousie University and the President of the Nova Scotia Historical Society, who compose the Board of Trustees of the Public Archives, hardly required the tenure during good behaviour with which they were once endowed,[38] it is certainly appropriate that the three members of the Board of Public Utilities, whose duties are primarily quasi-judicial in nature, should hold office during good behaviour subject to retirement at 70,[39] and that members of the Liquor Commission, who are especially vulnerable to political pressure, should be appointed for terms of ten years and removable only for cause. For a similar reason the commissioner-manager of the Power Commission enjoys a tenure during good behaviour, but at least one of the other commissioners must be a minister of the Crown and therefore in a position to facilitate loans from the government, obtain the necessary amendments to the Power Commission Act, and bring an outside judgment to play upon the Commission's work.[40]

Yet a mere statutory guarantee is not sufficient in itself to ensure for the members of these boards the independent character which is desirable. If they are to be treated like judges, they must act like judges. Integrity of character, professional pride, and above all the avoidance of appearance of sympathy for any one political party are intangibles which go a long way to establish a special status in the eyes of the public. That they do so is especially desirable in Nova Scotia where a change of government is rare and the convulsion is all the more likely to be violent when it does occur. After 1925 a Conservative government actually resorted to the argument that the incumbent members of the Board of Public Utilities and the Compensation Board were partisan, in order to defend the bills which destroyed the independent character of the Boards.[41]

The members of most boards and commissions, however, do not possess an extraordinary tenure, nor do they require it. Often, as in the Engine Operators Board, the intention is simply to confer a legal status upon a group of civil servants who collectively perform regulatory or administrative functions. In other instances, as in the Public Accountants Board, the provisions are designed to permit the enlistment of experts to perform similar functions in a part-time or

[38]21 Geo. V, c. 63.
[39]R.S. 1954, c. 243.
[40]Brady, *Report on Electric Power*, s. 81.   [41]*Infra*, 221n.

occasional capacity. Sometimes, as in the Nova Scotia Economic Council or the Board of Governors of the Research Foundation, the outsiders may be academicians, industrialists, and business men whose knowledge and judgment can be turned to good account usually without remuneration, or they may be men of mature judgment and wide experience, even if they are defeated politicians, who are not averse to being recompensed for serving on such authorities as the Old Age Assistance Board. Not all the boards and commissions can be justified as easily as these, but enough has been said to indicate that the diversity of their character is not to be accounted for primarily by the incapacity or lack of thought of legislators.

III

The need for an adequate civil service has become all the more compelling because of the expert knowledge which is required to administer the foregoing array of governmental activities. "Modern administration does not consist of merely adding a few figures and dictating a few letters; it involves an understanding of many activities, a thorough knowledge of one or two special fields, a capacity to deal with many kinds of people, an ability to think straight and to make quick, accurate, wise decisions."[42] Some concern as to the quality of the provincial civil service has been expressed by academicians who were acting in the capacity of royal commissioners. One of them, Professor R. MacGregor Dawson, emphasized particularly the need for encouraging the higher civil servants to hold independent views which would always be at the disposal of the government; ministerial sycophants, he pointed out, fail in their primary duty.[43]

This recommendation deserves special attention inasmuch as most of the departments are small and few contain more than two or three officials whose status places them at the policy discussion level. Furthermore, some of these are quite incapable of doing more than the routine work of administration. While critics may charge the Nova Scotian bureaucrat with being bound up in red tape, none may accuse him of exceeding his legitimate functions. The one instance to the contrary—a Provincial Health Officer's attempt, allegedly on his own initiative, to formulate a policy for the tuberculin testing of school children[44]—was a unique circumstance and is not likely to be repeated.

While a high ranking official may become acutely conscious of

[42]R. MacGregor Dawson, *Report on the Civil Service*, no. XVIII of the *Report of the Royal Commission on Provincial Development and Rehabilitation*, s. 1.
[43]*Ibid.*, s. 2.   [44]See *Halifax Herald*, Nov. 5, 1928.

defects and anomalies in the acts which he has to administer, he will initiate steps to effect a remedy only after consulting with his minister. In bills of a highly technical nature his role may be somewhat magnified, although even then he is subject to effective checks. But when the proposals fall within the category of basic policy-making both the initiative and the final decision remain as securely in the cabinet as ever. It is not the administrator's deeply rooted patterns of thought nor even his notions of sound business which count in the end; the ultimate action depends upon ministers whose opinions are determined by their own political predilections, by the exigencies of the moment, and by their antecedent political commitments. Yet this in no wise alters the fact that a major problem in Nova Scotian administration is to ensure that the top civil servants are capable of providing upon request the information and advice which are indispensable to intelligent policy-making.

In 1935 Professor Dawson pointed out two other weaknesses in the civil service: the overriding influence of political patronage and the lack of an adequate system of gradation and classification.[45] Until recently the general attitude of the Nova Scotian politician in making appointments to public office has been no better than that of Fielding in 1892:

One of the principles of party politics is that "to the victors belong the spoils," that is, providing we can agree as to what the "spoils" are. There are some persons who would clear out every Tory who holds an office under the government. I do not agree with that, but I hold that vacancies as they occur, and patronage within legitimate bounds should be given by the government to its friends and supporters, and I am prepared to give such patronage every day in the week provided the person who receives it does a dollar's worth of work for every dollar he gets.[46]

Sometime earlier the Conservatives had suggested that the local officials should be appointed only after consultation with a county's representatives in the Assembly, but the government of the day rejected this "new form of responsible government."[47] Instead, the assemblymen lost their one right in respect to patronage, that of nominating road commissioners, and Charles Tanner once decried a government "so deeply rooted in partizanship that he had never yet succeeded in as much as getting a man appointed a justice of the peace."[48]

[45]See the memorandum on the civil service, Royal Commission, Provincial Economic Inquiry, Appendices, 53.
[46]Halifax Herald, Oct. 17, 1892.
[47]Assembly Debates, 1873, 19.   [48]Ibid., 1907, 17.

The two changes in party rule prior to 1925 brought in their wake sufficient dismissals to evoke the comment that government was being entrusted to "mere political wire-pullers, coming in and going out as their party was up or down."[49] But both were entirely dwarfed by the events of 1925 when the new Conservative government was confronted with an unparalleled scramble for office by its supporters who had been deprived of the loaves and fishes for forty-three years. Since the offices which were held during pleasure were insufficient to relieve the pressure, the government proceeded to build up a case for interfering with the civil servants who had been appointed during good behaviour.

> Every official of the late government seemed to think it natural that Nova Scotia would never have anything else but a Liberal government. . . . There were officials who got the happy idea that they could go on as they like and certain of these we deem it necessary to discipline.[50]
> An unprecedented situation . . . had arisen from the long tenure of one Government; a civil service . . . had grown up, in partisanship, and became part of a political organization. . . . There have been leakages in confidential matters of Government.[51]

Although these statements had a patently clear purpose, it may be argued in extenuation that some of the leading civil servants were former political opponents of the government and a few at least evinced an unsympathetic, if not hostile, attitude towards it. The instrument of discipline was to be a Tenure of Office Bill which was designed to convert the tenure of every official without exception to one of pleasure. But in 1926 and 1927 the Legislative Council thwarted the government's intentions, and in 1928, when it might have had its way, it contented itself with amending specific statutes so as to permit the removal of the officials whom it found thoroughly obnoxious.[52] Some of its newly won powers were used immediately; others were reserved for the so-called Christmas executions of 1928 and the "grand slaughter of the innocents."[53]

All in all the Liberals alleged the dismissal of 601 persons by order-

[49]*Acadian Recorder,* Nov. 29, 1878.
[50]*Halifax Herald,* Feb. 13, 1926.
[51]*Halifax Chronicle,* Feb. 11, 1927.
[52]The tenure of the registrars of deeds was changed to one of pleasure (18 Geo. V, c. 44); sheriffs who had reached the age of 75 might be removed (18 Geo. V, c. 21); the incumbent members of the Board of Public Utilities and the Compensation Board had their tenure altered to one of pleasure, but their successors were to hold office for ten years removable for cause (18 Geo. V, cc. 41 and 42).
[53]*Halifax Chronicle,* Dec. 28, 1928.

in-council alone during the eight years of Conservative government.[54] But with their own advent to office in 1933 another flood of dismissals followed, estimated this time by their opponents to be of the order of 500. Yet they too put forward a plausible justification by proving a closer direct connection between civil servants and a party's organization than had ever before existed.[55]

It was with this background that the Macdonald government, in conformity with the recommendations of the Jones Commission, sponsored the Civil Service Act of 1935 and thereby embarked upon the course of building up a permanent body of properly selected and qualified civil servants. The opposition was naturally dubious of the practicability of this objective. According to their leader patronage had been "a matter of acute interest in this province for many generations. Frequently the view is held that if some personal advantage is not to be secured from some party then that party will not be supported. If that feeling is general then it is useless to . . . consider [this] bill."[56] He wondered also if the period which followed an orgy of head-slashing was propitious for setting up a Civil Service Commission. Premier Macdonald contended in reply that the number of provincial employees appointed by Liberal governments was not substantially larger than the number which their opponents had appointed. "When was the service to be established," he asked, "if not when the two were fairly evenly balanced."[57]

While nothing in the Act[58] impaired the legal right of the Governor-in-Council to remove the provincial employees,[59] it contained the mandatory requirement that no appointment should be made to the civil service except "upon competitive examination . . . at the instance of the Commission and upon the written request of the head or deputy head of a department."[60] Furthermore, it debarred any employee who came under its provisions from engaging in partisan activities of any kind.[61]

In the one inquest[62] into the operation of the Act, Professor Dawson doubted whether the Commission was fully meeting the purpose for which it was designed. The deplorable feature was that it had not

[54]*Ibid.*, March 8, 1934.
[55]*Ibid.*
[56]*Halifax Herald*, March 15, 1935. The *Herald* itself (March 14, 1935) was of the opinion that "Nova Scotian partizan politics will require a great deal of purging and overhauling before [the British] 'security of tenure' will obtain in this Province.
[57]*Ibid.*, March 15, 1935.
[58]25–26 Geo. V, c. 8.
[59]S. 27.   [60]S. 17.   [61]S. 28.   [62]Dawson, *Report on the Civil Service*.

attained the position in the public eye which it should possess. Part of the fault lay in the part-time functions and the miserable salary of the Civil Service Commissioner, both of which robbed the office of prestige and diminished its importance.[63] Little improvement could be expected until a full-time Commissioner with the rank of Deputy Minister was appointed.

The position of the Commission was also weakened by the inexcusable omission of many public servants from its oversight. Unskilled labourers appeared to be tacitly excluded since patronage was clearly evident in the appointment of manual labourers, elevator attendants, and messengers. Yet the investigator saw no harmful effects if the practice was confined to this group of employees; in fact, he recommended their removal from the jurisdiction of the Commission. He was highly critical, however, because other employees, particularly those of boards and commissions, who might have been brought under the Commission by order-in-council, were permitted to remain outside its surveillance thereby diminishing materially the effective field within which it operated.[64]

Even more serious was the continuing lack of an adequate system of classification.

The classification provided in the Act has been amplified in the regulations and, as a supplement, schedules of compensation which give a range of salary for each position have been issued for each department. The result is scarcely a happy one. The first is supposed to form a classification of positions and the second a classification of salaries, but the former indicates (as indeed, it must) salaries also, so that even the Commission is hard put to it to merge the two together in an intelligible whole. They both bear the marks of stop-gap measures which have never been properly worked out. . . .[65]

This criticism appears to have borne fruit, for subsequently the Commission conducted a survey of the staffs of the various offices with a view to determining the proper classification of the employees. This culminated in a genuine attempt to reconcile the salaries paid by each of the departments to employees with equivalent ability and at the same time to bring them into line with those paid by the Dominion and the other provincial governments, and private industry.[66]

The second major weakness had developed in the method of making

[63]Ibid., s. 6.
[64]Ibid., s. 7.
[65]Ibid., s. 8.
[66]See JHA, 1950, Appendix 33. The Director of Organization and Classification of the Dominion Civil Service Commission assisted in the survey.

appointments to skilled positions. It was made possible because one of the regulations which the Governor-in-Council had passed by virtue of its powers under the Civil Service Act contained a loop-hole for avoiding the strict mandatory provisions of the Act. As a result, examinations for entrance into the public service need be held only "where practicable and necessary." This had made it difficult to insist on genuine competition in the filling of any vacancy.[67]

A Minister may at any time assert that the appointment is urgent, that there are no other qualified candidates for the position, that competition is neither "necessary" nor "practicable," and that an "appraisal of documents" would be sufficient for the purposes of the test. Unless the Commission is prepared to resist demands of this nature, the entire principle of open competitive examinations is, in effect, struck out of the Act.[68]

While the complexity and skilled nature of many civil service jobs often render a resort to patronage inexpedient, the ills which may flow from the very existence of the loop-hole are none the less obvious. A Liberal government normally holds office for long periods before it is displaced, thus making it certain that its successor will be deluged with demands for appointments. It will find it difficult to resist these pressures if its predecessors have allegedly manipulated the act to their own ends even in a small number of instances. In 1945 Dr. Dawson expressed the opinion that "*so long as the Civil Service Act is applied and interpreted as it is to-day, there is no reason to expect anything but an outburst of dismissals following a change of Government.*"[69] Nevertheless, Mr. Stanfield gave assurances during the 1956 election that no civil servants would be disturbed in the event of a Conservative victory unless they had actively campaigned for the government, and despite the controversy which has since occurred on the subject of dismissals, no official under the jurisdiction of the Civil Service Commission appears to have been disturbed.

IV

Nova Scotian governments have been criticized almost as much for favouring their political friends in the purchase of supplies as in the making of appointments. This is understandable because a typical attitude has been that of the Commissioner of Public Works and Mines who once admitted the existence of a patronage list on his desk and avowed that he would "sacrifice his seat in this House [of Assembly] before he would concede the proposition that he had not the right to deal with his political friends rather than with his political opponents,

[67]Dawson, *Report on the Civil Service*, s. 11.   [68]*Ibid.*   [69]*Ibid.*, s. 15.

other things being equal."[70] The tendency was, and is, to rationalize such conduct in the following terms:

Patronage in some form or another is inseparable from any kind of government whether democratic or autocratic, as long as human nature is what it is. Other things being equal, a party has a perfect right to prefer its political friends to its political enemies. The interests of the public generally must *always* be safeguarded, but this does not necessitate the granting of favours to enemies. Where two men offer the same thing at the same price and of the same quality for sale, one a supporter, the other an enemy, a government has a perfect right to give the preference to its friend. To deny this would be an evidence of imbecility. . . .[71]

In 1921 the Murray administration sought to make its position more defensible by setting up a Purchasing Bureau presided over by the Minister of Public Works and Mines, and by appointing a General Purchasing Agent to superintend the purchase of most of the government's supplies under a strictly competitive system.[72] But since the appointee to the new post had recently resigned from the Legislative Council to facilitate the Premier's plans for reconstructing his cabinet, he was unable to dispel the suspicion that he was merely a figure-head behind which the government continued to practice the old devices almost as it pleased.[73]

For this reason one of the first acts of the new Conservative administration of 1925 was to abolish the office of General Purchasing Agent and, while retaining the Purchasing Bureau, to set up a Purchasing Committee composed of departmental officials who, under the direction of the Minister of Public Works and Mines, were to have a general control over purchasing.[74] In essence these provisions remain, but so, it is alleged, do the old practices. On one occasion a cabinet minister was accused of usurping the powers of the Purchasing Committee;[75] on another the Conservative assemblymen were "struck by the number of faithful supporters of the Government when you look at the list outlining the provisions purchased by the Government departments."[76] Each time the Provincial Treasurer, who now supervises the Purchasing Bureau, insisted that he did not interfere with its discretion. A favourite defence in recent years has been to single out a few Conservatives who have likewise been the recipients of government beneficence, but this form of argument is by no means convincing. One consolation is that the straining of the machinery for purchasing supplies to favour the government's

[70]*Assembly Debates*, 1909, 177–8.
[71]*Acadian Recorder*, April 1, 1909.
[73]*Halifax Herald*, April 7, 1923.
[75]*Halifax Herald*, March 19, 1941.
[72]11–12 Geo. V, c. 11.
[74]16–17 Geo. V, c. 15.
[76]*Halifax Chronicle-Herald*, May 4, 1950.

friends probably results in little harm to the public interest so long as the opposition makes searching probes into the public accounts.

V

As Nova Scotian government expanded, it did not escape the striking development in the use of administrative powers which has been characteristic of modern government.   In the last century only a few statutes, such as the Public Health Act of 1888,[77] exhibited marked deviations from Dicey's exposition of the rule of law, but not even the conservative nature of the government of the day and its abhorrence of anything which savoured of radicalism could stem the tide which set in about 1910. The pressure for more positive action along social and humanitarian lines forced the government into new spheres of activity, and required it to adopt new procedures to make its legislation effective.   The new problems were first revealed in their true light in the regulation of public utilities.   The Murray government soon discovered that the Governor-in-Council, which in 1903 and 1907[78] had been constituted the final authority over telephone and electric rates, was

rather an unwieldly body for this purpose because for one thing it could not have a session in the town in which the dispute might arise. . . . [So] the Government came to the conclusion that it would be better to have a Board which would be practically a Court appointed to deal with such matters. . . .
The very object of establishing a Commission was to see that the price was fair and just . . . that the charges should be uniform, that there should be no discrimination. . . . The Board was empowered to make rules for the carrying out of the Act. . . . These rules would have to be approved by the Governor-in-Council and would have the force of law. . . .[79]

The Act[80] creating the Board of Commissioners of Public Utilities thus violated all the canons of the old order—board-made law displaced the ordinary law of the land and a quasi-judicial body with wide discretionary powers administered it instead of the ordinary law courts. Furthermore, one avenue of appeal open to an aggrieved person, the Governor-in-Council, was eliminated within three years.[81] So the ice had been broken and features which had once been

[77]51 Vic., c. 9.
[79]Assembly Debates, 1909, 75–7.
[78]3 Edw. VII, c. 33, and 7 Edw. VII, c. 40.
[80]9 Edw. VII, c. 1.
[81]2 Geo. V, c. 64.   An appeal lies to the Supreme Court in banco from an order of the Board upon any question of law or jurisdiction. 7 Geo. VI, c. 2, s. 96.

exceptional in legislation won general acceptance. Yet the development proceeded so gradually and in such conformity with the needs of a new day that no one subjected it to theoretical speculation. Only when the administrative powers were likely to affect some particularly vocal interest or to offer the prospect of political advantage were their dangers brought to the attention of the political community.

The new trend in legislation made itself apparent in the delegation of both legislative and quasi-judicial power. The arguments which were used to justify the former followed the normal pattern. The Assembly simply had not the time to do otherwise; it was forced to rely on specialists because of its own incompetence in technical matters; it had to provide some means of enabling legislation to be adapted to unforeseen circumstances and of permitting the government to act quickly in the event of an emergency. At first the legislators made an effort to limit the scope of the delegated authority. The Theatres and Cinematographs Act of 1915, for example, empowered the Governor-in-Council to make regulations on fourteen specific matters and no others. But within two years that power was widened to include the regulation of any other matters which the Governor-in-Council considered "necessary or expedient for the purpose of giving full effect to the provisions of this Act."[82] Today more than half the public bills include rule-making authority of this nature. Yet although the power which they confer is wide, the courts are usually not debarred from determining whether the regulations are germane to the act.

Nevertheless, Nova Scotia has also not escaped the growing tendency to delegate legislative authority on matters of principle. The Industrial Loan Act,[83] for example, enables the Governor-in-Council to designate the type of industry to which its provisions are to apply, to prescribe the purposes of the loans, and to regulate their size. Yet in legislation of this nature no alternative appears to be possible since new ground is being broken and the Legislature is deficient in the information which will enable it to determine how its objectives can best be achieved. If it were vigilant, however, it would insist upon these acts being placed in a more desirable shape when the experience which accrues from their practical operation renders that course possible. It is difficult to see in any event why the minister who administers the Hotel Regulations Act should, with

[82]7-8 Geo. V, c. 76.
[83]15 Geo. VI, c. 6.

the approval of the Governor-in-Council, be permitted to make regulations "for the creation of offences."[84]

Whenever the delegated legislative authority appears to be greater than is required, the fault can be ascribed more to the periodic failure of the electoral system to produce a strong and critical opposition than to any deliberate attempt to assume excessive power. Even the occasions on which the delegated powers are alleged to have been used objectionably are rare. Perhaps the greatest safeguard has been the practice of requiring the regulations and orders to be confirmed by the Governor-in-Council, which is certain to take into account the likelihood of political repercussions.

No suggestion has ever been made in Nova Scotia that subordinate legislation is shrouded in secrecy. From the beginning many statutes provided that the rules and regulations which were made by virtue of their authority would be effective only after being published in the Royal Gazette. In 1941 an even more adequate assurance of publicity was provided by statute on the initiative of the government itself.[85] As a result, all rules and regulations whether made by the Governor-in-Council, or by a minister, departmental official, or major board or commission, with or without the approval of the Governor-in-Council, must be tabled within twenty days of their passage if the Assembly is meeting; if not, within twenty days after its next session convenes. Failure to comply with these provisions results in the automatic repeal of the regulations. Since 1943 most of the subordinate legislation of more than a purely limited application has also been published in the annual volume of provincial statutes. It is doubtful if more adequate provisions for giving publicity to delegated legislation exists anywhere.

VI

The delegation of quasi-judicial authority has followed the haphazard, sporadic and unsystematic course which it has exhibited elsewhere. The number of instances in which almost purely judicial power has been delegated or in which recourse to the courts upon matters of law has been denied have been rare, but whenever the decision to be made clearly involves discretion on the part of the determining body—in other words when it is a quasi-judicial decision —the general practice has been to leave it to some administrative authority. The reasons are the usual ones—the inability of the common

[84]R.S. 1954, c. 116, s. 9(d).
[85]R.S. 1954, c. 249. This is the so-called Regulations Act.

law courts to handle the great volume of decisions of this character; their lack of criteria to explain the meaning of terms like "reasonable" or "proper" or "fair" which are commonplaces in modern legislation; and their natural tendency to emphasize the rights of the individual rather than social objectives.

So today the Provincial Secretary may "in his absolute discretion" suspend or cancel the licence of any seller under the Instalment Payment Contracts Act;[86] an individual aggrieved by the decision of an inspector under the Engine Operators Act may appeal to the Minister of Labour and "the decision of the Minister shall be final";[87] the Minister of Lands and Forests may revoke the licence of a scaler for an infringement of the Scalers Act or "for any other reason which the Minister in his discretion deems sufficient."[88] These examples illustrate the type of subject-matter which it has been thought desirable to place under the discretionary control of ministers and officials; they indicate too the possibility of that discretion being used as a political weapon. But suggestions that it is actually so used have been rare, and the most serious complaints against an excessive delegation of discretionary authority have been registered by the strong non-partisan pressure groups who merely anticipate undesirable consequences. The Union of Nova Scotia Municipalities once protested the vesting of a wide discretion in the Governor-in-Council to deal with local governments which were about to, or might, fail to meet their obligations.[89] Similarly the lumbermen were highly vocal in 1930 against Bill 151 because it required the owners of the larger woodlots to obtain licences from the Minister of Lands and Forests prior to cutting pulpwood.

It is loaded dynamite. It is confiscation in one of its worst forms. It gives arbitrary power to the Minister to permit or refuse as he sees fit, a licence to cut "trees" on any and all lands in Nova Scotia over a thousand acres in extent. . . .

The Minister at his own sweet will may cancel the terms of "any grant, deed, transfer agreement, lease, license, Order-in-Council, Rule, Regulation or the like heretofore made, whether by the Crown, Legislature or otherwise. . . .

Such a thoroughly unsound, unjust, un-British and revolutionary proposal is unheard of in any British Legislature.[90]

[86]R.S. 1954, c. 131, s. 4.
[87]R.S. 1954, c. 84, s. 5.
[88]R.S. 1954, c. 258, s. 5.   [89]Infra, 312.
[90]Halifax Chronicle, April 21, 1930. On this occasion the opposition did not question the extent of the discretionary power so much as the purpose for which it was conferred. Was it to ensure the continuance of the pulpwood industry?

The delegation of discretionary authority to boards and commissions has also proceeded apace since the establishment of the Board of Public Utilities in 1909. The continual expansion of the power of this Board has been due in no small measure to the calibre of its performance. Throughout its long history only its administration of the Gasoline Licensing Act of 1934 invited substantial criticism. In this instance the opposition in the Legislature once alleged that any Liberal who had previously sold gasoline was able to secure a licence through political pressure.[91] The eventual deletion of the objectionable clause, which required a prospective retailer of gasoline to prove "public convenience and necessity," meant the end of the one function of the Commission which had raised doubts respecting its political impartiality.

The principal safeguard against an excess of discretionary authority ought, of course, to be the Legislature itself. When the bill to set up the Nova Scotia Liquor Commission was first introduced, it was alleged that it placed the Commission above the law.

Its actions are not subject to review in any court. It may make judicial decisions of its own motion. It may drive a coach and four through every penalty contained in the bill itself, nullify the effort of the Provincial Police set up under it, make void the judgment of any court, release any offender from the penalty of his conviction, give back the fine which any offender has paid, open the prison doors for any of its friends, and render the whole machinery of the law a mockery and a sham. . . . Its actions are subject to no review either by a court of law, by the Government of the day or the Legislature of the Province. It is to be clothed with absolute and autocratic powers and holding office for ten years may snap its fingers in the face of all public authority.[92]

On this occasion the criticism of a large and vociferous opposition resulted in major amendments which defined the duties of the Commission more explicitly, brought it more effectively under the control of the Governor-in-Council, and subjected its accounts to the examination of an auditor appointed by the Governor-in-Council.

An alert and vigorous opposition, however, has been an uncommon phenomenon over an extended period. Hence, just as in the case of delegated legislation, the main deterrent to abuse of discretionary powers has been the political executive which is often the final authority in such matters. This at least affords a measure of protection whenever the powers appear to have political significance.

Or was it to create a monopoly in favour of the Mersey Paper Company which the government had recently been instrumental in establishing?
[91]*Ibid.*, April 4, 1935.
[92]*Halifax Chronicle*, March 28, 1930.

CHAPTER XV

THE LEGISLATIVE COUNCIL

CONSTITUTION

WHILE NOVA SCOTIA retained its second chamber until 1928, scarcely a session went by after 1870 without some criticism being levelled at its activities, and every administration after 1878 at least professed sanctimonious hopes for its extinction. Curiously enough all of them possessed ample power to abolish the Council without their knowing it;[1] it continued to exist simply because no one took the trouble to determine what its constitution actually was, or at least what the courts said it was.

That constitution was by no means simple. In essence it consisted of a statutory and conventional superstructure resting on a base which was prerogative, and it was this base which finally proved unsound and undermined the entire edifice. The major portion of the prerogative component was contained in the Commissions and Instructions of the pre-Confederation Governor-in-Chief, since the Commission to Lord Durham dated February 6, 1838, constituted the Council, and those of his successors maintained it. Only two major alterations were made in the course of time—the Council's normal membership was increased from fifteen to twenty-one to enable the quorum of eight to be more readily secured, and the Governor was empowered to appoint its President[2] to prevent an office which required very considerable parliamentary knowledge from being filled by seniority. The provisions of the Commission and the Instructions which are especially relevant to this discussion accorded the councillors a tenure during pleasure and restricted to twenty-one the number of appointments which could be made provisionally by the Governor. By implication the Crown in the right of the Sovereign retained an unrestricted power of appointment.

The other portion of the prerogative component—the dispatches of the Colonial Secretary which amplified and explained the Commissions and the Instructions—was just as authoritative as if it had been con-

[1]Provided, of course, that the Judicial Committee would have given the same opinion as it did in 1927.

[2]Pursuant to a suggestion of Alexander Stewart. See copy of Stewart's letter to Russell, Aug. 3, 1840, included with Russell to Falkland, Aug. 31, 1840, in P.A.N.S. 79, 7–10.

tained in the original instruments. One example was Lord Stanley's requirement that any bankrupt Councillor who declined to resign should be suspended.[3] But the proper interpretation to be placed upon two other dispatches was not so clear. While Lord Stanley peremptorily rejected the Council's request for remuneration in 1845, his reply to its alternative demand—a "defined constitution" which would provide at least a statutory guarantee of a life appointment for its members[4]— was subsequently interpreted by some as an outright conferment of that tenure, by others as merely a willingness to confer. Certainly he gave an assurance that, if councillorships were vacated in case of bankruptcy, extended absence without leave, or commission of an infamous crime, he would be "prepared to accede to the suggested change in . . . tenure,"[5] and his successor, William Ewart Gladstone, appeared to have accepted the new tenure as a *fait accompli*.[6] Nevertheless, the subsequent Commissions of the Governor-in-Chief made no such alteration, and in later years the interpretation of these pronouncements became a species of legal exercise for a number of constitutional authorities. Eventually the Judicial Committee dismissed them as tentative proposals which had never been fully consummated.

The first statutory component, although not expressly so intended, was that portion of the B.N.A. Act of 1867 which provided that the constitution of the Nova Scotian Legislature should continue unaltered until it was changed by the action of the Legislature itself.[7] This left the size of the Council in doubt. Was it the twenty-one which constituted the normal membership before 1867, or the eighteen which actually constituted its membership at Confederation, or the unlimited number which the Sovereign had always possessed the right to appoint? Since the Legislature failed to establish a fixed membership by statute, it was again left to the Judicial Committee to decide sixty years later that the third alternative was the correct one.

Three Nova Scotian statutes explicitly altered the constitution of the Council. The first (1872)—a belated sequel to promptings both from London and Ottawa[8]—gave to the Lieutenant-Governor-in-Council

[3]Stanley to Falkland, Dec. 7, 1841, P.A.N.S. 80, 167–8. Falkland made immediate use of this directive to force the resignation of J. L. Starr, *Journals of the Legislative Council (JLC)*, 1842, 10. Forty years later Adams G. Archibald put it to similar use in the case of James S. Macdonald. *JLC*, 1883, 34–5.
[4]See *JLC*, 1845, 60–1.
[5]Stanley to Falkland, Aug. 20, 1845, *JLC*, 1846, Appendix 1.
[6]Gladstone to Falkland, May 4, 1846, *JLC*, 1847, Appendix 4.
[7]Ss. 88 and 92 (1).
[8]See Meredith to Doyle, Oct. 26, 1867, *Journals of the House of Assembly (JHA)*, 1868, Appendix 13, 6–7.

the power of making absolute, rather than merely provisional, appointments.[9] The act did not state explicitly, however, if the provincial authority was restricted to appointing the normal maximum of twenty-one or if it had been vested with the power of the Queen-in-Council to appoint an unlimited number. The latter alternative had likely occurred to no one, and certainly not to the Council, but the Judicial Committee eventually accepted it as the correct interpretation of the act.

The second statute (1873) had the effect of repealing those clauses of the Commission and Instructions which permitted the suspension and removal of councillors for extended absence by assimilating a provision of the Senate of Canada to the Legislative Council. As a result, a Councillor vacated his seat automatically if he failed to make an appearance during two successive sessions.[10] In the third statute (1925) the Council made a last valiant gesture to stave off extinction by acquiescing in a reduction of its powers and an altered tenure for its members.[11]

Conventions and rules also made their contribution to the constitution of the Council. While the conventions were not explicitly stated, they were often as effective as if they had been decreed by law. Typical examples were the practice which grew up after 1848 of appointing members on a partisan basis, and the custom which prevailed after 1887 of prescribing representation on a rigid geographical basis. The latter was the result of two widely separated actions. The provision of a sessional indemnity in 1854 had enabled the councillors to be recruited more readily from a wider area[12] and on March 10, 1887, Fielding brought a long-term development to its ultimate conclusion by appointing a member for each of the four counties then unrepresented. From that date it became as securely woven into the constitutional fabric of the upper House as if it had been provided by legal enactment that Halifax County would have three councillors and all the other counties at least one.[13]

The constitutional student J. G. Bourinot felt that the tenure of councillors during life had been similarly established. For "while the Crown had not given up its theoretical right to appoint members of the council only during pleasure, it had," he said, "by agreement and usage for many years previous to 1867 practically yielded its right,

[9]35 Vic. c. 13.
[10]R.S. 1873, c. 2. Apparently this provision was operative only in the case of George Whitman in 1912.   [11]*Infra*, 249.   [12]*Supra*, 103.
[13]After 1912 most governments recognized the claims of populous Cape Breton by allotting it two seats.

and conceded a tenure for life, subject to certain rules and conditions."[14] Yet he himself admitted and history amply confirmed the futility of citing mere understandings in a court of law.

The Council's rules of procedure, and particularly the stipulation that those of the House of Lords were to apply when not incompatible with the Nova Scotian circumstance, completed its constitutional structure. A few modifications—not always formal in character—occurred with the passage of time. Some rules passed practically into desuetude, such as the one which required voting to proceed from the junior to the senior member so as to prevent the veteran councillors from exerting an undue influence over their less experienced colleagues. There were additions, too, usually prompted by the exigency of the moment, as in 1849 when the President assumed the right of the Lord Chancellor to vote on all decisions, instead of merely to break a tie.[15]

THE COUNCIL IN ACTION

After 1848 the Council tended to adopt a course of slavish concurrence or factious opposition depending upon whether or not its majority was sympathetic to the administration of the day.[16] Until 1882 the second of these courses was the rule and constituted a serious embarrassment to newly instituted ministries. While fortuitous circumstances such as a heavy mortality rate at propitious moments sometimes provided a remedy, a government often found itself forced to rely on its own ingenuity to circumvent its opponents in the Council. Thus the first administration after Confederation could put into effect its proposals for the repeal of Confederation only by appropriating the requisite funds without the consent of a hostile Council. Even more unsavoury were the attempts of the Conservatives to get Councillor James McNab to abstain from voting on a highly contentious bill at a time (1871) when the political complexion of the Council was in doubt.[17] Ten years later a Conservative government was accused of refunding to the 96-year-old R. M. Cutler the sessional indemnity which he had lost as the means of securing his resignation,[18] and the

[14]"The Constitution of the Legislative Council of Nova Scotia," *Transactions of the Royal Society of Canada*, 1896, vol. II, sec. II, 171. The rules and conditions were those elaborated in the despatch of Aug. 20, 1845. *Supra*, 102.
[15]*Supra*, 103–4.   [16]*Supra*, 103.
[17]By the promise of a federal appointment to his son Peter.
[18]Although Cutler was a Conservative, his advanced age prevented anything like a regular attendance. His successor was William H. Owen who remained in the Council until 1928. Together Cutler and Owen filled the one seat during the whole ninety years of the Council's existence.

same year the ailing Liberal Councillor William C. Whitman of Annapolis swore out an affidavit to the effect that a prominent Halifax Conservative had offered him $1,000 for his resignation.[19]

The last two sorry episodes indicate the desperate straits of the only administration which experienced the factious opposition of the Council throughout its entire life. Activated by a partisan of the first water, Thomas F. Morrison, the upper House severely checked any display of initiative by the Conservative administration of Simon Holmes between 1878 and 1882. Any reconciliation of its actions before and after 1882 is entirely out of the question. It rejected an $800,000 debt-funding bill of Holmes, yet it gave Pipes and Fielding almost a blank cheque in adding to the provincial debt; it turned down the Bridge Bills of 1881 and 1882 to prevent a large sum of money being placed under "the control of the two-penny-half-penny members supporting the Government, at the next elections,"[20] yet it acquiesced in similar bills of Fielding which were geared even more closely to Liberal campaign strategy; it denied Holmes the right to withdraw the control of the Insane Asylum from a Public Charities Board which was dominated by Liberals for fear an act of gross partisanship might be perpetrated, yet it permitted Pipes first to reappoint or reject the incumbent sheriffs at his pleasure and then to convert their tenure to one during good behaviour. To argue in reply that the Conservative government's conduct was characterized by dullness, imbecility, and folly[21] made no sense, for no administration merited interference less than the all-too-cautious Holmes ministry. The Council's action can, in fact, be justified only on the premise that Conservative governments do no right, Liberal governments no wrong. That the Conservatives developed an ineradicable dislike of the second branch during this period is understandable.

There were, however, a few brighter areas in this generally dismal picture. William Stairs and his son William J. Stairs both resigned from the Council when they found themselves basically opposed to the administration which appointed them. On rare occasions, too, the Council rejected or at least lessened the worst effects of partisan legislation. A Conservative Council prevented a Conservative government from giving the Conservative Judge in Equity a status equivalent to that of the Liberal Chief Justice. A Liberal Council rejected more than once the attempts of a Liberal Assembly to repeal the Ballot Act after its first use had not been to the advantage of the Liberal party, and

[19]See *Morning Chronicle*, May 17, 19, 21, 24, and 27, 1881.
[20]*Acadian Recorder*, April 11, 1881.   [21]*Ibid.*, April 9, 1881.

it introduced some degree of fairness into the bill to disfranchise Dominion officials in provincial elections by extending the disqualification to a restricted number of provincial officials as well.

But the basic conclusion remains sound. No administration needed to fear a Council which contained a majority of the same political allegiance, and controversial bills normally experienced rough treatment only when they emanated from an unfriendly government or a private member. With this unfortunate background the Council entered upon a 43-year period of Liberal rule in 1882 during which its prestige sank to a new low.[22] Four factors contributed to its steadily diminishing role.

Foremost among them was its lessened influence in the counsels of government. Until 1882 the Executive Council normally included a Legislative Councillor with portfolio and usually one without portfolio. The Pipes government (1882-4) ushered in a new era. From its inception dated the custom of appointing the government leader in the Council a minister without portfolio, and of providing the upper branch no other cabinet representation. Even before this innovation the legislative councillors in the cabinet had more than once shown themselves deficient in information on governmental policy; henceforth the Council's position came to resemble that of the modern Canadian Senate. The government's legislation was introduced without exception in the lower chamber and the upper branch simply registered a second opinion. Actually it had become an outsider in the scheme of government.

At the same time there was an increasing tendency on the part of the public to disregard its transactions altogether. The Council's acquiescence in the policy of the government after 1882 meant, of course, an almost complete black-out of its proceedings in the newspapers. Even those of its acts which were deemed worthy of cognizance,

[22]Normally some of the evils which are inherent in selecting the members of a second chamber on a purely partisan basis are submerged when each of two parties shares in the making of appointments over reasonably equal periods, but in Nova Scotia this factor was inoperative for almost half a century. Some of the striking abnormalities in the composition and the functioning of the Council which resulted from the almost continuous period of one-party rule were: the appointment by Liberal governments of 89 of the 105 members who were chosen between 1848 and 1927, 59 of them consecutively between 1882 and 1925; an unbroken Liberal majority from 1871 to 1927; no divisions along party lines after the early 1890's; no Conservative leader from the death of Hiram Black in 1896 until the appointment of F. P. Bligh in 1926; and only one Conservative member from 1913 to 1926. The latter, William H. Owen, outlasted a 43-year-old government and concluded a 47-year term by casting a successful vote in favor of the abolition which he had previously opposed.

particularly its refusals to vote for its own abolition and to increase the indemnity of the assemblymen unless its own members were accorded the same treatment, brought only unfavourable notoriety. But since these incidents were few, the caustic comments of its unfailing critic, the *Herald*, were likely not far off the mark:

The common belief is that the Legislative Council passed from nothingness to absolute oblivion some years ago. At least there has been for some years no sign, sound, or symbol that such a body of executives exist. No one ever sees their names in the press. No one ever hears of their doing any thing. Oh, yes,—once a year, to be exact, it is bruited that the members of the Legislative Council have been paid their honorarium. The people read, gasp, and snort in disgust, exclaiming, "We thought that those legislative futilities were long ago dead and buried and turned to dust."[23]

Occasionally some far-sighted Councillor would warn his colleagues of the inevitable consequences of the lack of recognition in the press. "You cannot go on for ever," one said, "and transact business and the public know nothing about it. . . . if there becomes a general notion abroad . . . that this is a useless body, occupied by a lot of old people who do no good, it will bring about the end if it is not contradicted."[24] Yet the additional publicity which he recommended would hardly have redounded to the Council's advantage. Certainly the few outsiders who ventured to gaze on its proceedings could not have been impressed by what purported to be a deliberative assembly. What they saw bore a much closer resemblance to an exclusive old gentlemen's club. Speech-making was at a minimum possibly because the wisdom of age had convinced the councillors of its futility. Even its rules of procedure worked against it. After 1899 it adopted the two-committee system of the Assembly,[25] but with an important difference—it referred all the bills to committees immediately after their first reading and thereby devolved upon them not only the amending function but the more vital task of approving the bills in principle. Thus the Council performed its real work far removed from the public eye. "The work of this body is largely done in committee," said one Councillor, "and we have really been hiding our light under a bushel."[26]

The Council's inability to keep its business moving at a moderate tempo—a fault beyond its own capacity to rectify—strengthened the unfavourable impression. Even if the Assembly rushed through a

[23]March 13, 1919.
[24]H. C. LeVatte in *Council Debates*, 1921, 10.
[25]The Law Amendments Committee dealt with the public bills; the Select Committee on Bills with the private and local bills.
[26]*Morning Chronicle*, March 10, 1926.

few bills early in the session to give the second chamber something to do, it was frequently inactive, and one who gazed upon its lethargic state adapted the "Ancient Mariner" to what he saw:

> There was no bill, no MOTION,
> They're as idle as a painted ship
> Upon a painted ocean.[27]

This, of course, was in marked contrast to the closing days of the session when there was always a "mad rush of business being crowded through, the House passing from session to . . . Committee of the Whole, and from one to the other, like a shuttle board."[28]

The critics of the Council often attributed its apparent lack of purposeful activity to the advanced age of its members, and the statistics[29] justify to some degree their charge that it constituted an old man's home. In 1910 the average age of its members was 71.5 years, and in both 1910 and 1920 one-third of the councillors had passed the 75-year mark. But whatever the cause the plain fact was that the Council could offer little justification for its existence to either the actual observer or the general public, and its vulnerability to attack without any effective means of self-defence constituted a constant threat to its very being.

The Council's tendency to become geared more and more closely to the political strategy of a particular party further weakened its position. In accordance with well-established practice the Liberal administrations from 1882 to 1925 appointed none but staunch Liberals to the Council. Twenty-one of their thirty-three appointees after 1896[30] had contested Dominion or provincial elections, ten of whom had suffered defeat in their last political ventures.[31] The remaining twelve appointees had performed yeoman service for the party on a lesser scale. All the evidence suggests that the Council had become a key adjunct of the Liberal organization and that Premier Murray in particular used all its potentialities to keep himself in office. It is far less difficult to secure suitable candidates for election when the prospect of even a small pension looms pleasantly ahead after a term or two as an assemblyman or even after a single electoral defeat; it is likewise easy to appease influential party supporters who have been denied other preferment by the promise of a safe haven in the upper House; it is even possible to facilitate the reorganization of a cabinet in a time of crisis through the power of appointment to the Council, and

---

[27]*Ibid.*, March 22, 1888.   [28]*Ibid.*, April 29, 1922.   [29]See Appendix J.
[30]The appointees of the Murray and Armstrong administrations.
[31]Eight in the provincial and two in the federal field.

Murray's practice of allowing a few councillorships to remain vacant fitted conveniently into this scheme of things.

The policy of demanding pledges in support of abolition from all the councillors who were appointed between 1884 and 1925 added a more sinister note to the government's relations with the second chamber. But although Murray continued to exact these pledges after 1896, for more than twenty years he evinced not the slightest interest in abolition. During that period the legislative record of the Council reveals an all too accommodating concern not to embarrass his government, and the cynic would have good grounds for alleging an arrangement which accrued to the benefit of both. Certainly no legislative body could be placed in this peculiar position and still be expected to maintain a proper independence.

Finally, the role played by the Council in the legislative process was, to a large degree, inconsequential and erratic. Long before the upper House had received its quietus, the Assembly had come to dominate the legislative process. The supporters of the second chamber, it is true, sometimes lauded its efficiency in checking legislation which was designed to promote the advantage of a particular party.

. . . it smothers out, unseen, [they said] many small and almost unsuspected political fires. It confines others within proper limits, and it stands ever ready to prevent any flagrant political wrong-doing. The mere fact of its existence serves to prevent real "jobs" from being attempted or even thought of.[32]

To support this contention they could point to the Liberal Council's rejection of a Conservative government's proposals in 1926 and 1927 to convert the tenure of all office-holders to one during pleasure. It is more than peculiar, however, that a Council of like political allegiance had permitted its power of rejection to remain quiescent in similar cases during the preceding forty-three years of Liberal administrations. A series of bills manipulating the boundaries of municipal districts for purely partisan purposes had afforded it more than one opportunity to check "small political fires," and the redistribution of seats in Cape Breton and Richmond counties in 1925, which was the most flagrant resort to gerrymandering in the history of the province, gave it the chance to oppose a real "job," but it let these party bills pass unchecked.

It was this obeisance to successive Liberal administrations, above all, which was seized upon by the Conservative government after 1925. Its first appointee to the Council bluntly condemned his fellow

[32]*Morning Chronicle*, March 17, 1924.

councillors: "You have been rubber stamps. . . . Was there ever a government measure that came to this House in the last 40 years that was defeated here. . . . Did you ever raise one word against government measures in the past. Were the past governments always right?"[33] Earlier one Liberal Councillor had suggested that, if "matters political continue[d] to run the same course much longer, it [would] be well for the government of the country to consider the appointment of a 'devil's advocate,' to point out the demerits of the various government measures."[34] But although matters political ran in the same direction for two more decades, a critic's voice was seldom heard.

An even more serious charge was that the Council, at the bidding of the government, occasionally rejected a bill which it was politically inexpedient for the administration to oppose in the Assembly.[35] Here the particular reference was to the Nova Scotia Temperance Act which had been handled gingerly by the politicians over a long period. While politically astute George Murray always permitted a free vote in the yearly amendments of this Act, both he and his ministers usually gave some support to the temperance forces, sometimes to secure a more extended application of the Act, sometimes to plug loop-holes which prevented its enforcement. In contrast, the Council, which had no need to placate a watchful pressure group, could adopt a more realistic view, and more than once it rejected the Assembly's concessions to the temperance forces. Naturally the critics were quick to accuse the Council of conspiring with the Premier for partisan purposes. They singled out the proceedings of 1917 in particular as "A Pitiable Exhibition of 'Playing the Political Game' at Both Ends and in the Middle by Premier Murray . . . [in a] plain effort to HOLD the liquor dealers for another election,"[36] and although they could produce no certain evidence of collusion, they were at least correct that the Council's assumption of an unpopular role accrued to the advantage of the Murray administration.

The Council's record as an upholder of conservatism and as a protector of property and vested rights admits of no easy generalization. Prior to 1900 it appears to have demanded clear proof of the need

---

[33]*Halifax Herald*, March 5, 1926.

[34]See speech of Jason M. Mack, *Council Debates*, 1903–4, 7.

[35]Premier Rhodes deprecated the passage of bills with all the outward forms of solemnity, "while the Premier of the day [Murray] was having negotiation with honorable gentlemen in another chamber preparing that same bill for slaughter, so they could go to the people and say 'we tried to get this bill through but it was defeated by the Legislative Council.' " *Halifax Herald*, Feb. 11, 1927.

[36]*Halifax Herald*, May 10, 1917.

for changes in the status quo before accepting them,[37] but its later record indicates an attitude no more conservative than that of the Assembly.[38] The upper House, it is true, always contained a few members who deprecated any interference with property and vested rights. In the early years of the century their spokesman was Jason Mack, who refused to alter the conditions of property held in trust even when the purpose of the trust had disappeared;[39] in later years it was C. P. Chisholm whose particular dislike was the conversion of quit claim deeds into guarantee deeds by statute. "This thing is like the Frenchman's soup," he declared; "it is coming a little too often. . . . We will wake up some day and discover that somebody sitting here is deeding away our lands and potato patches."[40]

The opposition of the Council on this score was noticeably less determined when bills were initiated by the government rather than by private members. Mack found little support for his opposition to a bill which affected the existing rights of the bondholders of the Dominion Iron and Steel Company, because it had the backing of the government,[41] but another which allegedly divested the pew-holders of the Presbyterian congregation of Baddeck of their seats became a highly contentious item.[42] Even within the narrow field of private bills and private members' public bills, however, the Council appears in one instance to have been seriously derelict in its duty. That was the celebrated Jane E. MacNeil case in which a Liberal government at Ottawa felt no compunction about disallowing a provincial act which deprived an outside corporation of a clear title to some of its property in Nova Scotia. In this instance the Council had accepted the measure even though a retired judge of the Supreme Court had accosted its members on the steps of Province House and bluntly accused them of wrong-doing.[43]

All in all, the Council's record in the initiation and rejection of bills

---

[37]For example, it permitted the repeal of the obsolete legislation having to do with imprisonment for debt and preferential assignments by insolvent debtors only after many years of debate. 53 Vic., c. 17, and 61 Vic., c. 11.

[38]One Councillor, A. W. Redden, was, in fact, a foremost advocate of the abolition of the exclusive fishing rights of riparian landowners, and in this instance the second chamber was noticeably less solicitous of property rights than the popular branch.

[39]*Council Debates*, 1903–4, 49.

[40]*Ibid*, 1922, 39.

[41]*Ibid.*, 1902, 25–9.

[42]*Ibid.*, 1909, 56–8.

[43]Of the councillors only C. P. Chisholm raised his voice against the bill. "I might as well come in and ask a deed of all the Crown Lands," he said. *Ibid.*, 1921, 78.

was not impressive. During two three-year periods[44] only twelve, or 3.3 per cent, of the 370 public bills enacted into law originated in the Council and none attempted any far-reaching changes. While forty-two, or 4 per cent, of the Assembly's bills failed to win approval in the upper House, none of them was of major importance. Yet 38 per cent of these bills became law only after the Assembly had accepted the Council's amendments, and if any justification existed for the continuance of the upper House, it was its record in revising those bills upon which the government was content that it should exercise a free hand.

In performing this function it was constantly advised by the press not to accept special, vicious, clandestine, or otherwise obnoxious legislation. It probably reached the high point of public approval in 1902 when all three Halifax newspapers agreed upon the utility of its work.[45] But there were bad moments as well. The worst of these, its failure to detect the inconsistencies in two bills which were passed in 1922 to change the rule of the road,[46] provided excellent ammunition for its Conservative critics after 1925.

Its sins of omission, however, were not nearly so serious as its sins of commission. In 1904 its fault lay in attaching to an inconsequential bill having to do with assessments a mysterious appendage which deprived the county magistrates of their jurisdiction within the incorporated towns.[47] Since for some unexplained reason the provision was made applicable to Pictou County only, the Council found it hard to deny the contention of the Conservatives that it had been introduced surreptitiously at the request of the liquor interests who preferred to have their cases tried by a sympathetic town magistrate. Yet by that time the clumsy procedure of the lower House had enabled the provision to be enacted into law without its members being cognizant of its existence. In the following year the Council, which had on several occasions prevented the Assembly from extending the franchise to Dominion officials in provincial elections, itself introduced the change as a thoroughly irrelevant amendment to a bill regulating the taking of oaths by presiding officers and poll clerks. Once again the lower House accepted the alteration without being fully aware of its purport. But this time the Conservatives denounced a highly irregular method

[44]See Appendix K.
[45]Even the *Herald* gave its approval: ". . . the general impression is that the councillors' work on other bills [the H.S.W. Railway Bill excepted] was such as to prove the council's right to be." *Halifax Herald,* March 28, 1902.
[46]To prevent confusion, Ottawa eventually disallowed the acts at the request of the provincial government.   [47]See 3–4 Edw. VII, c. 37, s. 3.

of making substantive changes in the law so vehemently that the Assembly amended its rules to prevent a recurrence.[48]

Yet neither these occasional shortcomings nor irregular modes of proceedings refuted the fact that the Council, through its committees, generally worked industriously and with sincerity. To the original Towns' Incorporation Act, it added forty or fifty manuscript pages of amendments and the House, unequal to the task of review in the closing days of the session, was forced to accept the opinion of the Council's law clerk that the alterations were in order.[49] Often, of course, its amendments were of dubious value.[50] Yet early in the century it displayed an infinitely greater regard for principle than the Assembly in dealing with a multitudinous crop of bills empowering municipalities to grant bonuses to industries. Previously it had taken the lead in adapting its rules to the more efficient working of the legislative process, in one instance by refusing to permit the introduction of local bills after the first twenty days of each session, in another by requiring the sponsor of a private or a local bill to furnish satisfactory evidence that he had given advance notification to any municipality, corporation, or private individual that might be affected by the bill.[51]

The conclusion seems to be that the Council performed its functions seriously within its self-restricted sphere. Up to 1928 the closing days of each session continued to be marked by the committees of the two Houses attempting to secure mutually acceptable compromises. Hence it is easy to see how a Councillor who once had been dubious of the second chamber's utility might conclude that it was rendering an indispensable service. He could come to agree wholeheartedly with the idyllic picture of its onetime legal counsel Benjamin Russell that it did its work "quietly and effectively making few long speeches and doing much good work, killing a number of bad bills and making the good ones better."[52] What he did not realize, or admit, was that the

[48]The statute in question was 5 Edw. VII, c. 21, s. 3, *Infra*, 260. The change in rules provided that "the amendments of the Legislative Council to Bills passed in this House shall be referred to the Committtee of this House which passed the original Bill."

[49]But not without an indignant Conservative Assemblyman questioning the propriety of Mr. Benjamin Russell's running the lower as well as the upper House. *Assembly Debates*, 1888, 377.

[50]Once when the Council added the clause "and have laid the rails thereon" to a bill for the completion of a particular railway project, it drew the caustic comment of Attorney-General J. W. Longley who felt "it would be difficult to complete a railway without laying rails on the track." *Ibid.*, 344.

[51]See *Council Debates*, 1898, 49.

[52]Letter to C. H. Cahan, *Halifax Herald*, Feb. 2, 1894.

meritorious performance of a severely limited function hardly justified the existence of the Council. Both Premiers Fielding and Rhodes were of the opinion that it could be performed adequately without the elaborate trappings and trimmings of an upper House. Neither saw "good reason to believe that the abolition of the Council would lead to the passing of hasty legislation. While the Council exist[ed] its services [were] utilized, but if the Council did not exist the Assembly would understand its greater responsibility"[53] by giving more careful attention to details.

EXODUS

For fifty-eight years the Council withstood a multitude of attacks on its right to exist. Only the inability of the proponents of abolition to get an apathetic public to express an opinion either upon the necessity of a bicameral Legislature or upon the adequacy of the existing Council prolonged the issue. Its solution was left, therefore, to the politician, and when the British government declined to interfere in a non-emergency matter within provincial legislative competence, an act of the Legislature became the one means of effecting abolition. There was no difficulty in securing the Assembly's assent, since after 1878 it always considered the second chamber redundant; the problem was to obtain one Council with a like opinion. That is the keynote of the abolition story as it unfolded in six distinct phases:

1869–71. For three years the ultra anti-Confederate wing of a solidly Liberal Assembly utilized without success the straitened financial conditions of the province under Confederation to reinforce its argument for getting rid of a body "filled with men . . . who became the assassins of the Constitution, and who received their seats . . . as the reward of their treachery."[54]

1872–8. Throughout two Assemblies the Conservative opposition kept insisting that the Council membership should be reduced by the simple expedient of leaving its vacant seats unfilled, the ultimate purpose being to effect abolition. But in the first few years the government refused to weaken its not overly strong position in the upper branch, while later the Council itself "decline[d] with thanks the kind suggstion that [it] become *felos de se.*"[55]

[53]See order of the Executive Council dated Feb. 24, 1894, in *JHA*, 1896, Appendix 16, 3.

[54]*Assembly Debates*, 1871, 267. The reference was to those councillors who as assemblymen had supported the resolution in favour of Confederation.

[55]*Acadian Recorder*, March 20, 1876.

1878–82. The worsened financial situation of the province, combined with a Liberal Council's obstruction of a Conservative government's legislative programme, led to the first real attacks on the second branch. Premier Holmes tried three different methods to remove a constant irritant to his administration. The first was to appoint to the Council only those individuals who were in accord with his policy of abolition.[56] Yet despite the inherent soundness of this course the state of the Council militated against its success, for, when the Conservatives assumed office, their supporters in the upper House were limited to five veteran members, while the Liberals, with one or two exceptions, were "either comparatively young or in the full vigor of middle life."[57] Nevertheless the plan made some headway. A majority of seven in 1879 was reduced to one of three in 1882[58] and only the defeat of the Conservative government after a single term of office saved the Council at this stage.

Holmes also requested the permission of the British government to appoint enough councillors to effect abolition and explored the possibility of united action with the two other Maritime Provinces which were also seeking to rid themselves of their Councils. But neither of these courses was more successful than the first, in the one case because of the British government's refusal to intervene,[59] in the other through the failure of any of the three governments to suggest specific ameliorative action.

1882–96. The Pipes and Fielding administrations accepted the policy of abolition in the interest of economy and promised to effect it "as soon as it [could] be done consistently with the existing law and the prerogatives of this legislature."[60] The method was to continue the appointment of persons who were known to be in favour of abolition. This time, however, the government gave assurances that it would be "able to place papers on record that would indicate the policy they had pursued."[61] Despite the demands of the Conservatives for immediate

[56]The manner in which the appointees made by Holmes signified their intention in this regard is somewhat uncertain, but there appear to have been pledges of some kind or other. *Infra,* 247n.

[57]See letter of Holmes to the Lieutenant-Governor, Oct. 17, 1881, *JHA,* 1882, Appendix 12, 15.

[58]In 1878 twelve Liberals and a dubious Conservative (James Fraser) opposed six Conservatives; in 1882 it was ten Liberals, one Conservative (John McKinnon), and the same dubious Conservative who opposed eight Conservatives and one Liberal (James Butler).

[59]The circumstances did not lead the Colonial Secretary to conclude that "an alteration of the constitution has been proved to be necessary." For full details, see *JHA,* 1882, Appendix 12, 5.

[60]*Ibid.,* 1886, 514.   [61]*Ibid.,* 1884, 286.

action, Fielding bided his time until his appointees, when combined with the previous advocates of abolition, constituted a majority of the upper House. Yet even then the Council rejected his first bill for its demise in 1888.

The division[62] on this occasion was the forerunner of many idiosyncrasies to follow. Two of the unpledged, pre-1878 appointees, an adherent of each party, reversed their previous pro-abolition stand. More significantly, two of the four Conservatives who were supposed to have been pledged by Holmes and one of the six Liberals who had definitely been pledged by Pipes voted against abolition. The latter, Monson Hoyt Goudge, placed on record the reasoning which was later to be developed by his colleagues into a flawless technique for preserving the Council. He denied first that he had ever regarded pledges as absolute; indeed, Pipes in exacting them had intimated that any members who later became convinced of the utility of the Council had a perfect right to renounce them.[63] He had discovered, in addition, two constitutional objections to the government's course of action. Not only did the introduction of an abolition bill in the Assembly constitute a violation of the Council's privileges, but "it was absolutely unconstitutional to pledge any man in coming to [the] House as to a course that he should pursue, and no man could vote independently unless he exercised his own judgment upon all questions."[64]

This double-barrelled constitutional argument was the means of defeating Fielding's two final efforts to secure abolition, both of which were attempted in pre-election sessions. In 1890 the Council resorted to the first of these points; in 1894 to the second. On the latter occasion everything augured well for abolition—a majority of councillors had been pledged by Liberal administrations and the government did its best to make the measure more palatable, first by having it introduced in the Council and secondly by making abolition contingent upon the favourable vote of the electorate at a plebiscite. But the upper branch had provided itself with protective insurance in anticipation—an opinion from distinguished legal counsel[65] that although the government had a

[62]The breakdown of the councillors was as follows:

Time of appointment	For abolition		Against abolition	
Pre-1878	1 Cons.		6 Lib.	2 Cons.
1878–82 (Holmes)	2 Cons.			2 Cons.
1883–8 (Pipes and Fielding)	5 Lib.		1 Lib.	
Total	5 Lib.	3 Cons.	7 Lib.	4 Cons.

[63]For Pipes's statement see *Assembly Debates*, 1884, 281.
[64]*Morning Herald*, April 10, 1888.
[65]Benjamin Russell and R. L. Borden, whose views were concurred in by Dean R. C. Weldon of the Dalhousie Law School.

perfect right to appoint councillors who were in agreement with its own views and intentions, anything further was unconstitutional and subversive of the general purpose for which the Council existed.[66] One of its legal advocates was particularly forceful in condemning the device of pledges on the ground that it made the Council "a mere collection of puppets to be worked from a key board in the provincial secretary's office" and necessitated its dependence upon "the existence, discovery and interpretation of a number of written memoranda that [might] be found in the provincial secretary's desk and partly in the coatpockets of the prothonotary of Halifax."[67] Thus fortified, the Council concluded that it could not give an independent judgment so long as these pledges deprived its members of their freedom of choice.[68] This line of conduct provoked a controversy which was to last for thirty years: "Has a gentleman the right to obtain an appointment to the council by means of a written pledge to vote for its abolition, and then, when he gets in the council, [either] violate his pledge and vote the other way,"[69] or refuse to allow the issue even to be raised?

Fielding showed no inclination to temporize with the Council's behaviour. He declared its constitutional arguments to be mere subterfuge and suggested that any Councillor who felt he had acted unconstitutionally in making a pledge should present his resignation as a matter of honour.[70] Yet he refused the one bit of advice which might have been successful—the suggestion of C. H. Cahan that the councillors who had broken their engagements should be dismissed forthwith[71]—and his own alternative—another address to the Queen re-

---

[66]See *Council Debates*, 1894, 22–3.

[67]These excerpts are from an exchange of letters in the *Herald* between Russell and C. H. Cahan. See particularly *Morning Herald*, Feb. 2, 1894. On this occasion Fielding made public all the pledges which he had exacted, but much to Cahan's annoyance, Holmes, who was at the time prothonotary of the Supreme Court at Halifax, declined to take similar action on the ground that the pledges were "personal, private and confidential, that it would be a violation of his oath as executive councillor to disclose them now." See telegram of Cahan to Sir John Thompson, Jan. 27, 1894, in Thompson Papers, (P.A.C.), item 24780.

[68]The vote was 14 to 5. See *Council Debates*, 1894, 49. As in 1890, all the councillors but five pledged Liberals adopted the constitutional pretext as a basis for their votes.

[69]*Morning Chronicle*, Jan. 30, 1894.

[70]*Assembly Debates*, 1894, 144.

[71]*Morning Chronicle*, Jan. 27, 1894. Cahan's position assumed that the tenure of legislative councillors was during pleasure, a viewpoint shared by few others of that day.

questing relief by way of an amendment to the B.N.A. Act—proved of no avail.[72]

1896–1925. Premier Murray's policy is by no means as easy to condone as that of his predecessors. His two proposals to abolish the Council were at best faint-hearted pre-election gestures designed to meet the criticism of his opponents, and the upper House had ample precedents for casting them aside with scarcely a ripple to disturb the political waters.[73] On the second occasion his inconclusive statement of policy was a clear case of playing both ends against the middle. He was all in favour of a unicameral Legislature, he said, but, after all, the movement for abolition had arisen because of financial stringency which no longer existed; the Council did no harm and some good; and the provinces which had abolished their second chambers were by no means certain that the results had been beneficial.[74] So, on the one hand, he continued to exact pledges, thereby placing himself in a position to lead any popular demand for abolition, while, on the other, he tolerated the Council and utilized it to further his own political ends. The result was to destroy the independence of the upper branch and to lower the dignity of public life.

Another course was possible. By 1901 the Liberal press had become decidedly favourable to the Council's continuance. "We might have to dispense with the Council if we could not afford it," said the *Chronicle*, "but, now that we can afford it, we cannot afford to dispense with it."[75] The *Recorder*, in its turn, pointed to the necessity of a second chamber in an "era of giant corporations, all clamoring for special privileges."[76] Murray, who had the alternative either of recognizing the utility of the Council and dispensing with pledges, or of taking active steps to extinguish it, did neither. In fact, during his last session as Premier he made the revealing admission that because of the lack of any real pressure for abolition he had "adopted the course of 'letting sleeping dogs lie.' "[77]

Naturally his behaviour drew the fire of the opposition groups in

[72]For the address see *JHA*, 1894, Appendix 17. It was stated in reply that "resort to Imperial legislation would be inexpedient except in circumstances of urgent necessity." See *JHA*, 1896, Appendix 16, 11–12.

[73]In 1897 the Council raised the same objections as in 1890; in 1901 the same as in 1894. On the second occasion it refused even to permit the introduction of a bill to effect abolition until the government gave an assurance that the pledges which it had exacted were not binding. See *JLC*, 1901, 148–55.

[74]*Assembly Debates*, 1901, 14.

[75]April 1, 1901.   [76]March 12, 1901.   [77]*Halifax Herald*, April 7, 1922.

the Assembly who, in the first decade of the century, denounced the Council as an anachronism, and in the second proposed that it should be reduced to exercising the suspensive veto which had been forced upon the House of Lords in 1911. Yet W. L. Hall's bill to that effect was defeated in 1916, as was one introduced by the Hon. R. M. MacGregor in his capacity as a private member in 1917.[78] The Farmer-Labour group, which provided the main opposition in the Assembly from 1921 to 1925, was even more critical of a temporizing government than the Conservatives, but when a joint committee of both Houses met in 1922 and 1923 to consider the position of the second chamber, the latter had discovered a new reason for its existence—it was to be a last barrier against J. B. McLachlan and his communistic activities in eastern Nova Scotia.

Nevertheless the evidence suggests that Premier Armstrong was unwilling to play the old game with the same regard for the convenience of the Council as his predecessor. It is true that the abolitionist of 1922 became the reformer of 1925, but the Council realized that he meant business. For that reason it was ready to discard the constitutional niceties of the past and to accept with amendments a bill which altered its constitution even though it was introduced in the Assembly. Yet there was still a bit of fight left in the ancient body. While it agreed that its members should in future be appointed for ten-year periods, it raised the age proposed for their retirement from 70 to 75 years, and as a last splendid gesture in protecting its own vested rights, it declined to make this provision applicable to the incumbent members.

Furthermore, even though it permitted its powers to be reduced to a suspensive veto in some matters, it retained all its old rights over money bills and bills which altered the constitution of the two Houses, thereby ensuring that the new provision could not be used to effect its own destruction.[79]

1925–8. The Rhodes government ushered in a new era for the Council. The days of temporizing were over, for the new government

---

[78]On the former occasion Premier Murray attributed to the Council part of the credit for ensuring that "more care, deliberation and caution had been exercised in the passing of legislation . . . than in perhaps any other Province of the Dominion." *Morning Chronicle*, May 3, 1916. On the latter he made the curious observation that "the fact of a public man signing . . . a pledge [to support abolition] would have an effect more or less some day or other in the bringing about of constitutional change." *Ibid.*, April 18, 1917.

[79]15–16 Geo. V, c. 16.

had no need to mollify a body which contained but a single Conservative whose political usefulness had long since passed. Heeding the lessons of the preceding forty years, it declined to fill vacancies as they occurred for fear the new members might become too enamoured of their new offices. In 1926 it contented itself with appointing F. P. Bligh to act as its spokesman in the Council; in 1927 it promoted him to the presidency of the upper House[80] and named R. H. Butts as the government leader. All its other appointments were to be geared to its grand strategy for establishing a unicameral Legislature.

To accomplish its purpose, it resorted to four different devices in 1926, and held an additional one in reserve.[81] First, it made tentative offers of ten-year pensions to the life members of the Council and five-year pensions to the ten-year appointees in the event of their agreement to abolition, but the Council, after considering these proposals in secret conclave, declined the mercenary approach. Next, the government requested the Lieutenant-Governor to appoint a sufficient number of councillors to effect abolition, basing its request on the ground that the pre-Confederation right of the Sovereign to appoint an unlimited number of members had been vested by virtue of the provincial statute of 1872 in the provincial chief executive acting on the advice of his responsible ministers. But the Governor-General-in-Council, upon whom Lieutenant-Governor Tory placed the onus for accepting or rejecting this request, was dubious of its legality and directed Tory to make no appointments above twenty-one until the questions at issue had been determined judicially.

Rebuffed twice, the government initiated bills in 1926 and 1927 to effect abolition, not with any hope of success, but to make certain that the responsibility for the retention of the Council would rest upon shoulders other than its own. Finally, it set the judicial machinery in motion to determine two disputed points, a favourable decision on either of which would mean that it could accomplish its end. Late in 1927 the Judicial Committee agreed with its contentions: (a) that no action prior to Confederation had limited the right of the Sovereign to appoint an unlimited number of councillors, and that the effect of

[80]Premier Rhodes considered this office to be held at pleasure, and in January, 1927, he requested the resignation of the Liberal Jason M. Mack whom he had reappointed in 1926. Mack declined because of the doubts respecting the tenure of the office, but his death later in the month obviated the necessity of obtaining an authoritative decision.

[81]That of "having a referendum and taking the direct voice of the people of [the] province." *Halifax Herald*, Feb. 11, 1927.

the provincial statute of 1872, if not of the B.N.A. Act itself, was to vest that power fully in the Lieutenant-Governor-in-Council and (b) that nothing had altered the original tenure of councillors, that is, appointment during pleasure, until the statute of 1925 provided for ten-year appointments, and that the tenure of all members who had been appointed prior to the effective date of this statute was at the pleasure of the Crown as vested in the Lieutenant-Governor-in-Council.[82] In effect, the decision placed the Council entirely at the mercy of the Executive Council which, by dismissing the members appointed prior to June, 1925, and by adding any number of new appointees, might effect whatever transformation it desired. To the councillors the wisdom of Alexander Stewart's long-past plea for a defined constitution based upon statute became painfully apparent as they observed how the independence which had once been conferred by a constitution based on the prerogative had been whittled away by the vagaries of constitutional change. Realizing the futility of attempting to conserve a structure which was rotten at its foundations, they proposed to assist in its obsequies, but Premier Rhodes could now afford to decline their belated offer.

Of the seventeen councillors, six were ten-year appointees and could not be disturbed. Two others, the Conservative W. H. Owen, who had not been formally pledged to abolition, and A. W. Redden, a convert to Conservatism and abolition, were permitted to retain their seats. The nine remaining Councillors, all of whom were Liberals and had been pledged to support abolition, were given the alternative of resignation or dismissal. Three resigned and six had their seats vacated by order-in-council. The simultaneous appointment of fourteen staunch Conservatives brought the total number of councillors to twenty-two for the second time. This act not only permitted the government to demonstrate its newly won powers, but also enabled each county to participate in a momentous constitutional change. To prevent the new councillors from developing too high an opinion of the functions of a second chamber, the government saw to it that they barely went through the motions as legislators in the session of 1928, and the councillors apparently had the time of their lives. President Bligh's carefully prepared valedictory with its concluding "Sic transitur gloria mundi" was barely audible amongst a babble of sounds. Critics alleged it was a regular "Feast of Belshazzar."

[82]For the judgments of the Supreme Court of Nova Scotia and the Judicial Committee, see JHA, 1928, Appendix 31.

It was said about the city that the old order of the Good Time, established at Port Royal so many centuries ago to while away the tedium, had been re-established and was set up in the Legislative Council Chamber and rooms adjoining. It was said that wine and wassail was the order of the day. That as the clock ticked solemnly away, every minute brought nearer the hour of its death, and the motto was adopted "let us eat and drink, for tomorrow we die."[83]

In this fitting manner the Legislative Council of Nova Scotia passed away, unwept, unhonoured, and unsung.

[83]*Halifax Chronicle*, March 28, 1929.

CHAPTER XVI

THE HOUSE OF ASSEMBLY:
REPRESENTATION AND PERSONNEL

REPRESENTATION

ALTHOUGH the House of Assembly is primarily a representative body, it owes whatever representative character it possesses almost as much to accident as to human ingenuity. A primary test of the adequacy of representation in a political system operating through parties is the degree to which it brings a party's popular vote and its representation in the Legislature into correspondence. In this respect it can at least be said that the party which polls the largest popular vote always controls the Nova Scotian Assembly. Thus the system performs the basic function of permitting the electorate to make a simple affirmative or negative decision upon whether the governing party, by virtue of its past record and the prospects which its continuance in power offers, deserves a renewal of its mandate. Its other merits are that it normally ensures strong one-party rule and that it is sensitive to small changes in public opinion. In 1933, for example, a 5 per cent turn-over in the popular vote was sufficient to defeat the Conservative government and to reduce the percentage of its members in the Assembly from 53.5 to 26.7, while in 1956 the Conservatives won by taking one per cent of the popular vote from the Liberal party, and 4 per cent from the C.C.F. Yet these merits are achieved at the cost of a glaring weakness, the failure to ensure a strong opposition. Although the total opposition vote has fallen below 40 per cent on only two occasions since 1867, the members to the left of the Speaker often constitute little more than a corporal's guard.[1] Their total for the elections of 1897, 1901, and 1906 was ten; for those of 1937, 1941, and 1945, eleven. Even Liberal premiers have recognized the lack of a strong opposition as an obvious weakness in an age when an ever more powerful executive needs to be constantly challenged. Never-

[1]The following results are illustrative (see also Appendix F):

Year of election	Party	Percentage of popular vote	Number of seats	Percentage of seats
1906	Conservative	43.3	5	13.6
1925	Liberal	36.3	3	7.0
1937	Conservative	46.0	5	17.7
1945	Conservative	33.5	0	0

theless the old-line parties do not advocate the thorough revamping of the electoral process which the removal of the ill requires. The Conservatives in particular are well aware that such a change could not help them to win an election and might embarrass them if and when they chance to be successful. For this reason the *Herald* has been almost a lone voice in urging electoral reform. Yet the merit of its proposal to adopt the alternative vote is dubious since its practical result would likely be to increase the majority of the usually overrepresented Liberals. Only some scheme of proportional representation which would divide the province into half a dozen multimember constituencies could effect any real amelioration, but that would necessitate something not far short of a political revolution.

The Nova Scotian electoral system is similarly incapable of providing an Assembly which represents a true cross-section of the electorate by religion, race, occupation, or age-group. This is, of course, only natural when the voter's freedom of choice is practically unlimited. A few extra-legal restrictions are introduced, however, by the parties' deliberate attempts to facilitate religious or racial representation in half a dozen counties. In Halifax County both parties have been nominating candidates on the basis of their religious faith since 1867, and although the voters have deviated occasionally from the straight party ticket, they have failed only once to honour the recognized religious convention. After the creation of five single-member constituencies in 1932 the usual practice was to nominate Catholics in Halifax North and South, and Protestants in the other three ridings. Under these circumstances the electorate had no alternative but to fall in line. A similar usage was operative in Inverness County before Confederation and was introduced in Cape Breton County during the 1880's. While the frequent changes in representation since 1925 have made it difficult to retain some of these usages, Inverness returned to its long-standing practice of electing a Protestant and a Catholic after it regained its second member in 1948. Elsewhere a wide degree of toleration prevails, and in most ridings a person who otherwise possesses suitable qualifications need not feel himself debarred as a candidate because the members of his religious faith constitute a small minority.

The only racial minority of sufficient size to justify separate representation is the French Acadian, and in Digby County after 1837, and Yarmouth and Richmond counties after 1897, each party invariably chose a candidate from this racial group. With the reduction of these counties to single-member ridings in 1933, party conventions subordinated racial considerations to general merit in their choice of candidates, but since 1949 they have been able to restore the old practices in Yarmouth and Digby.

The disparity between the age of its members and that of the adult population generally applies no less to the Nova Scotian House of Assembly than to the Canadian House of Commons[2]—far too few assemblymen are between the age of twenty-one and thirty-five, far too many between forty and sixty. Yet the Assembly has never constituted an old man's home, since no member has been elected after eighty, few after seventy.[3] Nor does the electoral process prevent the introduction of reserves of new blood. Every election between 1920 and 1949 resulted in a turn-over of at least 40 per cent of the Assembly; in 1945, thirteen of thirty members, and in 1949, seventeen of thirty-seven, were elected for the first time. In 1953 only twelve of thirty-seven members were new, but in 1956 the number was twenty-two out of forty-three.[4]

Occupationally the House of Assembly has altered materially over a long-term period. Of the lawyers, merchants, and farmers who dominated the early nineteenth-century House, the last group appears to have lost its ranking position much the earliest, the country merchant retained his influence almost to the turn of the century, while the lawyers' hold on the Assembly remains as secure as ever.[5] Since 1925 they have constituted 30.7 per cent of the members returned at general elections: in 1953 they numbered thirteen in a House of thirty-seven members and in 1956 seventeen out of forty-three. Although a broader representation of occupational groups is undoubtedly desirable, any serious reduction in the number of lawyers might produce a vacuum in the Assembly. In the Forty-fourth Assembly (1949-53) they formed a majority on the government front benches which gave guidance and leadership to the House, and three of them to the left of Mr. Speaker provided the major opposition to the government's measures and kept the cabinet ministers on their toes during the consideration of the estimates; in the Forty-fifth they played a lesser, though still vital role.

Although the Assembly allowed its power of changing the system of representation to remain dormant in the forty-six years following Confederation, it has made no less than six alterations since 1914. On these occasions ostensible motives cannot easily be separated from the real. In 1948 redistribution was allegedly designed to constitute

[2]See Norman Ward, *The Canadian House of Commons: Representation* (Toronto, 1950), 128–31.
[3]See Appendix L.
[4]The percentage of new members in the last four elections was 43.5.
[5]See Appendix M.

an Assembly of the optimum size. The cabinet, it was felt, might gain an excessive dominance over a House in which it could constitute more than half the government members. But an even more impelling consideration was that the Assembly should be large enough to "give committees an opportunity to sit while the House is also in session, otherwise the sessions will be unduly long or public business will suffer."[6] On these grounds the size of the House was increased from thirty to thirty-seven in 1948, and to forty-three in 1955.

Changes have also been prompted by the desire to secure a system based more nearly on population. That was particularly true in 1914 when Tupper's half-century-old act had developed striking abnormalities in the unit of representation, which ranged from 4,955 in Victoria to 26,752 in Halifax. Similarly the changes of 1929 and 1932 were effected with the deliberate intent of reducing the representation of the eleven counties smallest in population from 51.2 to 36.7 per cent of the total, while the last redistribution in 1955 was purportedly designed to bring the representation into conformity with the census returns of 1951. The general principle underlying these new arrangements is that every county is entitled to one member for each 15,000 of its population, and one member for any remainder greater than 3,000.[7] Yet a close correspondence between population and number of members by no means solves all the problems of representation because not only is it less difficult to represent the electors who reside in a few hundred acres in Halifax city than to represent a similar number spread over sixteen hundred square miles in Guysborough County, but also the highly populous industrial areas possess an influence out of all proportion to their representations.[8] So, for purposes of redistribution, the special select committee of 1955 considered cities and towns with more than 7,500 people to have a population half their actual size.

A secondary objective of the changes since 1932 has been to eliminate multi-member constituencies. The defects of these constituencies were that they introduced a long ballot in Halifax and Cape Breton Counties, and permitted the voters in one county to ballot for five members, while most of their counterparts elected only two. Of the original eighteen multi-member ridings, there now remain only three dual constituencies—Yarmouth, Colchester, and Inverness.

[6]See Journals of the House of Assembly (JHA), 1948, 76.
[7]See JHA, 1955, 162–7.
[8]Wishart Robertson (Liberal-Shelburne) once intimated that ten or twelve business men in Halifax exercised as much influence upon any government as all its supporters in the Assembly. Halifax Chronicle, March 14, 1929.

But the experimentation of the last thirty years proves that no scheme can be free from objections and that the one likely to be adopted is a compromise that appears to favour the party in power. While no party has sponsored a change in representation which was certain to be to its disadvantage, in only one instance—the comparative minor alterations of 1925—could a government not offer a plausible justification on grounds other than those of party advantage. The Conservatives undoubtedly expected to secure some advantage from their legislation of 1929 and 1932, particularly if the industrial areas continued to give them a large measure of support, but neither act created an obvious injustice, for the succeeding Liberal administration retained the second act unamended for three successive elections and then practically reinstituted the former in 1948. Actually no ministry has benefited from its own alterations in the system of representation. The moral is obvious—a further convincing demonstration of the political acumen of Premier Murray, who considered it dangerous to tinker with a status quo already favourable to himself.

No definite procedure has been laid down for effecting the redistribution of seats, but the general practice has been to appoint select committees to make recommendations to the Assembly. These committees usually possess nothing like freedom of action. Sometimes they are narrowly circumscribed by their terms of reference, and always their composition is such that the government guides their deliberations. Yet the use of elaborate machinery like an independent commission is difficult to justify. Certainly the cutting up of individual counties and municipalities for partisan purposes has never constituted a major ill.

In contrast with the problems centring around redistribution of seats, those associated with the franchise have long been settled. Yet several intermediate stages of voting qualifications were employed before the property franchise of 1863 was finally converted to universal suffrage. After 1885 the Conservatives supported complete manhood suffrage because they hoped it would sweep away a system which, by its very complexity, facilitated electoral malpractices and provided the dominant party with an additional means of political manipulation. But the Liberals would not agree that twenty years of public schools had raised the general educational level sufficiently to justify universal suffrage,[9] and in 1885 Attorney-General Longley was still

[9]See comment of the Conservative member Adam Bell in *Assembly Debates*, 1885, 347.

resorting to Howe's arguments of the early sixties that it would bring
in the dregs who supported the Tories.[10]

A Liberal government continued, therefore, to have an eye to property when it extended the franchise in 1885.[11] As a result, its only
concessions were to accord the yearly tenant the same voting privileges as the owner of a property,[12] and to permit as many sons to
vote upon the property of a father or widowed mother as might have
voted if the property had been divided among them.[13] Nevertheless
Premier Fielding contended that, if it had been possible to add an
income franchise as in Ontario, the system would have been "almost
perfect."[14] The Municipal Assessment Act of 1888, by introducing
a moderate income tax for municipal purposes, provided the machinery
which enabled this deficiency to be overcome, and in 1889 an annual
income of $250 was made an alternative to the other qualifications
for voting.[15]

For thirty years no other changes were effected. By 1910, however, even the Liberals were beginning to admit that the difficulties
of administering the restricted franchise hardly compensated for the
benefits which it was supposed to confer. Yet they prolonged the old
voting qualifications on the ground that they were obligated to consult
the towns and municipalities before making a change.[16] It required
another decade, further pressure from the Conservatives, and the
precedent established by the Dominion Parliament before universal
suffrage finally became a reality in 1920.[17]

The equality of voting rights for males and females which this
act conceded was not won easily. The first break in the complete
exclusion of women from voting privileges occurred in 1887 when
widows and unmarried women with the requisite property qualifica-

[10]*Ibid.*, 352–3.

[11]48 Vic., c. 2.

[12]"We provide that the owner shall not have any more privilege than the occupant," said Premier Fielding. *Ibid.*, 345–6.

[13]Previously it had not been unusual for the assessors to "admit the sons of
certain farmers, of the right political faith, to the privileges of this arrangement,
and to refuse similar privileges in the cases of opposite political belief." *Acadian
Recorder*, Feb. 23, 1885.

[14]*Assembly Debates*, 1885, 345.

[15]52 Vic., c. 1.

[16]Since the municipal government used the same machinery to prepare both the
municipal and provincial voters' lists and since it was proposed to leave the
preparation of the provincial lists in their hands, it was considered necessary to
have conversations with them before the basis of the provincial franchise was
made to deviate from that of the municipal.

[17]10–11 Geo. V, c. 49.

tions were permitted to vote in municipal elections.[18] After 1890 the leaders of a militant women's temperance movement sought to have the privilege extended to provincial elections. In the Assembly their chief spokesman was A. M. Hemeon of Queens, who contended that the privileges already granted women had made them none the less womanlike, and had, in fact, checked disorder and wrangling at the polls. In contrast, his chief opponent, Attorney-General Longley, maintained that the issue was simply "whether the gentler sex should be unsexed or whether women should continue to exercise the functions which nature had imposed upon them with no unfaltering voice."[19] Despite his "brilliant pyrotechnic display"[20] Longley sometimes found it difficult to put down his own backbenchers in the early nineties, but by 1897 Hemeon was dead and only six assemblymen still supported his principles.[21]

The renewal of the agitation awaited another two decades and a period in which old ideas and dynasties were crumbling. This time the proponents of female suffrage did not have to go far afield for precedents, since the three Prairie Provinces had adopted it in 1916, and Ontario and British Columbia were to follow their example the next year. In 1917 Premier Murray opposed the energetic campaign of the Local Council of Women in Halifax on the ground that the women of Nova Scotia ought not to have the franchise before the women of England,[22] but the repercussions of his refusal were such that women's suffrage became a reality in the following session under the government's own sponsorship.[23]

One interesting quirk in the franchise law during the past century was the restriction upon Dominion office-holders. Some culprit had to be discovered for the defeat of an anti-Confederate in a provincial by-election in Halifax in 1870, and the Liberal press found it in the 250 federal officials resident in the county—those "dishonest, toadying busy-bodies who, whilst holding office under the Dominion Government, run fussying about and thrusting their fingers and their noses into Local Legislative elections, without any comprehension of propriety . . . or decency.[24] In 1871, therefore, they debarred most of these officials from voting in provincial elections,[25] purportedly to

---

[18]50 Vic., c. 28. For a complete account of women's suffrage in Nova Scotia, see C. L. Cleverdon, *The Woman Suffrage Movement in Canada* (Toronto, 1950), 158–76.

[19]*Assembly Debates*, 1893, 204.   [20]*Ibid.*

[21]*Ibid.*, 1897, 94.   [22]Cleverdon, *Woman Suffrage Movement*, 175n.

[23]8–9 Geo. V, c. 2.   [24]*Acadian Recorder*, Dec. 16, 1870.

[25]34 Vic., c. 3. The act affected a limited number of provincial officials as well.

enable them to retain their offices without outraging their consciences by voting for the Confederates under the pressure of Ottawa.[26]

For the next thirty-five years periodic skirmishing occurred around this provision. Once the Liberals formed a government at Ottawa in 1896, the real reason for the disqualification had disappeared. Yet the cycle of events which concluded the issue was somewhat bewildering—the Legislative Council, after rejecting the Assembly's bills to remove the disqualification in three successive years, itself initiated the change in 1905 as a thoroughly irrelevant amendment to a bill sent up by the Assembly, and the latter accepted it without realizing its purport.[27]

Of even greater concern than the qualifications for voters has been the determination of the persons who are qualified by law to exercise the franchise. The Franchise Act of 1863,[28] which required lists to be prepared annually by assessors and revisal boards, augmented rather than diminished the difficulties, and as early as 1872 the Conservatives were suggesting universal suffrage and a simple registration system as the only practical remedy. Before this proposal materialized, however, the province was to experience a host of singular events in the preparation of electoral lists. In 1901, for example, the Attorney-General himself was guilty of providing incorrect information to the assessors of Richmond County,[29] while the affidavits in which credible persons attested to the qualifications of specific individuals by virtue of their personal knowledge were especially productive of chicanery real or alleged.[30]

In this murky story the Conservatives were generally the sufferers. Their organizer for the election of 1890, C. H. Cahan, fully appreciated the hardships under which they laboured.

. . . the past fortnight, I have discovered that our grit friends are playing with loaded-dice. The assessors are grits in nearly all . . . of the counties, and they have been instructed to place the name of every grit voter on the assessment roll, and leave every "tory" off where it was possible. I have sent out 1,500 circulars of instructions and 10,000 blanks for income qualifications; and unless they arouse our friends to look very actively after the local lists, we will work under very great difficulties throughout the rest of the campaign.[31]

[26]Assembly Debates, 1872, 100ff.
[27]5 Edw. VII, c. 21. Supra, 242–3.
[28]Supra, 117–18.
[29]Assembly Debates, 1901, 113–18.
[30]See Halifax Herald, May 4, 1910; Assembly Debates, 1911, 91 and 96–7.
[31]Cahan to Thompson, Jan. 2, 1890, Thompson Papers (P.A.C.), item no. 11, 394.

Thus Cahan learned that an election campaign began in the first three weeks of the year when applications were required to be filed under the income provisions of the Franchise Act. To him it was obvious that $3,000 spent legitimately at this stage of the campaign could be used to better advantage than many times that amount on the eve of the election.[32]

The Liberals, on the other hand, could be fairly certain that the lists were compiled in a manner not uncongenial to themselves, and in the rare instance when they were not, they did not hesitate to take advantage of their continual control of the Legislature to enact special legislation in their own interests. One such measure (1905) modified the Franchise Act so as to prevent the Conservative City Council in Halifax from devolving the duties of registrar—then being performed by the Liberal City Clerk—on another of its officials; a second in 1911 permitted the town of Glace Bay to dismiss its Conservative registrar and appoint a Liberal during good behaviour; a third in 1913 enabled a Liberal sheriff to review the work of two Conservative revisers in Kings County.[33]

Even after the introduction of universal suffrage in 1920 the old influences were at work because the lists continued to be prepared annually in the same manner as before. It is not surprising, therefore, that the Conservative government which was elected in 1925 began to toy with the idea of a revolutionary change in the making of election lists. Its near defeat in 1928, and its loss of two Halifax seats, allegedly as a result of the partisan conduct of the city registrar, strengthened its resolve. The outcome was the Electoral Franchise Act of 1931,[34] which provided for the preparation of voters' lists immediately prior to each election by provincial officials. While the measure was excellent in its conception, it was faulty beyond belief in its details. But although the Liberals warned that its provisions actually empowered the party in power to make up the lists in populous centres,[35] their suggestions went unheeded, and all the evils which they portended were realized in full measure.

For one thing the obscurity of the act permitted the returning officers to adopt the interpretation that they need appoint only one registrar for each of the Halifax city constituencies, which contained populations ranging from 15,000 to 25,000. The Liberals were forced, therefore, to seek a mandamus from the Supreme Court requiring the appointment

[32]*Ibid.*, Feb. 11, 1890, item 11, 732.
[33]See 5 Edw. VII, c. 25; 1 Geo. V, c. 64; 3 Geo. V, c. 132.
[34]21 Geo. V, c. 3.   [35]*Halifax Chronicle*, April 14, 1931.

of additional registrars. But this was merely the first episode in a melancholy series of events. The preliminary lists of the registrars revealed a host of omissions, particularly in the Halifax city ridings, and enabled the Liberals to wage a completely uninhibited campaign on the premise that the Conservative organization in the Pentagon Building had concocted a diabolical scheme to destroy the democratic process. Joseph Howe made the front page once again. "As I walked passed the Provincial Building," a prominent Conservative is reported to have stated, "I would not have been surprised had Joseph Howe stepped off his pedestal." "So deplorable is this Frankenstein," said the *Chronicle*, "that it is enough to make Howe, the Great Emancipator, turn in his grave."[36] In these circumstances Premier Harrington's inability to dispel the taint of suspicion resting on the government itself destroyed any possibility of his retaining office. A subsequent inquiry[37] threw further light upon the astonishing ineptitude of Conservative strategists who, unlike their Liberal predecessors, had failed to ensure that their manipulation of the electoral rolls would not be of sufficient dimensions to permit public attention to be focussed upon it.

Yet some good resulted from the Great Franchise Scandal of 1933. Certainly it should act as a deterrent to any political schemers of the future who may contemplate the use of the franchise machinery in their own interest. More concretely it induced legislation which provided for the compiling of the preliminary lists by two enumerators of different and opposed political interests in urban districts and instituted adequate machinery for their revision. As a result, electoral lists have finally ceased to be a prominent part of the political struggle.

In other respects the laws relating to elections exhibit little of the unusual. The Quadrennial Act of 1840 remained in effect until 1897 when the life of an Assembly was extended to five years[38] simply because "there appeared to be no necessity for holding elections for provincial purposes any more frequently than for Dominion purposes."[39] George Murray took advantage of the change three times and survived, but two of his successors who in more difficult times waited the full five years suffered cataclysmic defeat. Today, therefore, a premier dislikes to be manœuvred into a position in which he can exercise no discretion in fixing the date of an election.

By-elections play a comparatively insignificant role in government since, because of their infrequency, they have no useful value as

[36]*Halifax Chronicle*, July 26, 1933.
[37]See Ross Franchise Inquiry, *JHA*, 1934, Appendix 32.
[38]60 Vic., c. 1.   [39]*Assembly Debates*, 1897, 195.

indicators. Some interest, however, has centred around a provision stemming from the Simultaneous Voting Act of 1847[40] which requires that if two or more vacancies exist in the Assembly they must all be filled at the same time. The opposition was outraged in 1907 when a member who vacated his seat automatically upon the acceptance of an executive councillorship was given an opportunity to contest a by-election while another seat remained unfilled.[41] On this occasion Premier Murray dismissed the objection as purely technical, but in 1918, when he wished to take another minister into his cabinet and was faced with six by-elections as a result, he sponsored legislation which exempted from the general rule by-elections necessitated by the acceptance of a ministerial appointment.[42] In 1927, however, when members were permitted to retain their seats after accepting executive councillorships with office,[43] the provision again became fully operative. Practically its only effect is to leave seats unfilled when any considerable number of vacancies occur.

Normally the Provincial Secretary has carried out many of the duties which the Chief Electoral Office performs in federal elections, but in 1947 the Governor-in-Council was empowered to appoint a barrister to be Chief Election Officer.[44] An official of the Provincial Secretary's Department acted in that capacity during the elections of 1953 and 1956. The election machinery in each riding is under the direction of a returning officer also appointed by the Governor-in-Council. From the earliest history of the province until 1928 the sheriffs were returning officers *ex officio*; then a change was made by a Conservative government which found it uncongenial to have elections directed by sheriffs for the most part appointed by previous Liberal governments.[45]

A candidate for election is officially nominated before the returning officer's court fourteen days prior to an election. His nomination papers must be signed by two qualified electors and accompanied by a deposit of $100. In the early provincial elections each candidate was required to pay fees for the remuneration of the election officials, but this was changed in 1875 to a fixed payment of $50 towards the general costs of the election.[46] When the province finally assumed the whole burden of election expenses in 1884, it required a deposit so that the contest would be confined to genuine candidates.[47] Otherwise any male British subject who had reached 21 years of age was

[40]*Supra*, 125.
[42]8–9 Geo. V, c. 34.
[44]11 Geo. VI, c. 2.
[46]38 Vic., c. 26.

[41]*Assembly Debates*, 1908, 2–4.
[43]17–18 Geo. V., c. 13.
[45]18 Geo. V, c. 20.
[47]R.S. 1884, c. 4.

eligible as a candidate. This meant that until universal suffrage was adopted in 1920, higher qualifications were demanded of an elector than a candidate. A candidate's deposit is returned if he polls at least half the number of votes cast for a winning candidate.

In the days of open voting the returning officer presided over a political meeting during the proceedings for the nomination of candidates, but after the introduction of the ballot in 1870 he was enjoined by statute not to give official recognition to a gathering of this nature. Until the late 1930's, however, joint political meetings continued to be held unofficially and thousands gathered at the county towns on nomination day for an afternoon of speeches, sport, excitement, and, not infrequently, heckling. The boisterous nature of the meetings and the wartime restrictions on gasoline then led to their elimination in most counties and the result has been to take much of the zest out of the contest. Certainly elections are not what they used to be.

Controverted elections have also lost much of their former significance. When the Canadian House of Commons transferred the trial of election petitions to the superior courts in 1868, the Nova Scotian Conservatives advocated a similar measure on the ground that "the trial of elections by committees was nothing more than the throwing of dice for the result, and depended on the way in which the names came out of the box."[48] Naturally the almost solid bloc of anti-Confederation assemblymen looked askance upon a proposal that they divest themselves of a power which had only recently enabled them to unseat the Conservative leader, and place it in the pro-Confederation judges of the Supreme Court from whom they could expect no favoured treatment. By 1875, however, the diminution of the anti-Confederation feeling and the passing of the die-hards from the political scene permitted the trial of election petitions to be vested in a single judge of the Supreme Court.[49]

Since the specific grounds for invalidating an election were not prescribed, the development of a body of law in this matter was, in effect, left to the judges as they tried specific cases. The subsequent dearth of election petitions, partly because of the substantial security which is required from the petitioner,[50] and partly because of the realization that the judges, unlike the committees of the Assembly, required evidence of substantial malpractices to invalidate an election, has

[48]A paraphrase of the words of Sir Robert Peel. See *Assembly Debates*, 1871, 31.
[49]38 Vic., c. 25.
[50]The persistent urgings of Charles E. Tanner eventually resulted in a reduction of the security from $800 to $400. 67 Geo. V, c. 8.

retarded the process. It has been established none the less that an election may be voided if a presiding officer's failure to perform his duties properly might have affected the result;[51] if a candidate's agents, even without his knowledge, have been guilty of substantial malpractices;[52] or if the number of unqualified persons who vote at an election are sufficient to determine its outcome.[53]

Some electoral malpractices, it was hoped, would be reduced by the secret ballot. Open voting was abandoned, in fact, as a result of the tactics alleged to have been used to secure the election of Joseph Howe in Hants County after his desertion of the anti-Confederation cause and his admission into the Dominion cabinet. The *Chronicle* warned that, unless the secret ballot were introduced, Canada could "nominate a candidate for any and every county in the province, and by direct bribery, . . . carry the elections."[54] Though adopted in 1870,[55] it failed to assist the anti-Confederates in its first test in a Halifax by-election. They concluded, therefore, that it provided no remedy for that army of Dominion government officials who "have to vote as they are told, or not vote at all."[56] But while they carried bills for its repeal through the Assembly in 1871 and 1873, the Legislative Council declined to allow the Legislature to look ridiculous by abandoning it without a fair trial.

Time has indicated, however, that neither the ballot nor any other device has broken down a two-hundred-year-old tradition that anything goes in politics. One provincial observer of the electoral process once stated that it "drags . . . many of our leading citizens down to the level of gangsters,"[57] and outsiders concur that Nova Scotia is anything but a shining exemplar in the matter of electoral purity.

Normally the parties behave as if an agreement existed which permitted their workers to break every section of the law relating to corrupt practices short of arousing complete public disgust. No matter how high-intentioned a candidate may be he is forced to fall in line with a system which operates on the principle that elections are not won by prayers. Between 1900 and 1910 Charles Tanner led a crusade to have electoral corruption extirpated by carefully framed legislation,

[51]The result of a Richmond County election trial in 1894. See *Morning Chronicle*, Aug. 10, 1894.
[52]The outcome of a Victoria County by-election in 1914. *Infra*, 266.
[53]*Blanchard* v. *Cole*, 25 M.P.R. 329.
[54]May 11, 1869.
[55]33 Vic., c. 24.
[56]*Acadian Recorder*, Nov. 21, 1870.
[57]See speech of R. H. Murray as reported in the *Halifax Chronicle*, Sept. 27, 1933.

but invariably he found himself in conflict with a Liberal Attorney-General who argued that "you could not make a people pure or . . . moral by any paternal or tinkering acts of legislation whatever."[58] When Tanner sought to make the law relating to corrupt practices more specific and at the same time more stringent, his critics took the view that the effect would be not only to "prevent ordinary canvassing , . . but unless a man was prepared to be offensive and insulting it would not be safe for him to go around, during an election campaign, with his mouth open at all."[59] When he suggested that a member-elect should be unseated for the corrupt practices of his agents performed without his own knowledge or consent, they argued that this was already possible under the common law.[60]

A controverted election case in 1915 proved the last contention to be correct.[61] But it also demonstrated that one provision of the Controverted Elections Act which was specially designed to discourage corrupt practices—the judge who tried an election petition might order the prosecution of a candidate or agent whose conduct warranted it—could not normally be invoked because of the limited time in which to institute the action. The Legislature remedied this deficiency in 1916,[62] but in that same year Charles Tanner departed from the Assembly and with him any attempt to reform the electoral law.

Members

Excluded from the Assembly today are senators, members of Parliament, and persons who permit themselves to be nominated as members of Parliament or who hold any provincial or federal office to which a salary or wage is attached.[63] The persons to be included in this last group have long been the subject of controversy. Early in the Confederation era the Legislature disqualified the full-time officials of both governments from holding seats in either of its branches,[64] but this proved insufficient to satisfy the anti-Confederates that the vast power of the federal government would not be employed through the medium of its henchmen to influence the Legislature, and in 1886 they

---

[58]*Assembly Debates*, 1905, 73.
[59]*Ibid.*, 1906, 304.
[60]*Morning Chronicle*, Feb. 23, 1905.
[61]See *JHA*, 1915, Appendix 29.
[62]6–7 Geo. V, c. 19, s. 5.
[63]1 Geo. VI, c. 2, Part III. Members of the Executive Council, stipendiary magistrates, justices of the peace, coroners, and Crown prosecutors are exempted from the disqualification.
[64]34 Vic., c. 6.

debarred from both the Council and the Assembly all persons in receipt of remuneration from any employment under the Dominion.[65] While the Conservatives offered no objections, they were surprised that the government was not equally sensitive about the influence which might be exercised upon the Legislature by the provincial government's own place-men.[66]

Their surprise changed to indignation after 1900 when, instead of tightening the provisions relating to provincial employees, the government made the restrictions upon federal employees less stringent. "Of thirty-six members of the Assembly," lamented the *Herald* in 1906, "at least twenty have been in receipt of public moneys as contractors with the Government or as paid employe[e]s of the Government. Such men are mere masqueraders when they pretend to be independent representatives of the people. . . . The Government wants the House filled with such men."[67] But although the Conservatives were perennial introducers of so-called Independence of Parliament bills while in opposition, they made no attempt to implement one after they assumed office in 1925, and still another reversal of viewpoint followed the change of government in 1933.[68] Each party apparently took the position that its return to power rendered nugatory the evils which such an Act was designed to prevent.

In 1937, the Macdonald government finally made a realistic reappraisal of the existing provisions, seeking to impose appropriate restrictions without limiting unduly the persons available as candidates.[69] It encountered little criticism for not disqualifying the shareholders of incorporated companies which had contracts with the government[70] since this exception had been tacitly recognized for at least half a century.[71] But two other provisions, one of which per-

[65]49 Vic., c. 6.

[66]*Assembly Debates*, 1886, 395.

[67]*Halifax Herald*, June 4, 1906.

[68]"There has been a great deal of political 'shadow-boxing' over this question," was the *Herald's* classic understatement on the last occasion (April 18, 1934).

[69]1 Geo. VI, c. 2, Part III.

[70]But the exemption did not apply if the contract was for the construction of a provincial public work which had not been let by tender to the lowest bidder.

[71]In 1888 Premier Fielding had pointed out that "so much of the business of the world to-day is done by joint stock companies that, if you were to lay down the rule that no member . . . should be a member of a joint stock company . . . it might be the means of preventing many men from coming into the legislature whom it would be highly desirable to have here." *Assembly Debates*, 1888, 319. But he insisted that if Attorney-General Longley was still a shareholder and director of the Nictaux and Atlantic Railway when it applied for a provincial subsidy, "one of us [will] no longer be a member of the government [of Nova Scotia]." *Ibid.*, 323.

mitted an Assemblyman to accept temporary or part-time employment with the Dominion or the province if the work required special qualifications or professional skill, and another which safeguarded the seats of members who chanced to be parties to contracts with the government of "a casual nature," were roundly condemned. The administration took the view, however, that no member's seat should be placed in jeopardy simply because his employee sold the government a gallon of gasoline or completed some other minor transaction without his knowledge. "We should guard against anything," said Attorney-General MacQuarrie, "which will cause a member of this House to be unseated through no fault of his own."[72]

Not unnaturally, the assemblymen have shown a greater interest in their indemnities than in their independence. The first change in their remuneration after Confederation (1872) resulted in a complete break with the past because it replaced the ninety-year-old system of payment on a *per diem* basis by a fixed sessional indemnity of $400. Since it meant also an extra charge of at least $6,000 upon the provincial revenues at a time when they could ill afford to bear it, it is not surprising that no one in the House was willing to accept the responsibility for the change.[73] The propriety of the next three increases—to $500 in 1889, $600 in 1907, and $700 in 1908—was also questioned. But when Charles E. Tanner maintained that the last two could have been avoided if the government had shortened the sessions by having its legislative work properly in hand, his opponents pointed out gleefully that he was "among the very first at the Treasurer's office to draw the swag."[74]

The next change was a highly unofficial one effected by the Murray administration in its later years. In keeping with its usual policy of avoiding the controversial it somehow found it possible to pay an additional allowance of $300 out of the contingent fund for legislative expenses without its becoming public knowledge. Hence when the Assembly finally got around to indemnities in 1921, it had to set them at $1,500 to provide anything like a substantial increase. That amount was to be short-lived, for within a year the Armstrong government felt it desirable to return to $1,000 in view of the deteriorating economic conditions and a falling wage rate. At the same time it placed the indemnities, which had heretofore rested on annual resolutions of the

---

[72]*Halifax Chronicle*, March 9, 1937.

[73]See *Assembly Debates*, 1873, 139–44. Perhaps C. J. Campbell of Victoria took the most sensible view when he suggested that "every man who took the $100 should hold his tongue and say nothing about it." *Ibid.*, 142.

[74]*Morning Chronicle*, April 22, 1908.

two Houses, upon a statutory basis. But its plan to require a minimum number of days' attendance before the full indemnity could be drawn failed because the more elderly councillors disapproved of too stringent rules in this respect.

It was not until 1938 that the augmented duties of the Assemblymen and the improved financial condition of the province once again enabled the amount to be set at $1,500.[75] In contrast, the provision of a statutory indemnity of $1,600 and an expense allowance of $800 in 1947[76] was dictated by the increase in the cost of living.[77] On similar grounds these amounts were further increased to $2,400 and $1,200 in 1954.[78] Whether this provides a reasonable compensation for the Assemblyman's interruptions from his normal vocation depends upon the individual representative. Certainly the expansion of the provincial government's activities and expenditures has given rise to a host of matters in every constituency to which the local member may give as much or as little of his attention as his inclination moves him.

Accompanying the most recent increases in the indemnities was a scheme of retiring allowances similar to that at Ottawa.[79] Its effect may be slight, but if it were to encourage the rise of a group of professional politicians who serve long terms, it might portend a radical, though not necessarily beneficial innovation in government.[80]

Even as the assemblyman's indemnities were being increased their privileges were expanded. While the British North America Act permitted the House of Commons to confer upon itself by statute the privileges, immunities, and powers which the British House of Commons possessed in 1867,[81] it made no explicit reference to the privileges of the provincial legislatures. The newly constituted ones[82] proceeded, therefore, to follow the example of the Ontario House of Assembly which in 1868 conferred upon itself the privileges and powers of the Canadian House of Commons. But none of these acts was permitted to remain on the statute book, because of John A. Macdonald's view that,

[75]2 Geo. VI, c. 54.
[76]11 Geo. VI, c. 45.
[77]See *Halifax Chronicle,* March 20, 1945.
[78]3 Eliz. II, c. 37.
[79]3 Eliz. II, c. 8. Upon retirement, members who have reached sixty years of age and served in three General Assemblies for at least ten years, may draw retiring allowances ranging from $1,200 to $1,800. To be eligible, they must elect to contribute 8 per cent of their sessional indemnity.
[80]For criticism in the legislature, see *Halifax Chronicle-Herald,* April 6, 1954.
[81]S. 18.
[82]Quebec in 1869 and Manitoba in 1873. The comparatively new Legislature of British Columbia adopted a similar measure in 1872.

if a provincial legislature could enact this type of provision at all, it might "confer upon itself and its members privileges in excess of those belonging to the House of Commons of England."[83] To counter his objection, the Quebec Legislature then adopted another course—it constituted itself a Court of Record with power to try and punish specific offences which it declared to be breaches of its privileges.[84] This time the Minister of Justice, although still somewhat dubious, declined to interfere on the ground that some provisions of this nature appeared to be "necessary to uphold the authority and dignity of the provincial legislature."[85]

To the continuing legislatures the omission of any reference to their privileges in the written constitution presented no immediate problem because they had built up a body of rules and conventions which seemed entirely adequate. When the authority of the Nova Scotian Assembly had last been questioned,[86] no doubt had been cast upon the sufficiency of its powers. Since then, however, the Judicial Committee of the Privy Council had denied to other colonial legislatures the right to assume "the same exclusive privileges which the ancient law of England had annexed to the House of Parliament."[87] Inherently, it said, they did not possess the power to punish for contempt, which was a judicial and not a legislative power, but only the self-preservative power of removing any immediate obstructions to their proceedings.[88] At the time these pronouncements passed unnoticed in Nova Scotia. It required one *cause célèbre* which convulsed the provincial political arena in the 1870's to indicate that the inherent privileges of a Canadian provincial legislature were in themselves inadequate, and another in the 1890's to demonstrate that it might overcome this deficiency by statutory action.

The first incident involved the Conservative Assemblyman Douglas B. Woodworth who, after harassing the Liberal administration with a long series of accusations of wrong-doing, went too far in 1874 when he charged the Provincial Secretary with making illegal alterations in the records of the Crown Lands Department. After a committee of the House found the accusation to be groundless, the Liberal members turned upon their tormentor for slandering one of their number.

---

[83]W. E. Hodgins, comp., *Dominion and Provincial Legislation, 1867–1895* (Ottawa, 1896), 83.

[84]33Vic., c. 5. Ontario and Manitoba followed suit in 1876.

[85]Hodgins, *Dominion and Provincial Legislation, 1867–1895*, 256.

[86]The Barry case in 1830. *Supra*, 48.

[87]*Kielley* v. *Carson*, 4 Moo. P.C.C. 63. This reversed *Beaumont* v. *Barrett*, 1 Moo. P.C.C. 59.   [88]*Doyle* v. *Falconer*, L.R. 1 P.C. App. 328.

Woodworth declined to apologize, suffered ejection for his contempt, and took legal action against his "persecutors." Ultimately he was successful, for the Supreme Court of Canada, in conformity with the previous findings of the Judicial Committee, ruled that he could not legally be removed because his conduct had not directly obstructed the deliberations of the Assembly.[89]

But even before the Supreme Court rendered its decision the Legislature had passed the all-inclusive act of 1876[90] by which it abandoned its reliance upon its inherent self-preservative powers for a complete statutory guarantee of its privileges, powers, and immunities. The act contained not only the provisions of the disallowed Ontario act of 1868 which provided privileges analogous to those of the Canadian House of Commons, but also those of the Quebec act of 1870[91] which created each branch of the Legislature a Court of Record with power to try and punish a comprehensive list of offences described as breaches of privilege.[92] These powers were so extensive that the Minister of Justice feared their "application to the subject in general would be to put [him] at the mercy of either House, no matter what might be the nature of the rule, order or resolution which it passed,"[93] but the Legislature declined to make any alterations, and for some unexplained reason Ottawa abstained from disallowance.

The fears for the ordinary liberties of the subject were, in fact, justified in the Thomas case. For a civic official—in this instance the mayor of Truro—to furnish the Legislature with *prima facie* evidence that an Assemblyman has surreptitiously used his position to obtain legislation beneficial to himself and detrimental to a town corporation appears at most to be a technical offence no matter how strongly the documents are worded. Nevertheless the ranks of the Liberal majority closed to defend a Liberal representative against a Tory mayor. Without investigating the charges against the Assemblyman it adjudged Mayor Thomas guilty of insulting a member, and upon his refusal to accept a reprimand, it proceeded to vindicate its honour by ordering him to suffer imprisonment.

[89]*Landers* v. *Woodworth*, [1878] 2 S.C.R. 158.   [90]39 Vic., c. 22.
[91]Actually Nova Scotia followed an Ontario act of 1876 which was based upon the Quebec act.
[92]The only subsequent addition of any consequence in Nova Scotia occurred as a result of a minor incident in 1903—it accorded immunity from civil action to an official who, on the instruction of either House, its committees, or its individual members, ejected from the precincts of the House a person guilty of creating a disturbance. 3 Edw. VII, c. 11 and *Assembly Debates,* 1903, 260–1 and 277–80.
[93]Hodgins, *Dominion and Provincial Legislation, 1867–1895,* 496.

The one merit of the episode was that the courts were required to pronounce upon the validity of the statute of 1876 which the Assembly relied upon to justify its action against Thomas.[94] The judgment of the Judicial Committee was that it could be supported either under section 5 of the Colonial Laws Validity Act of 1865 which gave the colonial assemblies full power to make laws respecting the constitution, powers, and procedure of such legislature or under section 92 of the British North America Act which empowered the provincial legislatures to amend their constitutions.[95]

In both the Woodworth and Thomas cases privilege had become inextricably connected with political motives. The same was true in 1914 when the Assembly had to decide if a newspaper's publications had passed beyond the tolerable limits. On that occasion the *Herald* and the *Mail*, as part of their crusade to forestall what they described as the bartering and plundering of a public franchise,[96] published a letter which alleged that, if the controversial bill became law, the electorate could only conclude that "some of the gentlemen sent to the House of Assembly to protect [their] interests, were unable to resist the temptation, and were bought, body and breeches." The outcome was that W. R. McCurdy, the news editor of the *Herald*, was adjudged guilty of contempt of the House and imprisoned for refusing[97] to divulge the source of the letter to its investigating committee.

While no clear-cut principles for guiding the Assembly's course of action can be deduced from any of these incidents, it seems obvious that unless the breach of its privileges is clearly intolerable it should refrain from exerting its authority in those cases in which its action is likely to be interpreted as just another excursion into partisan politics.

The converse of an outsider libelling or slandering an Assemblyman is an Assemblyman making scandalous attacks on private citizens. The difference is that the Assemblyman, because of his privileged position, operates under far fewer inhibitions. For that reason the *Recorder* once described a representative guilty of this abuse as being "several degrees lower than the goat which railed at the wolf from the top of the house. Such things might be pardonable in a goat, but they are

---

[94]As a result of a suit for damages instituted by Thomas.

[95]*Fielding* v. *Thomas*, [1896] A.C. 600.

[96]Its aim was to prevent the Robert interests of Montreal from using the assets of the Halifax Electric Tramway Company to finance a doubtful hydro-electric venture on the Gaspereau River.

[97]On the ground that it would be "a violation of the ethics of journalism and and a grave breach of the time-honoured tradition of the press the world over." *JHA*, 1914, 193.

simply contemptible in a man."[98] Members of the government in particular have little to fear from the only body which can effectively discipline them, the House itself. Hence a premier was once permitted to describe the editor of an opposition newspaper, a former clergyman, as "a renegade clerk in holy orders."[99] In these circumstances only the good sense of the House can prevent freedom of speech and debate from degenerating into an unwarranted abuse of that high privilege.

[98]*Acadian Recorder,* April 10, 1877.

[99]*Halifax Chronicle,* April 30, 1932. Premier Harrington defended his position thus: "Apparently . . . the Editor of the *Chronicle* can sit behind his desk and smear filth and abuse over me, but forsooth, if I say anything back then his friends in the House begin to squeal. Why don't they and he take their medicine the same as I have to do 365 days of the year?"

CHAPTER XVII

THE HOUSE OF ASSEMBLY:
PROCEDURE

THE PROCESS of adapting the rules and procedures of the Mother of Parliaments to the needs of a small provincial Legislature continued after 1867 much as before. In the course of time the Assembly tended more and more to follow the rules, conventions, and forms of the Canadian House of Commons, but it also developed its own usages, and in 1955 it officially authorized its Speaker to be guided by them in making his decisions. On only four occasions has it modified its formal rules substantially, the last time in 1928 to meet the needs of a unicameral Legislature.[1] Then some means had to be devised which would permit the Lieutenant-Governor to instruct a new Assembly to name its Speaker.[2] The form decided upon calls for the Premier, pursuant to a commission issued by the Governor, to make known the chief executive's pleasure to the assemblymen.

In choosing a Speaker the normal practice in recent years has been for the Premier to propose a candidate and the leader of the opposition to second the nomination. Ordinarily the Premier's choice is a veteran member who has been denied other preferment. One Liberal government of the last century suffered a humiliating experience because it selected a member without previous parliamentary experience, and within a matter of weeks its own backbenchers united with the opposition in declaring him devoid of "the necessary qualifications to fit him for the discharge of such onerous and sometimes technical duties as are imposed upon the Speaker of a Legislative Assembly."[3] The last time the opposition objected to a government's choice dates back to 1907 when the Conservatives opposed the re-election of a Speaker whose conduct as a Liberal agent had contributed to the voiding of a Dominion election.[4]

[1]The rules were modernized in 1955, but the changes, which went into effect in 1956, were relatively minor.

[2]Prior to 1929 the unorganized assemblymen were summoned to the Legislative Council chamber where the President of the Upper House issued the Governor's directive.

[3]*Journals of the House of Assembly (JHA)*, 1875, 109–10.

[4]*Assembly Debates*, 1907, 1–4.

Immediately after choosing a Speaker the Assembly proceeds to select its Sergeant-at-Arms. At one time it also chose its Clerk, Assistant Clerk, messengers, and pages, often after sharp debate and a series of divisions strictly along party lines, but this power has now passed to other hands.[5] The Assembly retains the right to name only the two officials who may be called upon to exercise disciplinary powers over its members.

The selection of the Speaker and Sergeant-at-Arms is timed to precede the Lieutenant-Governor's arrival at Province House, which is accomplished with all the ceremonial and fanfare which normally accompany the opening of legislative sessions. Since 1759 the Governor's first act in the Assembly chamber has been to confirm the choice of the Speaker and to accord the assemblymen their customary rights and privileges. He then reads the Speech from the Throne which in recent years has been an inordinately long treatise upon the economic and financial conditions and prospects of the province. Since the Assembly now boasts a mace—the gift of a Chief Justice in 1930—Dickens, were he to attend another opening, "might change his writing and say that it was . . . like looking through the right end of a telescope."[6]

The formalities concluded, the Assembly proceeds in the usual manner to demonstrate its independence of the Crown by temporarily abandoning the Speech from the Throne and turning to other business. But instead of giving first reading to a bill *pro forma* and then forgetting about it—the normal course of British representative bodies—its practice since 1937 has been to introduce and give first reading to one or more genuine bills.[7] Its powers thus vindicated, two government members move and second an address in reply to the Speech from the Throne, and another session of the General Assembly of Nova Scotia is well under way.

The trend towards permanent activity which has been developing in the major parliamentary bodies by no means applies to the Nova Scotian Assembly since its sessions normally last only seven or eight weeks. Recent experience indicates that even a vigorous opposition extends the usual period by no more than a week. Since 1956 speeches

[5]The Chief Clerk and the Assistant Clerk are appointed by the Governor-in-Council; the messengers and pages by a Legislative Internal Economy Board consisting of the Speaker, two executive councillors, and one or more members of the Assembly appointed by the Governor-in-Council.

[6]*Halifax Chronicle*, March 6, 1930. *Supra*, 100.

[7]Unlike the British and Canadian Houses of Commons, the Nova Scotian House did not possess a prescribed bill for this purpose even before 1937.

have been limited to one hour, but this restriction will have little practical effect. While occasional complaints have been registered against the prolonged debate on the Address in reply to the Speech from the Throne, it is undoubtedly superior to that at Ottawa in several respects. Because of the comparatively small number of members it cannot be continued *ad nauseam*; the assemblymen usually exhibit a laudatory capacity for self-restriction; their speeches, even when confined to the problems of a single constituency, are more meaningful to their fellow members since Nova Scotia is, after all, a small community.

In any case the time factor is not of pressing concern in the transaction of legislative business. Only occasionally has a premier been accused of railroading his measures through the House by over-working its members in post-midnight sessions. Furthermore, this charge is heard only when a numerically large opposition has let its conduct degenerate from legitimate criticism into pure obstruction. The rules of the Assembly provide a type of closure in that a member may move that the question before the House be now put, and if his motion is resolved in the affirmative, the original question must be voted on without amendment or debate.[8] In practice, however, the device has seldom been employed.

No opposition can, in fact, complain of being "gagged." When it is numerically weak, a Speaker not infrequently permits a lenient interpretation of the rules in its favour, sometimes by allowing a debate upon a motion for adjournment to discuss a matter of urgent public business even though a motion in similar circumstances would be summarily rejected at Ottawa, occasionally by permitting the consideration of a private member's bill which indirectly involves the expenditure of public money. But the opposition need rely, neither on the good-will of the Speaker, nor on its right to discuss grievances on a motion to go into Committee of Supply. Normally it presents its point of view in the form of resolutions, and while the latter are usually defeated, they are certain to be fully discussed because the rules give precedence to private members' business on Tuesdays and Thursdays. Much more frequently the opposition pries into the performance of the public business by asking the House to order a detailed return upon some expenditure or other matter which has aroused its curiosity, and no government dares to refuse a reasonable request. The opposition resorts only rarely to oral questions addressed

[8]If the motion is negatived, the debate proceeds until interrupted by some other motion.

to ministers, perhaps because they were not accorded official recognition until 1956.

The procedures connected with the legislative process are much more distinctive than those relating to the debate discussed above. Three categories of bills are presented to the Legislature—public bills, which deal with matters of a public or general nature; local bills, which are, in effect, public bills applicable to a single city, town, or municipality; and private bills which confer rights on, or relieve from liability, a particular person or group of persons. Except for the Appropriation Act, all of them pass through the legislative mill in identical stages. After two readings by the House proper, they are considered first by one of two legislative standing committees, then by the Committee of the Whole House. The report stage and third reading follow before the bills are submitted to the Lieutenant-Governor for his assent.

In accordance with the usual practice first reading is merely a formality which serves the purpose of introducing a bill into the legislative stream. But an apparent aberration from the normal occurs at the next stage, for during the four sessions of the Forty-fourth General Assembly (1949–53) only one bill was denied second reading. The major bills, all of which are sponsored by the government, could not, of course, be rejected without necessitating an election or a change of administration. In their case a full-dress debate normally occurs on second reading and reference to a committee means acceptance in principle. Private members' public bills, almost without exception, are likewise accorded a hearing in committee, but this is not so unusual as it might appear since few of them are of major importance or controversial, and second reading in this instance does not necessarily constitute approval in principle. In the case of private bills second reading simply signifies that the House requires a legislative committee to determine whether they are in accord with public policy.

The most distinctive feature of the Nova Scotian legislative process is its committee system for dealing with bills after their second reading. With few exceptions they are committed at this stage to the Committee on Law Amendments or the Committee on Private and Local Bills. This procedure was not adopted at one fell swoop, but evolved over a period of almost half a century as a means of avoiding the difficulties which were inherent in the reference of bills either to a host of standing committees or to the Committee of the Whole House.

A committee on expiring laws and private bills was already well established when in 1858 a committee was instituted to consider in detail any bills which proposed to amend the chapters of the revised statutes.[9]   During the next forty years, as a result of a steady although uneven development, its duties were augmented to include the consideration of the public bills which had previously fallen within the purview of the standing committees on Crown lands, railways, humane institutions, and the like.   Meanwhile the committee on expiring laws and private bills, even as it was losing its power to consider public bills, was being entrusted with hearing an ever increasing number of local bills—it was becoming a Private and Local Bills Committee.   By 1900 the two developments were practically complete and henceforth it was unusual for a bill to undergo examination by any other standing committee.

Today the allocation of bills is made by the Speaker, but it involves little discretion on his part since the division normally follows that in the statute book—public bills go to the Law Amendments Committee and all others to the Committee on Private and Local Bills. Yet the system is flexible for, when a bill relating to a particular area or interest involves considerations of the type presented by public bills, it may be referred to the former committee.[10]

In the course of its development the two-committee system was alleged to contain features which were destructive of parliamentary institutions.   One criticism was that most of the legislative work was being entrusted to "small and practically irresponsible committees sitting behind semi-private doors, instead of in open House"; another that the members were being "so overworked in committee and so trained to regard the Houses as mere machines for registering committee legislation that the proper functions of Parliament [were] falling into not innocuous desuetude."[11]   Nevertheless time has vindicated the usefulness of the two-committee system.   The unwieldly Committee of the Whole had long been condemned as unsuitable for the minute examination of bills; one smaller committee would have found it physically impossible to examine the total legislative output; the bills fall naturally into two subdivisions; and the membership of the Assembly permits two capable committees to be selected

[9]*JHA*, 1858, 458.

[10]Such as a local bill which proposes to alter the civil courts of either Halifax or Sydney, or a private bill which is intended to confer some privilege on a specific professional group in return for which it is expected to assume responsibilities towards the public.

[11]*Morning Chronicle*, April 2, 1902.

without resort to duplication. Over the years they varied in size from 13 in 1907 to 29 in 1928, but since 1933 neither committee has numbered more than 12. The result has been to promote the round-table type of discussion which is desirable, and to prevent the proceedings from degenerating into a public meeting unsuitable for the discussion of details. Any member may pursue his examination without being subjected to the signs of impatience which the large majority on the government benches often makes little effort to conceal in Committee of the Whole.

The two committees have also served to keep the statutes uniform in principle and in form. The Committee on Private and Local Bills not only deals with each bill on its own merits, but it ensures, in addition, that the bill is not inconsistent with the general policy which the Legislature is currently adopting towards the granting of privileges to individuals, corporations, and municipalities. Similarly the Law Amendments Committee reviews the public bills in the light of the existing public statutes and sees that they do not run counter to them in tenor or form. To make sure that this function is performed satisfactorily the Attorney-General has been acting as its chairman *ex officio* for the last three-quarters of a century. The continuity in membership which the two committees possess from session to session and even from one Assembly to the next also contributes to securing the optimum measure of uniformity.

Finally, the legislative committees have been useful vehicles for conducting public hearings on controversial bills. Neither has been known to turn down a reasonable request for a hearing by any party which may be affected by the provisions of a bill. One of the most difficult single items with which the Committee on Private and Local Bills has to deal is the annual bill to amend the charter of the city of Halifax. Often it finds itself in a quandary when it has to decide whether to intervene in favour of individuals or groups against the local authority which represents them in a lesser sphere of government. The Law Amendments Committee conducts a larger number of hearings on a far wider range of topics. Sometimes the requests for a hearing do not come until the discussion of the principle of a bill on second reading has focussed public attention upon its contents. In recent years the representatives of the Union of Nova Scotia Municipalities and the temperance organizations have been the most regular attendants before the Committee, the former to oppose the imposition of additional burdens upon the municipalities, the latter to protest the extension of the sale of liquor. But the representations of any influential pressure group always receive serious consideration, and modifications to remove or allay the major cause of complaint are not infrequent.

Thus the two legislative committees have assumed, in effect, the function of making decisions on matters both of principle and of detail. Over the ten-year period from 1946 to 1955 they recommended the deferment of 3.7 per cent of the bills which they considered. In addition, the Law Amendments Committee amended 339 or 50.1 per cent of its bills, the Private and Local Bills Committee 437 or 68.2 per cent of its bills.[12] An Attorney-General who appreciated the extensive character of these duties once expressed regret that "the general public does not have more opportunity to see the work of the committees of the Legislature."[13]

If the committees recommend that a bill be deferred, the House almost invariably concurs although not always without debate; if they report a bill with or without amendments, the House commits it to the Committee of the Whole usually without discussion. Undoubtedly the work of the smaller committees adds to the difficulty of making a clause by clause examination in the Committee of the Whole, for unless their amendments have been so extensive as to require a reprinting, the larger committee is forced to rely upon the Clerk's reading of the proposed changes for its acquaintance with the amended bill. This fact, together with the rapid tempo at which the committee works, sometimes makes it difficult for even those individuals who are trained in the examination of bills to appreciate fully what the committee is being called upon to approve. Many members, realizing the futility of attempting to understand precisely what is happening, lose all interest in the proceedings.

Nevertheless the consideration of bills by the Committee of the Whole still possesses some merit. In particular, it provides every assemblyman with an opportunity to oppose the recommendations of the smaller committees and therefore places the larger committee in the role of arbiter. Nor is the opportunity lost, for although the Committee of the Whole approved the work of the smaller committees on 93.0 per cent of the bills between 1946 and 1955, it deferred four on its own initiative and amended 86 others, thus demonstrating that it had renounced none of its former power.

When the Committee of the Whole reports a bill without amend-

---

[12]For the action taken by the Assembly on all bills introduced between 1946 and 1955 see Appendix N.
[13]See *Halifax Chronicle*, May 10, 1947.

ment, the House orders it to be read a third time at a subsequent sitting; otherwise the bill is subject to further debate and amendment. While its sponsor occasionally uses this opportunity to try to have the amended clauses restored to their original form, he is seldom successful.

Third reading is normally a formality. Fewer than 0.6 per cent of the bills were amended at this stage between 1946 and 1955, and in every instance the changes were not substantial.

In addition to the two legislative committees, the House constitutes a committee on privileges and rules, and eight select standing committees on a functional basis to deal with particular aspects of the public business. In selecting them each party ensures that its representation is arranged to suit the interests and the capabilities of its own assemblymen. But despite this apparent concern for their composition seven of these committees—agriculture, lands and forests, education, mines and minerals, industry, humane, and temperance—now play no significant role in the governmental process. None of them is entrusted with the consideration of legislation; few meet more than one or two hours during the session and then only because an energetic chairman feels the committee should be going through the motions of doing something; only rarely does any of them present a recommendation which is not already under consideration by the appropriate department.

The one exception is the Public Accounts Committee. While it too has been dormant over long periods, it is spurred into activity whenever a vigorous opposition senses the possibility of uncovering something which will be highly embarrassing to the government at an approaching election. In self-defence the government members of the committee utilize every plausible means at their disposal to confine the inquiry within the narrowest limits possible. Since political considerations are thereby joined to those of public interest, it is only to be expected that the functioning of this committee is highly troublous during its most active periods.[14]

Special select committees have at no time played a significant role in the functioning of the Legislature. Within recent years their use has been confined largely to the redistribution committees which recommend changes in the representation of the Assembly. More

[14]In 1933 the Liberal minority on the committee was outraged because it had not been permitted to see the report which was presented to the Assembly; in 1953 a Conservative member walked out on the committee because the Liberal majority had set up a "veil of secrecy" and a "virtual iron curtain." Both incidents occurred in election years.

and more the tendency has been to employ a royal commission rather than a committee for purposes of investigation.

To ensure an adequate measure of control over the provincial finances, the Assembly has long been adapting the financial procedures of the British and Canadian Houses of Commons to the needs of a small provincial Legislature. It is now a long-established practice for the Provincial Treasurer to deliver his budget in two parts—by the tenth day of the session he tables the public accounts and comments upon their significance; by the twentieth[15] he presents his estimates and forecasts the financial prospects of the province in what may be called the budget speech proper. On the first occasion the House orders the accounts to be referred to the Public Accounts Committee; on the second it resolves itself into Committee of Supply, that is, the Committee of the Whole House which examines the proposed expenditures for the coming year.

These proceedings deviate considerably from the practice at Ottawa where the estimates are presented separately on a motion to go into Committee of Supply, and the budget speech, which is especially concerned with taxation proposals, is accompanied by a motion to go into Committee of Ways and Means. The latter committee appears to have become obsolescent in Nova Scotia since its last recorded use dates back to 1892 when it considered a resolution for the imposition of succession duties.[16] Its demise may be attributed partly to the long intervals which have often occurred between the introduction of taxation bills, and partly to the doubtful utility of the elaborate procedures which its use entails. In any case, other than that a member of the government must introduce them, taxation measures follow the same sequence of stages as non-financial bills in their passage through the legislative mill.

The Nova Scotian procedures afford the Assembly three opportunities to review the provincial finances in their general or particular aspects. One comes in the debate on the budget proper, which, while not nearly so discursive as that at Ottawa, permits the broad financial policies of the government to be brought closely under review. Another occurs during the review of provincial accounts by the Public Accounts Committee when the opposition singles out specific expenditures for minute scrutiny.[17] The third arises during the consideration of the estimates in Committee of Supply, but since this committee normally works at an even more accelerated pace

[15]The former period is statutory; the latter customary.
[16]JHA, 1892, 101-2.   [17]Supra, 281.

than at Ottawa, a small opposition must be well prepared in advance if it is to use its opportunities to the full.[18]

The opposition is especially interested in providing procedures which will permit a genuine control to be exercised over the provincial expenditures. In the 1890's it sought to prevent the government from spending greater amounts than were specified in the various sections of the Appropriation Act, and when the government approved overexpenditures by order-in-council in 1890 and 1892, it warned that "the functions of [the] legislature are at an end and his honor the lieut governor might as well send us home."[19] At the same time it denounced the practice which allowed the government to make unauthorized expenditures in the first three or four months of the calendar year before supply had been voted. Although Premier Fielding dismissed both these criticisms as technical, he took immediate steps to counteract them.[20] Henceforth the Governor-in-Council was authorized by statute to approve an overexpenditure whenever a minister or principal officer certified that it was required in the public interest, while the Provincial Treasurer might permit funds to be expended upon the usual services in the interval between the close of the fiscal year in December and the passage of a new Appropriation Act in March or April.[21]

Yet neither provision introduced any real limitations upon the cabinet's control of the provincial finances. One of them was, in fact, rendered almost nugatory when, as a result of a change in the fiscal year, it was found necessary to authorize the payment of one-half of the normal expenditures before the passage of a new Appropriation Act.[22] Two further months of legislative control were added after 1935, but only by virtue of another change in the fiscal year[23] which made it increasingly difficult to have the public accounts and

[18]Actually the proceedings relative to supply follow the normal pattern much more closely than those pertaining to the raising of the revenue. The estimates are presented to the House on the authority of the Lieutenant-Governor; the Committee of Supply, after due consideration, reports them back to the Assembly in the form of resolutions, which when approved by the House are incorporated in the Supply Bill; it receives the normal three readings and the Governor's assent, and passes into law as the Appropriation Act. While supplementary estimates are seldom necessary, the practice in recent years has been to present the capital estimates separately towards the close of the session.

[19]*Morning Herald*, April 3, 1890. See also *ibid.*, March 8, 1892.

[20]*Assembly Debates*, 1892, 9; 56 Vic., c. 4.

[21]But these sums were in no case to exceed one-third of the entire sums appropriated during the previous year.

[22]2 Geo. V, c. 29.

[23]24 Geo. V, c. 18.

departmental reports prepared and printed by the time it was customary to convene the Legislature.

In 1950 the Macdonald government sought a way out of this difficulty by introducing a fiscal year starting on April 1 as was the practice of the Dominion and a majority of the provincial governments. This meant that the last complete fiscal year for which public accounts could be presented at any session of the Legislature would have ended twelve months earlier. The Conservatives protested a change which would "substantially diminish public interest in examination of the public accounts and . . . substantially weaken the position of the Opposition in respect to dealing with public expenditures," but the Premier had a simple answer for all their arguments: "This is the way it is done in the other provinces."[24] The change eliminated the need of machinery for legitimatizing unvoted expenditures for the ordinary services, since the Appropriation Act can now readily be passed in time, but the old provisions for authorizing unavoidable overexpenditures are still required. Since 1909 they have permitted the Governor-in-Council, upon the report of the Provincial Treasurer and the appropriate minister, to approve the repair of any public building or work which is damaged by accident, or the carrying out of any other work "not foreseen or provided for by the Legislature [which] is urgently and immediately required for the public good."[25]

Associated with the attempts to maintain an effective control over provincial finance has been the endeavour to secure a proper audit of the public accounts. Because a standing committee is unable to examine critically more than a few specially selected items, the opposition has been striving since 1901 to secure the appointment of a Provincial Auditor possessing a status similar to that of the Auditor-General of Canada. At first Premier Murray contended that a provincial cashier who issued cheques only after the departmental heads had certified to the authenticity of the accounts performed all the useful functions of an Auditor-General, but he changed his mind in 1909 when the direct responsibility for paying out the road and bridge moneys was transferred to the Provincial Treasury. Yet his appointment of a Provincial Auditor with a tenure similar to that of the Auditor-General of Canada and the setting up of a Treasury Board with a composition and powers comparable to that at Ottawa[26] won no favour. The Treasury Board continued to exist on paper until

[24]*Halifax Chronicle-Herald*, April 6, 1950. The relevant statute was 14 Geo. VI, c. 47.   [25]9 Edw. VII, c. 3.   [26]*Ibid.*

1926, but there is no evidence that its role was ever of any real significance, while the Provincial Auditor was accused from the start of being lax in the performance of his duties[27] or of being "tied hand and foot by the government."[28]

When a Conservative government finally managed to secure an independent probe of the public accounts in 1925, it was revealed that the departments had "systematically postponed the payment of accounts for no other purpose than to disguise the fact that their appropriations ha[d] been overrun," and that the financial records were "incomplete, inaccurate and wholly inadequate for recording the transactions of the Province."[29] Yet the Conservatives themselves can lay no great claim to consistency since their own Audit Act did no more than authorize the Governor-in-Council to appoint chartered accountants on an annual basis to examine and audit the public accounts.[30] Their report was to be presented to the Provincial Treasurer and tabled in the Legislature not later than the tenth day of each session. Succeeding Liberal governments have retained these provisions, but in 1942 they appointed, in addition, a Provincial Auditor with powers comparable to those of the Comptroller-General at Ottawa during a tenure of good behaviour.[31] To all appearances, however, the government still lacks a genuine critic of its financial procedures. That is why the Conservatives have reverted to the position that the Provincial Auditor should be a servant of the Legislature rather than an employee of the Department of the Provincial Treasurer. Their electoral success in 1956 permits the implementation of these views.[32]

[27]*Assembly Debates*, 1912, 562; see also *Halifax Herald*, May 3, 1916.

[28]*Halifax Herald*, March 5, 1925.

[29]See the Ross Report, *JHA*, 1926, Appendix 38, 6–7. The Liberals described the report as a political document, more "in the nature of one a detective agency would prepare and not a firm of auditors." See *Halifax Chronicle*, April 20, 1934.

[30]16–17 Geo. V, c. 1. The Governor-in-Council was also to determine their remuneration.

[31]6 Geo. VI, c. 3, s. 23. His duties are now defined in the Provincial Finance Act. R.S. 1954, c. 229.

[32]The Hicks administration re-established the Treasury Board in 1954, but its effectiveness in checking the departments is still to be determined.

CHAPTER XVIII

THE JUDICIARY

CONFEDERATION did not introduce far-reaching changes in the basic structure of the courts. The Dominion Parliament, it is true, used its power to "provide for the Constitution, Maintenance, and Organization of a General Court of Appeal for Canada"[1] by setting up the Supreme Court of Canada in 1875. This Court, since the abolition of appeals to the Judicial Committee of the Privy Council in 1949, has acted as the final court of appeal from the provincial courts in both civil and criminal cases. But Parliament's right, notwithstanding anything in the B.N.A. Act, to constitute "any additional Courts for the better Administration of the Laws of Canada"[2] has been confined to setting up the Exchequer Court of Canada which exercises original and appellate jurisdiction whenever claims are made by or against the Crown in the right of Canada.[3] Thus the Canadian practice differs from the American, for although Congress might have vested original jurisdiction in cases arising under the laws of the United States in the state courts, it preferred to establish separate federal courts for this purpose.

The pre-Confederation system of provincial courts as described in chapter VIII was preserved intact by section 129 of the B.N.A. Act until the appropriate authority—the Dominion Parliament or the provincial legislatures—made such alterations as the Act permitted. The power of the Nova Scotian Legislature to regulate "the Constitution, Maintenance, and Organization of Provincial Courts, both of Civil and of Criminal Jurisdiction"[4] has been used only once to create a new court of major importance. That was in 1874 when a system of county courts was established. A more important effect of the B.N.A. Act was to introduce a combined Dominion and provincial authority in the major provincial courts. The provincial Legislature, in addition to constituting, maintaining, and organizing them, regulates their pro-

---

[1]S. 101 of the B.N.A. Act.

[2]*Ibid.*

[3]The judges of the Court also exercise an admiralty jurisdiction throughout the country. But since Nova Scotia constitutes one of six admiralty districts, they share this function with a District Judge in Admiralty who is appointed by the Governor-General-in-Council.

[4]S. 92 (14) of the B.N.A. Act.

cedure in civil matters and the administration of justice in general.[5] Parliament, on the other hand, prescribes the law and procedure in criminal matters[6] and provides the salaries, allowances, and pensions of the judges of the superior, district, and county courts,[7] who are appointed by the Governor-General-in-Council.[8] Over the minor provincial courts the Dominion authority is slight, but it at least regulates the scope of their jurisdiction and their procedures in criminal matters.

The courts which are constituted by virtue of the provincial authority are the Supreme Court of Nova Scotia, the Court for Divorce and Matrimonial Causes, the county courts, the probate courts, and the minor courts.

THE SUPREME COURT OF NOVA SCOTIA

The pre-Confederation Supreme Court was continued after 1867, and, as was indicated above, the power to regulate its constitution, although not to appoint and pay its judges, still remained in the provincial Legislature. Today the Court consists of a Chief Justice and six assistant justices.[9] The last additions—two assistant justices in 1870 —were secured with difficulty. At Confederation the advanced age and infirmities of the judges, combined with a steady increase in the number of causes, had resulted in extensive unfinished business both in Halifax and on the circuits.[10] Since there was no immediate prospect of relief, the onus was upon the Legislature to augment the Supreme Court, but neither it nor the government of the day evinced any enthusiasm for taking remedial action. Not only did they appear to enjoy the predicament of the judges, who, with one exception, had supported Confederation, but they were all too well aware that any appointments which they might facilitate would mean preferment for Confederate lawyers. Hence their only proposal was to appoint barristers who might try causes on circuit if a regular judge were unavailable, and this was rejected by the Legislative Council which agreed with the judges that it was thoroughly undesirable. Meanwhile the condition of the Court steadily became more intolerable:

[5]*Ibid.*   [6]*Ibid.*, s. 91 (27).
[7]Including those of the admiralty court. *Ibid.*, s. 100.
[8]Except those of the probate courts in Nova Scotia and New Brunswick. *Ibid.*, s. 96.
[9]The Judicature Act of 1950 continues to make reference to a Judge in Equity, but legislation which was enacted in 1948 effectually abolished the office.
[10]See the address of the Chief Justice to the grand jury of Halifax in the *Morning Chronicle*, Oct. 28, 1868.

The Chief Justice has long since passed the period fixed in Holy Writ for the life of man, and is now verging on eighty years of age. . . . In consequence of the age and infirmity of the Judge in Equity, the Island of Cape Breton . . . has been deprived of the administration of justice for a whole year. . . . Mr. Justice Dodd is very old and infirm. Over and over he has pronounced himself unfit to endure the enormous responsibility and fatigue of a judge-ship of the Supreme Court. . . . Mr. Justice DesBarres is an older man than "brother Dodd" and much less intellectually energetic. . . . Judge Wilkins we would leave as a kind of nest egg, and he will do for some years longer—perhaps to be Chief Justice. . . .[11]

Ultimately even an anti-Confederate ministry was forced to initiate steps for the appointment of two additional judges and thereby provide a sufficient number to travel the five circuits and perform the chambers duties at Halifax.[12]

To be eligible for appointment as judge of the Supreme Court, one has to be a barrister of ten years' standing who has practised for at least five years. To what extent these qualifications are to be con-sidered a part of the constitution of the court and subject, therefore, to provincial regulation is a matter of controversy, but the Minister of Justice has always successfully maintained the position that, except for pre-Confederation statutes, the Dominion government's power of appointment cannot be limited by provincial enactments.[13]

Since Confederation the most significant change in the powers and the jurisdiction of the Supreme Court was effected by the Judicature Act of 1884[14] which adapted the corresponding English statute of a decade earlier to the Nova Scotia circumstances. Broadly the measure conferred upon the Supreme Court the powers which were formerly exercised by the Courts of Queen's Bench, Common Pleas, Chancery, and Exchequer in England.[15] More particularly, it abolished the Equity Court and gave to all judges alike an equitable jurisdiction. To satisfy those who were wont to complain that Nova Scotia had been "plodding along in the old ruts for years" with a practice "unlike any other in the world,"[16] it created an entirely new system of practice. "It sweeps away all forms of technical pleading," said the *Recorder*, "and puts the Courts of this Province on the same footing as those of Ontario and Great Britain."[17]

[11]*Ibid.*, Aug. 2, 1870. [12]33 Vic., c. 2.
[13]F. H. Gisborne, comp., *Provincial Legislation, 1896–1920* (Ottawa, 1922), 271. [14]47 Vic., c. 25.
[15]Later it was declared to possess, in addition, all the powers exercised by the Court of Appeal and the High Court of Justice on Oct. 1, 1884, excepting those conferred solely upon the Probate, Divorce, and Admiralty Division or by the statutes relating to bankruptcy. See R.S. 1900, c. 155.
[16]*Acadian Recorder*, Feb. 1, 1884. [17]*Ibid.*, April 19, 1884.

Although the Judicature Act of 1950 repeats the same general grant of power, federal and provincial statutes serve to define the Court's functions more precisely and to limit them. Today it has original jurisdiction in civil cases whenever the amount at issue is in excess of $100,[18] but it shares that jurisdiction with the county courts in amounts up to $1,000. In criminal cases its original jurisdiction is restricted to indictable offenses, but except in the most serious cases the accused may waive a preliminary hearing and consent to be tried by a magistrate, or after being committed for trial may elect to be tried by a county court judge without a jury.

Sitting individually, a judge of the Supreme Court acts as a trial division judge; sitting *in banco* the Court hears appeals in both civil and criminal cases, most of which have been tried in the first instance by either a single judge or the county courts. For many years this capacity was exercised in a thoroughly undesirable manner. On their return from the circuits the judges met to reconsider the causes which were appealed, and it was only natural for them to assist one another in upholding their previous rulings or judgments.[19] Eventually the judges themselves removed the worst feature of the process by prohibiting any one of their number from participating in the appeal of a cause which he had tried in the first instance.[20]

By Dominion statute the Supreme Court, like the superior courts of the other provinces, is constituted a bankruptcy court, a single judge possessing original jurisdiction and the full court appellate jurisdiction. By provincial statute it has been required since 1890 to express an opinion upon any matter which the Lieutenant-Governor-in-Council may refer to it for consideration. This opinion is to be deemed a judgment of the Court and an appeal is to lie from it as in ordinary actions.[21] The adoption of this provision followed what the Attorney-General of the day described as one of the most surprising events ever to occur in the judicial affairs of the country. When asked to give an opinion upon a legal point in connection with the provincial licensing act of 1886, one judge declined to be a party to making the Supreme Court a moot court and withdrew with all his papers.[22] Although the Governor-in-Council has rarely resorted to a test case,

[18]14–15 Geo. V, c. 55.   [19]See *Morning Chronicle*, April 8, 1870.
[20]By exercising their power to make rules under the Judicature Act of 1884. See the *Royal Gazette*, April 16, 1890.
[21]53 Vic., c. 9, and 4 Geo. VI, c. 30.
[22]*Assembly Debates*, 1890, 102. This judge was following the practice of the American courts which permit their judgment to be invoked upon a constitutional issue "only when [it is] inextricably entangled with a living and ripe law suit."

in two instances the Court has been required to express an opinion
on matters of substance, in 1926 upon the constitution of the Legislative Council and the tenure of its members, in 1947 upon the legal
right of the Dominion and the provinces to delegate their legislative
powers to each other.[23]

THE COURT FOR DIVORCE AND MATRIMONIAL CAUSES

Until 1948 the Court for Divorce and Matrimonial Causes possessed
the form and performed the functions prescribed by the act of 1866.[24]
Although the British North America Act had jeopardized its very
existence by empowering the Dominion Parliament to legislate on the
subject of divorce, the politico-religious implications which militate
against the establishment of a federal divorce court have enabled it
to survive. Yet since serious doubts were long entertained about the
right of the provincial Legislature to alter its constitution, no government attempted to adapt its form or functioning to new needs. Indeed
a measure which did no more than alter the description of its judge
was rescinded before it became practically operative.[25]

The deluge of divorce cases after 1945 finally brought about a
change. "It is beyond the capacity of any man—or machine—working
day and night to handle them," said the Attorney-General in 1948.[26]
Now that a higher conception of the provincial legislative power prevailed, his remedy was simply to empower the Governor-General-in-
Council to name all the justices of the Supreme Court as judges of the
Court for Divorce and Matrimonial Causes.[27] While the new provisions

[23]*In re Constitutional Validity of Bill No. 136 of the Nova Scotia Legislature,*
22 M.P.R. 83.   [24]*Supra*, 132.

[25]After the Judicature Act of 1884 deprived the Judge in Equity of his special
duties in equitable causes, his title was a misnomer since he was then to be distinguished from the other judges only because he was *ex officio* Judge ordinary of
the Court for Divorce and Matrimonial Causes. For that reason the Legislature
took steps to distinguish the title on the death or retirement of the incumbent
judge, at the same time empowering the Governor-General-in-Council to name any
of the judges of the Supreme Court to act as Judge ordinary. 47 Vic., c. 25, s. 3,
and 48 Vic., c. 30. But since the validity of this legislation was questioned at the
time of the first vacancy in 1889, there was no alternative but to resurrect the
title in order to preserve the Court. 52 Vic., c. 8. See the statement of Attorney-
General Longley, *Assembly Debates*, 1897, 141.

[26]*Halifax Herald*, April 13, 1948.

[27]12 Geo. VI, c. 8. The federal government gave practical effect to this provision
almost immediately. The act also repealed the historical anachronism which
permitted the Judge ordinary to collect a fee of $4 for each day's sitting of the
Court. This was a relic of the time when the Governor, the judicial vice-president,
and the executive councillors were each allowed £1 for every day they spent
in actual attendance at the Court.

had the additional merit of permitting divorce cases to be heard on circuit, the Attorney-General was careful to deny that it made divorce any easier. There was never any good reason, he said, why all divorces should be heard in Halifax "unless it was the belief of those involved that, under such a system, news of the proceedings would be kept out of their home-town papers."[28] The provincial Legislature is, of course, still debarred from regulating the constitution of the Court in most respects. For example, it cannot widen the grounds for which divorces may be granted. But unlike the other provincial courts, which are empowered to grant divorces only on the ground of adultery, the Nova Scotian Court still possesses its pre-Confederation right to recognize the additional ground of cruelty.[29]

THE COUNTY COURTS

The vacuum which had existed since 1841 between a single judge of the Supreme Court and two justices of the peace was filled in 1874 when the Legislature instituted a system of county courts.[30] Parliament, however, did not provide for the salaries of the judges until 1876, and the federal government then made the appointments. The new arrangements, according to the Attorney-General, "simply took from the Supreme Court a portion of its jurisdiction. . . . it saved the Supreme Court from frittering away a whole day in the hearing of appeal and summary causes."[31]

To enable the new courts to perform their functions, the province was divided into seven districts,[32] over each of which a judge, who before his appointment had been a barrister of not less than seven years' standing, was to preside. The formal constitution of the courts still remains practically unaltered, but their functions have been constantly extended. Today they try civil causes where the amount at issue does not exceed $1,000.[33] In 1889 they were empowered to hear all but the

[28]*Halifax Herald*, April 13, 1948.
[29]29 Vic., c. 13 (1866). Cruelty, in this context, is established only by "proof of actual violence of such a character as to endanger physical or mental health or safety, or by proof of a reasonable apprehension thereof." *Jones* v. *Jones*, 20 M.P.R. 213.   [30]37 Vic., c. 18.   [31]*Assembly Debates*, 1874, 126.
[32]The districts were: no. 1, Halifax; no. 2, Lunenburg, Queens, and Shelburne; no. 3, Annapolis, Digby, and Yarmouth; no. 4, Kings, Hants, and Colchester; no. 5, Cumberland and Pictou; no. 6, Inverness, Antigonish, and Guysborough; no. 7, Cape Breton, Victoria, and Richmond.
[33]9 Geo. VI, c. 5. They have no original jurisdiction in these cases, however, when the amount at issue is less than $20, and they are still debarred from hearing any action where the validity of a devise or bequest is disputed or where the title to land is in question.

most serious criminal causes whenever the accused elected speedy trial without a jury;[34] in 1897 to assume the functions of the Judges of Probate when vacancies first occurred in that office;[35] in 1936 to make the recommendations which are required for the restoration of the licences of motor vehicle operators;[36] and in 1953 to conduct the recounts in provincial elections.[37]

COURTS OF PROBATE

The probate courts have been altered radically only once since Confederation. That change, effected in 1897, was made possible by the power conferred upon the Nova Scotian government to appoint Judges of Probate.[38] Its object was to simplify the machinery of the courts and reduce the cost of their procedures by eliminating one of the two sets of fees hitherto required from every estate large or small. In effect, the functions of the existing Judges of Probate were to be assumed by the registrars of probate and the county court judges, the former transacting the uncontested probate business, the latter dealing with the contested cases and hearing appeals from the decisions of the registrars.[39]

The practical method of effecting this result was a novel one. The incumbent Judges of Probate were to retain their offices for the time being, but were required to assume the registrarships whenever they fell vacant. ". . . in this country," said Attorney-General Longley, "there had always been a certain amount of sacredness attached to the vested interests of persons in offices held by them, and for this reason it was considered desirable not to proceed in too hasty or drastic a manner."[40] When the Conservatives took the view that if the change was desirable it should be introduced at one fell swoop,[41] the two parties appeared to have completed a full turn on vested rights since 1848.

While it required thirty-six years to bring these provisions fully into

---

[34] 52 Vic., c. 11.   [35] See below.   [36] 1 Edw. VIII, c. 42.

[37] 2 Eliz. II, c. 39. They had previously been authorized to conduct the recounts in federal elections.

[38] S. 96 of the B.N.A. Act made this provision applicable to Nova Scotia and New Brunswick.

[39] The county court judges were to receive no extra remuneration since the majority were "not overworked officials and . . . by adding the contested business of the probate court . . . it would not . . . impose upon them any greater duties than they were expected to discharge when their office was first created." See statement of Attorney-General Longley, *Assembly Debates*, 1897, 29.

[40] *Ibid.*, 28.   [41] *Ibid.*, 51.

operation,[42] they proved to be well conceived and have required only small modifications. Consequently the principal concern with probate matters in recent years has been associated with the general problem of eliminating officers who are remunerated by fees. Only three registrars of probate are at present on a fixed salary,[43] but the government's intention is to extend the practice whenever it can be accomplished without serious financial loss to the province.

THE MINOR COURTS

Until recently the complexity and lack of uniformity of the courts below the county courts and the incapacity of their presiding officers, all appointed and paid by the province, provided the main source of complaint against the judicial structure. At the lowest level are the courts presided over by the justices of the peace, which possess much the same powers as at Confederation—a single justice may try actions for debt where the amount at issue does not exceed $20; two justices may deal with amounts up to $80.[44] In addition, a justice of the peace may exercise the limited jurisdiction in minor misdemeanours which is prescribed by the Nova Scotia Summary Convictions Act.[45]

One step higher in the hierarchy of courts are those presided over by the stipendiary magistrates,[46] who, in addition to all the powers possessed by one or two justices of the peace, exercise jurisdiction in most personal actions involving sums not exceeding $80,[47] and some of whom possess powers in criminal cases as prescribed by the Criminal Code.[48] Stipendiary magistrates preside, in addition, over the municipal courts of the towns, which were first established by the Towns' Incorporation Act of 1886. The town stipendiaries not only possess

[42]Halifax County, which was originally excluded from the act, came under its provisions in 1933. 23–24 Geo. V, c. 49.

[43]Elsewhere the registrars retain approximately two-thirds of the fees which they assess, but since 1914 they have been guaranteed a minimum annual return which is now fixed at $500. 1 Eliz. II, c. 40.

[44]R.S. 1954, c. 141, s. 1.

[45]4 Geo. VI, c. 3.

[46]Originally both the towns and the municipalities were empowered to appoint their own stipendiary magistrates, but this function was assumed by the Governor-in-Council in the case of the towns in 1891 (54 Vic., c. 43) and the municipalities in 1900 (63 Vic., c. 18).

[47]R.S. 1954, c. 141.

[48]The Lieutenant-Governor-in-Council may authorize a stipendiary magistrate who is a barrister of five years' standing to exercise the extended jurisdiction conferred upon a magistrate by Part XVI of the new Criminal Code. The terms of such appointments are judicially noted. 4 Eliz. II, c. 43. All provincial magistrates (infra, 295) possess these powers.

the normal power of a magistrate or two justices of the peace in civil cases, but they also exercise a jurisdiction in all actions upon contract where the amount does not exceed $100.[49] The city courts of Halifax and Sydney, as established by their charters, possess analogous functions.

These courts, their jurisdictions, and their procedures were the result not of any coherent plan to provide the most efficient and workable system that could be devised, but a haphazard growth designed to meet specific needs as they arose. In 1913 the Bar Society registered its opposition to the multiple framework of justices', stipendiary magistrates', municipal, city, and county courts each with jurisdiction up to $80, and concurrent from $20 upward with the Supreme Court.

If a market gard[e]ner belonging to the Eastern Passage wish[ed] to sue a Haligonian or a Dartmouthian for $20 worth of produce sold in Halifax, he could sue in the justices' court and have a jury of three persons to decide the case, or in the county stipendiary's court with a similar procedure, but at an increased cost; or in the Dartmouth town court where he could get a certificate of judgment to bind real estate; or in the Halifax city court where he could get no such certificate, but solicitor's costs were taxed and a written defense had to be filed; or he could go to the county court and have the case hung up for a whole season from term to term and have it tried with a jury of five men, or else go to the supreme court and, perhaps, have it tried at chambers without a jury, at once, or at all events in a materially different way from other courts.[50]

The result, in the opinion of the critics, was to work not only inconvenience but frequently injustice as well. Even after the most glaring ills of these overlapping jurisdictions had been remedied, the administration of justice continued to be plagued by the type of individual who presided over the lower courts. On various occasions assemblymen complained that "some of the magistrates . . . have no more conception of the law than an ordinary school boy"[51] or that four-fifths of the Cape Breton magistrates were crooked and dishonest,[52] while Mr. Justice Hall was "loathe to see the grand jury system abolished under the present conditions of magistracy."[53] The de-

[49]The limit in such cases was raised to $200 in 1923 (13 Geo. V, c. 27) and $500 in 1924 (14–15 Geo. V, c. 51, and 15–16 Geo. V, c. 28) on the ground that individuals who were empowered in certain circumstances to deal with crimes, the sentence of which might be life imprisonment, should not be too narrowly circumscribed. *Morning Chronicle*, March 22, 1923. Later (1928) the amount was reduced to $100. 18 Geo. V, c. 51.

[50]See address of J. J. Power in *Halifax Herald*, March 26, 1913.

[51]See address of R. W. E. Landry, *ibid.*, April 6, 1929.

[52]*Ibid.*, March 30, 1916.

[53]*Halifax Herald*, April 1, 1932.

pendence of judicial officials of this low calibre upon fees for part of their remuneration could not fail to introduce other evils which were periodically characterized as vicious.[54]

It was not until 1938 that the first step was taken to put the magistracy upon a better basis. The method which was adopted was the appointment of lawyers of at least three years' standing at the bar as police magistrates on a full-time basis with adequate salaries to perform the judicial functions of a stipendiary magistrate and one or two justices of the peace.[55] Each was to try causes in the leading centres of the magisterial district in which he exercised his jurisdiction. By this means it was proposed not only to improve the calibre of the magistracy, but eventually to eliminate the fee system altogether. The incumbent magistrates were not to be ousted, but the new system was to be extended gradually as they retired.[56]

In 1942 the new magistrates were empowered to preside over the municipal courts whenever the Attorney-General requested it,[57] and in 1945 their title was altered to the more accurate designation of provincial magistrate.[58] The volume of judicial business which they transacted from the start made it clear that they were filling a long-felt need. In referring to the leave of absence which two of them requested in 1950, the Attorney-General commented: "No wonder . . . the poor men have been overworked."[59]

While the structure of the courts has imperfections, changes will not be made easily because two authorities must act in concert to effect them. The provincial Legislature may make modifications in the constitution of the provincial courts which affect the status and the number of judges, but the Dominion government and Parliament must agree to the new salary arrangements which are required.[60] A

[54] One Attorney-General adverted to the general belief that justices and even magistrates, "anxious to obtain fees connected with the issue of process in their courts . . . were disposed to find in favor of the plaintiff." *Assembly Debates*, 1895, 34.

[55] 2 Geo. VI, c. 19. In 1955 the qualification became one of five, rather than three years' standing at the bar. 4 Eliz. II, c. 43.

[56] See speech of Attorney-General J. H. MacQuarrie, *Halifax Chronicle*, March 23, 1938. By 1956 the number of provincial magistrates had grown to ten.

[57] 6 Geo. VI, c. 27.   [58] 9 Geo. VI, c. 4.

[59] See speech of Attorney-General M. A. Patterson, *Halifax Chronicle-Herald*, March 13, 1951.

[60] For a long time the Dominion and the province were in disagreement upon which authority was to defray the cost of criminal prosecutions. After 1867 the anti-Confederate government took the view that the prosecution of criminals, although incident to the administration of justice, formed no part of it. See

provincial government may decline to sponsor an increase in the size of a court which is clearly needed in the hope that a change of administration at Ottawa will enable a member or members of its own party to secure preferment. The circumstances may clearly call for a reduction in the number of senior judges and an enlargement of the facilities of the lower courts, but complications will arise because a different authority is responsible for the payment of the two levels of judicial officials.

Recently the more extensive resort to the facilities of the lower courts has brought out in bold relief the faults which have long existed in the judicial structure. In 1950 when the seven provincial magistrates were trying cases at the rate of 13,000 a year, the seven judges at the top of the judicial hierarchy in the Supreme Court were hearing a total of 66 ordinary cases, 31 appeals, and 84 divorce cases,[61] while the county court judgeships, with the possible exception of District No. 1, were little more than sinecures for the want of judicial work.[62] "Now is the time to have a shuffle of jurisdiction," said the Attorney-General, "and if the present situation is going to remain the privilege of the Supreme and County Courts, then surely we can find some more work for them to do."[63]

His was the fourth plea since 1897 for a basic alteration in the framework or the jurisdiction of the courts.[64] The first three were motivated, not only by the unsatisfactory distribution of judicial business between the various courts, but also by a fault which was completely structural—the absence of a genuine court of appeal. Unlike the other provinces,[65] which have established separate trial and appellate divisions in their superior courts, the Nova Scotian Court still continues to sit in banco

Journals of the House of Assembly (JHA), 1871, Appendix 6. But when it attempted to repeal the legislation which made the cost of prosecutions a charge upon the Provincial Treasury, the Legislative Council flatly declined to imperil the administration of justice. Journals of the Legislative Council (JLC), 1871, 41. Although an Attorney-General was still doubtful in 1887 if the responsibility for paying prosecutors was a provincial one, his successor soon learned to appreciate the usefulness of this new source of patronage.

[61]See Halifax Chronicle-Herald, March 13, 1951.

[62]In 1913 J. J. Power observed that the county court judges with one exception did not have enough to do and could spend their time publishing books. Halifax Herald, March 26, 1913.

[63]Halifax Chronicle-Herald, March 13, 1951.

[64]See the proposals of Attorney-General J. W. Longley (Assembly Debates, 1897, 141–2), the resolutions of the N.S. Barristers' Society (Halifax Herald, March 26, 1913), and the proposals of Attorney-General W. J. O'Hearn (Morning Chronicle, April 19, 1923).

[65]Except Prince Edward Island where the number of judges is insufficient to constitute separate divisions in the Supreme Court.

to hear appeals. Those who are conversant with this procedure have long held that it can provide neither the dignity nor the respect which a proper court should possess. One critic once referred to

the intolerable mischief of a group of judges of the same court reviewing the judgment of a brother judge, and that judge in turn making up a group which would revise the opinion of another judge that composed the first named court. It was too much of a draft . . . on human nature to think that mortal beings could make up an ideal appellate court under these circumstances. . . .[66]

Two attorneys-general have demonstrated how a more suitable appeal court might be constituted without increasing the cost of the judicial establishment. Broadly their proposals were to abolish the county courts and to designate some of the incumbent judges of the Supreme and county courts as district judges of the Supreme Court with original jurisdiction only, the others as an appellate division of the Court.[67] Yet a bill to this effect has never been placed before the Legislature even though no Minister of Justice nor Dominion Parliament has yet declined to provide the salaries if the judicial system is generally in accord with the job it has to perform.

The circumstances of the moment present still further difficulties. The basic need is for an increase in the number of provincial magistrates, but the funds for this purpose cannot be obtained by reducing the number of judges in the top layers of the judicial hierarchy since the salaries come from different sources. The one thing which may be safely inferred is that Nova Scotia will not set a precedent by reducing the number of judges who are paid by another authority.

Equal in significance to the structure of the courts is the calibre of the persons who preside over them. As a general rule, government officials perform their duties within a system of rewards and punishments which is designed to keep them politically responsible. Judges, on the other hand, are in an entirely different position because their opinions must be founded, not on the wishes or the needs of the public, but on the law of the land. Hence, as Dr. R. MacGregor Dawson demonstrates, "rewards and punishments . . . become not merely inappropriate, but dangerous; for they at once introduce the possibility that the judge may give his decisions . . . influenced to some degree by the effects of these decisions on his own personal career and fortune."[68] To avert this, a condition known as the inde-

[66]*Halifax Herald*, March 26, 1913.   [67]*Supra*, note 64.
[68]For a full discussion, see R. MacGregor Dawson, *Government of Canada* (Toronto, 1947), 472–91, and Dawson, *The Principle of Official Independence* (London, 1922), chap. II.

pendence of the judiciary is created whereby members of the judiciary are freed from most of the restraints, checks, and punishments to which other public officials are subject. Security of tenure, difficulty of removal, adequacy of salary, and care in selection and promotion are essential if this independence is to be meaningful.

The judges of the Supreme Court hold office during good behaviour and may only be removed for deliberate wrongdoing by a federal order-in-council subsequent to a joint address of both Houses of Parliament. While county court judges enjoy a similar tenure, the grounds for removal are the wider ones of misbehaviour or incapacity because of age or infirmity, and it may be effected by simple order-in-council pursuant to a commission of inquiry. Actually no judge of the Supreme Court of Nova Scotia has acted in such a manner as to warrant even the initiation of steps leading to his removal, but during the 1930's two county court judges vacated their offices under discreditable circumstances. One resigned prior to his being tried, convicted, and imprisoned for felony; the other was removed by order-in-council after an inquiry by a judge of the Supreme Court into his judicial conduct.[69] It would be grossly unfair, however, to measure the quality of the county court judges by two isolated cases, for often the appointees to this court possess character and ability in no wise inferior to that of their fellow jurists on the Supreme Court. Their relegation to the lesser role may be determined solely by the limited number of higher appointments which are available and the necessary relinquishment of their claims to others who have rendered political service of a higher order. Yet once they accept a county court judgeship, they automatically forego any prospect of higher preferment since there is no instance in Nova Scotia of a direct promotion to the Supreme Court.[70]

One problem of judicial tenure still remains to be solved. Whereas the county court judges must retire on reaching the age of seventy-five, the superior court judges have not been subjected to a similar provision since the British North America Act guarantees them a tenure during good behaviour. Furthermore, the Dominion government hesitates to

[69]Prior to the judge's removal in 1932 the Premier had declined to permit the county court judges to exercise powers under the Liberty of the Subject Act in respect to persons imprisoned under criminal process because of an "insurmountable obstacle" which he could not mention with propriety (*Halifax Herald*, March 24, 1932); in 1933 he agreed to a restoration of the power (23–24 Geo. V, c. 47).

[70]This is, of course, in accord with the general, although not invariable practice. The one Nova Scotian who sat in both courts, D. D. Mackenzie, had a long political career between his two appointments.

resort to a stoppage of salary in the event of their inefficiency or non-performance of duties because of age or infirmity. While there are few instances in which a disabled judge fails to resign, only recently an ailing Chief Justice of Nova Scotia attempted to emulate the record of two of his predecessors who were on active duty at ninety. When, as in such instances, a judge continues to serve beyond the age of seventy-five, there is always the suspicion that he is withholding his resignation until a government is returned at Ottawa which will appoint someone of his previous political leanings to succeed him.[71]

Certainty and adequacy of salary are also required to induce the best lawyers to accept judicial position and indirectly to ensure judicial independence. With this intent Parliament voted an increase of 20 per cent in the salaries of the superior and county court judges in 1951 and a further increase of $2,500 in 1955. As a result the Chief Justice of the Supreme Court now receives $18,500; its assistant justices $16,900; and the county court judges $10,500. Of comparable importance to salary are provisions for the pensioning of judges. Their absence in the pre-Confederation era had been responsible for eleven of the fifteen judges appointed before 1867 clinging to their offices until death. Thus, when Mr. Justice Bliss requested a retiring allowance because "the infirm and delicate state of [his] health warn[ed] [him] that his day of labor and usefulness [was] well nigh over," he was told that it would be preferable for him to perform only those services which his health and strength would permit rather than establish a costly precedent.[72] The system of pensions which the Dominion government established for the superior and county court judges shortly after 1867 ought to have redressed the evil, but, as indicated above, it failed to be entirely successful in the case of the Supreme Court.

While security of tenure and adequate remuneration are conducive to judicial independence, the selection of political partisans as judges naturally acts as a counteracting factor. Within recent years a Liberal government at Ottawa has occasionally appointed non-Liberals to the bench in other provinces, but in the case of Nova Scotia no party has shown preferment to individuals outside its ranks except in two instances of ancient vintage.[73] Human nature being what it is, the

[71]In 1951 the Attorney-General promised a thorough investigation of the tenure of these judges. See *Halifax Chronicle-Herald,* March 13, 1951.

[72]*JHA,* 1864, Appendix 30.

[73]In appointing the first county judges the Mackenzie government made the selections from both parties, and in 1907 the Laurier government promoted an ex-Conservative, C. J. Townshend, from an assistant justice to Chief Justice of the Supreme Court.

subsequent conduct of appointees may at times be coloured by their past, however circumspect their intentions. Certainly it is difficult to explain in other terms the opinion of the Supreme Court judges in the test case revolving around the constitution of the Legislative Council[74] and in a controverted election case in 1949–50.[75]

Fortunately incidents of this nature have been so rare that no doubts have been cast upon the integrity of the Court. Nevertheless the Legislature has not been sufficiently alert in taking steps to reduce the shocks which may damage the judiciary. The law in many matters is not some hidden truth which emerges with absolute finality after a careful examination of the facts and the legal precedents. In the election law particularly—which every judge ought to approach with fear and trembling—the statutes are often silent, the precedents are few, and the judiciary has no alternative but to legislate.

Yet despite the resort to political considerations in their appointment the calibre of the Nova Scotian judges has generally been high. Only rarely can they be considered too youthful or lacking in judicial experience, since the average Supreme Court judge at the time of his appointment has been 53.5 years of age and a barrister of 28.4 years' standing while the corresponding figures for the county court judges have been 50.5 and 25.3 years. Moreover, even though the method of appointment sometimes has the effect of excluding approximately 50 per cent of the eligible candidates over an extended period, the judges have, with few exceptions, possessed the qualities of mind and character which are needed to perform their duties meritoriously. To the generally high quality of the judiciary may be attributed the disappearance of the venomous attacks which the newspapers were wont to lavish upon them prior to 1870.[76] That had been particularly true during the debate upon Confederation, which four of the five judges of the Supreme Court openly supported. Chief Justice Young, for one, was characterized as "a political partizan of the hottest type" and advised to "cease talking unnecessary platitudes to Grand Juries,

---

[74]JHA, 1928, Appendix 31. Supra, 250–1.

[75]See Blanchard v. Cole, 25 M.P.R. 329. This is the only provincial controverted election case which has been carried to the full bench of the Supreme Court.

[76]The Recorder (Sept. 6, 1856) taunted Mr. Justice Wilkins that his "long, long struggle over a foul, dark, and crooked way more loathsome than that of Belzoni among the mummy crammed catacombs, [had] only sufficed to make [him] an assistant judge of the Supreme Court in a third rate British Colony," and accused (Feb. 7, 1857) Mr. Justice DesBarres of "impeding, instead of accelerating the progress of counsel and witnesses and driving the jurymen half mad with the pompous prolixity of orations which mean nothing."

and confine himself to expressions of penitence for the evil he ha[d] done."[77] Subsequently the judges scrupulously avoided any utterances which might prove objectionable and thereby raised their prestige in the public eye. Beyond doubt the weaknesses of the judicial system flow less from the frailties of the judges than from the failure of the politician to provide them with an improved *modus operandi.*

[77]*Morning Chronicle,* Oct. 11, 1869.   At the time of Young's appointment the *Recorder* (July 28, 1860) came out in mourning, charged him with outraging all the proprieties of public life, and described him as "utterly unfit for any office of trust."

CHAPTER XIX

MUNICIPAL GOVERNMENT

THE MOST FAR-REACHING CHANGES in Nova Scotian government since 1867 have occurred at the local level, for where there was one self-governing community, there are now 66: 2 cities, 40 towns, and 24 rural municipalities. The abandonment of the old non-elective system must not be attributed, however, to any sudden change of attitude on the part of the local authorities, but rather to serious exigencies at the provincial level. The clue to the origin of the County Incorporation Act of 1879[1] is to be found in the section which transferred the management of the road and bridge service to the municipal councils instituted by the Act. To balance the public accounts, the Holmes administration reduced the provincial government's expenditure for this service from \$140,000 to \$85,000, and put it squarely up to the new elective councils to maintain the former standards by supplementing the sum out of their own revenues.[2] Hence although the measure was generally defended on the grounds of increased efficiency and reduced expenditure, its principal object, as its sponsor, the forthright J. S. D. Thompson, admitted, was to "compel the Counties to tax themselves directly to keep up their roads and bridges."[3] ". . . you will have to face the melancholy fact," he said, "that additional taxation stares you in the face. . . ."[4] So for the second time[5] in fifteen years the Conservatives took their political life in their hands by forcing the local communities to resort to the direct taxation they abhorred.

In one respect the title of the new act was a misnomer, for while twelve of the counties were incorporated as such, the other six were

[1]42 Vic., c. 1.
[2]The argument has been used that the real intention of the Conservative government was to obviate the need of large additions to the sessions to destroy the Liberal ascendancy in local administration (see speech of R. M. Fielding, *Proceedings of the Union of N.S. Municipalities*, 1935, 52), but although it was undoubtedly aware of this not unpleasant implication, the real motivating factor was quite different.
[3]*Acadian Recorder*, April 7, 1879.
[4]*Morning Herald*, April 11, 1879.
[5]The former occasion was Tupper's introduction of schools supported by compulsory assessment in the 1860's.

divided into two municipalities each.[6] It is to these 24 divisions, and not to all the 66 self-governing communities, that the average Nova Scotian refers when he uses the designation "municipalities." Although the powers of the municipal councils were generally those of the sessions and the grand juries, they also assumed the functions of the town meetings which had previously provided for the support of the poor, and undertook the allocation and expenditure of both the provincial and county road moneys.

Naturally the thrusting of a previously unacceptable system upon the local communities without warning did not escape criticism. In its first year of operation, Yarmouth Township petitioned for permission to revert to its former status, and in 1883 and 1886 the Legislature itself debated proposals for a return to the optional system.[7] The arguments against the councils were the increased cost of administration, the introduction of politics into their deliberations, and above all, the inefficient spending of the road moneys. In place of the county's two or three assemblymen, a myriad of councillors now asserted their right to a share of the spoils and allegedly frittered away the funds in small amounts without an adequate return.[8] On each occasion, Premier Fielding championed the County Incorporation Act as an essentially liberal measure: ". . . if we are not able to administer it we are not fit for self-government, but should have that wholesome form of despotism which is sometimes called the best of all governments."[9] This unequivocal support played a substantial part in the municipal corporations' gaining recognition as a basic part of the governmental system after 1886. In time the 24 original municipalities acquired a sacrosanct character and every attempt to divide or combine them as a result of altered circumstances has ended in failure.[10]

Naturally these far-flung and sparsely populated rural municipalities were unable to provide all the amenities which their thickly populated

[6]Guysborough and St. Mary's, Lunenburg and Chester, Shelburne and Barrington, Yarmouth and Argyle, Digby and Clare, Hants East and Hants West.

[7]*Supra*, 139–40.

[8]It was to be expected that the assemblymen who resented the loss of a cherished privilege would paint a blacker picture of the new system than it warranted.

[9]*Assembly Debates*, 1886, 163.

[10]Such as the movement (1888) to have the northern half of Inverness set off as a separate county and the contrary proposal (1922) to amalgamate Shelburne and Barrington municipalities. The former was motivated by the poor system of communications; the latter by the improvement of the hitherto difficult means of travel.

settlements demanded. To meet the needs of the latter, five towns had been incorporated by special acts of the Legislature prior to 1879,[11] three others were set up during the 1880's,[12] and further requests were pending when the Legislature finally confessed its inability to give them all its special attention. The result was an enabling act—the Towns' Incorporation Act of 1888[13]—which prescribed the conditions under which subsequent charters would be granted. At one time or other 44 towns have come within its provisions, 25 before 1900 and none since 1923. Since 1946, however, three have found the overhead of town organization too heavy a burden and reverted to their rural municipalities.[14] Each of them had been incorporated under a provision which required a minimum population of 700 to be resident within 500 acres.[15] The hard lesson of experience has been that a minimum of 1,500 inhabitants living within an area of 640 acres[16] is a much more realistic requirement.

In its almost complete separation of the towns and cities from the countryside Nova Scotia adopted a course markedly dissimilar to that pursued by most of the Canadian provinces and the American states. Neighbouring New Brunswick, for example, has county councils which include representatives who are elected or appointed by the towns and cities; in contrast, the only connection between these two bodies in Nova Scotia is the slight tie which permits joint expenditures for a few limited purposes.[17]

In addition to the cities, towns, and rural municipalities, several other forms of organization have been created in response to the demands of the more populated areas of a rural municipality which desire amenities not otherwise provided. The Village Service Act[18] enables villages to be organized for such purposes as the operation of a waterworks, the provision of street lighting, and the laying out

[11]Dartmouth (1873), Pictou (1874), Truro (1875), New Glasgow (1875), and Windsor (1878).

[12]Sydney (1885), North Sydney (1885), and Kentville (1886).

[13]Its provisions, which were made applicable to the earlier towns, closely followed those relating to Kentville, the last town to be incorporated by a special act.

[14]Port Hood (1946), Wedgeport (1947), and Joggins (1949). These towns lost their corporate status by virtue of the general enabling act of 1945 (9 Geo. VI, c. 17); Sydney changed its status from town to city in 1903 (3 Edw. VII, c. 174).

[15]54 Vic., c. 39.   [16]5 Geo. VI, c. 3.

[17]See D. C. Rowat, *The Reorganization of Provincial-Municipal Relations in Nova Scotia* (Halifax, 1950), 1; *infra*, 306.

[18]The original statute, the Village Supply Act, was 13 Geo. V, c. 3 (1923); the present act is R.S. 1954, c. 307.

of streets and sidewalks; and empowers the elected commissioners who administer these services to make by-laws on such matters as curfew regulations and the removal of garbage. These commissioners assess the villagers for the cost of the services but may leave the collection of the levy to the municipal treasurer who superimposes it on the ordinary municipal rates.

Of a lower order still is the community which is completely dependent upon the rural municipality. When the residents of a community request it, a municipal council may provide a hall and lands for cultural, social, and amusement purposes, and establish a Board of Managers to consist of two municipal councillors and five officers of the community's organizations. To defray the cost the municipal council levies a special rate upon all the assessable property within the community.[19] There are also approximately twenty local commissions incorporated and operating under special acts of the Legislature, generally set up to provide street lighting or fire protection.

Seven other administrative mechanisms, some of which are optional and others compulsory, also perform local governmental functions. The result is that six different types of organization may be established to function at the same time within a town or city, eleven within a rural municipality.[20] This complex system developed in a completely piecemeal fashion, not in conformity with theoretical considerations, but in response to clearly felt needs. It is, in fact, the result of the Legislature's periodic response to demands for an organization which will enable localities of diverse sizes to provide a variety of services, some on a mandatory and some on an optional basis. Undoubtedly much of the machinery was adopted without any real comprehension of how it would fit into the existing pattern; some parts of it have since become clearly unsuited to modern needs and conditions. Hence a major problem of modern government is to

[19]R.S. 1954, c. 40.

[20]Every town and city has an elected council and is obliged to constitute itself a separate poor district, fire district, health district, and school section; it may also come within the jurisdictional area of a Joint Board of Health. A rural municipality has an elected council and must contain one or more poor and fire districts, a varying number of local health boards and perhaps a County Board of Health (it may also come within the jurisdictional area of a Joint Board of Health), a varying number of local school boards, and a Municipal School Board; one or more villages, communities, and local commissions may also operate within its confines. See G. A. McAllister, "Development of Local Government in N.S.," *Public Affairs*, Autumn, 1943, 29.

reassess the entire structure of municipal government with a view to discarding what is redundant, unsuitable, and inefficient, and reorganizing it to provide a significant proportion of the provincial services at reasonable efficiency.

The actual mechanics and structures of the elected councils exhibit little of the unusual. Except for Halifax, where the term is one year, the mayors who preside over the councils of the cities and towns are elected for two years. In contrast, the wardens who act as chairmen of the rural municipal councils are chosen by the councillors from among themselves. Half the city councillors are elected each year by the wards into which the cities are divided. The same procedure is followed in the case of the towns except that the smaller ones, which constitute the great majority, elect their councillors at large. The rural municipalities, on the other hand, are divided into districts for election purposes, and choose all their councillors at one time for three-year terms.

The school boards of the cities, towns, and municipalities are in no case elective, but are appointed partly by the local councils and partly by the Governor-in-Council. Since the adoption of the larger school unit during the 1940's, the dominant control over education in the rural municipalities has passed in two stages to twenty-four Municipal School Boards. But the 1,700 school sections have been permitted to retain a few of their former powers in order to maintain local interest in education. The success of this innovation has strengthened the position of those who advocate larger units of administration for other purposes.

Because of the separation of the urban units from the countryside, the single municipalities were financially too weak to construct and operate court houses, jails, and welfare homes, or maintain offices for the sheriff, registrar of probate, and registrar of deeds. So by law the rural municipalities are required to provide these services for themselves and for the towns and cities within their limits. Arbitration committees consisting of representatives of all the interested councils meet annually to adjust the objects of expenditures which are for their joint benefit and to determine the amounts to be borne by each municipal unit. "This . . . is the basis for the scheme, peculiar to Nova Scotia, known as Joint Expenditure."[21] Each unit pays a proportion of the cost of the joint services based upon its total assessment rather than upon the benefit it receives from the services. Thus the lack of

[21] Rowat, *The Reorganization of Provincial-Municipal Relations in Nova Scotia*, 5.

a uniform standard of assessing property is a serious impediment to making the device work without friction.[22]

II

The responsibilities of the rural municipalities were at their apex in 1879. The first substantial reduction in their powers occurred in the administration of the road moneys which had determined their creation in the first place. Fielding's policy of making capital expenditures on bridges and roads as provincial projects and charging the interest to the counties' road moneys steadily diminished the amounts which were available to the municipal councils.[23] By 1907 the impracticability of the system of dual control had long been evident and in view of the failure of other expedients[24] the province reassumed the expenditure of all the provincial moneys.[25] For the time being the councils continued to administer the statute labour on the highways, but in another decade they lost this last vestige of control when its commutation was made mandatory.[26] Thereafter both the rural and urban municipalities collected a highway tax for the province, which assumed the full control of road maintenance outside the incorporated towns and cities.

The councils found their control over their own officials similarly whittled away step by step under the ostensible reason that they needed to be protected from the aftermath of partisan strife in the local communities. The town councils lost the right to appoint their stipendiary magistrates in 1891;[27] the rural municipalities lost theirs in 1900.[28] In time the municipal clerks and treasurers were accorded the same protection from removal and reduction in salary which the corresponding officials in the towns had always enjoyed.[29] But the crowning point in regulation occurred in 1910 when the municipalities

[22]Infra, 320–1.

[23]The Legislature always maintained a close supervision over any municipal councils which the Conservatives controlled to prevent them from distributing the road moneys on a partisan basis. Hence, when the Victoria County Council allotted $2,310 to the ten Conservative districts and $585 to the eight Liberal districts, the Governor-in-Council was empowered to take steps for a re-division. See 54 Vic., c. 122 and Assembly Debates, 1892, 129–33.

[24]The government enacted optional measures in 1892 and 1900 in an attempt to provide a more efficient system, but the rural voters, who were allowed to express an opinion in plebiscites, rejected the first because it meant the imposition of an additional tax on real estate, the municipal councillors the second because it would have deprived them of much of their patronage. 55 Vic., c. 5, and 63 Vic., c. 23.

[25]7 Edw. VII. c. 2.

[26]7–8 Geo. V, c. 3.

[27]54 Vic., c. 43.

[28]63 Vic., c. 18.

[29]55 Vic., c. 39.

were required to appoint and pay a fixed salary to a Temperance Act inspector whom the Governor-in-Council might dismiss and replace with another if the local government failed to fill the vacancy.[30] In some of these instances the Legislature was undoubtedly far too zealous in protecting local officials who espoused the Liberal cause when it might well have devoted some of its concern to protecting the provincial employees.

The municipalities were also aggrieved on occasion by legislation which had the effect of imposing increased expenditures upon them or of reducing their revenues from such minor sources as licensing. Although normally the Legislature had no intention of treating them in a capricious manner, it gradually dawned upon them that they needed a vehicle through which they might present a collective opinion upon their common problems to the government at Halifax. In the Union of Nova Scotia Municipalities (established in 1906) they remedied the deficiency. Its purpose now, as then, is to "hold annual Conventions for information, discussion and resolutions, to promote and strengthen what is best in municipal government and service, to protect the rights and privileges of responsible government in municipal affairs, and generally by co-operation to further municipal interests."

Sometimes, in its early days, it was criticized for daring to oppose the government. Once the *Chronicle* reminded it that its status was only that of "a body of private individuals banded together for the furthering of what they conceive to be social progress. The Independent Order of Good Templars is another such." Hence it should "leave politics severely alone if [it] wish[ed] to accomplish any good."[31] But in a province in which partisanship has been infused into almost every nook and cranny of political life, that advice has not always been easy to follow. While partisan politics were never vigorously pursued in the town governments and are normally non-existent today, the rural municipalities inherited the plague of the old sessional districts, and the practice of nominating candidates for the municipal councillorships along party lines has not been entirely eliminated. Yet its gradual discontinuance is reflected in the history of the Union itself since it was able to abandon its practice of selecting an executive composed equally of Liberals and Conservatives more than three decades ago. "We never think about that now," said one official in 1919. "We have no politics."[32] In recent years some of the most

[30]10 Edw. VII, c. 2.   [31]March 15, 1911.
[32]*Proceedings of the Union of N.S. Municipalities*, 1919, 33–4.

outspoken criticism of a Liberal provincial government has come from municipal leaders who espouse the Liberal cause.

Essentially the Union of Nova Scotia Municipalities is an influential pressure group which is continually striving to reduce the financial burden of its member municipalities and to prevent their autonomy from being impaired. Where the two objectives conflict the former is almost certain to be given precedence. The Union's initial successes in regaining for the towns the control over their streets and in bringing the property of banks under the provisions of the Assessment Act established its prestige as something more than a mere discussion group.[33] By 1929 every municipality had become a member and until 1957 that record had remained intact. From long experience, its members have been taught the cardinal virtue of patience in their dealings with the provincial government.[34] They have learned also to keep their legislative, if not their financial, proposals within the realm of the practicable and to secure fairly general agreement, rather than a mere majority, for their programme before presenting it as the will of the Union.

III

The modern history of provincial-municipal relationships begins with the depression of the thirties and the practically concomitant and continuing drive for a more adequate system of social services. The outcome of the former has been a greater measure of planned regulation than had existed heretofore, while the second has altered the old balance of responsibilities and cast serious doubts upon the adequacy of the existing units to fulfil the present demands upon them.

The regulation of the local governments by the provincial authorities has proceeded along three lines, the most significant of which is the supervision of municipal finance. Every provincial administration has insisted that "no municipal government . . . should be allowed to conduct its affairs in such a manner as to harm other municipal governments and the Province as a whole. . . ."[35] The principal reason for the creation of the Department of Municipal Affairs was, in fact, to provide a more adequate means of regulating the finances of the municipalities. In 1931, after the Legislature had long spurned the Union's request for its establishment, the Assembly's Committee on

[33]1 Geo. V, c. 21, and 2 Geo. V, c. 39.
[34]It required twenty-five years to bring their demands for a Department of Municipal Affairs to a successful conclusion.
[35]Statement of Hon. J. H. MacQuarrie, *Proceedings of the Union of N.S. Municipalities*, 1945, 68.

Private and Local Bills admitted its inability to deal properly with thirty-six borrowing bills involving over $1,500,000 and emanating from twenty-seven different local governments. During the same period one town was in danger of defaulting upon its obligations; four others were experiencing serious financial difficulties which adequate supervision might have averted; several had used their sinking fund moneys to purchase their own debentures; thirteen were in arrears in their sinking fund payments; and the general handling of their finances was in many cases irregular, if not chaotic.

Hence the Department of Municipal Affairs which the Harrington government proposed to set up in 1932 was to possess such powers as the strict regulation of municipal borrowing, the periodic inspection of municipal accounts by qualified auditors, the exercise of wide discretionary powers over defaulting municipalities, and the provincial management of the municipal sinking funds. But the opposition of the efficiently managed municipalities to the last two of these powers, and particularly to the payment of 5 per cent of the income from their sinking funds towards the cost of the department, forced the government to drop its plans until it had time to "go back over the ground and dispel the opposition and distrust that ha[d] been built up."[36] Another three years were required, therefore, to establish the Department,[37] and even then it was deficient in the powers to which objection had been taken.

Undoubtedly the primary functions of the Department are those which relate to municipal borrowing—its consent is required whenever a local government borrows for any purpose which in its essence pertains to municipal government; borrowing for other purposes requires a special act of the Legislature.[38] But these provisions leave many questions unanswered. Should the Department permit a municipality with a heavy funded debt to incur a burden which may in time cause a default?[39] What degree of pressure should it employ to ensure that capital expenditures are applied in the most judicious manner? Should it require these expenditures to be delayed until construction costs are cheaper or a more propitious occasion presents itself? What policy should the Legislature adopt when a municipality in a strong financial position requests permission to

[36]*Proceedings of the Union of N.S. Municipalities*, 1932, 110.
[37]25–26 Geo. V, c. 5.
[38]9 Geo. VI, c. 6. In the case of the towns and the city of Sydney the consent of the ratepayers is also required for most forms of borrowing.
[39]J. H. MacQuarrie, "Municipal Borrowing," *Proceedings of the Union of N.S. Municipalities*, 1944, 94.

borrow money for a non-municipal purpose such as the erection of a rink? If it permits borrowing of this nature, will it establish a dangerous precedent for dealing with the other municipalities?[40] Since these questions do not lend themselves to explicit answers, the Department's policy is simply that laid down by the Minister in 1950. "We boast we have never had a municipal default in Nova Scotia— and we intend to maintain that record. Borrowing applications must be scrutinized carefully."[41]

Yet the Department has usually managed to perform this function effectively without resort to the strong arm tactics which might bring the concentrated oppositon of the Union to bear upon it. For although the total municipal indebtedness is once again on the increase, a substantial improvement has been effected in the financial status of the municipal governments generally, and the credit is due in large measure to the oversight of the Department. Naturally it has experienced set-backs as well. Although it has always insisted that each local government is to prepare a sound budget and adhere to its provisions, sometimes, even after the Department's own officials have supervised the adoption of proper procedures, a municipality will still fail to collect sufficient sums to pay its current obligations and continue to operate at a deficit.[42]

The municipalities in their turn have a legitimate grievance when the government sponsors measures which increase their financial burdens during the current year and thereby upset their budgetary arrangements.[43] Unless there are compelling considerations to the contrary the municipalities ought to be notified in advance of any proposals which add to their financial burden or substantially affect their interests in any other way. [44]

There are, of course, strong forces at work which tend to minimize any shirking of responsibilities by the individual municipalities. One

[40]See the opinion of W. E. Moseley, Deputy Minister of Municipal Affairs, *Halifax Chronicle-Herald*, April 15, 1950.

[41]See *Proceedings of the Union of N.S. Municipalities*, 1950, 73.

[42]See MacQuarrie, "Municipal Borrowing," 1944, 91.

[43]On this ground the Union denounced two proposals in 1950, one to increase the charge upon the local governments for indigent patients in hospitals from $3 to $4 a day, the other to raise their share of the cost of maintaining female prisoners in reformatories from $125 to $350 annually. In the end, it managed to prevent the second bill, which would have increased the expenditure for Halifax city alone from $6,000 to $18,000, from coming into immediate operation. See the *Halifax Chronicle-Herald*, May 3, 1950.

[44]The administration of the day introduced drastic legislation in 1939 and 1943 without prior consultation. For its condemnation by the Union, see *Proceedings of the Union of N.S. Municipalities*, 1939, 89.

is an intangible type of moral coercion which results from member-ship in the Union—clearly no municipality wants to appear as a member by sufferance only in the eyes of the other municipal govern-ments. A second and more cogent type of coercion is provided by the Municipal Affairs (Supervision) Act of 1939.[45] Whenever a munici-pality has failed, or in the opinion of the Governor-in-Council may fail, to pay its sinking fund instalments and other obligations, or to rate, levy, and collect sufficient moneys to cover its expenditures, the government may supplant the elected mayor (or warden) and councillors with an appointed commission which is endowed with sweeping powers to restore the financial solvency of the munici-pality.[46] The wide measure of potential discretionary power did not pass unnoticed:

It is not enough to say that care will be taken to prevent abuses—the Act should be drafted so as to ensure that there can be no possibility of abuses. The Minister apparently does not trust the municipalities to attend to their obligations, but the municipalities are required to trust the present and all future Ministers to exercise the rights given by the Act only in a proper case and then only in a wise, judicious and efficient manner. If the Machinery is deemed necessary, let it be more strict as to what shall constitute a default, let it contain restrictions as to who shall be members of the Commission, and let it impose much more rigid regulations on the operations of that Commission; for it would seem to be a primary rule of legislation, that laws which encroach on the rights either of persons or municipalities, should not be wider than absolutely necessary and certainly should not confer more powers than are intended to be exercised.[47]

But despite their objectionable features these provisions, simply by virtue of their existence, have tended to act as a deterrent to bad financial procedures.

The Department has acted in a more positive way to introduce uniformity into the accounting and reporting practice of the munici-palities, the intention being to allow comparisons to be made which would enable one local government to benefit from the mistakes and guard against the weaknesses of the others in determining its financial policies.[48] To have real meaning, the facts to be compared must refer to the same thing, and after 1942 the Department urged the local governments to follow the *Manual of Instructions* issued

[45]Now simply the Municipal Affairs Act, R.S. 1954, c. 186.
[46]See 3 Geo. VI, c. 3, Part V.
[47]W. E. Moseley, "Preventing Municipal Default," *Public Affairs*, June, 1939, 198.
[48]J. H. Lowther, "Interpreting Municipal Statistics," *Proceedings of the Union of N.S. Municipalities*, 1942, 87.

by the Dominion Bureau of Statistics in these particulars. As a result the Department is now in a position to "publish separate operating statements and balance sheets for all the funds or activities administered by each municipal unit . . . of a truly comparable nature."[49] This makes it possible for investment brokers to turn to the Department for information relating to the financial condition of any municipality and consequently relieves the local municipal officials of a burdensome duty.

In addition to supervising municipal finance, the government and Legislature are sometimes confronted with the problem of determining when to insist upon uniformity and when to permit local differences in legislating for the municipalities. After half a century of ineffective action they have finally adopted a reasonably satisfactory procedure for regulating the bonussing of industries by municipalities,[50] but they have yet to decide whether a uniform set of municipal by-laws is either practicable or desirable.

Occasionally the provincial administration has sought to reduce the control of the local governments over their own officials, but never without arousing strong criticism in the Legislature and before its committees. Thus proposals to require deposits from the candidates for elective municipal offices and to effect the suspension of the elected officials for non-payment of taxes were denounced in 1943 as an unnecessary interference with the municipalities. But the real fire was concentrated upon other clauses which provided that the clerks, treasurers, and auditors of the local governments must possess qualifications of a specified order, except as the Minister of Municipal Affairs in his absolute discretion might otherwise determine, and that the Minister could remove or suspend a municipal official for any reason which he deemed sufficient. Thus an incompetent official might have been got rid of despite an unwilling Council. Ultimately the government gave way, but only after it was shown that the Minister would have possessed more power over the town and municipal officials than the elected body which placed them there and more control over them than over the officials of his own department.[51]

Subsequently the Department adopted less objectionable means to build up a sound permanent service made up of "persons who take up [municipal] work as their life's work, who train and prepare for it as such . . . who . . . give their best to it, and who . . . receive adequate

---

[49]With the exception of the city of Halifax. See *Annual Report of Municipal Statistics*, 1948, Introduction, V.   [50]*Supra*, 217.

[51]See statement of W. E. Moseley, *Halifax Chronicle*, April 7, 1943.

compensation, adequate security of tenure, and adequate superannuation."[52] More particularly, it has for some time been conducting courses of instructions on accounting and reporting, budget preparation and control, and methods of tax collection in which virtually all the municipal finance officers participate, and in 1952 it introduced a similar school for the training of assessors.

At the same time that the municipalities were being increasingly subjected to regulation they were losing the primary responsibility for providing educational and social services. Fundamentally this stemmed from their lack of any flexible source of income. Approximately 90 per cent of their revenues came from the direct taxation of property, and the ratepayers, through their councils, continually insisted that this source had reached its upper limit whenever they were confronted with additional expenditures. The local governments were hard pressed, therefore, to provide direct poor relief during the depressed thirties and to carry out their normal duties in the period of inflated costs in the forties. So, instead of relying upon them to provide new social and educational benefits, the province has been helping them to perform even their ordinary functions for the past two decades.

For one thing it has taken steps to increase their general revenues. In 1938 it recognized the principle that a publicly owned commercial enterprise should pay its share of the municipal services when it permitted the property of the Nova Scotia Liquor Commission to be assessed and taxed in the normal way; the same year it agreed to share with the municipalities the payments which were made by the Canadian National Railways in lieu of provincial and municipal taxation. In 1947, after it had surrendered the provincial income taxation field to the Dominion, it reimbursed all the municipalities by a sum which was equivalent on a per capita basis to 150 per cent of the highest income tax raised by any local government, and in 1952, after it had concluded a second agreement with the Dominion, it increased these payments by a further 50 per cent.

At the same time it assisted the local governments in performing some of the functions imposed upon them by statute. In 1930 it assumed part of the cost of the administration of justice in connection with convictions for violation of its liquor control enactment. In 1948 it set up a municipal loan and building fund account from which the local governments might borrow funds on advantageous terms for municipal projects. By far the most significant assistance occurred,

[52]See MacQuarrie, "Municipal Borrowing," 1944, 92.

however, in the field of education where the provincial contribution increased more than fivefold in the decade after 1941 and its share of the total expenditure rose from 27 to 55 per cent, the highest of any Canadian province.

Finally, the province's assumption of a variety of health and welfare services has accrued directly or indirectly to the financial advantage of the municipalities. Indirectly it made a significant contribution through its old age pensions and assistance legislation which became effective in 1933 and 1952 respectively, directly by relieving the municipalities of the full cost of maintaining their tubercular patients at provincial sanatoria in 1946 and their mentally ill patients at the Nova Scotia Hospital in 1948. In the latter year, too, it abolished the provincial highway tax insofar as it was applicable to the towns and cities, and two years later it relieved the rural municipalities of the poll tax portion of the same tax.[53]

This series of developments explains why in 1950 the province was paying 65.7 per cent of the combined cost of provincial and municipal services in contrast with the 56.9 per cent paid by the other provinces. Yet despite its apparent generosity, it was continually chafing the municipalities after 1940. For although, from the strictly legal point of view, they possess only the powers which are conferred upon them by statute in express words and any incidental or implied powers which are indispensable to their performance—in other words a limited and delegated rather than a residuary power[54]—they dislike to be treated as the creatures of an overriding authority. Their contention is that local self-government is not merely a privilege conceded by the Legislature at its discretion, but the keystone of democracy itself.

That our councils are statutory is no more in point than it is to say that the Provincial Government as it is today is the product of Imperial legislation. Independent local self government is part of our freedom, part of our inheritance from the "Mother of Parliaments," and is well recognized as the only foundation upon which a successful democracy can be built and maintained.[55]

One warden has described the existing state of municipal autonomy as "tons and tons of responsibility, and not one ounce of authority";[56] other municipal representatives are chagrined because even though "practically stripped of self government for the purpose of raising

[53]12 Geo. VI, c. 54, and 13 Geo. VI, c. 48.
[54]See Frank Rowe, "Municipal Government—Its History and Limitations," *Proceedings of the Union of N.S. Municipalities*, 1928, 90–9.
[55]See "Report of the Executive of the Union," *ibid.*, 25.
[56]*Halifax Herald*, Sept. 10, 1948.

revenue" they are still "censured in some quarters for not giving service, for which money is the essential element."[57] They would undoubtedly be in agreement with the chairman of the Private and Local Bills Committee of the Assembly who felt that the municipalities were treated with "a little too much grandmotherly care"[58] or with the Conservative Assemblyman who wanted the Legislature to "stop being a father, a mother, a brother, a sister, an uncle and an aunt to the towns and municipalities of Nova Scotia."[59]

Others, however, have questioned the right of the local governments to exist in view of their less than mediocre performance of some functions. The deplorable condition of many jails and court-houses is continually put forward as eloquent testimony of their failure to provide for the administration of justice. Dr. George F. Davidson, in his report for the Dawson Commission, was equally condemnatory of the county homes and asylums. In his opinion, the former were "little more than indiscriminate dumping grounds for all the various types of unfortunate misfits who happen to be a burden on the community,"[60] while the worst of the latter were "dark, dismal, evil-smelling and filthy to the point of almost nauseating the visitor who passes through them," and the best provided little more than custodial care.[61] The C.C.F. assemblymen have also been critical of the municipal public welfare services, especially poor relief and the care of the harmless insane. One of them characterized the municipalities as outworn and inefficient, and looked forward to the day when they would be non-existent as in Prince Edward Island.[62] In the late forties, when provincial expenditures caught up with provincial revenues and the local governments still continued to press for financial assistance, even the provincial government's attitude towards them hardened. The new gospel preached by Premier Macdonald came to be that of municipal self-help.

But at the same time the Premier recognized that the problem was highly complex and tacitly admitted that the basic arrangements of 1879, modified in an unplanned and unco-ordinated piecemeal manner, could not be suited to a radically altered set of circumstances. That is why his government undertook a re-examination of the entire basis of provincial-municipal relationships in October, 1947. In convening

[57]*Ibid.*, Sept. 10, 1947.
[58]*Halifax Chronicle-Herald*, May 2, 1950.
[59]*Ibid.*, May 8, 1950.
[60]*Report on Public Welfare Services*, no. IV of the *Report of the Royal Commission on Provincial Development and Rehabilitation*, 107.
[61]*Ibid.*, 123.   [62]*Halifax Herald*, April 12, 1947.

a provincial-municipal conference to that end, its intention was to follow the course which it had been recommending for the solution of Dominion-provincial financial problems, and which was to prove unsuccessful in both spheres. Its expectation was that the first undertaking of the conference would be to study the division of authority between the provincial and municipal levels of government with a view to determining which services each authority could perform more effectively. Only after the proper areas of responsibility were defined would it be appropriate to consider the allocation of adequate financial resources to the local governments. Thus constitutional arrangements were to come first, financial arrangements afterwards.

Within this general framework the province expressed its opposition to extreme centralization. "I am opposed," said Premier Macdonald at the outset of the negotiations, "to remote control and to the idea of planning everything at some one great centre, and to all other theories of that sort." He hoped, therefore, that the municipalities would not press the province to take over too many of their responsibilities. But if they insisted that the province should assume the financial burden of any service, they could not expect to control its administration.[63]

The province was also hopeful that the municipalities themselves would play a significant part in determining the new form of provincial-municipal relationships. Hence it declined to present any cut-and-dried scheme of its own and suggested instead that the municipal representatives should initiate the proposals which were to serve as a basis of discussion. But for all its good intentions it could not avoid the weaknesses and pitfalls of the Dominion-provincial conferences. Possibly the time was not propitious, for however widely the municipalities differed on other points they were all bent on securing a share of the increased revenues which would accrue to the province as a result of its taxation-rental agreement with the Dominion. Even though they were reminded on several occasions that the purpose of the conference was not to make spotty grants, they showed little or no interest in a reallocation of responsibilities. Their single conclusion was that grants of $4 per capita or a percentage of their individual tax revenues would meet their requirements until it was possible to establish permanent grants on the basis of fiscal need. Thereupon the Minister of Municipal Affairs expressed his regrets that "the real purpose for which the meeting had been called had only been discussed by the way," diplomatically accepted the local governments' brief for further consideration, and promised a study of provincial-municipal

[63]*Ibid.*, Oct. 24, 1947.

relations which would not be "a makeshift or stopgap piece of work," but the blue print of arrangements which would last for many years to come.[64]

The outcome was the comprehensive *Rowat Report* of 1950.[65] It found that the basic weakness of local government lay in the nature of the municipalities themselves since they were "too small to administer education and the social services efficiently and too financially weak to afford a desirable level of service."[66] At the same time an outmoded assessment system prevented the comparisons between municipalities which could provide an objective criterion for allocating provincial grants in such a way as to permit local governments with varying capacities and requirements to sustain an average level of these services. The result had been that the municipalities had not shared to any extent in developing some of the public health services and had forfeited to the province the responsibility of administering and paying for others. Furthermore, those public welfare services which the local governments financed and administered, such as poor relief and the care of the harmless insane, were generally supplied at an undesirably low level.[67]

Yet some of the services which had been assumed by the province could not be administered most satisfactorily at that level. The provincial government had itself recognized that fact by decentralizing its health and welfare services. It was essential, therefore, if local control was to be preserved and strengthened, to create a more efficient administrative unit, and with that end in view the *Report* recommended that a second tier of local government should be introduced between the provincial government and the existing municipalities. While the latter would remain with diminished powers, the province would be divided into nine municipal regions each containing a population of not less than 40,000, and regional councils would administer substantial portions of such services as health, welfare, the administration of justice, and education, some of which were presently being undertaken by the province and some by the local governments, and all of which were of greater than local concern.[68]

[64]See *Halifax Herald*, Jan. 24, 1948.
[65]The full title is *The Reorganization of Provincial-Municipal Relations in Nova Scotia*. The work was largely that of Donald C. Rowat, Director of Research of the Institute of Public Affairs, Dalhousie University.
[66]*Ibid.*, 54.   [67]*Ibid.*, 55.
[68]Earlier, in his *Report on Public Welfare Services* for the Dawson Commission, Dr. George F. Davidson had indicated the need for "a progressive shift of all social service responsibilities to higher and larger administrative units." See Recommendation E, ss. 78–86.

Since opposition was expected to its major proposal, the *Report* suggested that the entry of towns and municipalities into the regions should be on a voluntary basis to avoid the impression of coercion. But in contrast with the provincial government's apathetic attitude towards the permissive municipal legislation of the past, it should make "the financial advantage to municipalities that join Regions . . . so great that no group of municipalities could afford to remain unorganized for very long."[69] This could be done by providing no increase in provincial aid to non-regional municipalities and granting an additional amount to the regions over and above the existing cost to the province of the services which they assumed.[70]

But whether the municipalities entered into regions or not, the *Report* proposed that the existing system of provincial aid should be revised, and that provincial funds should in future be allocated to municipalities on the basis of a formula which took account of both their relative tax-paying ability through an index of total taxable assessments, and their expenditure requirements for social services through a population index weighted by such factors as the density of population and the percentage which fell within specific age-groups.[71] For the calculation of these equalization grants a reform of the mode of assessment was obviously essential, and this was to be effected by establishing a Provincial Assessment Commission and a system of regional supervisors of assessment to supervise local assessors and to institute a province-wide equalization of assessments.[72]

Scattered throughout the *Report* are unmistakable signs of faith in the local governments and their elective officials. It describes as overworked the argument that the municipalities could not be trusted to maintain proper social and educational services and prefers to attribute their failings to the weakness of their financial and administrative positions.[73] It argues that the raising of revenue by one level of government and its distribution by another does not necessarily lead to irresponsibility, particularly if the lower level of government is made responsible for raising through taxation a portion of the cost of the services which it is to administer.[74] It admits that a major reason why the expenditures per capita on provincial and municipal services in Nova Scotia are $13 less than the Canadian average results from the low level of municipal taxation—property taxes per capita being 31

[69]Rowat, *Provincial-Municipal Relations in Nova Scotia*, 72.
[70]*Ibid.*, 127.
[71]*Ibid.*, 61. For a discussion of the application and calculation of the formula, *ibid.*, 123–9.
[72]*Ibid.*, 94.   [73]*Ibid.*, 60.   [74]*Ibid.*, 66.

per cent less than those in the other provinces[75]—but it apparently sees no difficulty in securing a greater return from property taxes and thereby bringing the level of the province's social and educational services up to the Canadian standard. If the worst came to the worst, the province could make part of the additional aid to a region contingent upon an increase of its expenditures for approved purposes above those for the year it was established.[76]

It is this faith in the local governments which appears to be the principal source of weakness of the *Report*. For however admirable and well reasoned its proposals may appear on paper they must also prove to be politically acceptable in the environment for which they are designed. To date, they have remained unimplemented and, in fact, almost unnoticed. Already they seem destined to pass to the limbo of forgotten things. The official attitude of the Union of Nova Scotia Municipalities was one of pained surprise that the *Report* paid so little attention to the matter of provincial and municipal autonomies, particularly with a view to defining clearly their responsibilities and sources of revenue, and thereby preventing irritating differences of opinion on that score in the future.[77] Actually the whole object of the *Report's* recommendations was to place the local governments in a financial position to administer efficiently and without undue direction from above a significant portion of the provincial services.

The Union also felt that a second tier of government would serve no useful purpose if the problems of assessment and joint expenditures were satisfactorily settled.[78] It appears self-evident, however, that neither of these matters penetrates to the core of contemporary municipal problems, and their solution would hardly effect more than a temporary *modus vivendi*. Yet any prospective remedial action even within this limited sphere is calculated to unleash all the forces in municipal government which resist change. When, in 1947, the government responded to the appeals of the Union for an improvement in the system of assessment by having legislation enacted in permissive form which authorized a Provincial Assessment Board to establish standards of qualifications for assessors and to issue licences to those who were entitled to act, a sufficient number of the local governments protested an allegedly unwarranted interference with their autonomy to secure its repeal.[79] To meet the Union's own demands the Department of

[75]*Ibid.*, 57.   [76]*Ibid.*, 129.
[77]See report of the executive, *Proceedings of the Union of N.S. Municipalities*, 1950, 25.   [78]*Ibid.*, 1951, 57.
[79]11 Geo. VI, c. 47, and 13 Geo. VI, c. 45. See also R. M. Fielding, "Provincial-Municipal Relations," *Proceedings of the Union of N.S. Municipalities*, 1950, 68.

Municipal Affairs has been limited, therefore, to the innocuous role of providing a training school for the assessors whom the local governments choose to send on a purely voluntary basis.

Joint expenditures by the municipalities within a county present an even thornier problem.[80] In 1952 the government sponsored legislation practically of the Union's own making which permitted the expenditures to be apportioned more scientifically,[81] but heeding the experience of the past, the Minister of Municipal Affairs took care to see that its provisions became effective only upon proclamation, thus permitting the response of the individual municipalities to be ascertained. At the same time, he confessed somewhat despairingly that there was little likelihood of unanimity either for or against the statute as drawn.[82]

But these diversions have by no means permitted the basic problems of provincial-municipal relations to lapse into quiescence. For unlike the recommendations of the *Report* of 1950 the financial difficulties of the local governments have not remained dormant. After 1951 they hinged upon the complex question of teachers' salaries which, despite the substantial contributions of the province, were still inadequate. The background of this problem—the most difficult one to confront the provincial government in recent years—goes back to 1938 when the Commission on the Larger Unit reported that a system containing 1,758 financially independent school units, instituted when rural communities were relatively self-contained and self-supporting and when educational needs were confined to the "three R's," had become obsolete. Among its notorious evils were inefficiency in business administration, inequalities in the ability to support education between the sections within a county and between the counties themselves, and an increasing tendency for the support of schools to break down altogether in the poorer sections. As the ideal solution, the Commission recommended that the province itself should replace the school section as a financial unit, that a minimum programme for purposes of finance should be defined in terms of teachers' salaries and classroom maintenance, that a uniform province-wide school tax should be

[80]The determination of the proportions of the expenditures to be borne by each member of a joint expenditure unit for the limited services which they performed in common became a source of unending controversy in the forties largely because the municipalities used varying standards of valuation for assessment purposes thereby effectually denying any objective criterion of measurement. It was for this reason that the Legislature enacted legislation in 1947 which permitted the existing proportions to be varied only by unanimous consent. 11 Geo. VI, c. 47.

[81]1 Eliz. II, c. 15.

[82]See *Proceedings of the Union of N.S. Municipalities,* 1952, 65.

imposed at a rate based on a $100 property assessment, and that the province should provide an equalization fund to make up the deficiency between the cost of the minimum programme and the receipts from the property tax. But since the adoption of these proposals at one fell swoop appeared impracticable, the Commission suggested that their operation should be confined to those municipalities in which a majority of school boards gave their approval. Thus the municipality would become the financial unit for purposes of education, and a municipality-wide school tax would be levied.[83]

An enabling act of 1942[84] permitted the larger administrative unit to be adopted, but it was not until 1946, after the public had been educated through a variety of channels—ratepayers' meetings, inspectors' conferences with trustees, home and school associations, study clubs, and the like—that all the twenty-four rural municipalities accepted it. Henceforth, for purposes of education, they levied on the general municipal assessment a tax rate which was 10 per cent less than the median of the local tax rates in the school year 1941-2. The innovation, while worth-while, possessed serious defects, one inherent and one unforeseen. It tended to equalize the educational burden within, but not between the municipalities, and resulted, therefore, in "uneven treatment as between the Provincial Government and some Municipalities as well as between one Municipality and another."[85] Still more serious was the lack of machinery to force the municipalities to assume greater responsibilities as the cost of the minimum programme rose. Hence, although the total municipal expenditures upon education increased a mere $44,000 between 1942 and 1948, the provincial share of the costs rose from 36.52 per cent in 1941-2 to 61.45 per cent in 1950-1. In self-protection the province then froze its equalization grants at their existing level, and by 1953 its proportion had dropped to 49.93 per cent.[86]

During the same period the province's payments towards teachers' salaries and pension funds, exclusive of the equalization fund, increased from one to five millions. Nevertheless the shortage of properly qualified teachers continued to be alarming. In this instance, however, the province steadily resisted the pressure of the Nova Scotia Teachers' Union and the municipalities for further assistance. Its position was that it already paid more than 50 per cent of the cost of education, and

[83]For the Report of the Commission on the Larger Unit, see Journals of the House of Assembly (JHA), 1940, Appendix 8.
[84]6 Geo. VI, c. 21.
[85]See Report of the Royal Commission on School Finance, 8.
[86]Ibid., 8-10.

to go further would likely reduce the proportion of local support below the level which makes for efficient administration by the local officials and the continuance of local interest.[87]

To centralize education seems to be the idea . . . control everything from Halifax, and ultimately, perhaps, from Ottawa. . . . the municipalities have an important place in our whole governmental system. . . . But if [the provincial] government is to take over everything, there will be nothing left for the municipalities to do; they will atrophy and disappear, and our system of government in the country will be the poorer.[88]

The opposition, which in its position could afford to champion the cause of the municipalities, criticized the two higher levels of government for absorbing such a large portion of the national income in taxation that the local governments found their own sources of revenue seriously reduced. In its opinion, Ottawa should be returning larger sums to the province under the tax-rental agreements, and the province should be paying more than a mere pittance to the municipalities instead of spending most of the Dominion payments for its own purposes and boasting what it had done for the people. These critics argued further that the major source of municipal revenue, the property tax, was approaching exhaustion in many, if not in all counties, and in any case it was an inequitable and anti-civic tax which should be avoided.[89]

The outcome was the appointment of Judge V. J. Pottier to study the financing of the entire educational system. His *Report on Public School Finance*, presented in November, 1954, proposed, in effect, the ideal solution of the earlier commission (1938–9), but broadened it to include all the sixty-six municipalities and clothed its skeletal outlines with the details needed to give it practical effect. The minimum programme became a foundation programme, which was to provide a basic level of educational services, including the maintenance of schools, the transportation of pupils, and teachers' salaries on a scale calculated to relieve the shortage.[90]

The contribution of the municipalities to this programme was to be determined by their ability to pay, which was measured, rightly or wrongly, by the value of their real and personal property. This necessitated the equalization of municipal assessment, and since a complete

---

[87]*Halifax Chronicle-Herald*, March 4, 1952.
[88]See comments of Premier Angus Macdonald, *ibid.*, Feb. 23, 1952.
[89]See the observations of R. L. Stanfield, *ibid.*, Feb. 21 and 22, 1952.
[90]Report of the Royal Commission on School Finance, 16, and chaps. 4, 5, and 6. Chap. 7 outlines the contribution which the provincial government was to make towards capital costs under the foundation programme.

reassessment at the individual unit level was impracticable, it had to be done at the municipal unit level. After an analysis of six thousand properties throughout the province, the Commissioner determined the ratio of the existing assessments to the full value of the property in the sixty-six municipalities, and arrived at an equalized assessment of approximately $1,000,000,000 for the entire province.[91] His next task —to decide the municipal rate upon each $100 of equalized assessment —was the crucial one, and necessarily involved his personal discretion. After ascertaining that the median rate levied by the municipalities on their equalized assessment was 62 cents in 1953, and knowing the total amount required for the foundation programme, he decided that 80 cents was a fair rate since, in his opinion, taxation on real and personal property could provide $8,000,000 towards the cost of salaries, maintenance, and transportation without undue hardship. Undoubtedly he was influenced by the consideration that this rate would require the municipalities to pay approximately 50 per cent of the programme, a fiscal relationship with the province which he believed desirable to retain if at all possible.[92]

These provisions meant that fifty of the municipal units would have to pay increased, and in many cases substantially increased school taxes, amounting altogether to an additional $2,000,000 per annum.[93] Nevertheless, within four months the government had introduced a bill which, for all practical purposes, implemented the basic provisions of the *Pottier Report*.[94] Although critical of the heavier burden which it imposed upon the municipalities and dubious of the "ability to pay" premise upon which it was based, the opposition permitted it second reading without a recorded vote, but when criticism of its contents was voiced in public hearings before the Law Amendments Committee, both the Conservative and C.C.F. assemblymen tried un-

[91]The validity of these conclusions are, of course, open to doubt. Both the *Report* and the subsequent enactment provided for their review at periodic intervals.

[92]*Report*, 71. In the Legislature G. I. Smith commented thus: "I think the use of the words 'ability to pay' in relation to this 80 cents rate is not correct. It was arrived at simply by multiplying the total equalized assessment by an amount necessary to provide one-half the education expense in Nova Scotia." *Halifax Chronicle-Herald*, March 26, 1955.

[93]*Report*, 128–30, Tables 23-A and 23-B.

[94]Premier Hicks, as Minister of Education, pointed out that in respect of scales of maintenance the bill "goes further than the recommendations of Mr. Justice Pottier, allows the local authority a degree of latitude which he had not envisaged and at the same time provides for additional participation [particularly in capital costs] . . . by the provincial government." *Halifax Chronicle-Herald*, March 25, 1955.

successfully to have the bill considered at an autumn sitting of the Legislature in order to give the municipalities further time for study and the making of representations. Premier Hicks was confident, not only that the bill provided a foundation for a financial system in public education as soundly based as any on the continent,[95] but that the Nova Scotia people were willing to pay its cost. Yet in view of past history and despite its acceptance by the Union of Nova Scotia Municipalities, the passage of the bill was an act of unprecedented political courage. To the average voter its full implications would become apparent only when he was confronted by successive annual increments to his tax bill, and these would inevitably occur in an election year.

Political campaigning in 1956 naturally centred to a considerable degree on Bill 66, the new Education Act. The Conservatives contended simply that the additional tax burden which it imposed on the rural municipalities would constitute a crushing blow to agriculture, and to rural industry in general. In reply, Premier Hicks showed that the municipalities had so far been required to bear only one-fourth of the $4 million increase in educational expenditures, and that the province still paid two-thirds of the entire cost of education in rural municipalities. To this argument he added a monetary inducement. Out of the additional revenues to become available to the province under the new taxation arrangements with the Dominion, the municipalities would be allotted an additional $1,000,000, "without any strings attached . . . to use as they see fit." The government's defeat resulted primarily from its losses in industrial Cape Breton and Pictou Counties, but it might still have weathered the storm if it had not also lost some predominantly rural constituencies in western Nova Scotia where increased property taxes were a key issue.

[95]*Halifax Chronicle-Herald*, March 25, 1955.

CHAPTER XX

NOVA SCOTIA
IN THE CANADIAN FEDERATION

NOVA SCOTIA has rested uneasily in the Dominion of Canada since its inception. Indeed, except for a brief period during the Laurier régime when it appeared that the province might achieve a higher destiny within the federation, a feeling of injustice and a sense of frustration have always existed in some quarters. It is not surprising, therefore, that in 1886 Nova Scotians pronounced in favour of secession at a provincial election; that in 1896 the Liberal majority in the Assembly indignantly voted down a proposal to have Dominion Day declared a holiday in the public schools;[1] and that within comparatively recent times some Nova Scotians have flown flags at half-mast on July 1.

Recent Nova Scotian governments have held that two conditions are essential in a well-adjusted and smoothly functioning federal system. Both the central and the provincial legislatures and governments should perform the functions for which they are best suited, and should possess the financial resources requisite to that end; the over-all economic policy of the country ought to be designed to foster the full development of the latent possibilities of each entity within the federation and precautions should be taken that the advancement of one entity is not achieved through the economic retardation or actual decline of the others.

This attitude has evolved over a period of more than twenty-five years during which Nova Scotia's position in Canadian federalism has been constantly agitated and no fewer than five royal commissions, three Dominion and two provincial, have conducted inquests into various aspects of Dominion-Nova Scotian relations. The federal government appointed the Duncan Commission on Maritime Claims in 1926 to examine "from a national standpoint . . . all the factors which peculiarly affect the economic position" of the Maritime Provinces and to make specific recommendations designed to alleviate their grievances; the White Commission in 1934 to determine the size of the monetary payments which the Duncan Commission had recommended; and the Royal Commission on Dominion-Provincial Relations (the Rowell-Sirois Commission) in 1937 to report on the financial and

[1]*Assembly Debates*, 1896, 123–7.

economic basis of Confederation, the distribution of legislative responsibilities and financial powers in the federation, and the financial relations of all the Canadian governments. The provincial government appointed the Jones Commission in 1934 to investigate the effect of the Dominion's fiscal and trade policies upon the economic life of Nova Scotia and the adequacy of the existing Dominion-Nova Scotian financial arrangements in the light of the powers, obligations, and responsibilities of the two governments; and the Royal Commission on Provincial Development and Rehabilitation.(the Dawson Commission) in 1943 to investigate and report on the possibilities of economic development especially with a view to assisting in the rehabilitation of war veterans. The significance of these commissions will appear in the discussion which follows.

I

Until 1867 the Nova Scotian government budgeted in the typical manner of autonomous governments. For many years customs duties had provided the degree of flexibility in revenue which ensured that no ministry would be thwarted in its efforts to meet an emergency or to provide any new services that were deemed desirable. From the financial point of view, therefore, Howe was not far off the mark in his prophecy that the province would revert to something like municipal status under federation, for after 1867 the provincial revenues lost their former flexibility, and successive governments were relegated to administering services which were in some cases inferior to those of pre-Confederation days or stooping to beggary at Ottawa.

It may be argued, however, that even if Nova Scotia had not given up its right to levy customs duties, the flexibility in provincial revenues was coming to an end. Reciprocity and the American Civil War, which had boosted trade and prices and produced a striking increase in the revenues from *ad valorem* duties, would soon have been things of the past. Furthermore, the province faced the immediate necessity of defraying the cost of its new Pictou Branch Railway. Consequently even without Confederation it would probably have been forced to increase its customs duties to a level which would, in effect, have destroyed their former flexibility. But this is a probability stated by students of a later day. Only a delay of two or three years in the entrance of the province into the federation could have afforded convincing proof to Nova Scotians that the basic conditions of their former happy state had vanished.

While the province might have resorted to direct taxation after 1867, to Nova Scotian legislators the power seemed incapable of practical use. The aversion to these taxes was still delaying the establishment of municipal self-government, and any party bold enough to have run counter to a dislike deeply ingrained in the consciousness of the Nova Scotian electorate would undoubtedly have committed political suicide. That is why the first advance into this field, succession duties on estates of substantial size in 1892, was noticeably along a line which could do little political damage.

The question is still raised: Did Tupper and his associates set the price of entrance into the federation at too low a level on the one occasion when they possessed strong bargaining power? Certainly the financial bargain made at Quebec, even when improved upon in London, was found insufficient almost at once to carry on the pre-Confederation services. Furthermore, Howe's "better terms" of 1869 did little more than guarantee their existing level and provided nothing substantial to venture into new undertakings. But to blame Tupper for Nova Scotia's modern financial difficulties is sheer folly, for there was no practicable allotment of financial powers in 1867 which would have enabled the provinces to meet both their immediate and long-run needs.

The sharply contrasting attitudes of the federal and Nova Scotian governments towards the financial strait-jacket in which the province normally finds itself first became apparent after 1877. By that time Nova Scotia had spent or guaranteed its augmented debt allowance of 1873 to promote further railway building; the special ten-year grant provided by the "better terms" agreement of 1869 was about to terminate; and economic depression was making its appearance. Yet for ten years Conservative and Liberal governments ineffectually besought Ottawa for assistance on what amounted to a "fiscal need" basis. Despite the utmost economy, they argued, the province had been forced to reduce its road expenditures to below the pre-Confederation level and to devolve part of the responsibility for road maintenance upon the local governments. In their opinion "policy, as well as justice, demand[ed] that each Province should have enough to maintain in efficiency its local services."[2] Ottawa's contention was that "Provinces, like individuals, should hold to engagements once made and settled as being binding" as the agreement of 1869 had been declared to be.[3] Furthermore, the financial woes of the province were of its own making since it had depleted its debt allowance to provide

[2]Memorandum of the Deputy Provincial Secretary, April 4, 1881. See *Journals of the House of Assembly* (*JHA*), 1882, Appendix 14, 44.
[3]Memorandum of the Deputy Minister of Finance, Oct. 29, 1880. *Ibid.*, 33.

unremunerative public works. Nevertheless, even now, "if a better system of check were instituted, and if the public moneys were husbanded with greater frugality . . . in course of time . . . an equilibrium might be established between receipts and expenditures."[4] This advice, singularly enough, was offered to Holmes, who headed the most economical of all the Nova Scotian administrations.

The natural inference to be drawn from this position was that the role of the Nova Scotian government was to be confined to performing the routine tasks of administration, and that if it ventured into new fields, it would have to be at the expense of normal services. A further general increase in debt allowances, it is true, was provided in 1884. But this occurred as the direct result of pressure from Quebec with which the fortunes of the Conservative party of that day were intimately connected and left the Nova Scotian politicians no false hopes about their ability to exert pressure with similar results. To strengthen their bargaining power they sporadically considered such expedients as maritime union, but genuine provincial autonomy remained an illusion none the less. After twenty years of federation Fielding, one of the ablest of Nova Scotian financiers, bewailed the failure to place something less objectionable than direct taxation within provincial control. "If we had some elastic source of revenue left to us," he said, "we could, by some form of that increase of taxation which is resorted to by finance ministers in case of need, deal with the difficulties of our position."[5]

The increased tempo in the development of the province's coal resources which began in the 1890's afforded a temporary measure of relief. After the turn of the century coal royalties surpassed the federal subsidy as the greatest single source of provincial revenue, and for the first time since Confederation the province was placed in a position of financial independence.[6] Under these circumstances it was able to expand its development services and make timorous advances into the social service field. Shortly before the outbreak of the First World War, however, conditions were reverting to what was unhappily becoming to be regarded as normal. Coal royalties and federal subsidies accounted for 89 per cent of the provincial revenues in 1913, and of these sources the former had about reached its peak, while the latter was completely inelastic in a province with a stationary population. Yet the provincial government was being confronted with insistent

[4]Memorandum of the same official, n.d. *Ibid.*, 7.
[5]*Assembly Debates*, 1886, 224.
[6]Under the Laurier régime, too, the province undoubtedly exerted greater influence at Ottawa.

demands for improved health and educational services, and although its expenditures on railways were coming to an end, two other development services, hydro-electric power generation and highway construction, were requiring its attention. For the time being the Murray government managed to delay extensive expenditures on power and road projects, but it was powerless to halt the other inexorable demands.

The result was that something not far short of a revolution occurred in provincial finance between 1913 and 1921. The yields from succession duties, motor licences and fees, and corporation taxes grew to comprise 56 per cent instead of a mere 10 per cent of the revenues, while federal subsidies and coal royalties accounted for only 21 per cent of the total.[7] The Murray and Armstrong administrations, by entering upon an extensive highway construction programme in the post-war period, provided a further threat to the financial structure and forced the Rhodes government to allot 57 per cent of its entire expenditures in 1926 to debt and highways, leaving only 21 per cent available for education and welfare—half the percentage allotted in the other provinces.

Hence when Nova Scotia presented its brief to the first of the royal commissions to conduct an inquest into its affairs—the Duncan Commission on Maritime Claims in 1926—it urged "sufficient subsidy allowances to assist [it] in maintaining services which modern requirements have enlarged to a degree not anticipated sixty years ago," and suggested "a special initial allowance . . . for the smaller provinces, graded according to population, or a recasting of the per capita basis."[8] Its case might well have rested on this broad ground, which, in effect, amounted to fiscal need, but following the customary method of bargaining between the Dominion and the provinces, it superimposed a number of other claims which obscured what was fundamental.

The Commission itself applied two simple tests to Nova Scotian financing. Were the expenditures reasonable and proper? Were the sources of revenue being employed to full advantage? Using what it considered the fairest basis of comparison, taxation yield per unit of production, it found Nova Scotians to be taxed more heavily than the

[7]For an extensive discussion see Stewart Bates, *Financial History of Canadian Governments* (Ottawa, 1939), 108–11.

[8]*Province of Nova Scotia—A Submission of Its Claims with Respect to Maritime Disabilities within Confederation*, 1926, 102–3.

Canadian average, but it could discover no fault in the size and nature of the provincial expenditures. It recommended, therefore, that the province should be accorded an annual payment of $875,000 until a full reassessment of its claims could be made.[9]

The White Commission, which undertook the determination of the definitive payment in 1934–5, was confronted with a demand by the Macdonald government that the principle of federal grants based on fiscal need should be applied as part of a new conception of federalism that it was beginning to enunciate. The majority of the Commission, however, feared that the proposal would result in the introduction of grave abuses since, in deciding whether a provincial government was spending its revenues wisely and efficiently and whether it had exhausted all its available sources of revenue, the Dominion government would inevitably show favouritism.[10] The Commission apparently forgot that the proponents of fiscal aid advocated the setting up of a quasi-judicial federal grants commission to determine the financial payments to the provinces, and that a major argument in support of their position was that it would eliminate the grab-bag type of proceeding which had characterized Dominion-provincial financial relations since 1870. Actually the White Commission itself provided the best argument for fiscal need when it acknowledged its inability to assess each of the provincial claims in detail, and then by some sort of hocus-pocus which involved the equitable consideration of all the claims in the aggregate recommended that the temporary annual grant of $875,000 to Nova Scotia should be increased to $1,300,000 as a final settlement.

Despite this initial set-back the Liberal governments since 1935 have never ceased their efforts to have a new *modus operandi* introduced into Dominion-provincial financial relations. The basis of their arguments lies in the brief which Norman McLeod Rogers presented to the Jones Commission on their behalf in 1934. Any attempt to neutralize the existing differences in taxable capacity between the provinces simply by providing a higher scale of subsidies to the weaker units, declared the brief, would "lead to invidious comparisons and recrimination. Instead of promoting harmony it would produce friction."[11] On the other hand, endowing the provinces with the sole

[9]See *Report of the Royal Commission on Maritime Claims*, 1926, 19.
[10]See *Report of the Royal Commission on Financial Arrangements between the Dominion and the Maritime Provinces*, 1935.
[11]*A Submission on Dominion-Provincial Relations and the Fiscal Disabilities of Nova Scotia within the Canadian Federation*, 1934, 188.

right to collect income taxes would accentuate the differences rather than neutralize them. The solution was to give this power to the Dominion on the understanding that it was to be used as an instrument for the redistribution of national income, "a conduit through which a portion of the income . . . transferred from the other provinces to Ontario and Quebec as a result of the protective tariff [should] be returned to those provinces [adversely] affected."[12] To ensure stability of payments for fixed periods and to remove their revision from the dangers and abuses of political manipulation, a commission would be appointed at the time of each decennial census which, as the basis of its calculations, would adopt a test of fiscal need bearing an intelligible relation to the relative wealth and revenue capacity of the various provinces.

Five years' experience in managing the provincial affairs resulted in some adaptation of the Macdonald government's views, but its basic position remained unchanged. Hence its submission to the Rowell-Sirois Commission in 1938 proposed that the absolute right to impose succession duties and income taxes should be conferred upon the Dominion Parliament on condition that part of the receipts would be employed to equalize the effect of inequalities in the taxable capacities of the provinces. Fiscal need would become the sole determinant of provincial subsidies, and a Federal Grants Commission modelled upon the Commonwealth Grants Commission in Australia would consider and report upon the needs of the provinces.

In essence, the Nova Scotian position coincided with the recommendations of the Commission itself although they were at variance upon whether the Dominion should be required to assume a portion of the provincial debts[13] and whether the province should be permitted entrance into the sales tax field. These differences and others may be explained in part by the differently coloured spectacles through which the Commission and the province viewed these matters. Since Premier Macdonald was not restrained by questions of political expediency, he could suggest substantial constitutional changes for the relief of financial ills; in contrast, the Commission realized more and more as its work progressed that it must at all costs remain within the realm of the politically practicable. The viewpoint of the province towards the *Report* of the Commission therefore becomes understandable. At the Dominion-Provincial Conference which was called in 1941 to con-

---

[12]*Ibid.*, 192.
[13]Macdonald's statement to the Commission was: "We've contracted the debts here and we should pay them here." See *Halifax Herald*, Feb. 5, 1938.

sider the implementation of its recommendations Premier MacMillan indicated that, if he were asked to give a categorical answer for or against the *Report*, the answer would have to be "no." Yet its main principles would be acceptable, he said, if the details and methods for applying them could be worked out satisfactorily.[14] Hence the Nova Scotia delegation was highly indignant when the Conference broke up in short order and the *Report* disappeared from the arena of practical politics.

The subsequent adoption of some of its recommendations by oblique means was also greeted with little enthusiasm since they were palatable only as part of a unified scheme in which the principle of fiscal need integrated and gave meaning to all the other provisions. On two occasions the provincial administration accepted objectionable terms only because they were the lesser of two distasteful alternatives. The MacMillan government acquiesced in the wartime tax agreement of 1942 by which each province withdrew from the income tax and succession duty fields and in return received compensation based partly upon its former revenues from these fields, but not before it expressed its opinion that Nova Scotia had not been dealt with as fairly as some of the other provinces.[15] Premier MacMillan himself was far-sighted enough to see that the legislation confirming the agreement might be "the most important . . . that has come before this House since Confederation,"[16] since it heralded radical changes in Dominion-provincial financial relations and in the nature of Canadian federalism. Time vindicated his prophecy and in its protracted post-war negotiations with the Dominion the Nova Scotian government's attitude was undoubtedly little different from that of the *Chronicle*:

Had there been no war, no Liberal Government would have had the temerity to dictate the proposals of 1942 without a long period of negotiation. Today we find we have put a horseman in the saddle who rides rough-shod over all Liberal tradition of the past. . . .[17]

The viewpoint of Angus L. Macdonald, who resumed his position as Nova Scotian spokesman in 1945, was that constitutional changes ought

[14]See *Proceedings of Dominion Provincial Conference*, 1941, 18.

[15]See speech of Premier MacMillan in *JHA*, 1942, 70–101. The major complaint was that Nova Scotia would be required to contribute equally to maintaining a status quo in which it had an inferior position. This was the result of some provinces' being compensated for abandoning the substantial income tax which they had levied to provide a high level of social services. Nova Scotia, on the other hand, had been content with a low level of services, levied no income tax, and received no compensation.

[16]*Ibid.*, 70.   [17]Dec. 19, 1946.

to come first, taxation arrangements afterwards.[18] Hence in April, 1946, he suggested that the proper course would be to conclude agreements for a three-year period during which the responsibilities and resources of all the Canadian governments might be reallocated. But this temporary agreement would not be permitted to become a backdoor method of effecting constitutional change.

We do not intend to let the Dominion government draw us into a permanent arrangement by getting us to make particular commitments here, there, or elsewhere, on a so-called temporary basis, and by then telling us, at the end of the temporary term, "What are you going to do about it now? You cannot withdraw. You must continue the temporary agreement and you must continue it on our terms."[19]

Macdonald condemned particularly the procedure of dealing separately with the provinces which was introduced subsequent to the budget proposals of June, 1946. Rather than having to rely on the newspapers for the terms of the agreements with the other provinces he insisted that they should be worked out in a general Dominion-provincial conference.[20] But his requests for a resumption of the adjourned conference and the regular convening of similar conferences at fixed dates were unavailing. Prime Minister King denied the first bcause of what he called the unchanged recalcitrant attitude of several provinces, the second because it would be "importing a principle foreign to our constitutional practice, involving undesirable rigidity."[21] So although the Nova Scotian Premier kept reiterating that "the conference question is fundamental, and Ottawa knows it,"[22] the only concession he could secure was a promise to consult the provinces at least one year prior to the termination of the proposed five-year agreement.

But most of all the Nova Scotian Premier deplored the abandonment of the principle of fiscal need. In March, 1945, he questioned "why the principles and conclusion of the Sirois Report . . . framed by a Commission appointed by the Dominion Government, approved by the Dominion government, should now be disregarded and abandoned by that Government."[23] In April, 1946, he declared population to be

[18]See "Preliminary Statement of the Province of Nova Scotia," *JHA*, 1946, Appendix 33, 2–3.
[19]See *Halifax Chronicle*, May 13, 1947.
[20]Macdonald to King, Dec. 18, 1946. See *Halifax Chronicle*, Dec. 20, 1946.
[21]King to Macdonald, Dec. 14, 1946. See *Halifax Chronicle*, Dec. 17, 1946.
[22]*Halifax Chronicle*, March 10, 1947.
[23]See "Preliminary Statement of the Province of Nova Scotia," *JHA*, 1946, Appendix 33, 3–4.

an unsound basis for determining grants to the provinces. Yet faced with the alternative of utilizing his province's own resources which would at best have yielded three to four million dollars less per annum, he finally accepted proposals in mid-1947 which failed to meet his test of adequacy. For a province like Nova Scotia which levied no provincial income tax the more favourable proposition was the one which provided a minimum grant of $15 per capita based on the 1942 estimated population in return for the province's relinquishing its corporation and income taxes and succession duties.[24]

Yet while Macdonald failed to have the principle of fiscal need recognized, he would have been the first to deny that the new per capita grants were as objectionable as the previous grants of this nature. The hostility to grants based on population arose in a period in which they constituted only a small portion of the provincial revenue and in which each province retained those sources of revenue that yielded grossly disproportionate returns per capita if levied at the same rate by the different provinces. The effect of the agreement of 1947 was to provide something approaching equal per capita revenue in the latter fields and hence to place the financial resources of all the provincial governments on more nearly the same footing. But the new device by no means nullifies the argument for grants based on fiscal need; its practical implications are merely to reduce the force of the arguments in their favour.

Back of the Nova Scotian position was the desire to preserve provincial autonomy, whatever the cost, and to maintain that decentralization of power which is an essential safeguard of democracy. Ottawa, annoyed at Premier Macdonald's obstinacy, kept reminding him that its plans were specially designed to ensure a degree of financial independence for a province like Nova Scotia by providing substantial unconditional grants for the abandonment of relatively unremunerative fields. Yet its own actions confirmed the Nova Scotian Premier's opinion that the concessions were to be all on one side. While the provinces were to withdraw completely from the major direct taxation fields, the Dominion initially refused to commit itself to withdrawing from the minor tax fields (which it had first entered after 1939) for fear its own budgetary policies might be hampered.

Although Nova Scotia admitted the relatively low productivity of these sources of revenue, it demanded their exclusive use as a matter

[24]The normal statutory subsidies and the additional grants awarded by the Duncan and White commissions were also to be continued. Furthermore the new per capita grants were to increase as the gross national product of Canada increased.

of principle and to preserve at least a vestige of autonomy. In this instance it made good its claim despite its lack of bargaining power. In December, 1946, Ottawa announced its intention to retire from the gasoline taxation field; in April, 1947, from the amusement and pari-mutuel fields. The latter concession, however, appears to have been more a means of inducing Nova Scotia to sign an agreement and hence of maintaining Liberal solidarity than a wholehearted recognition of a genuine claim. Hence Premier Macdonald was still undecided whether the agreements constituted a danger to Canadian federalism. "We must be satisfied that [their] trend . . . is in the right direction," he said, "before we can even contemplate any extension of this agreement beyond the five-year term."[25] Yet the bald facts are that whatever his opinion was in 1952 he had no alternative but to renew the agreement.

Premier Hicks followed in the Angus L. Macdonald tradition. Noting the steady ingress of the central government into fields traditionally and constitutionally provincial, he warned that although he was not opposed to a well-considered reallocation of legislative powers in the light of contemporary conditions, he objected to the loss of the federal system by default without the Canadian people being given the opportunity to pronounce upon its desirability.[26] Like Macdonald he realized the necessity of surrendering the major direct taxation fields to the Dominion, but he criticized some features of the tax agreements which were in force between 1947 and 1957. A major defect, in his opinion, was their impermanency. To avoid the province's dependence for 40 per cent of its revenues upon their successful re-negotiation every five years, he suggested the incorporation of renewal provisions in the rental agreements themselves or the adoption of a constitutional amendment with like effect.[27]

At the Dominion-Provincial Conference in October, 1955, Premier Hicks also objected to the method of calculating the rental payments. The tax agreements gave approximately equal per capita payments to the contracting provinces, but they had to supplement those amounts by recourse to local taxation. Because of the wide variation in

[25]*Halifax Chronicle,* May 13, 1947.

[26]*Halifax Chronicle-Herald,* Jan. 25, 1955. In its editorial comment (Jan. 26, 1955) this paper supported Prime Minister St. Laurent's "spreading the national wealth across the country" in preference to "appeals to the shibboleths of the past." This is one illustration of its long-standing myopia in regarding Dominion-provincial financial negotiations as having no constitutional implications.

[27]*Ibid.,* March 15 and April 27, 1955. Premier Hicks pleaded also for greater permanency in conditional grants. His particular grievance was Ottawa's recent termination of its agreement to pay 50 per cent of the cost of physical fitness programmes.

the tax potentials of the provinces, their ability to provide even essential services differed markedly and the objective of minimum standards for the Canadian people had therefore not been achieved. To augment the revenues of the have-not provinces, Premier Hicks suggested that the calculation of federal payments to the provinces should not be based solely on population and the gross national product. Some factor which would compensate for a low tax potential should also be taken into account, and the most appropriate index of measurement might be provincial per capita incomes.[28]

This position was natural for a Premier who feared that the activities of his government were about to be closely circumscribed by the normal financial strait-jacket. Today about 90 per cent of the provincial revenues stems from three sources, Dominion payments and subsidies, the sale of liquor, and highway and gasoline taxes and licences. Since the third source is barely sufficient to meet the outlay on highways, the first two must, in effect, sustain most of the other provincial services. While their yields still show no signs of contraction, the present indications are that neither will continue to match the inexorable annual increases in expenditure which an entrance into social services always entails. Furthermore, each of them is almost certain to decline with the slightest falling off in economic activity. Notwithstanding these considerations neither of Premier Hicks's principles is recognized in the Dominion-provincial fiscal arrangements which came into effect on April 1, 1957. For Nova Scotia the best option was another rental agreement which guaranteed a higher annual return to the province but otherwise retained the essential features of the old. Yet during the election campaign of 1956 Liberal politicians conveniently overlooked the failure of Premier Hicks to have his principles recognized and extolled his skill as a negotiator in enriching the Provincial Treasury by five or six millions per annum.

II

Financial relations constitute only one facet of Nova Scotia's relations with the Dominion. Sporadically prior to 1933 and consistently since then, the province has held that the mere provision of money grants by the federal government provides no solution of its basic ills, which are economic. Naturally it denies that poverty of resources and remoteness of position have constituted too formidable a challenge for

[28]See *Proceedings of the Federal-Provincial Conference 1955* (Ottawa, 1955), 45.

the resourcefulness of its people and attributes its ills largely to the Dominion's fiscal and transportation policies.

Yet every commission which seeks to make a mathematical appraisal of these disabilities immediately encounters a complex series of relationships from which immeasurable "buts" and "ifs" cannot be excluded. The conclusion of the Duncan Commission in 1926 was that "the responsibility of Confederation [for the Nova Scotian failure to progress] can only be a matter of speculation and not of proof."[29] Norman McLeod Rogers, in his brief prepared for the Jones Commission, estimated that Nova Scotia's net loss in 1931 as a result of the protective tariff was roughly $4,500,000,[30] but most economists declined to accept the assumptions upon which his calculations were based. Professor W. A. Mackintosh of Queen's University concluded that it was "not possible to give a quantitative statement of the long-run effects of the protective policy on the different regions of the country," but that "some descriptive probabilities [might] be stated."[31] Chief Justice Rowell discounted the opinions of the economists respecting the effect of the tariff because they dealt with too many unknowns, and requested Premier Macdonald for his opinion on what Nova Scotia's position would be outside federation. "We'd be making treaties tomorrow [with the United States] whereby we'd be getting [our] automobiles free of duty and they'd be taking [our] fish,"[32] was the Premier's reply, but his insistence that he could treble the provincial market for fish in ten years if he had complete control of tariff policy undoubtedly needs to be tempered by considerations of economic nationalism within the United States itself.

Yet even if the effect of National Policy is not subject to strict mathematical analysis, the general impact on Nova Scotian industry is more than mere probability. A few provincial industries, notably coal and steel, have been subsidized by the tariff, but by and large the province contributes to the bonussing of central Canadian industry, the result being to place a heavy burden upon its consumers and particularly upon its export industries which find their competitive position in world markets deleteriously affected by the increased costs.

In these matters each section within a federal system is theoretically supposed to have its interests safeguarded by its representation in the central legislature. This raises the question whether Nova Scotian

[29]*Report of the Royal Commission on Maritime Claims*, 1926, 10.

[30]*A Submission on Dominion-Provincial Relations and the Fiscal Disabilities of Nova Scotia within the Canadian Federation*, 102.

[31]*The Economic Background of Dominion-Provincial Relations* (Ottawa, 1939), 87.　　　　　　　　　　　　　　　[32]*Halifax Herald*, Feb. 5, 1938.

members of Parliament have been more concerned with maintaining party solidarity than with safeguarding provincial interests. While the western Canadian provinces have undoubtedly found it to their advantage to return third-party representation in strength, the Maritimes have rarely deviated from the old-party lines to the extent of more than a single member, and the political leaders at Ottawa have had no difficulty in keeping them in line by what might be alleged to be little more than temporary sops. The Conservative members of Parliament who in the late twenties used an almost hysterical "Maritime rights" agitation to harass a Liberal government at Ottawa cooled noticeably on the return of their own party to office in 1930 although the partially adopted recommendations of the Duncan Commission satisfied little more than a fragment of their original grievances. Premier Macdonald secured no vocal support from Liberal members of Parliament during his protracted negotiations with Ottawa between 1945 and 1947, although they may have used their influence behind the scenes to secure the concessions which made an agreement possible before the Halifax federal by-election of mid-1947.

The main Nova Scotian pressure upon the federal government has, in fact, been exerted by the local Legislature and cabinet. But here, again, inconsistency and a resort to political expediency have marked the course of Dominion–Nova Scotian relations. Since the early 1880's the tariff handicap has been alternately paraded as the chief exhibit in the province's disabilities or withdrawn completely from the public eye as it suited the purposes of party strategy. In 1886 the Fielding government campaigned for the repeal of Confederation, stressing the disastrous effect of the Canadian fiscal laws upon the provincial economy, but its victory in the provincial election was more than counterbalanced by the success of the Nova Scotian Conservatives in the Dominion election of 1887, and the last serious repeal movement petered out.

The Fielding of 1886 became the Fielding of 1896, who, as the minister responsible for the Dominion's fiscal policy, retained the tariff framework as an instrument of Canadian development despite his hitherto pronounced opposition. Altered circumstances rather than inconsistency were largely responsible, however, since after 1900 Nova Scotia was itself progressing under "N.P." as its coal and steel industry expanded to meet the needs of western development with which central Canadian industry was for the moment unable to cope. Curiously enough, when Fielding at length proposed some relief for the primary producer, he found the electorate strangely apathetic, and in the reciprocity election of 1911 the best he could secure in his native province was an even break.

The apathy disappeared in the face of the province's chronically depressed condition after 1918 and gave way to a concerted "Maritime rights" movement which helped the Conservatives to win the provincial election of 1925. Under their guidance the movement took a peculiar turn. Their brief to the Duncan Commission in 1926 showed a distinct orientation of the general Nova Scotian viewpoint to make it accord with Conservative support of "N.P." While it did not condemn the protective tariff as a national instrument, it could find "no reasonable defence . . . of a system under which Nova Scotians are compelled to buy what they consume in a substantially protected home market, and to sell what they produce in a virtually unprotected one."[33] All it asked, however, was that "the accepted principles of the National Policy of protection to Canadian industries be extended frankly and intelligently to this basic Nova Scotia [coal and steel] industry."[34] Clearly the brief was on much happier ground when it turned to analyse the transportation disabilities under which the province laboured.[35]

The Commission itself carefully refrained from considering the effects of the tariff on the economy, ostensibly to avoid interference with the functions of the Tariff Advisory Board, but allegedly in obedience to instructions issued by the Meighen "shadow" cabinet to protect the central Canadian manufacturing interests. "No blacker record of betrayal, no darker story of disregard of promises can be found in the political annals of the country," was Premier Macdonald's comment.[36]

It was, in fact, the Duncan Commission's failure to consider the

---

[33]*Province of Nova Scotia—A Submission of Its Claims with Respect to Maritime Disabilities within Confederation*, 146.   [34]*Ibid.*, 149.

[35]The Commission recognized as an understanding of the Confederation agreement that "to the extent that commercial considerations [respecting the I.C.R.] were subordinated to *national, imperial* and *strategic* considerations, the cost would be borne by the Dominion and not by the traffic that might pass over the line." See *Report of the Royal Commission on Maritime Claims*, 21. Until 1912 this stipulation had been honoured, but subsequently the rates on the I.C.R. had increased a cumulative total of 92 per cent compared with 55 per cent elsewhere in Canada. The Commission therefore recommended a reduction of 20 per cent in the rates charged on traffic which originated and terminated in the Atlantic Division of the C.N.R., and on traffic originating in the Atlantic Division destined to outside points over the I.C.R. portion of the journey. The Maritime Freight Rates Act of 1927 incorporated this recommendation, and a continuing struggle since then has been to maintain it, not only in theory, but in practice as well.

[36]*Halifax Chronicle*, March 8, 1934.

burden of the tariff upon the province which led Macdonald to appoint the Jones Commission in 1934 to rectify the omission. At its hearings both he and Norman McLeod Rogers urged either that the tariffs should be revised downward to relieve the handicaps resting upon the Nova Scotian primary producer or that they should be retained as a constituent element of national economic planning, but modified and supplemented so "as to provide deliberately for the economic recuperation of those provinces which, like Nova Scotia, have been prejudiced by [their] operation."[37] The latter suggestion is open to criticism because it limits the power of the national government to initiate policies which it conceives to be in the general interest; if it is forced to resort to the principle of "compensating advantage," the tendency will be to wipe out the net national gain.[38] The Nova Scotian reply is that a net national loss has already resulted from the effects of federal policies which operate to the advantage of only two provinces.

The *Dawson Report* (1944) indicated that the policy of concentrating war contracts in Ontario and Quebec had further weakened the position of the outlying provinces since its result was "the development of a vast new industrial machine which [would] add economic and political power to the central provinces in the post-war era."[39] Thus once again Nova Scotia has suffered from being dominated by a St. Lawrence Valley economy with its tendency towards centralization and government intervention. In both the private and governmental spheres Nova Scotians have been left with nothing but the most limited control over their own destiny. Remote control has become the dominant feature of the human forces which direct the provincial economy. Financial policy, formerly determined by Nova Scotian banks in Halifax, is now dictated from Ottawa, Montreal, and Toronto. A host of smaller industries have fallen, not necessarily through inefficiency, but in the face of practices which, "while justified legally under the régime of competition, are in fact forms of discrimination which are without economic or social justification."[40]

Larger industries have for the most part become subject to remote control with generally tragic results. Perhaps no complaint should be

[37]*A Submission on Dominion-Provincial Relations and the Fiscal Disabilities of Nova Scotia within the Canadian Federation*, 124.

[38]See, for example, J. A. Maxwell, "Aspects of Canadian Federalism," *Dalhousie Review*, XVI (Oct., 1936), 283–4.

[39]*Report of Transmission, Royal Commission on Provincial Development and Rehabilitation*, 41.

[40]*A Submission on Dominion-Provincial Relations and the Fiscal Disabilities of Nova Scotia within the Canadian Federation*, 120.

raised because the sympathetic attitude towards a local community and the genuine desire to maintain operations which once existed have been replaced by a stern insistence upon profitable operations, but when the result is planned neglect or the operation of Nova Scotian industries as pure ancillaries merely to improve the position of a not necessarily more efficient industry in central Canada, the grievance is real and justified.[41] The federal regulation and control of various aspects of the provincial economy raises similar considerations. One provincial minister, for example, blamed past policies and lack of attention by Ottawa for the decline of the fishing industry in Nova Scotia and advocated that "absolute dominant control" be vested in the province.[42]

Thus Nova Scotia illustrates convincingly the difficulty of making federalism work when one of its entities is grossly disproportionate in wealth, population, and bargaining power to some of the others. But whenever maritime union is suggested as a means of creating a province which could make its influence felt to greater advantage at Ottawa, it always has to contend with an insuperable obstacle latent in the intangibles of Nova Scotian history.

For over a century and a half prior to 1867 this Province was a distinct community under the British Crown. It is not a matter for wonderment, therefore, that the traditions and the loyalties engendered in this long period of separate existence should create in this Province a distinct consciousness and sense of independence. These sentiments have never been wholly superseded by the larger idea of Confederation. Nova Scotia[ns], to a larger extent perhaps, than the people of most of the other Provinces, cherish a double loyalty . . . a loyalty to their own Province and a loyalty to the Dominion as a whole. . . .[43]

For a time the device of the royal commission was a popular substitute for more revolutionary proposals. After the fifth in nineteen years reported in 1945, the *Chronicle* wondered "whether the time is not very nearly at hand when we shall have to choose, once and for all, between Royal Commissions on the one hand, and outright revolt against the iniquities of federate domination on the other."[44] Actually the government accepted the conclusion of the *Dawson Report* that

[41]For a specific example see the report of Mr. Justice Carroll on the closing of two departments of the Trenton Steel Works. *Halifax Herald*, Oct. 12, 1944.

[42]See speech of the Hon. Harold Connolly as reported in the *Halifax Chronicle*, Feb. 28, 1945.

[43]See the *Submission by the Government of the Province of Nova Scotia to the Royal Commission on Dominion-Provincial Relations*, 1938, 1.

[44]*Halifax Chronicle*, March 29, 1945.

there was no easy panacea for the solution of provincial problems, but that

Provincial progress can be achieved primarily by meeting and dealing intelligently with the very practical problems which will continue to arise in never-ending series. Such a programme throws the province back upon the ability and character of its citizens, and hence special care must be taken to arm them in advance by such long-range measures as education and research. "Line upon line; precept upon precept; here a little, and there a little" might well serve as the text for the province's future guidance.[45]

But despite the best efforts of the Department of Trade and Industry, the Research Foundation, and associated agencies the results in the way of new industries have been somewhat meagre for the money and energy expended to encourage their establishment. Doubts have been expressed whether they even compensate for the loss of other industries which has been occurring at the same time. Furthermore, the provincial coal industry, which with its allied industries supports almost one-fourth of the province's population, is at present experiencing a serious crisis of which none can safely predict the result.

The pessimist might suggest that Nova Scotia should abandon the idea of maintaining its present population at anything like the Canadian standard of living or that of retaining all its people within its borders. If so, it would only mean the intensification of a process which the province has been undergoing for many years, the exodus of its youth to areas which can offer greater opportunities. Federal hand-outs through the medium of expensive public works are doing nothing to solve the basic difficulties. Central Canadians, or Nova Scotians who have prospered elsewhere, periodically call upon the province to give itself a hoist by its own bootstraps, and Nova Scotia and the adjoining provinces are now making such an attempt through the Atlantic Provinces Economic Council.[46] The Council's work is still in the initial stages, but by avoiding premature publicity and by beginning with a careful inventory of the area's resources and possibilities it is at least making a good start. It is equally encouraging that, when the old line parties made economic development the principal plank of their platforms in 1956, they neither blamed outsiders for the province's failure to prosper, nor looked to them for assistance. Both insisted that it was the duty of the Nova Scotian government itself to provide the appropriate climate for that development.

[45]*Report of Transmission, Royal Commission on Provincial Development and Rehabilitation,* 28.

[46]For the purposes and functioning of the A.P.E.C., see Nelson Mann, "Atlantic Provinces Economic Council," *Dalhousie Review,* XXXV (Winter, 1956), 309–22.

APPENDIXES

APPENDIX A

Governors, Lieutenant-Governors, and Administrators of Nova Scotia (1749–86)

(The dates indicate their actual time in office)

Governor	Lieutenant-Governor	Administrator	Time in office	
			From	To
Edward Cornwallis			July 13, 1749	Aug. 2, 1752
Peregrine Thomas Hopson			Aug. 3, 1752	Oct. 31, 1753
		Charles Lawrence	Nov. 1, 1753	Oct. 20, 1754
	Charles Lawrence		Oct. 14, 1754	July 22, 1756
Charles Lawrence			July 23, 1756	Oct. 19, 1760
	Jonathan Belcher		Oct. 19, 1760	Nov. 20, 1761
		Jonathan Belcher	Nov. 21, 1761	Sept. 26, 1763
	Montague Wilmot		Sept. 26, 1763	May 30, 1764
Montague Wilmot			May 31, 1764	May 23, 1766
		Benjamin Green	May 23, 1766	Aug. 23, 1766
	Michael Francklin		Aug. 23, 1766	Nov. 26, 1766
Lord William Campbell			Nov. 27, 1766	Oct. 7, 1773
	Michael Francklin		Oct. 1, 1767	Sept. 10, 1768
	Michael Francklin		Nov. 4, 1768	Dec. 4, 1768
	Michael Francklin	Benjamin Green	Oct. 17, 1771	June 1, 1772
	Michael Francklin		June 2, 1772	July 10, 1772
Francis Legge			Oct. 8, 1773	May 12, 1776
	Mariot Arbuthnot		May 13, 1776	Aug. 16, 1778
	Richard Hughes		Aug. 17, 1778	July 30, 1781
	Andrew Snape Hamond		July 31, 1781	Oct. 18, 1782
John Parr			Oct. 19, 1782	April 24, 1786

APPENDIX B

LIEUTENANT-GOVERNORS AND ADMINISTRATORS (1786–1867)
(The dates indicate their actual time in office)

Lieutenant-Governor	Administrator	Time in office	
		From	To
John Parr		April 24, 1786	Nov. 25, 1791
	Richard Bulkeley	Nov. 25, 1791	May 13, 1792
John Wentworth		May 14, 1792	April 12, 1808
Sir George Prevost		April 13, 1808	Aug. 25, 1811
	Alexander Croke	Dec. 7, 1808	April 14, 1809
	Alexander Croke	Aug. 26, 1811	Oct. 15, 1811
Sir John Sherbrooke		Oct. 16, 1811	June 27, 1816
	Duncan Darroch	Aug. 26, 1814	Sept. 20, 1814
	George Stracey Smyth	June 27, 1816	Oct. 24, 1816
Earl of Dalhousie		Oct. 24, 1816	June 1, 1820
	Michael Wallace	Mar. 29, 1818	April 25, 1818
Sir James Kempt		June 2, 1820	Aug. 23, 1828
	Michael Wallace	May 1, 1824	Aug. 18, 1825
	Michael Wallace	May 26, 1828	July 17, 1828
	Michael Wallace	Aug. 23, 1828	Nov. 27, 1828
Sir Peregrine Maitland		Nov. 28, 1828	Oct. 8, 1832
	Michael Wallace	Oct. 14, 1829	May 30, 1830
	T. N. Jeffery	Oct. 9, 1832	July 1, 1834
Sir Colin Campbell		July 2, 1834	Sept. 30, 1840
Viscount Falkland		Sept. 30, 1840	Aug. 2, 1846
	Sir Jeremiah Dickson	Aug. 3, 1846	Aug. 28, 1846
Sir John Harvey		Aug. 29, 1846	Mar. 22, 1852
	John Bazalgette	May 30, 1851	Sept. 29, 1851
	John Bazalgette	Mar. 22, 1852	Aug. 5, 1852
Sir Gaspard le Marchant		Aug. 5, 1852	Feb. 15, 1858
Earl of Mulgrave		Feb. 15, 1858	Sept. 17, 1863
	Hastings Doyle	Sept. 18, 1863	June 21, 1864
Sir Richard Graves MacDonnell		June 22, 1864	Sept. 28, 1865
	Hastings Doyle	Sept. 29, 1865	Nov. 7, 1865
Sir W. Fenwick Williams		Nov. 8, 1865	June 30, 1867

APPENDIX C

A Nova Scotian Family Compact

(M.C. = Member of the Council; M.E.C. = Member of the Executive Council)

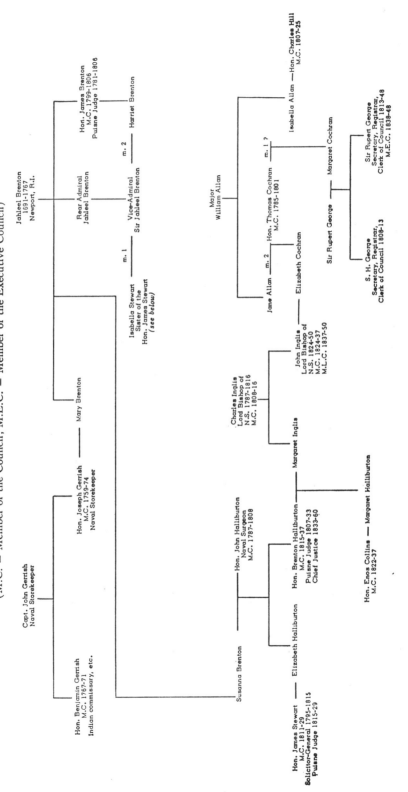

APPENDIX D

LIEUTENANT-GOVERNORS SINCE CONFEDERATION

Sir William Fenwick Williams	July 1, 1867
Sir C. Hastings Doyle	Oct. 28, 1867
Joseph Howe	May 10, 1873
Sir Adams G. Archibald	July 23, 1873
M. H. Richey	July 4, 1883
A. W. McLelan	July 10, 1888
Sir Malachy B. Daly	July 14, 1890
A. G. Jones	Aug. 7, 1900
Duncan C. Fraser	March 30, 1906
J. D. McGregor	Oct. 21, 1910
David MacKeen	Oct. 22, 1915
MacCallum Grant	Dec. 2, 1916
J. Robson Douglas	Jan. 23, 1925
James C. Tory	Oct. 1, 1925
Frank Stanfield	Dec. 2, 1930
W. H. Covert	Oct. 9, 1931
Robert Irwin	May 1, 1937
F. H. Mathers	June 10, 1940
H. E. Kendall	Nov. 30, 1942
J. A. D. McCurdy	Aug. 19, 1947
Allistair Fraser	Oct. 1, 1952

APPENDIX E

NOVA SCOTIAN MINISTRIES UNDER RESPONSIBLE GOVERNMENT

Premier		Party
J. B. Uniacke	Feb. 9, 1848	Reform (Liberal)
William Young	April 4, 1854	Liberal
J. W. Johnston	Feb. 24, 1857	Conservative
William Young	Feb. 10, 1860	Liberal
Joseph Howe	Aug. 3, 1860	Liberal
J. W. Johnston	June 11, 1863	Conservative
Charles Tupper	May 11, 1864	Conservative
Hiram Blanchard	July 4, 1867	Confederate (Conservative)
William Annand	Nov. 7, 1867	Anti-Confederate (Liberal)
P. C. Hill	May 11, 1875	Liberal
S. D. Holmes	Oct. 22, 1878	Conservative
J. S. D. Thompson	May 25, 1882	Conservative
W. T. Pipes	Aug. 3, 1882	Liberal
W. S. Fielding	July 28, 1884	Liberal
G. H. Murray	July 20, 1896	Liberal
E. H. Armstrong	Jan. 24, 1923	Liberal
E. N. Rhodes	July 16, 1925	Conservative
G. S. Harrington	Aug. 11, 1930	Conservative
A. L. Macdonald	Sept. 5, 1933	Liberal
A. S. MacMillan	July 10, 1940	Liberal
A. L. Macdonald	Sept. 8, 1945	Liberal
Harold Connolly	April 13, 1954	Liberal
Henry D. Hicks	Sept. 30, 1954	Liberal
Robert L. Stanfield	Nov. 20, 1956	Conservative

APPENDIX F

RESULTS OF GENERAL ELECTIONS

Party	Popular vote	Percentage of popular vote	Seats	Percentage of seats
1867				
L	44,339	58.6	36	94.7
C	29,095	38.5	2	5.3
Others	2,182	2.9	—	—
1871				
L	39,213	52.2	25	65.8
C	32,808	43.7	13	34.2
Others	3,128	4.1	—	—
1874				
L	37,025	54.7	24	63.2
C	29,283	43.3	14	36.8
Others	1,383	2.0	—	—
1878				
L	45,972	45.3	8	21.1
C	52,310	51.5	30	78.9
Others	3,268	3.2	—	—
1882				
L	49,945	51.8	24	63.2
C	45,251	46.9	14	36.8
Others	1,205	1.3	—	—
1886				
L	61,822	54.7	29	76.3
C	49,216	43.6	8	21.1
Others	1,943	1.7	1	2.6
1890				
L	71,202	52.2	28	73.7
C	63,720	46.7	10	26.3
Others	1,407	1.1	—	—
1894				
L	75,121	51.9	25	65.8
C	68,455	47.3	13	34.2
Others	1,073	0.8	—	—
1897				
L	84,000	55.0	35	92.1
C	67,779	44.4	3	7.9
Others	968	0.6	—	—
1901				
L	78,375	56.7	36	94.7
C	57,689	41.7	2	5.3
Others	2,147	1.6	—	—
1906				
L	84,359	53.2	32	84.2
C	66,638	42.1	5	13.2
Others	7,423	4.7	1	2.6
1911				
L	99,192	51.1	27	71.1
C	88,114	45.4	11	28.9
Others	6,851	3.5	—	—

APPENDIX F—*continued*

Party	Popular vote	Percentage of popular vote	Seats	Percentage of seats
1916				
L	136,315	50.4	30	69.8
C	131,844	48.8	13	30.2
Others	2,215	0.8	—	—
1920				
L	154,627	44.4	29	67.4
C	85,736	24.7	3	7.0
F.-L.	107,591	30.9	11	25.6
1925				
L	161,158	36.3	3	93.0
C	270,544	60.9	40	7.0
Ind.	12,260	2.8	—	—
1928				
L	209,380	48.3	20	53.5
C	218,974	50.6	23	46.5
Ind.	4,862	1.1	—	—
1933				
L	166,170	52.6	22	73.3
C	145,107	45.9	8	26.7
Others	4,805	1.5	—	—
1937				
L	165,397	52.9	25	83.3
C	143,670	46.0	5	16.7
Others	3,396	1.1	—	—
1941				
L	138,915	52.7	23	76.7
C	106,133	40.3	4	13.3
C.C.F.	18,583	7.0	3	10.0
1945				
L	153,513	52.7	28	93.3
C	97,774	33.5	—	—
C.C.F.	39,637	13.6	2	6.7
Others	634	0.2	—	—
1949				
L	174,269	50.9	27	73.0
C	134,190	39.2	8	21.6
C.C.F.	32,998	9.7	2	5.4
Others	750	0.2	—	—
1953				
L	169,921	49.1	23	62.2
C	149,973	43.4	12	32.4
C.C.F.	23,700	6.9	2	5.4
Others	2,065	0.6	—	—
1956				
L	159,656	48.2	18	41.9
C	160,996	48.6	24	55.8
C.C.F.	9,878	3.0	1	2.3
Others	812	0.2	—	—

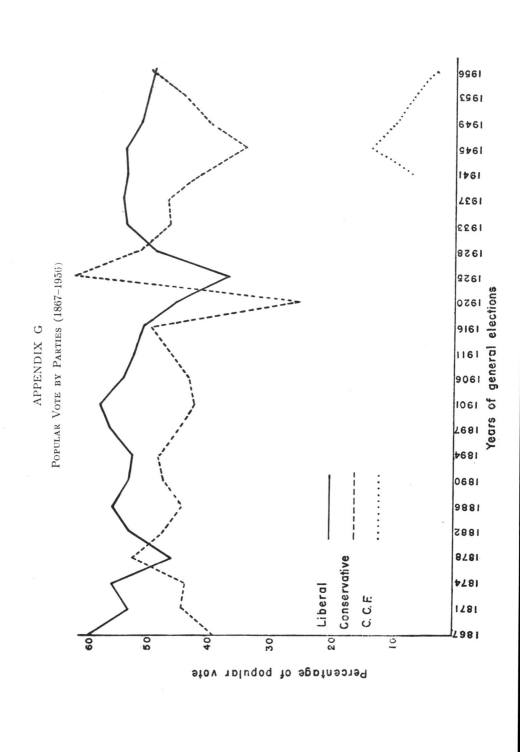

APPENDIX G

POPULAR VOTE BY PARTIES (1867–1956)

APPENDIX H

CABINET REPRESENTATION BY REGIONS

Ministry	Halifax	South Shore*	Valley†	North-ern‡	Eastern§	Cape Breton‖	Number of lawyers
Annand	1	1	3	1		2	
Hill	3	1	1		1	2	
Holmes	1	1	2	3	1	1	5
Thompson			1	3	1		2
Pipes		3	1	2		2	2
Fielding	1	2	1	1		2	2
Murray	1	2	2	1	1	1	3
Armstrong	1	2	3	1	2	1	5
Rhodes	2	2	1	1		3	4
Harrington	2	1	2	2		1	3
Macdonald (1933)	1	1	3	1	1	1	2
MacMillan	1	1	3		1	1	2
Macdonald (1945)	2	1	1	1	1	1	3
Macdonald (1950)	4	2	1	1	1	2	5
Hicks	2	1	1		2	2	3
Stanfield	1	1	1	3		2	5

*Lunenburg, Queens, Shelburne, and Yarmouth
†Digby, Annapolis, Kings, and Hants
‡Cumberland, Colchester, and Pictou
§Antigonish and Guysborough
‖Cape Breton, Victoria, Inverness, and Richmond

APPENDIX I

NUMBER OF MINISTERS WITH PORTFOLIO IN THE PROVINCIAL GOVERNMENTS (1867–1918)

Year	N.S.	N.B.	P.E.I.	Que.	Ont.	Man.	Sask.	Alta.	B.C.
1867	4	5	3	6	5	–	–	–	–
1871	5	5	3	6	6	4	–	–	3
1873	5	5	3	6	6	4	–	–	3
1877	4	5	3	6	6	4	–	–	or
1878	3	5	3	6	6	4	–	–	4
1885	3	5	3	6	6	5	–	–	
1900	3	5	3	6	7	5	–	–	5
1905	3	5	3	7	7	6	4	4	5
1910	3	or	3	7	7	7	5	4	6
1915	3	6	3	8	7	7	7	8	6
1918	4	6	3	8	7	7	7	8	8

APPENDIX J

Age Brackets of Legislative Councillors

					July 1					June 1,
Age bracket	1880	1885	1890	1895	1900	1905	1910	1915	1920	1925
90 and up	1									
85–89					1		2	1		
80–84	1		3			3	1	1	2	3
75–79	1	4	1		5	1	4	4	5	
70–74	5	1	1	5	1	5	4	4		1
60–69	2	7	6	6	5	7	5	2	5	5
50–59	5	3	4	6	6	3	2	5	7	5
40–49	4	2	4	1	2					
30–39	1	1		1						
20–29			1							
Average ages	61.5	61.4	60.5	61.6	63.2	67.6	71.5	68.5	64.8	66.4

APPENDIX K

Legislative Record of the Council During Two Three-Year Periods

A. *Action of the Council on the bills which were initiated by the Assembly*

	Introduced in, and passed by Assembly	Deferred by Council or not proceeded with because of disagreement or other reason	Passed by Council	Amended by Council	Per cent amended by Council
1910	137	3	134	65	48.5
1911	160	10	150	48	32.0
1912	238	16	222	117	52.7
1920	221	2	219	71	32.1
1921	197	10	187	61	32.6
1922	131	1	130	34	26.2

B. *Action on the bills which were initiated by the Council*

	Introduced in Council				Deferred or abandoned in Council	Deferred or not proceeded with by Assembly	Passed into law	Category passed into law		
	Public	Private	Local	Total				Public	Private	Local
1910	8	20	21	49	3	3	43	6	18	19
1911	1	5	5	11	1	0	10	0	5	5
1912	3	5	15	23	2	0	21	2	5	14
1920	4	5	5	14	2	3	9	1	5	3
1921	3	4	7	14	0	2	12	1	4	7
1922	4	8	11	23	1	4	18	2	5	11

Ages of Assemblymen

Age	1878	1882	1890	1901	1916	1925	1928	1933	1937	1941	1945	1949	1953
21–30	2	1	3	0	0	4	1	0	0	0	1	1	0
31–40	18	16	4	11	11	4	4	4	3	4	7	11	9
41–50	8	13	15	10	12	14	13	11	11	9	9	10	10
51–60	6	4	8	12	16	16	17	9	6	8	8	10	10
61–70	2	2	3	2	1	2	4	6	9	6	4	2	7
71–80	0	0	1	1	0	0	0	0	0	0	1	0	0
Not known	2	2	4	2	3	3	4	0	1	3	0	3	1
Total	38	38	38	38	43	43	43	30	30	30	30	37	37
Average age	42.2	42.7	48.3	47.9	47.2	47.3	50.5	50.5	52.9	51.2	49.6	46.4	49.7
Oew members	27	20	18	12	16	33	17	16	12	14	13	17	12
Nld members	11	18	20	26	27	10	26	14	18	16	.17	20	25

Occupations of Assemblymen*

Occupation	Date of election												
	1878	1882	1890	1901	1916	1925	1928	1933	1937	1941	1945	1949	1953
Law	7	11	6	14	15	12	11	6	7	7	11	15	13
Merchants and sales	10	11	15	8	9	8	8	6	5	5	3	3	5
Agriculture	3	3	5	6	2	2	3	2	1	1	2	3	4
Lumber operations	1	1	1	1	1	2	2	1	1	2	2	2	1
Printing and journalism		1	2	1	1			1	1	2	1	1	2
Manufacturing	1		2		1	3	2	1	2	3	1	3	1
Building and contracting		1	1	2	1	1	3	1	1	2	1	1	
Medicine and dentistry	1	2	2		5	4	5	6	4	1	2	1	3
Pharmacy	1	1			1		2	2	2	2	1	1	1
Finance and insurance				3	4	6	3	1					
Labour (trade unionist)													
Retired	1		1						3	3	2	2	4
Unclassified	13	7	3	3	3	5	4	3	3	2	3	3	1

*Many assemblymen have several occupations; the main one is indicated here.

ACTION OF THE ASSEMBLY ON BILLS (1946–55)
(Appropriation Act not included)

	1946	1947	1948	1949	1950	1951	1952	1953	1954	1955	Total
Number of bills introduced	127	131	174	146	134	131	154	100	135	107	1,339
Number combined with other bills or not proceeded with	3	1	6	4	1	0	4	0	1	0	20
Proceeded with	124	130	168	142	133	131	150	100	134	107	1,319
Refused second reading	0	0	0	0	0	0	0	1	0	0	1
Action taken by Law Amendments Committee											
Referred to committee	59	72	82	67	67	68	85	58	64	55	677
Approved without amendment	11	25	25	31	34	31	50	33	36	36	312
Approved with amendment	45	44	53	35	30	34	35	21	26	16	339
Not reported back	0	0	0	0	0	0	0	0	0	2	2
Recommended for deferment	3	3	4	1	3	3	0	4	2	1	24
Action taken by Private and Local Bills Committee											
Referred to committee	65	58	86	75	66	63	65	41	70	52	641
Approved without amendments	22	12	21	16	14	15	14	19	28	17	178
Approved with amendments	38	44	60	56	49	45	49	22	40	34	437
Not reported back	0	0	0	0	0	0	0	0	0	1	1
Recommended for deferment	5	2	5	3	3	3	2	0	2	0	25
Action taken by the Committee on the Whole House											
Accepted committee recommendation for deferment	8	5	9	4	6	6	2	3	4	1	48
Rejected recommendation for deferment	0	0	0	0	0	0	0	1	0	0	1
Accepted without further amendment	108	115	152	131	120	115	137	87	120	90	1,175
Accepted with amendments	8	10	5	6	7	10	11	8	10	11	86
Deferred without committee recommendations	0	0	1	1	0	0	0	0	0	2	4
Recommitted and not reported back	0	0	0	0	0	0	0	0	0	0	1
Amended on third reading	1	1	2	0	0	1	0	1	1	0	7
Total given third reading	116	125	157	137	127	125	148	96	130	101	1,262

INDEX

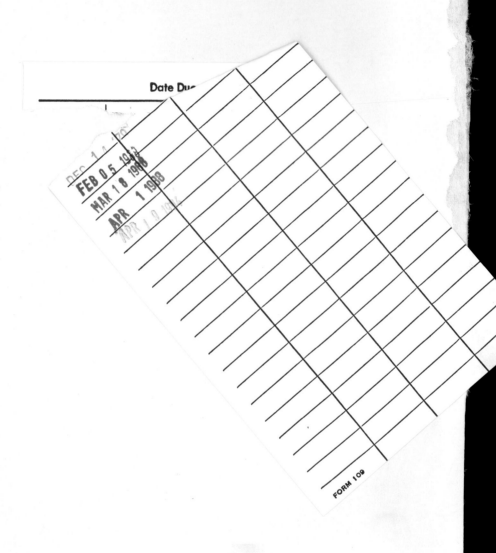

Date Due

FORM 109